Smart urban and rural planning techniques

Other titles of interest:

Best Practices in Urban Transport
Edited by Dr. M. Ramachandran

Fixing Flawed Urban Planning: The Case of Delhi
B.G. Fernandes

Humane Approach to Urban Planning
Priya Choudhary

Geographic Information System for Smart Cities
Prof. TM Vinod Kumar and Associates

Local Area Planning in India
Rishi Dev

Metropolitan Governance: Cases of Ahmedabad and Hyderabad
Dr. Vinita Yadav

India's Urban Confusion: Challenges and Strategies
Edited by Dr. M. Ramachandran

Designing Better Architecture Education: Global Realities and Local Reforms
Dr Manjari Chakraborty

The Ekistics of Animal and Human Conflict
Rishi Dev

Water Conservation Techniques in Traditional Human Settlements
Pietro Laureano

The City Observed: Notes from an Unfolding India
Pallavi Shrivastava

Tirtha at Mukteswar: Understanding its Architecture
Dr. Ranjana Mital and Prabhjot Singh Sugga

Smart urban and rural planning techniques

Harmit Singh Bedi

COPAL PUBLISHING GROUP
Inspiring for a better future through publishing

Published by Copal Publishing Group
E-143, Lajpat Nagar, Sahibabad,
Distt. Ghaziabad, UP – 201005, India

www.copalpublishing.com

First Published 2016
© Copal Publishing Group, 2016

This book contains information obtained from authentic and highly regarded sources. Reprinted material is quoted with permission. Reasonable efforts have been made to publish reliable data and information, but the authors and the publishers cannot assume responsibility for the validity of all materials. Neither the authors nor the publishers, nor anyone else associated with this publication, shall be liable for any loss, damage or liability directly or indirectly caused or alleged to be caused by this book.

Neither this book nor any part may be reproduced or transmitted in any form or by any means, electronic or mechanical, including photocopying, microfilming and recording, or by any information storage or retrieval system, without permission in writing from Copal Publishing Group. The consent of Copal Publishing Group does not extend to copying for general distribution, for promotion, for creating new works, or for resale. Specific permission must be obtained in writing from Copal Publishing Group for such copying.

Trademark notice: Product or corporate names may be trademarks or registered trademarks, and are used only for identification and explanation, without intent to infringe.

ISBN: 978-93-83419-26-5 (hard back)
ISBN: 978-93-83419-27-2 (e-book)

Typeset by Bhumi Graphics, New Delhi
Printed and bound by Bhavish Graphics, Chennai

Dedication

To Bimla Kumari, my mother, who guided me and believed in me, and Surinder Bedi, my wife, for her unconditional support and companionship.

About the Author

Harmit Singh Bedi is a professional urban planner and designer. He has been involved in building harmonious and livable communities for many years. As director of planning and development department, he has planned for various progressive and dynamic communities. He holds degrees from  University of Pittsburgh, USA, Indian Institute of Technology, Kharagpur, and Panjab University, Chandigarh, India. He has been associated with Georgia Southern University, Kennesaw State University, and Georgia Gwinnett College, Georgia, USA as Affiliate Assistant Professor. He has authored and published articles in Planning magazine, published by the American Planning Association. He managed the preparation of Master Plan and Design of Indian Institute of Technology, Ropar, Punjab, India. He is an expert empanelled member of Lal Bhahadur Shastri National Academy of Administration (LBSNAA), Mussoorie, India. He is a Member of American Institute of Certified Planners. He has made presentations at various institutions and organization in both USA and India. He resides in the USA.

Contents

Preface   xxi
Acknowledgements   xxv
Introduction   xxvii

1. Urban and rural planning 101   1

1.1	Introduction	2
1.2	A city	3
1.3	The city as an economic entity	3
1.4	Exchange	4
1.5	Manufacturing	4
1.6	Extraction	4
1.7	Government	4
1.8	Education	5
1.9	Religion/spiritual	5
1.10	City as a social cradle	5
1.11	City as a legal entity	6
1.12	City as a physical organism	6
1.13	What is planning	7
1.14	What planners do	8

1.15	A typical day for a planner, and with whom do planners work	9
1.16	Common specializations in the planning profession	11
1.17	How are planners educated?	12
1.18	What skills do successful planners possess?	12
1.19	Good city planning	13
1.20	Planning as a team effort	14

2. Evolution of urban planning — 16

2.1	Indian evolution of town planning	16
2.2	Evolution around the world	21
2.3	Medieval cities	22
2.4	The Middle Ages	22
2.5	Renaissance cities	23
2.6	European new towns	23
2.7	Spanish colonial new towns	23
2.8	Urban concepts	23

3. Planning portfolio — 28

3.1	Plan for planning	28
3.2	Role of plans	28
3.3	Plan authority	29
3.4	Basic plan structure	29
3.5	Types of plans	33
3.6	Elements of plan	35
3.7	Regional plans	38
3.8	Redevelopment area plans	40
3.9	The plan	41
3.10	Public policy analysis and planning/engineering/architecture	42
3.11	Policy relevant information	43
3.12	Process of policy making	44
3.13	Policy problem structuring	44

3.14	Forecasting	45
3.15	Recommendation	46
3.16	Implementation	46
3.17	Monitoring	47
3.18	Evaluation	47
3.19	Process of policy communication	48
3.20	Conclusion	48

4. Planner's tool kit — 49

4.1	Role of community participation	49
4.2	Surveys	50
4.3	Community visioning	51
4.4	Charrettes	51
4.5	Asset mapping	54
4.6	Development standards	56
4.7	Land use distribution	58
4.8	Infrastructure standards	58
4.9	Social services	59
4.10	Recreational	59
4.11	Traffic and transportation	59
4.12	Other facilities	59
4.13	Context-sensitive solutions/design/planning	59
4.14	Underground development planning	69
4.15	Project management	71
4.16	Project management knowledge areas	75
4.17	Management of planning department	79

5. Education of planning — 80

5.1	Why learn planning	80
5.2	How to learn planning	80
5.3	Planning in India	81
5.4	From where planners will come	84
5.5	Planning and other professions and disciplines	87
5.6	Education, Education, Education	87

	5.7	Teaching the teachers	88
	5.8	Other planning elements	89
	5.9	Code of conduct of ITPI members	90
	5.10	Conclusion	93

6. Smart cities 94

	6.1	Introduction	94
	6.2	The concept	96
	6.3	Sustainability	98
	6.4	Wireless sensor and network for smart cities	98
	6.5	Geographic information systems in smart cities	100
	6.6	How GIS works	100
	6.7	GIS and smart cities	101
	6.8	The smart city model	102
	6.9	Economic infrastructure	103
	6.10	Governance infrastructure	103
	6.11	Physical infrastructure	103
	6.12	Institutional infrastructure	104
	6.13	Technical infrastructure	104
	6.14	Smart city project in India	104
	6.15	Telescopic view	105
	6.16	Lessons learnt – Case of Chandigarh	109
	6.17	Forward thinking	111
	6.18	Planning for Smart Cities	112
	6.19	Suburbs and new cities	113
	6.20	Internal and external transportation links	114
	6.21	Environmental balance	114
	6.22	Social and cultural integration	114
	6.23	Cities of future and future of cities	115
	6.24	Spirituality for spiritual living	118
	6.25	Integrity and honesty	119
	6.26	Communication	119
	6.27	India clean and beautiful	119

	6.28	Green India Green	120
	6.29	Love your home, *galli*, street, neighborhood, city, town, village, and country	121
	6.30	How many Indians in India	121

7. Land use planning — 124

	7.1	Introduction	124
	7.2	Uses, land, and planning	125
	7.3	Capabilities, values, and planning	127
	7.4	Types of land uses	129
	7.5	Retail mall / Big-box retail	131
	7.6	Wholesale / warehouse	133
	7.7	Temporary and mobile vendors	133
	7.8	Institutional	134
	7.9	Industrial	134
	7.10	Digital industry	134
	7.11	Environment and planning	135
	7.12	The ecology	135
	7.13	Environmental planning	136
	7.14	Environmental land use regulations	138
	7.15	Sustainable water supply and planning	139
	7.16	Hydrology	140
	7.17	Watersheds and surface water	141
	7.18	Sustainable air quality and planning	141
	7.19	Environmental land regulations	143
	7.20	Conclusion	144

8. Zoning — 145

	8.1	Introduction	145
	8.2	Definition of zoning	145
	8.3	The objectives	146
	8.4	The purpose of zoning	146
	8.5	Implementing zoning	147
	8.6	Zoning map and zoning ordinance	148

8.7	Districting	148
8.8	Variety of districts	149
8.9	Planned unit development	156
8.10	Mixed-use development / new urbanism	157
8.11	Non-conforming uses or buildings	159
8.12	Exclusion of named uses	160
8.13	Cumulative use restrictions	160
8.14	Exclusion of those uses not specifically permitted	160
8.15	Exclusionary zoning	160
8.16	Inclusionary Zoning	161
8.17	Transitional Zoning	161
8.18	Spot Zoning	162
8.19	Development limitations	162
8.20	Bulk requirements	163
8.21	Floor Area Ratio	164
8.22	Lot area retractions	165
8.23	Parking	165
8.24	Signage	165
8.25	Traffic impact	167
8.26	Impact on social services	168
8.27	Utilities impact	168
8.28	Enforcement	168
8.29	Subdivision regulations	169
8.30	Principles of good design	170
8.31	Aesthetic and architectural control	172
8.32	Zoning in operation	172
8.33	Form-based codes (FBC)	174
8.34	Addressing	177
8.35	Gated communities	180
8.36	In-laws apartments	181
8.37	Servants' employment and planning	181
8.38	Home business / home occupation	182

8.39	Planning for "wallas"	183
8.40	Planning process	184
8.41	Telecommunication tower planning	185
8.42	Animals in the city	186
8.43	Farm housing	187
8.44	Staff	188
8.45	Planning commission	189
8.46	Board of Adjustment or Appeals	189
8.47	Governing body	189
8.48	Zoning powers	189
8.49	Pros and cons of zoning/conclusion	190

9. Urban design — 191

9.1	Introduction	191
9.2	Indian cities' context of urban design	192
9.3	Urban form	194
9.4	Economic advantages of design	195
9.5	Good design makes better places	196
9.6	Design reflects people	199
9.7	Design is an essential skill	200
9.8	Design in context of place	201
9.9	Innovative planning techniques	202
9.10	Urban design perspectives	202
9.11	Urban design controls	204
9.12	Restrictive zoning	205
9.13	Indicative zoning	205
9.14	Incentive zoning	206
9.15	Performance zoning	206
9.16	Urban design plan	206
9.17	Urban landscaping design	207
9.18	Urban forestry	209
9.19	Campus communities	211
9.20	Military bases/cantonments	221

10. Transportation planning — 223

10.1	Introduction	223
10.2	Roads, streets, sidewalks	227
10.3	Road systems	228
10.4	Freeway	231
10.5	Expressway	231
10.6	Arterial	232
10.7	Sub-arterial roads	232
10.8	Collector	232
10.9	Local streets	233
10.10	Alleys	233
10.11	Sidewalks	234
10.12	Pedestrian planning – Sidewalks	236
10.13	Planning and design considerations	239
10.14	Cul-de-sac	240
10.15	Transportation modeling	241
10.16	Using the models	242
10.17	Land use trip generation	243
10.18	Residential trip generation	243
10.19	Commercial trip generation	244
10.20	Industrial trip generation	244
10.21	Recreational, religious, spiritual, and social trip generation	244
10.22	Transportation study/survey terms	245
10.23	Seasonal average and special events daily traffic	245
10.24	Annual average daily traffic	246
10.25	Traffic volume study	246
10.26	Classified traffic volume	246
10.27	Origin–destination study or survey	246
10.28	Traffic congestion	247
10.29	Safety	247
10.30	Traffic-calming techniques	249
10.31	Mass/public transit	253

10.32	Light rail transportation	254
10.33	Bus service transportation system	255
10.34	Rail transportation system	257
10.35	Waterways/boats means of transportation	259
10.36	Traffic management	259
10.37	Temporary traffic control	262
10.38	Street lights	263
10.39	Parking	263
10.40	Parking design	266
10.41	Shared parking	267
10.42	Taxis, three-wheelers, rickshaws, and tongas	268
10.43	Bicycles	270
10.44	Freight transportation and commodity transfer	272
10.45	Stray animals on roads	273
10.46	Old city transportation planning	274
10.47	Airport planning	274
10.48	Economic action of airports	278
10.49	Environmental issues of airports	279
10.50	Airport-planning process	281
10.51	Conclusion	282

11. Historic preservation — 283

11.1	Introduction	283
11.2	Historic districts and ordinances	285
11.3	Documentation and designation of individual historic properties	286
11.4	Historic buildings	286
11.5	Architectural style	287
11.6	Architectural character	287
11.7	Identify character-defining elements	287
11.8	Design issues	288
11.9	Buildings not listed	288
11.10	Walk-through and walk-around	289

11.11	Preservation economics	289
11.12	Other features	289

12. Utopian planning — 290

12.1	Sustainable communities	290
12.2	Mixed-use design	290
12.3	Efficient use of limited land resources	291
12.4	Transportation alternatives	291
12.5	Optimum use of urban resources and services	292
12.6	Human scale designs	292
12.7	Green built environment	293
12.8	Green environment	293
12.9	Implementation	293
12.10	Implementation and enforcement	294
12.11	Accountability and education	295
12.12	Evaluation and monitoring	295
12.13	Infrastructure planning	296
12.14	Infrastructure challenges for the cities	298
12.15	Infrastructure delivery	302
12.16	Steps in preparation of the infrastructure plan	302
12.17	Development regulations	303
12.18	Wastewater planning	305
12.19	Wastewater treatment	307
12.20	Planning for natural areas	308
12.21	Planning for wildlife habitat	310
12.22	Planning and managing wetlands	312
12.23	Coastal zone management	313
12.24	Planning for natural hazards and natural disasters	315
12.25	Principles of disaster preparedness	317
12.26	Emergency/disaster preparedness	318
12.27	Solid waste and recycling management	319
12.28	Waste generators	320

	12.29	Solid waste management and sustainability	321
	12.30	Sanitary landfills	323
	12.31	Other strategies	323
	12.32	Conclusion	324

13. Smart rural planning — 325

	13.1	Introduction	325
	13.2	What makes rural	327
	13.3	Smart approach	328
	13.4	Regional understanding	328
	13.5	Future role of rural settlements	329
	13.6	Rural comprehensive plan	331
	13.7	Redevelopment plan	332
	13.8	Smart rural areas	333
	13.9	Conclusion	334

14. Making India good to great — 335

	14.1	Urban overview	335
	14.2	Fairness and equity	339
	14.3	Urban diffusion	339
	14.4	Assumptions and reality	339
	14.5	The urbanization model	340
	14.6	Slums to utopia model	349
	14.7	Human growth and planning	360
	14.8	Salient features of making India good to great	364
	14.9	Conclusion	367

Conclusion — 369
Index — 371

Preface

The increased urbanization is posing challenges to maintain and upgrade quality of life in towns and cities of India. Migration from rural areas has added numbers to the natural urban population growth. Urban areas, undoubtedly, are the economic engines of the country by contributing major portion of the national gross domestic product. Economic opportunities are creating jobs and opening doors of entrepreneurship for the masses. Urban areas provide opportunities, choices, variety, options, openings and styles for all sections of the society. Simultaneously urban areas are becoming chaotic due to the increased number of people, traffic, commercial activities, structures, building new and expanding existing slums, environmental deterioration and pro-growth policies are just adding fuel to the fire. Professionals, administrators, elected officials, and policy makers must understand the complex urban phenomena and strive to provide infrastructure and services in the city to keep the economic growth phenomenon gearing up and supportive.

The challenge to maintain balance between better quality of life and urban problems is more at front stage than ever before. More opportunities attract people to move to urban areas with the hope of having a better quality of life. Therefore, many questions need to be asked. Are existing urban centers ready and equipped to provide required infrastructure, services, amenities, and social and cultural needs of the existing and new incoming people? Can India build smart and sustainable communities for today and tomorrow? Can India be catalyst by building smart cities for today and tomorrow? What is smart planning in Indian context? Is urbanization necessary for growth? And finally, can India lead the world in planning, designing, and developing futuristic cities? The book is attempting to explore answers to these questions.

This book is a concise document to understand built environment and human activities in urban and rural settings and provide practical and smart planning solutions. Furthermore, this book will explain theory and practice of many elements and facet of urban and rural planning ranging from need of planning, planners' identity, zoning, land use planning, transportation, urban design, landscaping, environment, and historic preservation. Modern urban issues of urbanization, sprawl, slums, implementation, and code enforcement are discussed. Local and micro level planning issues of role of religious/spiritual institutions, importance of addressing, and incorporation of *"wallas"* in local plans are mentioned in detail. The text explores innovative ideas like context sensitive design, form-based codes, preparation of smart development plans, project planning, smart city elements and futuristic cities and many other elements of day-to-day planning processes, urban governance and planning department management in Indian context. While understanding the urban dynamics and built environment, the book presents scenarios to balance between quality of life and growth and development in urban areas. The book provides understanding of the urban built environment, natural environment, and space elements. Techniques to make cities healthy, safe, convenient, comfortable, happy, aesthetically appealing, morally sound, vibrant, harmonious, and with the sense of place and preparing communities for today and future generations are explained. The book explores the potentials and opportunities of rural areas of India.

The intent of this book is to assist in improving quality of life, through planning and design processes, for citizens living in urban and rural areas. The book offers practical and smart scenarios to tackle urban issues and challenges. The text provides scenarios to build harmonious, sustainable, and futuristic communities through smart planning processes. The text outlines smart, simple, and practical urban planning tools and techniques to plan cities. Further, the text suggests a model to improve the quality of life of urbanites through "Urbanization Model." The model explore opportunities to improve living conditions, and explore socio-economic opportunities for both urban and rural area citizens.

A model suggesting solution to urban slums is introduced in the text. Slums are cropping up and expanding in and around urban areas. They are unacceptable human living conditions from any standards. The book suggests solutions and alternatives to make Indian cities/towns and rural areas to be more attractive and livable. Furthermore, with smart and innovative ideas, addressing each planning element, to make Indian settlements more efficient, effective, functional, operational, and seamless. A model to manage human growth is introduced from the perspective of human quality than quantity. Ultimately it matters how we live; how we represent our urban areas and rural areas to the world.

This book is designed for practicing, academics, and students of urban/city/town/rural/regional planning, civil engineering, architecture, landscape architecture, urban design, environmental studies, Indian Administrative Services (IAS) trainees, faculty/trainers, and practitioners, elected officials (local, regional, state, and center), policy makers, city managers/administrators, urban and rural sociologists, urban and rural geographers, urban designers, environmentalists, land-use and zoning lawyers, judicial judges, religious/spiritual priests/associates, urban economists, development studies, builders, developers, contractors, business practitioners, civil society groups, certain NGOs, citizens active and interested in improving quality of life, informed general readers, and organizations with goals to improve conditions for humanity such as World Bank, various foundations, United Nations, and Shack-Slum Dwellers International (SDI).

By implementing and executing the suggested solutions, scenarios, alternatives, plans, and models can help towns, cities, and villages to be the most beautiful places to live, work, play, learn, invest, worship and raise a family in the most beautiful place on earth – India.

> *Let us make our India a beautiful place to live, work, play, learn, worship, invest, and raise a family.*

Acknowledgements

Initiation of this book started when I was a student at the Department of Geography, Panjab University, Chandigarh. I am thankful to Prof. A. B. Mukerjee, for guiding and counseling me to be a town planner, rather than doing PhD in Geography. Prof. Dr. Swaranjit Mehta further inspired me by training me to see things in simple perspective. The book got inspiration when I was a student of planning at Indian Institute of Technology, Kharagpur. Prof. Satyavir Singh, groomed and trained me to be a town planner. After graduating, his inspiration remained with me. Prof. B. C. Chattopadhya and Prof. R. N. Chatterjee and other faculty members at Indian Institute of Technology, Kharagpur, showed me the path of being a true planning professional. I remember one of the professors used to challenge students by saying, "planners are next to God." I realize now, it is a tectonic responsibility.

Phil McLemore, my Guru, my mentor, showed me the path to practical and realistic urban planning and design.

I am thankful to Dr. Datar Singh and Mrs. Bina Singh for their unconditional support throughout my career and always being supportive – no matter what. Architect Pallavi Singla worked tirelessly to provide technical assistance in preparing this manuscript. Mrs. W. Worsfold, 83, provided me with her lifelong wisdom, when I asked her how to make India a better place to live. Her ideas are incorporated in the book.

The staff of Georgia Gwinnett College, Lawrenceville, USA, Holly Heitman, Kay Chatham, Sara Housworth, Colin Eade, David Menchew, Robert Aaron, Lisa Jones, Vicki Parson, Cecelia Saunders, and Maxine Small helped me to stay in good books with the library's laws and procedures. I admire their professionalism and patience. Without their help this book could not have been possible.

I am very thankful to Brig. P. D. Tewari, a true friend, for his time and efforts to keep me disciplined to complete this book. His guidance helped keep many loose strings together. His moral support was endless and kept me motivated. He spent endless hours to help keep the text in order and me in reality world. 'Thank you' word is not enough for Tanika Bedi for her many hours of time to review the draft manuscript. Prof. Dr. Rano Ringo helped me stay connected with local realities by reviewing the draft manuscript.

COPAL Publishing Group deserves special thanks for assisting in making publishing process a seamless endeavor. Rishi Seth with his professional, courteous, and amicable guidance took lot of pressure off my mind and made the process easy and smooth.

As always, my wife, Surinder, maintained continuous momentum and inspiration to write this book and my first critic, editor, and supporter for everything. Without her support, help, and wisdom this book never would have happened. Throughout the research and writing process she exhilarated and motivated me. I am lucky to have her by my side. Most importantly, special thanks to Vikram Singh Bedi, Kabir Singh Bedi, Shawn Singh Bedi, Aria Bedi and Kaden Singh Bedi for their whole-hearted support to write this book.

It was hard work – and lots of fun, you all made it happen. Thank you.

Introduction

Planning and managing our cities, towns, and villages is vital. Planned developments make cities more attractive, functional, and livable. Planning and management helps maintain desired quality of life in cities. Together – planning and management – strive to achieve the goals and objectives established by the community, for the community. Planning guides and helps to establish the goals and objectives of the community and assist in shaping the future of the cities and towns. Planned and managed development lay path for harmonious communities. Planning is a process and management is a cumulative action of various forces to achieve desired end results. Cities' form, social, and economic values change with time. Planning processes help communities keep track of these changes and variations. Planning helps understand and analyze changes, incorporate changes into the plans and assist in preparing and designing the future by acting at present times. Professionals use available expertise, experiences, and knowledge to prepare for the future. The quality of plans are further enhanced with smart, innovative, and creative ideas. It takes a community to plan for the community. The traditional and fundamental role of planning is to make cities safe, healthy, and morally sound, and aesthetically appealing. The new concept of smart cities will incorporate additional elements to the planning processes such as online submission and approval of development plans, smart traffic management, and identifying traffic bottleneck through traffic cameras.

Computers, wireless sensors, and networking together helps to activate Smart Cities. Geographic Information Systems (GIS), Global Positioning System (GPS), Management Information Systems (MIS) and other systems will help cities to plan and manage development better. The goal is to create a smartly distributed network of intelligent sensors nodes which can measure and track many parameters for a more efficient operation and management of a city. The data is delivered wirelessly and in real-time to the concerned citizens and the appropriate authorities to make a well-informed decisions. For example, if water pipe ruptures in a neighborhood, the residents will know, through electronic connections, the cause and effect. The authorities, through sensors, network, GIS, and GPS will know where the problem is and can dispatch the crew in a timely manner to correct the situation or bring it under control. Whereas, in the same situation, in a traditional city it may take long time to detect the problem and may take a longer time to correct the situation. In this scenario valuable resources can be saved or wasted.

Smart cities, traditional cities, old cities, new cities, metro city or small cities or villages, irrespective of the size, it matters how we live. It matters how we reflect ourselves to the world. We plan our house. We keep our house organized. We keep our house and surroundings clean. We landscape areas surrounding the house. Likewise, India needs to plan its neighborhoods, villages, towns, and cities. The citizens of India should be responsible to keep the country organized, planned, clean, and green. Villages, towns, and cities should be managed to reflect the best of Indian society, culture, heritage, and history. The new growth and development push for bigger responsibilities of planning and managing our cities for today and tomorrow.

Indian villages, towns, and cities, with the exceptions of some, have witnessed long periods of history. The history has impacted the urban form. Political, social, cultural, economic, monarchy, colonialism, and psychological forces have impacted the cities in the past and continue to impact in present times. These forces will impact in the future as well, joined by technology and smart and intelligent ideas and forces. There is an old but presently fiercely effective force – globalization – actively impacting our cities. They are becoming more competitive. Globalization is impacting India's social-cultural life style more than ever. It is changing quality of professionalism and understanding needs of the communities. Are Indian cities, new and old, ready to incorporate technology and smart operational tools and techniques?

Cities and towns are like organisms and they must grow with time. The growth diversify and solidify the revenue and economic sector. Some cities vanish or become ghost towns because of their anti-growth policies. If cities are not managed responsibly, they become chaotic, nuisance, and unsafe. Throughout the world, cities are striving to progress, grow, and develop responsibly. Cities, around the world, are planning their growth and development. In the West, especially in the developed countries, cities compete with each other to attract new economic opportunities and invite talented, creative, and innovative citizens to strengthen their social and economic base. This system help cities to progress by providing attractive activities, services, and technology to meet the needs of the creative and talented class. Are Indian cities doing the similar?

Historically, Indian villages, town, and cities have been neglected by the administration and citizens. That has magnified its challenges and issues. There are two forces at tug-of-war in cities. On the one side, cities are offering opportunities, choices, options, and variety. On the other side, ironically, the cities are not ready and equipped to provide infrastructure and services to the increasing number of urbanites to maintain quality of life. The increased urbanization due to the migration of people from rural to urban areas and cities being not equipped to handle the influx of people has made urban problems, such as population congestion, shortage of housing, traffic congestion, pollution (air, water, noise, and light), lack of services, lack of infrastructure, and deteriorating quality of life even worst. The push of automobiles by the automakers into the cities with the people with resources have worsen the existing situation and have added additional problems in the cities, such as parking, air pollution, congestion, accidents, reduced spaces for pedestrians, allocation of resources, and urban sprawl.

The increased urbanization is posing challenges to maintain and upgrade quality of life in towns and cities of India. Migration from rural areas has added numbers to the natural urban population growth. Interestingly, the urbanization concept has made reverse impact on the rural areas of India as well. Urban areas, undoubtedly, are the economic engines of the country by contributing major portion of the national gross domestic product. Economic opportunities are creating jobs and opening doors of entrepreneurship for the masses. Thus urban areas are providing opportunities, choices, variety, options, openings, and styles for all sections of the society. Simultaneously urban areas are becoming chaotic due to the increased number of people, traffic, commercial activities, and building new slums, expanding existing slums, and pollution of air, water, light, and holding the key position of being integral part of the national gross domestic product system. Rural areas provide raw material for the factories and industries in the cities. Villages and cities are two wheels of economic engines. *Like smart cities, villages can be smart as well.*

The idea of "good design" has been undergoing a transformation to include the elements of context – how new development can integrate and interact with the dynamics of the existing natural and manmade environment, and what can be done to preserve or even enhance those features. Context-Sensitive Design/Solutions/Planning (CSS/D/P) is a process for achieving design excellence by developing planning solutions that require continuous, collaborative communication, and consensus between various professionals, related agencies, and any and all stakeholders. A common goal of CSS/D/P is to develop a facility that is harmonious with the community, and preserves character, aesthetics, history, and the environmental resources, while integrating these innovative approaches with traditional developmental goals for safety, health, welfare, and performance.

Built environment of Indian cities are jeweled with architecture richness. The built areas of one city after another, one street after another, one neighborhood after another, one building after another is a marvel of planning, design, and architecture. Gardens, palaces, mansions, *havelis*, forts, and other buildings with architectural and art details are legacies in themselves. Family residences are garlanded with art and design. Gurudwaras, mosques, temples, churches and other worship/spiritual buildings are legacies of their time. A book could be filled with the examples of each category.

Form-based codes can provide a compromising platform in modern times of contemporary versus traditional choices. Ironically, the new unplanned, unthoughtful, insightful, undetermined, arrhythmic, unrhymed, and unsystematic development is covering the great architecture and art work done by the past generations. Art and design of buildings is patched up with grey plaster, facades are covered by signboards, *chajhas* and *chatris* are eloping and disappearing fast, and verandahs and courtyards are missing in the shades of high-rises. The history is being replaced with modern times with no detailing, art, and design work.

Modern architecture is a class in itself. Zoning is a component of public policy. Policy is one of a trio of controls that shape land and building development along with design and management. Design, policy, and management vary according to the type of environment and community. Form-based codes are vision-based and perspective, requiring that all development work together to create the place envisioned by the community. This requires that the community creates a detailed vision at the start of the coding process and then draft and administer the form-based codes to enforce the vision, and inherently proactive process.

Charrettes are modern public design exercises with great and extraordinary results. Charrettes are an integral part of many of the urban planning and design processes. A charrette involves a multidisciplinary team of professionals developing all elements of a plan. The team works closely with stakeholders through a series of feedback loops, during which alternative concepts are developed, reviewed by stakeholders, and revised accordingly.

The charrette is a sophisticated process that best serves controversial and complicated urban design and planning problems.

Its capacity to bring all the decision makers together for a discrete amount of time to create a solution makes it one of the most powerful techniques in a planner's tool kit.

The book is a concise document to understand built environment and human activities in urban and rural settings and provide practical and smart planning solutions. Furthermore, this book will explain theory and practice of many elements and facets of urban and rural planning ranging from need of planning, planners' identity, zoning, land use planning, transportation, urban design, landscaping, environment, and historic preservation. Modern urban issues of urbanization, sprawl, slums, implementation, and code enforcement are discussed. Local and micro level planning issues of role of religious/spiritual institutions, importance of addressing, and incorporation of *"wallas"* (road side mobile/static vendors, fulfilling many daily needs for produce, vegetables, eatables, repair, cooked food, and other services) in local plans are part of the book. The text explores innovative ideas like context-sensitive solutions/design/planning, form-based codes, preparation of smart development plans, project planning, smart city elements and futuristic cities and many other elements of day-to-day planning processes, urban governance, and planning department management in Indian context. While understanding the urban dynamics and built environment, the book presents scenarios to balance between quality of life and growth and development in urban areas. The book provides understanding of the urban built environment, natural environment, and space elements. Techniques to make cities healthy, safe, convenient, comfortable, happy, aesthetically appealing, morally sound, vibrant, harmonious, and with the sense of place and preparing communities for today and future generations are explained. The book explores the potentials and opportunities of rural areas of India.

The text outlines smart, simple, and practical urban planning tools and techniques and models to improve the quality of life of urbanites, explore opportunities to improve living conditions of urban and rural poor, and explore socio-economic opportunities for the urban and rural low income citizens. A model addressing urban slums problem with solutions. The book suggests solutions and alternatives to improve the living conditions with ideas to make Indian cities/towns/urban/rural areas to be more attractive and livable. Furthermore, with smart and innovative ideas, addressing each planning element, to make Indian cities/towns/villages more efficient, effective, functional, operational, and seamless. The intent of this book is to assist in improving quality of life, through planning and design processes, for citizens living in urban and rural areas. The text provide guidance to build harmonious, sustainable, and futuristic communities. A model to manage slums is discussed in detail in this text. The resources are limited but the population growth issue is not emphasized enough in any policy formulation at central, state, and local level. A model to address population scenario in Indian context is presented in this text.

A proposal to consider various elements while planning educational campuses are presented here. New IITs, Central universities, State universities, and private universities and colleges are being built in India. These institutions are formed with many different types of buildings, such as classrooms, meeting rooms, offices, lecture halls, lecture auditoriums, laboratories, workshops, amphitheaters, conference halls, theaters, play grounds, gymnasiums, recreational centers, and many other types of buildings depending on the type and nature of the educational institutions. Staff, faculty, students, and visitors fill these institutions.

Dynamic ecosystem provides environmental services such as clean air and water. Trees cool cities and save energy; improve air quality; strengthen quality of place and local economies; reduce storm water runoff; improve social connections; complement smart growth; and create walkable communities. Important element of "urban ecology" is the role of trees in providing wide variety of environmental, economic, and social benefits are part of this presentation.

There is lots of literature and writings available about planning sustainable communities. Many other names have been employed to identify the sustainability concept, such as new urbanism, walkable communities, smart communities, livable communities, life-style communities, and other titles. Many definitions have been proposed to explain sustainable communities. The present urban designs have official or unofficial, professional or unprofessional, and civic or non-civic fundamental responsibilities to build communities considering environment to the extent to conserve and protect resources for the next generation. Sustainability is the key to survival of settlements in present time high consumption society.

This text provides an overview of the public policy analysis processes. Planning, engineering, architecture, and other related professional departments are tangibly involved with public policy analysis from three perspectives: (i) Creation of public policy, (ii) Interpretation and implementation of public policy, and (iii) Being part of a team to create public policy. In a democratic political world and professional domain, both the creation and/or implementation of policy play an important role. Understanding of theory of public policy analysis is as important as implementation for planners, engineers, architects and related professionals.

The methodology of policy analysis draws from and integrated elements of multiple disciplines: political science, sociology, economic, philosophy, psychology, and technical disciplines, if the policy formation is about technical field. Policy analysis is partly descriptive, drawing on traditional disciplines that seek knowledge about cause and consequences of public policy. Yet policy analysis is normative, an additional aim is the creation and critique of knowledge claims about the value of public policies for past, present, and future.

In this book, a brief description of salient features of project management is depicted. Planning departments gets overwhelmed by various projects. These projects are related to community planning, social planning, physical planning, and economic planning. Preparing a comprehensive plan, zoning ordinance, or assessment of parks and open spaces in the community are projects. Imagine handling of a mega project – preparation of planning and management processes for 100 Smart Cities and 500 cities under Atal Mission for Rejuvenation and Urban Transformation (AMRUT). Planners and planning departments are sometimes dragged into the projects at various stages of a project.

A little while ago economists used the statement, "India is a rich country, inhabited by poor people." They wrote many treatises to justify this statement. Their research proved that though abundance of resources yet majority of people live in poverty and slums. The country is still plagued with poverty, slums, and more. The present-time economists, demographers, and population specialists should focus on "India is a rich but poor country, inhabited by too many people." India's population policies should educate citizens on preference of quality of children than having them in quantity. The country should make its citizens' understand, practice, and demand better quality of life. The population policies should emphasize on *education, education,* and *education* about the negativities of having too many children.

India's big problems have very simple solutions. For example, illiteracy among citizens can be solved in a simple way at a very nominal cost. Every educated person, student (high school, college, university), master, teacher, professor, should adopt an illiterate person (besides who attend school) to literate him or her. A volunteer can plan to spend and devote only couple of hours a week to literate a citizen – young or old. For the need to have a notebook, pen/pencil, and a basic book, for the student, the volunteer should contact an NGO, civil organizations (Rotary club, Kiwanis Club, Lions Club, Women's Networking Clubs, etc.) rich person, neighbor, relative, friend or stand in front of a worship/spiritual place with a sign that you need few bucks for this cause. Many NGOs in the foreign countries, run and managed by Indians, are looking for the opportunities to help people in India with needs. Within a short period of time, a large number of population will be educated at a nominal cost. This model will not need a national, state or local level budget and policy formulation. For this endeavor, no involvement of Central Government or politicians or administrators or World Bank or a national policy is required. Any educated citizen with zeal can do this endeavor. In addition, every worship/spiritual place should organize classes to educate illiterates. Every priest, cleric, deacon, or religious authority or institution should take initiative to educate people. All he or she will need is a couple of hours in a week to spare for this cause. The social, economic, psychological, and societal benefits are enormous. For example, an illiterate driver will enter in "no-entry zone" and may cause fatal accident. But educated driver will follow the instructions. The literate person can board the right train or bus without asking anyone. This will enhance self-confidence and self-esteem among citizens. Urban Local Bodies (ULBs), civil organizations, educational institutions, worship places, and other active entities should recognize such citizens for their contributions and accomplishments and to encourage others to participate in this endeavor.

Garbage and trash is a common site everywhere in India. Children should be educated about civic sense and integrity at early stages. Every child should be trained, early on, at school and home to dispose of trash at a proper and designated place. Once children are trained, they can teach the same to adults. Schools and parents can train young generation about this responsibility without any cost and without any national level "yojanas," "schemes," and "abhiyans." This training and way of life will make and keep the country clean. Clean places do not need frequent cleaning. Likewise, the children should be educated, early on, to follow the instructions, directions, signs, and information to maintain civic integrity. Children should be educated about the role and responsibilities of various level of governments and about the rights and duties of citizens. Young people are the future adult citizens, managers, professionals, work force, leaders, entrepreneurs, and politicians of India – to make India Good to Great.

The fundamental role of government is to perform responsibly by protecting its people and providing services according to the Constitution, ordinances, acts, and policies. The citizens have rights and responsibilities too. Both sides have to act responsibly. The citizens should question candidates running for elections about their agenda for the community. The strategies to fulfil community's goals and objectives. In democracy, the citizens are equally responsible for incompetency, irresponsibility, and inefficiency of the elected officials. Because general masses elect them – vote for them. The citizens should question the candidates, how they plan to make communities livable and harmonious. By virtue of their positions, elected officials cannot comprehend beyond winning next elections. In the democratic political world, anyone can run for elections, however, to be a physician one has to go a medical school, engineer has to go to an engineering school, and a teacher has to have enough education to teach and so on. But there are no minimum qualifications required to be an elected official. The citizens must think twice, whom they vote for – do not vote if the candidates are not responsible and honest. The citizens must take their positions seriously to the extent from voting to performing duties and their job(s) responsibly.

In India, rivers Ganga, Yamuna, Saraswati, Chambal, Gomti, Godavri, Kaveri, Ravi, Satluj, Bias, and other hundreds of them were the source of providing basic human necessity of water for centuries. Indian civilization and culture blossomed along the rivers and lakes. By protecting them, citizens do not have to drink bottled water. People with resources can afford bottled water, and show as status reflection, but people with meager resources should not be deprived of basic human right – clean drinking water. Every citizen is entitled for clean drinking water from public supply of water in urban areas. Ironically, elected officials bring and drink bottled water at the public meetings. It symbolizes that the municipal water is not up to the standards. Municipalities (ULBs) should strive and make top priority to provide clean drinkable water to citizens. This will protect human health, provide basic human necessity, and protect environment from trashed plastic bottles.

Ample sunshine, in India, should be tapped to generate renewable solar energy. The technology is readily available. The shortage of energy problem can be solved by smart energy planning. Every building and structure, where feasible, should be equipped with solar panels to generate renewable energy. Through smart planning local laws, the communities should be required installation of solar energy generating equipment on structures, buildings, open spaces, vacant lots, and other available sites.

In India, people are buying more cars today than ever. Additional cars are creating or expanding problems of congestion, parking, pollution (air, water, and noise) and other related problems such as junk cars and abandoned cars along public rights-of-way. Cities need more roads to accommodate additional cars. New roads and widening of existing roads are hijacking pedestrian spaces in cities. Flyovers are damaging cohesive urban fabric. There are simple solutions. "No Parking – No Car." A citizen must provide proof of available parking space prior to buying a car. Automobile manufacturers and dealers should pay to cities to install additional transportation infrastructure as required to accommodate their product. They are responsible for automobile-related generated problems and should compensate the communities. Planners should advocate to build walkable, lifestyle, livable, sustainable, smart, and mixed-use type communities – discourage car ownership. Transit system should be efficient, effective, comfortable, convenient, and economical to lure ridership. Walking and bicycling should be encouraged by providing special dedicated lanes for such uses.

Not long ago, I visited India for a spiritual tour and to thank God for his generosities. I realized that God, in any shape or form or under any name, such as Ram, Krishna. Brahma, Vishnu, Mahesh, Shiv, Parvathi, Hanuman, Ganesh, Sri Venkteshwara, Guru Nanak, Guru Gobind Singh, Buddha, many saints and peers and many other names of Himself preferred to walk in India than any other place on earth. I have my reasonings for HIS selection of India. The reader may carve his/her own reasonings. I am thankful to God for selecting India during His visits to earth. We, all Indians should challenge ourselves to make India welcoming and inviting and prepare for HIS next visit to earth – whenever that is. And God, instead of giving us another Geeta or Guru Granth Sahib or Quran or Bible or a new holy book about life, rather say Thank You to earthlings for keeping his kingdom clean, green, colorful, joyful, safe, and peaceful.

The country of Taj Mahal, phenomenal temples, gurudwaras, mosques, churches, and other worshiping/spiritual buildings and places, elegant palaces, spectacular mansions, unmatched architecture, and with long history, historic features, rich culture, and many other elements of pride is being tarnished, tainted, and spoiled. The country of spirituality and worshiping is at the cross-roads to select the right path of harmonious living by extracting and identifying the concepts of planned living as directed in our "Granths" and "Puranas" and "Vedas", and learn from our fore fathers whose wisdom and futuristic vision gave us the built environment we enjoy and relish today. The onus is on us now what kind of county we live in and leave for the coming generations.

"Bharat Hamara Desh Hai. Jaisa Banayenge Vaisa hee Banega."

"Bharat is our country. It will be what we make of it."

> *Let us make our India a beautiful place to live, work, play, learn, worship, invest, and raise a family.*

Chapter 1
Urban and rural planning 101

Urban planning is considered a rational process that seeks the orderly, cost-effective, and sustainable development of the urban environment, oriented to the formulation and attainment of objectives and application of standards that specify desirable built environment. Latest innovative concepts of smart growth, context sensitive design/solutions/planning, and form-based codes are incorporated in this text with the notion that they are more practical, professional, innovative, and functional in the old city/town realm than application of "standards" only. This view of urban planning assumes that the orderly physical development of urban areas is in the best interest of public health, safety, general welfare, aesthetics, morals, and not to furthering particular special interests. This text is more oriented towards providing a comprehensive binocular view of cities in Indian context, processes to understand them, and with emphasis on action of implementation with practical and functional solutions.

This text is intended to introduce to the concepts, principles, and practices underlying urban planning and design in general in Indian context. Emphasis are placed on the concepts of the smart cities, urban design, land uses, including comprehensive planning, urbanization, transportation, public utilities, community services, and implementation tools such as zoning, land subdivision controls, mapping, and capital improvement programming. Further, the text introduces innovative ideas of urbanization management, slum management, project management, and importantly historic preservation. Many other micro-level elements have been elaborated such as addressing, operation and confinement of *"wallas"*, airport planning, underground development, and environmental issues. The concepts of smart cities, new urbanism, smart growth, life-style neighborhoods, context-sensitive solutions, and mixed-use development have been perceived through Indian context.

The purpose of this text is to direct urban planners and designers to more microscopic understanding of the built environment and help other professionals such as municipal engineers, traffic and transportation engineers, transportation planners, environmental planners and specialists, architects, landscape architects, geographers, economists, demographers, attorneys, and ecologists and more proficient practitioners of their respective professions and active and informed citizens. Other professionals working in urban environment should be exposed to the planning processes and make them more effective members of urban planning teams, particularly at the municipal level of government.

1.1   Introduction

A good understanding of the principles and practices of urban planning requires prefatory terminology and an understanding of the basic concepts of the terminology. Throughout this text the terminology of terms, such as planning is used as urban planning, city planning, town planning, and the terms city, town, and urban are interchangeable. Urbanization, derived from the Latin 'Urbs' – a term used by the Romans to a city, is the increase in the proportion of people living in towns and cities.

The National Commission on Urbanization describes urbanization as a process whereby the surplus population of workers from rural areas resettles in urban centers where non-agricultural job opportunities are available.

1.1.1 Indian definition of urban area

All statutory places with a Municipality, Corporation, Cantonment Board, or Notified Town Area Committee, and all places satisfying the following three criteria simultaneously: (i) a minimum population of 5000; (ii) at least 75 per cent of male working population engaged in non-agricultural pursuits; and (iii) a population density of at least 400 per sq km (1000 per sq mile).

Urban agglomeration is defined as an urban spread constituting a city and its adjoining urban outgrowths or two or more physically contiguous cities/towns together and any adjoining urban outgrowth of such cities/towns.

1.2 A city

The rise of cities and towns marked a great revolution in human culture and, unlike the agricultural revolution that preceded it, was predominantly a social process – a change in the way humans interacted with one another, rather than in the way human interacted with the environment. A city may be defined as a relatively large, dense, and permanent settlement of people engaged in diverse economic activities. In addition, a city must have a government and social institutions to serve the needs of the resident population, a population that must be agglomerated rather than isolated. A traditional planning definition of city is complex arrangement of land uses, linked together by circulation systems and made viable by other systems of utilities such as piped water supply, sewer, sewage, electric power, telecommunication, and communication. Basically, cities are economic entities, social cradle, a legal entity, and a physical organism.

1.3 The city as an economic entity

Economists regard the cities as an economic entity existing to serve certain highly organized economic functions that act as an urbanizing force. These include four general functions that are performed by every city regardless of age, size, or location, and that remain unchanged over time. These four functions are production, distribution, consumption and amenity service. The last of these four functions is concerned with providing a suitable human life. More specifically, special urban economic functions include exchange, manufacturing, extraction, government, education, and religion/spirituality. These special functions differ between cities and will determine, to a large extent, the characteristics of the city. These special functions may also change over time due to, among other factors, technological innovations.

1.4 Exchange

The special urban function of exchange, also known as trade and commerce, acts as an urbanizing force for cause of cities to locate and grow at points of transshipment also known as *nodes*; at termini of trade routes; and at centers of agricultural regions.

1.5 Manufacturing

Manufacturing as an urbanizing force acts to cause cities to locate and grow at sources of raw materials, in proximity to markets, at sources of power and fuel, in areas marked by concentrations of labor and capital, and in areas of favorable climate. The momentum of an early application or adaption of a new technology, and even historic accident, may also be important factors determining the location of such cities. Examples of expansions are of Hyderabad and Bangalore.

1.6 Extraction

Extraction as an urbanizing force acts to cause cities to locate and grow at or in proximity to major mineral deposits, forests, and fisheries.

1.7 Government

Government as an urbanizing force is usually directed by political considerations and actions, e.g. state capitals, New Delhi.

1.8 Education

Educational incentives are a force for cause of cities to locate, stabilize, and grow.

1.9 Religion/spiritual

In Indian context, many towns and cities have been established and flourished over time because of religious/spiritual affiliation. Worship places become force for cities' complex activities.

Economists and geographers have developed various quantitative measures of these general and special urban functions such as employment structure, industrial structure, and economic base. The employment structure of a city or urban area may be defined as the ratio of the employment in each major endeavor – manufacturing, construction, mining, forestry, trade, government and other sectors; also known as formal and informal sectors. The informal sector or informal economy is a part of the economy that is not organized to be taxed or monitored by any form of government or included in any gross national product, unlike the formal economy. Industrial structure of a city may be defined as the ratio of the employment in each type of industry to total manufacturing employment. Economic base of a city, or urban area, may be defined as those functions that bring flow of purchasing power into the city – that is, that export of goods and services. The economic base of a city is always associated with its special economic functions.

1.10 City as a social cradle

Sociologists regard the city as a social cradle, that is, as a complex network of institutions that operate for the welfare of the residents. In this respect, the city may be regarded as a "community" that is a group of people with more or less common experiences, problems, issues, and interests, able to act in a corporate capacity. Although, it may often be difficult to attach this definition of "community" to larger cities and urban areas, a strong sense of community by a substantial number of residents will make the city planning process both easier and more effective. The sociologists also regard the city as a form or mode of life, wherein the associated beings acquire certain traits and create certain organizations for social action. Sociologists have also developed quantitative measures of these social characteristics such as population characteristics: size, age, gender, and race. Institutional structure of a city may be defined as the formal associational groupings that can be distinguished as either administrative agencies or organized groups. Value system of a group consists of the morally binding customs and attitudes of the group – that is, of the things the members of the group hold dear. Social satisfaction may be defined as the structure and process through which rights and privileges, and duties and obligations, are distributed unequally among socially designated, or ranked, grades of people. Power structure of a community may be defined as the locus of the real power to make decisions concerning the development of community. The power structure is not necessarily synonymous with the nominal leadership in a community that functions through the governmental structure.

1.11   City as a legal entity

The concept of a city as a corporate entity is one that is apt to be used by the legal profession and is probably the only truly strict definition of the term city. The entities may be district, city, town, village, and union territory.

1.12   City as a physical organism

The city may also be regarded as a large and complex physical organism. This view point holds that although the city be an economic entity, a social cradle, and a legal entity, it is also a large and very costly physical organism. That physical organism comprises the buildings and structures that house the individual land uses; the utility facilities that serve those buildings and structures with power, light, heat, communications, sewerage, water supply, drainage; streets, roads, transit, and transport facilities that provide for the movement of people and goods between those buildings and structures, and that connect the city to the rest of the nation and world.

1.13 What is planning

Planning, also called urban planning or city and regional planning, is a dynamic profession that works to improve the welfare of people and their communities by creating more convenient, equitable, healthful, efficient, and attractive places for present and future generations. Planning is a process striving to improve quality of life. Planning is often defined as one of the five basic functions of management, those being planning, organizing, directing, coordinating, and controlling. Planning is a rational process concerned with identifying needs or problems, gathering and analyzing relevant data concerning the problems, developing and testing alternative solutions to the identified problems, and selecting for adoption and implementation the solutions that is judged best. Planning enables civic leaders, businesses, and citizens to play a meaningful role in creating communities that enrich people's lives.

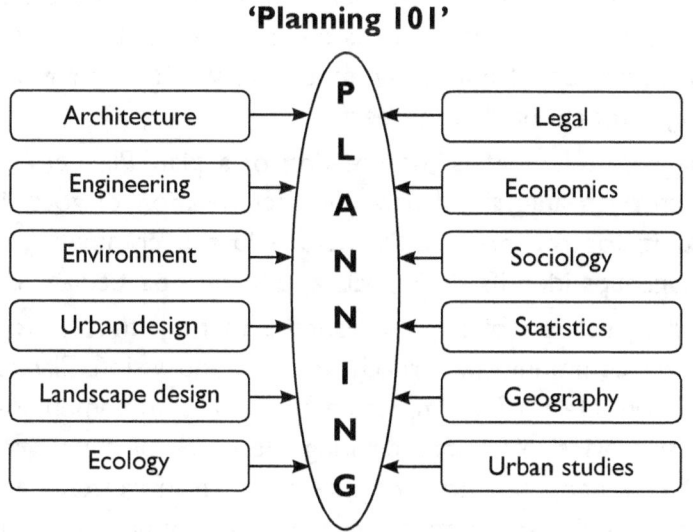

Figure 1.1 Planning is a cumulative discipline of many specialities

Planning does not work independently. Many disciplines and specialities provide elements to make planning shine, workable, appreciable, and recognizable. Planners have to have a peculiar sense to fathom, recognize, and incorporate elements from other disciplines to make planning a specialized and complete field in itself. Many interesting and dynamic disciplines such as architecture, engineering, landscape architecture, urban design, ecology, environment, economics, geography, sociology, legal, urban studies, population studies/statistics, and many others make the discipline and profession of planning more interesting, dynamic, and challenging. (Fig. 1.1)

Good planning helps create communities that offer better choices for where and how people live. Planning helps communities to envision their future. It helps them find the right balance of new development and essential services, environmental protection, and innovative change.

1.14   What planners do

Professional planners help create a broad vision for the community. They also research, design, and develop programs; lead public processes; effect social change; perform technical analyses; manage; and educate. Some planners focus on just some of these roles, such as transportation planning, but most will work at many kinds of planning throughout their careers.

The basic element is the creation of a plan. Planners develop a plan through analysis of data and identification of goals for the community or the project. Planners help the community and its various groups identify their goals and form a particular vision.

In the creation of a plan, planners identify the strategies by which the community can reach its goals and vision. Planners are also responsible for the implementation or enforcement of many of the strategies, often coordinating the work of many groups of people. It is important to recognize that a plan can take a variety of forms including: policy recommendations, community action plans, comprehensive plans, neighborhood plans, regulatory and incentive strategies, or historic preservation plans.

Other examples of plans include: redevelopment plans, smart growth strategies, economic development strategic plans, site plans, environment protection plans, context-sensitive plan, and disaster preparedness plans.

Planning used in the broadest sense is concerned with the future. The planners must, however, seek to understand the probable nature of future, estimating the probabilities of existing trends continuing, and must attempt to identify possible occurrence. Decisions exist only in present. The issue that faces planners is not what should be done tomorrow, but what must be done today to get ready for an uncertain tomorrow. Planning is necessary just because decisions can only be made in the present, and yet cannot be made for the present alone.

1.15   A typical day for a planner, and with whom do planners work

Planning is a highly collaborative field, and planners spend much of their time working with others. A planner's day may start with a staff meeting to discuss the management of a planning project. Other meetings might include a team meeting with engineers, architects, health professionals, and landscape architects to review the specifics of a plan. Yet other meetings might take place with developers as part of a pre-application process. The planner's role is to provide the big picture and to relate the project to various goals and guidelines, such as ordinances or design review, in order to achieve a final project that meets the needs of the community. This might include appropriate design, environmental considerations, support for the local economy, and removal of slums, or equitable access for all members of the community.

Planners are also responsible for knowing state and federal legislation and court rulings that relate to the project, plans, or guidelines. For example, planners must know how the certain *"yojna"* or "scheme" or "project" or "plan" or "central and state government policy" can work for his/her city or village. Once again, planners are responsible for providing this technical knowledge to the projects. In complex projects, a developer will likely consult his or her own legal experts.

Some part of the planner's day use variety of sources, including economic development or market research studies, from census reports, or from environmental studies. The planner tests assumptions about the meaning and importance of the data by using a variety of technologies. One common tool used in planning is Geographic Information Systems (GIS) that link data and electronic mapping. Other tools may include scenario-building visualization tools, electronic poling systems, financial analysis spreadsheets, and demographic databases. Planners prepare reports on their findings and analysis. Often, they will provide alternatives for policy makers to consider. Writing and synthesis skills are necessary for this part of the job.

Planners also do presentations. Presentations are made by top-level manager, mid-level staff, department heads, or the planning director. Planners frequently provide presentations to the city council, business groups, neighborhood groups, and professionals. These presentations place the specific project or issue in the context of the community's plans and guidelines for development and change. Today, planners are proficient in using PowerPoint and other visual technologies to present information and ideas in planning. Presentation skills are very important for private sector planners who have to present projects at various stages to clients, officials, or the public.

Project management is another important skill for planners, especially for those working in the private sector. Planners manage a variety of projects from neighborhood planning programs to the design and development of a new bike path to much larger scale projects. They also oversee grant programs, such as historic preservation or Rajiv Awas Yojana, or United Nations Development Program or other community development programs.

Planners also engage in more lengthy processes of public participation. In these projects, planners call upon their skills as facilitators working with a broad spectrum of community members. These processes have become very creative and planners often use exercises, charrettes, visualization techniques, and group work in the development of a plan.

A planner's day often extends into the evening as he or she provides staff support to the monthly planning commission meeting.

Public sector planners provide reports to the commission and provide support to the public meeting. Private sector planners present projects to the commission. It is not uncommon for a planning attorney to present proposals to the planning commission or, on occasion, to provide legal counsel to the planning commission. Other evening meetings may include neighborhood meetings or staffing the historic preservation review board.

1.16   Common specializations in the planning profession

Most planners perform their work in one or more particular fields of specialization within the larger planning profession. These specializations represent specific bodies of planning knowledge that jointly further the welfare of people and communities. While some planners spend their entire career within one of these specializations, most will move between them or find employment opportunities that combine specializations. Here are several of the most common specializations within the planning profession:

- Community Development
- City/Town Planning
- Rural Planning
- Regional Planning
- Land Use & Code Enforcement
- Transportation Planning
- Environmental/Natural Resources Planning
- Economic Development
- Urban Design
- Planning Management/Finance
- Housing
- Parks & Recreation
- Historic Preservation
- Policy Formulation and Analysis
- Community Activism/Empowerment

In Indian context, there are potentials for additional specializations such as slum planning and smart city planning.

1.17 How are planners educated?

Three main degrees are awarded in the field. The first is an undergraduate degree in planning. Many with undergraduate degrees will go on to receive a master's degree in planning. However, planners with undergraduate degrees do work in planning practice, often in entry-level positions. Institute of Town Planners, India, offers opportunities for professional advancement.

A master's-level graduate degree is considered the standard for those who are planning practitioners. Some planning graduate students have an undergraduate degree in planning, but others may have studied geography, urban studies, architecture, economics, statistics or sociology. When hiring for professional planning positions, many organizations require or give strong preference to candidates holding graduate degrees. For example, in 2004, 43 percent of all American Planning Association (note: approximately one-sixth of the APA members are planning commissioners, officials, or students, who do not have a degree in planning) had earned a master's degree in planning. In the United States, many employers also give preference to those who are certified by the American Institute of Certified Planners (AICP).

The third level of planning degree is the Ph.D. Most often, those who obtain a Ph.D. in planning pursue a career in academia or with research or policy institutions.

1.18 What skills do successful planners possess?

In addition to a formal educational background, planners possess a unique combination of skills that enhance their professional success. Because planning is a dynamic and diverse profession, individual skills vary depending on a planner's role and area of specialization. Successful planners possess a combination of these skills:

- Knowledge of urban spatial structure or physical design and the way in which cities and towns work.
- Ability to analyze demographic information to discern trends in population, employment, and health.
- Knowledge of plan making and project evaluation.
- Mastery of techniques for involving a wide range of people in making decisions.
- Understanding of local, state, and federal government programs and processes.
- Understanding of the social and environmental impact of planning decisions on communities.
- Ability to work with the public and articulate planning issues to a wide variety of audiences.
- Ability to function as a mediator or facilitator when community interests conflict.
- Understanding of the legal foundation for land-use regulation.
- Understanding of the interaction among the economy, transportation, health and human services, and land-use regulation.
- Ability to solve problems using a balance of technical competence, creativity, and hardheaded pragmatism.
- Ability to envision alternatives to the physical and social environments in which we live.
- Mastery of geographic information systems and office software.

1.19 Good city planning

Good city planning should meet at least three criteria:
1. It should be comprehensive, considering all aspects of physical development of the community and relating those to common unifying objectives. A comprehensive approach is essential to the making of intelligent decisions concerning relative needs and the effective allocation of resources to areas of greatest needs.

2. It should be relatively long range, looking well beyond obvious needs of the moment, and attendant expedient solutions.
3. It should encompass a geographic area that permits a sound technical approach to the issues and problems concerned.

There are no models or standard recipe for urban planning that can be applied everywhere. The communities/neighborhoods/cities/towns/ rural areas have to decide their expectations, establish goals and objectives, and monitor and evaluate the results. The communities have to be firm and flexible. They have to be firm on acting on the established goals and objectives and flexible to make changes if certain element or goal is not achieving its established expectation.

1.20 Planning as a team effort

Urban planning is so broad in scope that few individuals can master all the disciplines and professional skills required for its successful execution. City planning organizations, in addition to urban planners, include urban designers, municipal engineers, traffic and transportation engineers, transportation planners, environmental planners and engineers, architects, landscape architects, geographers, economists, demographers, attorneys, and ecologists.

The attendant undesirable effects of poorly planned or unplanned urban growth include:

- High capital and operating costs related to the provision of municipal infrastructure and services, with the customary tax revenues being inadequate to meet rising costs of providing municipal services to widely dispersed, rapidly expanding population
- Unstable tax bases for both older central city and first ring suburban areas and newer outer ring suburban and rural–urban fringe areas
- Pollution of streams, rivers, lakes, and water courses
- Drainage and flooding problems
- Air, noise, and light pollution

- Piped water-supply problems
- Power failures
- Overcrowded and inadequate transportation facilities, and overcrowded and inadequate community facilities and services, such as schools
- Traffic bottlenecks – congestion and unsafe conditions
- Often irreparable misuse of the land
- Slums formation
- Inadequate parks and open space areas
- Exacerbation is already serious problem of the central city core and surrounding core areas together with the appearance of blight in the older first ring suburbs
- Substandard areas of housing lacking essential public facilities and services, and inadequate housing for the needed work force in proximity to employment concentrations
- Imbalanced provision of utilities and services

Monetary savings are important but the most important value of planning lies not in such savings but in the objectives that good planning makes possible to attain. Good planning is its own best justification because it enables communities to achieve agreed-upon objectives. Planning is important primarily for what it achieves. Good planning can protect, preserve, and enhance the natural environment and built environment.

In conclusion, the central and state governments should focus on promoting town/city/urban planning discipline at colleges and universities. They should also create jobs in planning and make mandatory for urban local bodies (ULBs) to employ planners to plan and manage their entities. In Indian context, slum planning and smart city planning specializations can be part of urban planning curriculum at university levels. Ministry of HRD must focus on these areas to balance the development processes and improve quality of life for all sectors of the society. This will help design the future settlements and sociological uplifting of masses in India.

Chapter 2
Evolution of urban planning

2.1 Indian evolution of town planning

The planning of cities, towns, and villages was done on scientific basis in India since Vedic times. Some of the planning principles and theories are contained in the ancient literature such as Rig Veda, Atharva Veda, Puranas, Samhitas, Shilpa-shastras, Niti-shastras, and Smirit-shastras. The profession of an urban planner possessed a high social and professional status in the ancient times. An intensive training was required for a Stahpati (establisher or town planner). The architects and town planners were chosen from the upper social strata of society. Vishvakarma is known as the divine architect and is credited with spreading knowledge of silpa-shastra.

The cities were organized and governed according to the site conditions. The towns were generally situated on riverbanks or near water bodies. A river was much preferred for many reasons, such as availability of water for human use, irrigation of farmlands, and sanitary purposes. Perhaps these are the reasons Indian culture respect(ed) and worship(ed) rivers, and other natural features who nurtured day-to-day human and cattle life.

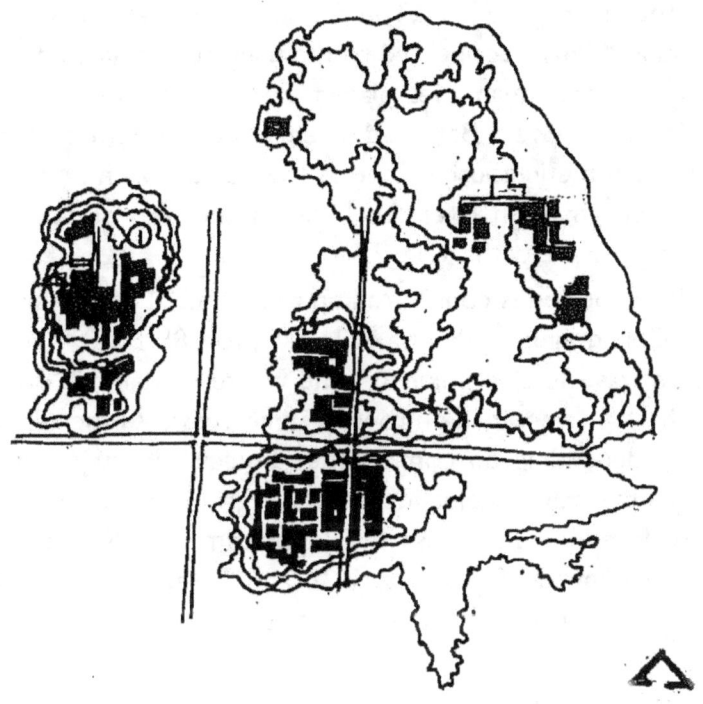

Figure 2.1 Plan of Mohenjo-Daro

Indus Valley civilization dates back to 3000 B.C., about five thousand years ago, along Indus River, now in Pakistan. The excavations for this civilization started only less than hundred years ago. The civilization covered areas Mohenjo-Daro, Harappa, Kalibangan in Rajasthan, Lothal, Sukortada, and Dhoulavira in Gujarat, Rakhigadhi in Haryana, show that the Indus Valley Civilization not only dates back to thousands of years but also was spread over large area or had many centers over large area. The excavations indicate that the cities had advanced systems of town planning. The streets were laid out on "grid pattern." Living quarters were of various sizes and stories. A series of rooms were arranged around an open-to-sky central court. The residences had no direct entrance opening to the main streets; and no windows were provided towards the subsidiary walkways. They depended on roof lighting and ventilation. Almost every house, built of kiln-brick, had complete bathing establishment. A common well provided to the groups of the buildings. They had a functional drainage system. The drainage lines were running under walkways and finally connected to the main sewers laid under main roads. There were manholes placed at difference for cleaning and inspections. The Great Bath had a remarkable system of filling and emptying and meticulously joined at the bottom with bricks. It was made watertight with layers of bitumen, and was surrounded by toilets and private baths. (Fig. 2.1)

Buddhist period is considered up to 320 A.D. During this period of King Chandragupta Maurya (321 B.C. to 185 B.C.), Kautilya or Chanakya was the chief minister who wrote the famous document "Arthashastra", a treatise on town planning. It states the regulations of zoning depending on communities, boulevards (Rajmarg) to be parallel to the main cardinal direction i.e. grid-iron pattern, Rajmarg to be wide enough, not less than approximately 30 feet. Ancient cities of Patliputra, Taxila (Fig. 2.2), and Nalanda were extreme examples of well-thought town planning.

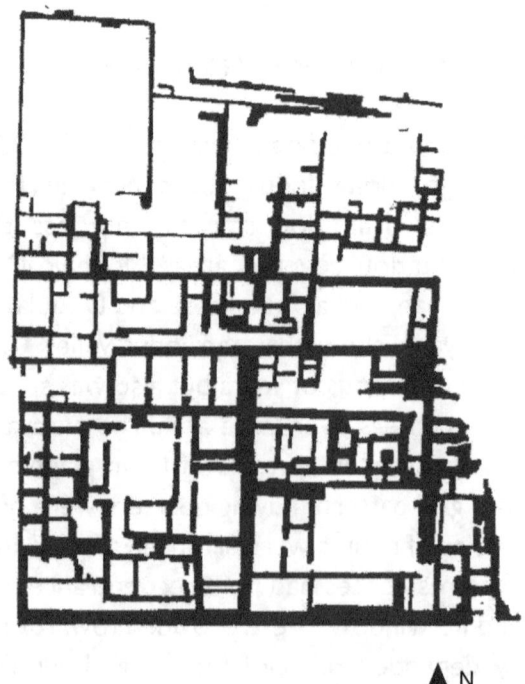

Figure 2.2 Plan of Taxila

In Vedic period, up to 400 B.C., the town planning was an organized activity. The principles of town planning are quoted in the ancient literature. It is written in "Vishwakarmaprakash" that first lay out the towns and then plan out the houses. This principle prevails even in modern town planning processes. In "Mansara Shilpa-shastra" some of the aspects of town planning like understanding soils, climatic conditions, wind direction, orientation of buildings to get maximum advantage of sun, topography, etc., are mentioned. Many town plan types, like "dandaka", "swastika", "padmaka", nandyavart", "prastara", "chatumukha", and "karmukha" are explained in the book. Historic foreign travelers have recorded descriptions of ancient Indian cities and towns. Ancient historians have also records of then cities and towns. Some names are Huen Tsang, Magasthenese, Iban-i-Batuta, Fahein, and others.

Records show a typical town consisted of shopping area, streets, public buildings, different types of residences for various status people, worship places, royal palace, recreation centers, ditches, shed for drinking water, gardens, water tanks, granaries, reservoirs, and other features like forts, boundary walls, and underground passages. Towards 14th century, known as medieval period, witnessed gradual development of trade and commerce. During this period, the country experienced cities of Dhaka, Krishnanagar, Agra, Murshidabad, and Jaipur.

Moghul period from 1526 to very early 18th century, cities like Agra, Delhi were redeveloped and expanded. Fathepur-Sikri was entirely planned. Cities of Bijapur and Lucknow were fortified. This era witnessed creation of a number of gardens. It was a new trend and addition to town planning with recognition of open spaces and beautification. Some existing examples are Kabul Bagh at Panipat, Shalimar Bagh and Nishat Bagh at Kashmir, Pinjor Garden, Haryana, and Lal Bagh at Bangalore.

The British period till the independence of India witnessed many changes to the town concepts. The British imported many town planning ideas from Europe including creation of parks, gardens, hill station cities, cantonment towns, and civil lines such as Shimla, Dalhousie, Darjeeling and Kasauli. They started independent colonies on and along outskirt of the existing towns. Civil lines were for residences for civilians and elite group of the city. They designed straight roads regardless of its social or economic impact to the existing communities. Regretfully, present engineers and planners are repeating the history by building flyovers and highways without any consideration to the existing community fabric. The new town of New Delhi, capital of colonial India, was planned and developed with modern town planning principles by Edwin Lutyens, who brought fresh planning ideas from England. The key buildings of Government House, Council Hall, and Secretariat were designed with monumental architecture style. Industrial use buildings were separated from residential uses. Then British left. Can Indian administration and planning sustain their creations?

Since the independence in 1947, India has taken many initiatives and built new towns around the country for various reasons. Industrial towns of Durgapur, Bhilai, Rourkela, Jamshedpur, Chittaranjan, and Bhadravati, and new capital towns of Chandigarh (Fig. 2.3), Gandhinagar, and Bhubaneswar.

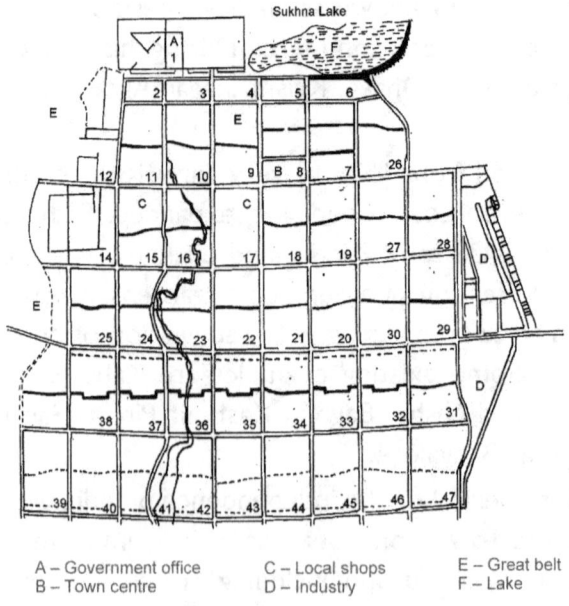

A – Government office
B – Town centre
C – Local shops
D – Industry
E – Great belt
F – Lake

Figure 2.3 Plan of Chandigarh

2.2 Evolution around the world

Major changes in human settlements occurred because of various reasons, such as climate, shift in water bodies locations. Agriculture, preserving food, domestication of animals, use of animals for agriculture, and irrigation methods helped make people together, in large numbers, and formation of settlements. Old civilizations provide account of their cities such as Tigris, Nile and Euphrates rivers and civilizations along them.

Egyptian cities developed along River Nile from 5000 B.C. The local soils were fertile because of annual deposition of fresh soils through floods by the river. The perennial water supply for irrigation and daily life uses helped flourish a remarkable civilization.

Greek civilization (750–350 B.C.) developed many state-of-the-art, of their time, elements of civilization. A great city-state was called as "Polis." Polis was community of families related to common ancestors. The ideal polis had 5000 citizens. The cities of ancient Greece during the Hellenic Age reflected the development of a democratic way of life. This age lasted from 1200 to 338 B.C. The city of Athens represented the highest development of the Greek culture, with many temples, public buildings, public markets, and political gathering places. The free citizens accepted responsibility for their government, lived modestly, and took pride in their public buildings and temples.

In time, Athens, weakened by the Peloponnesian War eruption, succumbed to the armies of Alexander the Great. However, the culture of Greece spread to the conquerors and gave rise to Hellenistic civilization. Throughout the Mediterranean region, Greek architecture and ideas influenced the development of large cities such as Alexandria, Syracuse, and Pergamon. These cities had many public buildings and monuments, and elaborate homes for the rulers and wealthy classes. The Hellenistic civilization persisted from 338 B.C. to 147 B.C.

While new cities were being built during the Hellenistic era, Rome began to emerge as a civilization. The Roman Empire eventually conquered most of Europe and the Mediterranean region, with the

Romans too, adopting much of Greek culture and architecture. The history of Romans began with the city of Rome, founded by Romulus and Remus in 753 B.C. As the empire grew, far away cities became part of the Roman Empire for self-rule by all the people. Rome was the center of a great empire and great civilization. Romans were great builders, which is evident through public buildings, temples, baths, and amphitheaters. Their engineering skills are well placed in their water systems and roads.

2.3   Medieval cities

By 500 A.D., the Roman Empire crumbled under the weight of its excesses and corruption. The Dark Ages had descended upon Europe, with a general decline in Western civilization. As Europe emerged from the Dark Ages, urban life improved considerably. Craftsmen and merchants formed guilds and challenged the nobility for economic and political power. The typical medieval town was walled and contained a castle, a market, and a church. The rest of the town was composed largely of shops and private dwellings. The medieval city was small, and the residents had ready access to the countryside. Life in the medieval town was pleasant and colorful. Marketplaces were filled with people and festivals were common. The physical beauty of the towns was one of subtle beauty.

2.4   The Middle Ages

The rise of mercantilism brought an end to the medieval town. The number of towns in Europe increased drastically during the Middle Ages, but most of the towns remained small due to confining walls. The power of the feudal lords and guilds declined, while the power of the merchants and landlords increased. Cities became congested, as garden spaces gave way to buildings. Second stories of homes and other buildings were extended over streets as more people crammed behind city walls. The quality of life declined due to overcrowding and poor sanitation. Plague swept across Europe, extracting their heaviest toll in the crowded cities.

2.5 Renaissance cities

Consolidation of power under monarchs and development of long-range artillery signaled the end of the walled cities. The arts and science expanded, and a desire to reintroduced monumental architecture into European cities prevailed. Without walls, cities expanded rapidly, and gardens, parks, and open space were the rule during this period. New homes were built for the wealthy, and broad avenues provided access to new churches and public buildings. In spite of these additions to cities, most residents were poor and lived in deplorable conditions.

2.6 European new towns

The European new towns were built primarily for military purposes. Plans for these towns were marked by rectangular, or sometimes radial street patterns, and by the provisions of public squares or plazas. Water supply and drainage were carefully considered in the planning.

2.7 Spanish colonial new towns

A number of new towns were planned and constructed in the North American Colonies. King Philip II of Spain in 1573 proclaimed a royal ordinance, known as the Laws of the Indies, governing the planning of new towns in the Americas. The ordinance contained detailed specification for the layout of major and minor streets, plazas, and sites for churches and other major buildings. The main plaza was to be starting point for the town. The plaza was to be either square or rectangular, if the latter, the length was to 1.5 times the width. The four principal streets were to begin from the middle of each side of the plaza, and eight other streets were to begin from each corner.

2.8 Urban concepts

2.8.1 The Columbian Fair

The growing dissatisfaction of Americans with the prevalent form of urban development was given impetus for action by the Columbian

Exposition of 1893. This World Fair held in what is now Jackson Park, Chicago, is said to have marked a renewal of interest in city planning within the United States.

The site plan for the Fair was prepared and the development of the site was directed by a team consisting of Daniel Hudson Burnham, an architect and chief of construction; Frederick Las Olmsted, landscape architect; and Abraham Gottlieb, consulting engineer. The site was developed into an impressive grouping of monumental buildings around a reflecting pool. The site had its own railway terminal and was also linked to Chicago central business district by an elevated rapid transit line, which is still in operation. The exposition is credited with changing architectural tastes of thousands of visitors, creating a widespread dissatisfaction with the dingy industrial cities of America and leading to the "city beautiful" movement and the renewal of interest in public planning within the United States.

Figure 2.4 Plan for Washington D.C., 1791

The Fair, which was held over a relatively short period of time, also introduced some important technical innovations, including the alternating current electric power and lighting system, and electric traction for elevated rapid-transit railway lines. The Fair was attended by 27 million visitors, of which 14 million were foreigners. One result of the Columbian Exposition was renewed interest in the L'Enfant plan for Washington, D.C. (Fig. 2.4). Another legacy of the Columbian Exposition was the preparation in 1909 of the Burnham plan for the redevelopment of Chicago. The plan proposed a focal point and radial street system, a half-crescent major boulevard, and a monumental entrance to the city from the Lake Michigan shoreline. The plan also addressed the need for improved rapid transit service, railway line and terminal consolidation, and the regulation of land subdivision.

2.8.2 The City Beautiful Movement

The city beautiful movement, in the United States, was focused on the planning and development of monumental civic centers, landscape parks, and parkways, and attractive boulevards.

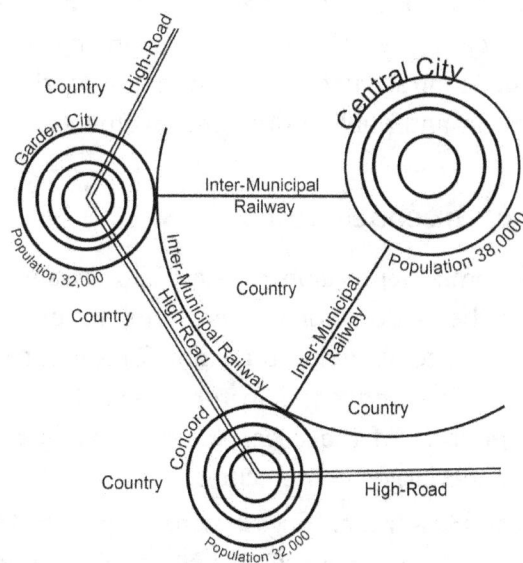

Figure 2.5 Garden city diagram (*Source:* Ebenezer Howard, 1902)

The city beautiful movement was further marked by:
- Renewed attention to the design of public buildings.
- Emphasis on planning for the remediation of existing problems.

- The public regulation of land use and building height and mass.
- The renewal of city planning as an essential function of local government
- The formation of the American City Planning Institute in 1917 – now the American Planning Association and American Institute of Certified Planners.

By 1913, states were beginning to enact planning enabling legislation. Other significant planning developments included the introduction of zoning and land subdivision control. (Fig. 2.5)

2.8.3   The City Efficient Movement

The city beautiful movement was initially dominated by the architectural and landscape architectural professions, and to a lesser extent by the legal profession. As city managers and municipal engineers became more active in planning, the city beautiful movements was gradually transformed into the "city efficient" movement. Increasing emphasis in city planning was placed on planning for public infrastructure development, particularly planning for transportation and public utility improvements.

2.8.4   The Greenbelt Towns

The great economic depression of the 1930s raised the question as to whether the nation could ever hope to provide full time, gainful employment to all within the labor force needed and sought such employment. This question, in turn, gave rise to the concept of resetting a portion of the urban force in satellite communities located around the larger center cities.

Sir Ebenezer Howard, an Englishman, proposed developing the countryside around the larger central cities with a number of new, largely self-contained town; each surrounded by its own permanent agricultural greenbelt.

Planning for American urban settlements is as old as the settlements themselves. The physical form of cities was of great concern to the founding fathers, who carefully set down those community forms they believed most conducive to realizing functional and humanly self-fulfilling settlements. The years from 1900 to 1920 saw the advent of the automobile as a major factor in American cities. The years of prosperity and depression, 1920 to 1940, saw the rapid spread of comprehensive zoning and subdivision controls. By the late 1950, city planning was well established in the United States, and most progressive communities were engaged in planning efforts with the assistance of resident or consulting staff. Initially, the resident staff were often provided by the engineering departments, but as the planning profession became well established, such staffs were provided in separate planning departments. The planning principles and practices applied were largely those developed during the city efficient movement. The planning efforts developed the quantitative relationships existing between land use and transportation and applied system engineering, including mathematical travel and traffic simulation modeling to the plan development process. These planning efforts also pioneered the application of digital computer technology to planning and helped foster the creation and application in urban planning of computerized geographic information systems, parcel-based information systems, and public works management systems.

The art – as opposed to science – of planning saw the refinement of zoning and land use subdivision design techniques and the development of the "new urbanism" and "smart growth" movements in reaction of the perceived disadvantages of urban sprawl. The new urbanism, however, is in reality a return to the old urbanism – new development, old values – higher densities of development, mixed land uses, and modified grid street patterns considered to be more amenable to pedestrian movement.

The cities around the world are experiencing dynamic changes due to the advancement in technology. Economies of scale is making technology available to masses. The world has become a smaller place. A person in a village or remote area with a smart phone may be as knowledgeable about the happenings as much a person in a metropolitan city. A race of making impacts on settlements through globalization is remarkable and creating new chapters in city planning.

Chapter 3
Planning portfolio

3.1 Plan for planning

A plan is an adopted description or statement of policy, in the form of text, graphics, and maps. The purpose of plan is to guide public and private actions that affect built environment and future of the community. A plan provides decision makers with the information they need to make informed decisions and affecting the short-range and long-range social, economic actions and physical growth of a community.

3.2 Role of plans

Plans are used when making decisions concerning the future of an area or a specific project or topic under consideration. For example, a plan may be used to identify:
- Market area – May be a new or redevelopment of a commercial area
- Transportation needs – Propose alternate mode, transit modes
- Housing needs – Propose program to meet housing needs
- Historic preservation plan – Propose means to preserve historic features

- Priority capital improvement plan – Propose programs to stimulate growth in a region
- Infrastructure plan to provide utilities equitably to the residents
- Improvement strategies for a specific area, such as neighborhood, corridor, or smart city transformation

Plans can be prepared and used for specific applications such as, providing citizens, local officials and others with interest in the area with an overview and projections of development and conservation in the planning area; serving as basis for local municipality enacting and administering regulatory measures such as, zoning, subdivision regulations, and establishing urban growth boundaries; and serving as basis for making resource allocation for services such as libraries, parks, streets and health centers; and serving as the basis for many other public programs, such as those relating to growth management, economic development, transportation system, historic preservation, and open space creation and preservation to name a few.

3.3 Plan authority

Plans may be authorized or required by statue, policy, or administrative rule, depending upon the type of plan and the jurisdiction of the community. For example, the 74th Constitution Amendment Act provides to constitute the district planning committee in every district to consolidate the plans prepared by the gram panchayats, nagar panchayats and the municipalities in a district and to prepare a development plan for a district as a whole, and metropolitan planning committees are also required to be set up in metropolitan areas with the purpose to prepare plans for the metropolitan area as a whole falling under the jurisdiction of metropolitan planning commissions.

3.4 Basic plan structure

The structure of a plan usually consists of three components: a core, number of elements, followed by recommendations. The specific contents of a plan depend upon numerous factors, such as type of plan being prepared, the purpose of plan, scope of plan, and type of plan.

The plan core generally includes:

- a statement of authority to prepare and adopt plan
- background data, including area history, topography, climate, existing conditions and trends, and data projections

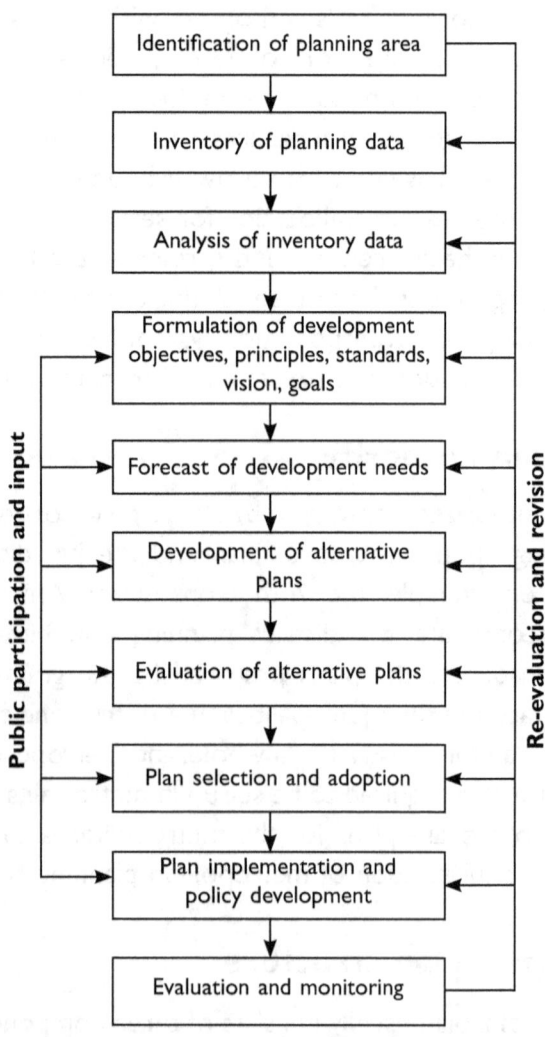

Figure 3.1 This figure illustrates the general process to be followed in the preparation of each of the elements of a comprehensive plan, whether the elements are individually prepared over time or whether the plan as a whole is prepared at one point in time.

- documentation of stakeholders' interests and stakeholders involvement process
- a mission statement, vision statement, and statement of goals and objectives for future conditions
- an evaluation of plan and design alternatives
- a program of implementation
- a program to monitor and evaluate the plan

The plan elements include plan's various topics. The elements must be included depend upon the plan's purpose. For a comprehensive plan, the land use, housing, infrastructure, services, transportation and communication, and economic activities are considered essential. Other elements are added as considered to be appropriate, based on the plan's scope and as required by the legal entity. (Fig. 3.1)

3.4.1 Goals, objectives, and assumptions

Universal to all plans is the identification and establishment of goals, objectives, and assumptions of the plan. Interestingly, reaching for a consensus on these three elements is quite a challenge – can be difficult sometimes. Intensive communication between the plan preparers and the stakeholders is an important part of plan preparation.

A goal is a statement that describes, usually in general terms, a desired future condition.

An objective is a statement of that describes a specific future condition to be attained within a stated period of time. Typically, these objectives are more numerous than the goals, and they are organized according to the topics in the goals statement. A set of measurable objectives should accompany the goals established for the plan.

3.4.2 Assumptions

An assumption is a statement of present and future conditions describing the physical, social, and economic setting within which the plan is to be used. At the outset of the process, it is necessary to identify the basic assumptions concerning the planning area. For example, it can be accepted boundaries of urban growth, probable rate of growth, and general desired character of the community.

3.4.3 Vision statement

Vision statement is different from goals. Vision includes the universalistic values and principles that will guide behavior. They provide a sense of direction. They help identify what the future holds. They provide glimpses of possibilities, not just probabilities. They evoke deeper meaning than mission statements or goals. They provide optimism and hope.

3.4.4 Typical data needed for plan preparation

Maps and images
- Base maps, GIS map layers, remote sensing data, aerial photographs, location maps and photos, and pictures from local and regional newspapers and other documents

Natural environment
- Topography, climate, floods information, seismic data, soils, vegetation, water bodies, habitat areas, and natural hazards

Existing land uses
- Residential, commercial, industrial, institutional, open space lands, public lands, vacant lands, agricultural lands, worship places, and forests

Housing
- Inventory of existing housing, inventory of conditions of existing housing, vacancy rate, rental and ownership records, and affordability

Public/private utilities
- Piped water supply, sewer, wastewater disposal, sewage treatment facilities, storm water management, solid waste management, telecommunication services, cable services, and internet services

Transportation

- Street network, street capacity, traffic flow volume, type of modes, parking supply and demand, transit facilities, non-motorized traffic, bicycle network, and pedestrian network

Community services

- Administrative centers, education facilities, libraries, post offices, health services, parks and recreation facilities, and public safety facilities
- Religious and spiritual entities

Population and employment

- Population size, historic population trend, population characteristics, vital statistics, and work force characteristics

Local economy

- Retail, wholesale, warehousing, employment, and cost of living

Special topics

- Historic buildings and historic features, archeological sites, urban design features, existing zoning and other existing ordinances
- Name of the plan, table of contents, time frame, acknowledgements and glossary and terminology are parts of a plan
- Identification of environmentally sensitive areas

3.5 Types of plans

3.5.1 Comprehensive/development/master plan

The document is addressed by comprehensive plan, development plan, or master plan. Comprehensive plans address a broad range of interrelated topics in a unified ways. The plan should be realistic, simple, and understandable for an average citizen. A comprehensive plan identifies and analyzes the important relationships among the land use, transportation, social activities, economic activities, housing, community facilities and services, environment, human services, and other community components.

It does so on community-wide basis and in context of wider region. A comprehensive plan addresses the long-range future of a community, using a time horizon of 5, 10, or 20 years, sometimes even more. The most important function of a comprehensive plan is to provide valuable guidance to those in the public and private sectors as decisions are made affecting the future quality of life of existing and future residents; how those decisions impact the natural and built environment in which they live, work, recreate, learn, worship, and perform other activities. The plans are guiding documents to citizens, elected officials, building community, and others interested in the community activities. The plans are fluid documents; in other words, they change with change of needs of the community.

3.5.2 Why a comprehensive/development/master plan

View the "whole community"

The local comprehensive planning process provides a chance to view broadly "community as whole" at programs related housing, transportation, public infrastructure, economic activities, environmental protection, and natural and manmade hazards, and how they relate to one another.

Coordinate local decision-making process

Local comprehensive planning results in the adoption of a series of goals and policies that should guide the local government decisions.

Give guidance to property owners and developers

In making its decision, the private sector can turn to a well-comprehensive plan to get some direction of where the community is headed in turn of the physical, social, economic, and transportation future. Because comprehensive planning results in a statement of how local government intends to use public investment and land development controls, the plan can affect the decisions of private landowners.

Sound basis for decisions

A plan through required information gathering and analysis, improves the factual basis for land-use decisions. Using the physical plan as a tool to inform and guide these decisions establish a baseline for public policies. The plan thus provides a measure of consistency to governmental actions, limiting the potential for arbitrariness.

Direction towards long-range future

Local comprehensive planning involves the active participation of local elected officials, appointed officials, various departments, stakeholders, civic groups, business community, non-governmental organizations, and citizens in a discussion about the community's major physical, environmental, economic, and social issues and challenges and opportunities. The plan gives their respective and varied interests an opportunity to share their ideas, better envisioning the community they are trying to create.

Informed constituency

The plan preparation process with its related workshops, informational meetings, public participation meetings and public hearings, allows two-way communication between citizens and planners and elected official regarding a vision of the community and how that vision is to be achieved. In this respect the plan is a blue print reflecting shared community values at a specific time.

3.6 Elements of plan

- Issues and opportunities element articulates the values and needs of the community and other affected interests about what the community should become. The local government or the plan preparer entity then interprets and uses those values and needs as a basis and foundation for its planning efforts.
- Vision and goals and objective statement is formal description of what the community wants to become.
- Existing conditions and characteristics description creates a profile of the community, including relevant demographic

data, related historical information, existing plans, regulatory framework, and other related information that broadly informs the plan.

- Opportunities, problems, issues, strengths, and weaknesses statement of the plan for growth and decline affecting the community.

- Public participation processes describe how the public was involved in developing the comprehensive plan. The types and methods employed to involve citizens are laid out.

- The land-use element is the dashboard of general distribution, location, and characteristics of current land uses and urban form. Many communities today use sophisticated land-use and land-cover inventories and mapping techniques, employing Geographic Information Systems (GIS), remote sensing, and new land-use and land-cover classification systems. These new systems are better equipped to accommodate the multidimensional realities of urban form such as mixed use, and time-of-day, and seasonal-use changes.

- Future land-use map show future intensity and density of uses. The land-use allocations shown on the map must be supported by land-use projections linked to population and economic forecasts.

- Land-use projections should envision all land-use needs for a certain period of time. That time period should be coordinated with the time frame of the comprehensive plan. All those needs should be designated on the future land-use plan map.

- The transportation elements commonly addresses traffic circulation, transit, bicycle routes, pedestrian network, bus terminals, railways, ports, airports, waterways, parking facilities, and other routes. The exact coverage of transportation element details varies from community to community depending upon the context of the community and region. The transportation element considers existing and committed facilities, and evaluates them against a set of service levels or performance standards to determine whether they will adequately serve future needs.

Street performance is measured for moving pedestrians, bikes, buses, trams, street cars, trolleys, light rails, two and three wheeler automobiles, rickshaws and *tongas*, in addition to moving cars. Urban design plans for the entire thoroughfares can augment the transportation element. A street connectivity plan showing degree of connectivity with various modes can affect pedestrian movement and traffic dispersal.

- Transit component takes into consideration bus and light rail facilities and intermodal facilities including transportation users to transfer from one mode to another mode conveniently.
- The community facilities element requires to inventory and assess the conditions and adequacy of existing facilities, and to propose a rage of facilities that will support the land-use elements' development pattern. Community facilities include buildings, equipment, land (above and below), and interests in land, easements, and whole systems of activities.
- A community facilities or services element may include parks, gardens, playgrounds, and open space component. They may be addressed as separate element depending upon the nature of the plan.
- Housing element assesses local housing conditions, inventory, and affordability and projects future housing needs by housing type and price to ensure that a wide variety of housing structures types, occupancy types, and prices (rental or ownership) are available for community's present and future needs. Housing element is an eminent issue in Indian cities. Many programs related to housing by the various levels of governments and private sector have been initiated. The plans must adhere to those existing and future housing projects.
- Economic development element describes the local government's role in the region's economy and identifies types of commercial, industrial, agricultural, and institutional uses desired by the local government. The purpose of this element is to create and retain job, increase employment diversity, diversify revenue sources, and stabilize local revenue sources.

- Hazard element includes both manmade and natural hazards. They can be part of the plan, again, depending upon the nature of the plan and local concerns about the hazards. The purpose is to identify the hazards before they occur and prepare the community for such hazards.
- Implementation is the most important element of the plan. The plan must contain implementation program to ensure that the proposals advanced in the plan are realized. Each listed action should assign responsibility for the task and include estimate of cost and a source of funding. The plan must establish a time limit to achieve the goals.
- Evaluation and monitoring is an important part of management and implementation of the plan. The plans must provide built-in system to evaluation and monitor the successes and hardships of the plan.

3.7 Regional plans

Regional plans cover geographic areas transcending the boundaries of local governments but sharing common characteristics that be economic, political, social, cultural, or transportation based. Region is a spatial entity. Many of the early studies in regional geography have been 'formal' regions that were identified on the basis of the presence or absence of peculiar identifiable features. The concept of functional regions which consist of spatial units tied to a nodal center connected through transportation and communication lines. These spatial centers are similar to each other in terms of connection with the same nodal center for either provision of goods and services or for trade of their commodities or movement of work force. The importance of regions and its system in planning, economic development came to be accepted not only by geographers but by other disciplines, such as economics. Regional planning emerged as a complimentary discipline for economic development and economic planning. The regional plan is more associated with new societal concerns of environmental and sustainability at local, urban, regional, and national level. No city works in isolation. Each settlement acts within push and pull factors. Thus have regional identity. The professionals must consider, while preparing plans, the regional impact and interaction between various factors.

Natural regions may be identified on the basis of physiography, soil, climate, vegetation. Regions can be formed to prepare plans for special purposes, such as multipurpose projects, industrial corridors, economic activities, or agricultural regions.

The concept of regions has been divided into two main categories: formal and informal. Formal regions are defined on the basis of homogeneity. The similarities or uniformity is based on the selected criteria. These regions are classified on the basis of topography, economic activities, political, and social factors. Functional region is a geographical area displaying certain functional similarities. The functional relationships are usually revealed in the form of movement, using various socio-economic criteria like trips to work, trips to shopping, and trips to services, newspaper circulation, and similar functions. The concept of functional regions brings into focus the importance of different modes of linkages or means of connectivity between places and areas for the functioning of those spatial units as human habitats. The functional regions are also referred as the nodal or polarized region consisting of heterogeneous entities, such as towns, cities, and villages which are functionally interrelated.

3.7.1 Defining the region

- Geographic and topographic features, especially watersheds
- Political boundaries to facilitate creation of region for a specific purpose
- Transportation pattern or system especially related to special projects
- Regions serving same characteristics, e.g. underdeveloped areas extended beyond political boundaries
- Intergovernmental relationships regions
- Metropolitan areas or urbanized boundaries, e.g. Delhi, Kolkata

Regional comprehensive plan elements can be same as comprehensive plan elements with the exception or addition of certain elements pertaining to the purpose of regional plan preparation. Regional plans are generally long range and take a long time to implement.

Planning is required for the purposes to achieve common goals for the identified region. The purpose could be economic development, provide social services, or connectivity between established nodes.

Based on the purpose of planning for a region, formal steps can be established and required elements can be identified. A generic model of regional planning includes the following steps:

- Identification of problems, challenges, and issues
- Formulation of vision statement
- Formulation of goals and objectives
- Identification of advantages and disadvantages
- Collection of data and information regarding existing conditions
- Analysis of collected information and data
- Projecting future, with a time line, of recognized elements
- Identification of alternatives and selection of preferred strategies
- Implementation plan with strategies
- Monitoring and evaluation
- Plan to revisit the plan and planning process

3.8 Redevelopment area plans

Conducting a visual or windshield survey of a city or town will provide noticeable run down, blighted, unmanaged, and undressed areas. One will notice deteriorating, dilapidated, and unsafe buildings around the city. They are in that condition due to many reasons, such as neglect by property owners, neglect by residents, lack of law enforcement, lack of management of properties, lack of property maintenance ordinance, decay over time, or just the old age. Other conditions could be open spaces, parks, playgrounds, vacant parcels, and establishments of inappropriate land uses, congestion, and lack of public utility services. The sites become civic nuisance and are in need of redevelopment.

Redevelopment areas are those identified as requiring specific action by the local government for revitalization to occur. The areas for which revitalization strategies can be formulated are:

- residential area with deteriorating living conditions or substandard living conditions;
- residential areas with dwelling units with marked state of deterioration and dilapidation;
- mixed-use areas with over population, congestion, and other alarming conditions by inappropriate uses;
- business district that is experiencing loss of retail, office and related residential activities;
- industrial areas where plants and facilities are abandoned, idled, dormant, underused, or sites are environmentally contaminated and must be remodeled before they can be reused.
- unsanitary or unsafe conditions that endanger life, health, and property;
- disaster area;
- defective or inadequate street or lay out plan;
- deteriorated public improvements, such as streets, roads, street lighting, curbs, gutters, sidewalks, and other streetscapes.
- unplanned, neglected, and haphazard developed area; and
- area affected by combination of such factors that substantially impede growth or affect public health and safety.

3.9   The plan

Redevelopment plans tend to be highly specific because of the local problem or issues with the certain section of the city. Depending upon the ownership of the land, it can create many speculative challenges. The redevelopment process can be delayed because of these reasons. Implementation process requires community commitment.

3.10 Public policy analysis and planning/engineering/architecture

Planning, engineering, architecture and other related professional departments are tangibly involved with public policy analysis from three perspectives: (i) creation of public policy, (ii) interpretation and implementation of public policy, and (iii) being part of a team to create public policy. In a democratic political world and professional domain, both the creation and/or implementation of policy play an important role. Understanding of theory of public policy analysis is as important an implementation for planners, engineers, architects, and related professionals. This section provides an overview of the public policy analysis processes.

Policy analysis is the activity of creating knowledge 'of' and 'in' the policy-making process. In creating knowledge of policy-making processes, policy analysts investigate causes, consequences, and performance of public policies and programs. Such knowledge remains incomplete, however, unless it is made available to policymakers and implementers and the public they are obligated to serve. Only when knowledge 'of' is linked to 'in' can members of executive, legislative, and judicial bodies, implementers along with citizens who have a stake in public decisions, use the results of policy analysis to improve or establishing a comprehensive policy process and its performance. Because the effectiveness of policy making depends on access to the stock of available knowledge, the communication and use of policy analysis are central to the practice and theory of public policy creation.

The methodology of policy analysis draws from and integrates elements of multiple disciplines: political science, sociology, economic, philosophy, psychology, and technical disciplines, if the policy formation is about technical field. Policy analysis is partly descriptive, drawing on traditional disciplines that seek knowledge about cause and consequences of public policy. Yet policy analysis is normative; an additional aim is the creation and critique of knowledge that claims about the value of public policies for past, present, and future.

The methodology of policy analysis, as noted above, aims at creating, critically assessing, and communicating policy relevant knowledge. In this context, knowledge refers to plausibly true beliefs, as distinguished from beliefs that are certainly true, or even true with a particular statistical probability. Statistical probability, in turn, has not direct bearing on the plausibility of knowledge claims.

3.11   Policy relevant information

The methodology of policy analysis provides information that is useful in answering questions like: What is the nature of problem(s)? What present and past policies have been established to address the problem (especially in Indian context)? What are their outcomes? How valuable are these outcomes in solving the problem, and what is their likely future of outcomes? What policies are available to address the problem, and what are their likely outcomes? What alternatives should be acted on to solve the problem? Answers to these questions yield information about policy problems, policy futures, policy action, policy outcomes, and policy performance. These questions are interdependent and interrelated. Policy relevant information is the basis for making knowledge claims of many kinds, the starting point in reasoned arguments which establishes the plausibility of knowledge claims in the face of criticisms, challenges, or rebuttals. Policy argumentation and debate is one of the principal vehicles for converting information into knowledge.

The methodology of policy analysis incorporates five general procedures that are common to most efforts at human problem solving: definition, prediction, prescription, description, and evaluation. These policy analytic procedures serve as a means of organizing particular methods and techniques of policy analysis.

3.12 Process of policy making

The process of policy analysis is a series of brain storming and intellectual activities carried out within a process comprised of activities that are essential political. These political activities can be described usefully as the policy-making process and visualized as a series of interdependent phases arrayed through time: agenda setting, policy formulation, policy adoption, policy implementation, policy assessment. Policy analysts may produce information relevant to one, several, or all phases of the policy-making process, depending on the type of problem faced for policy analysis.

Policy analysis seeks to create, critically assess, and communicate policy relevant knowledge within one or more phases of the policy-making process. These phases represent ongoing activities that occur through time. Each phase is related to the next, and the last phase is linked to the first.

Agenda setting is characterized by elected or appointed officials. They place problem on the public agenda. Not all problems are acted on while some may be addressed only after a long time.

Policy formation is formulation of alternative policies to deal with a problem by officials. Alternative policies assume the form of executive orders, and court decisions.

Policy adoption is a policy alternative adopted with the support of a legislative majority, consensus among entity directors, or a court decision.

Policy implementation is characterized by execution of an adopted policy by administrative division, which mobilize financial and human resources to comply with the policy.

Policy assessment is auditing and accounting units in government, which determine whether executive agencies, legislature, and courts are in compliance with statutory requirements of a policy and achieving its objectives.

3.13 Policy problem structuring

Problem structuring can supply policy relevant knowledge that challenges the assumptions underlying the definition of problem reaching policy-making process through agenda setting. Problem structuring can assist in discovering hidden assumptions, diagnostic causes, mapping possible objectives, synthesizing conflicting views, and designing new policy options.

3.14 Forecasting

Forecasting can provide policy relevant knowledge about future states of affairs which are likely to occur as a consequence of adopting alternatives, including doing nothing. Forecasting can examine plausible, potential, and normatively valued futures; estimate the consequences of existing and proposed policies; specify probable future constraints on the achievement of objectives; and estimate the political feasibility of different options.

- A projection is a forecast which is based on the extrapolation of current and historic trends into the future. Projections may be supplemented by arguments from authority.
- A prediction is a forecast based on explicit theoretical assumptions. These assumptions may take the form of theoretical laws (for example, the law of diminishing returns of money).
- A conjecture is a forecast based on informed or expert judgment about future situations. These judgments may take the form of intuitive arguments, where assumptions about the insight, creative intelligence, or tacit knowledge of stakeholders are used to support designative claims about the future.
- Regression analysis is a useful technique for estimating linear relationships among variables in theoretical forecasting. Regression analysis is general statistical procedure that yields precise estimates of the pattern and magnitude of a relationship between a dependent variable and one or more independent variables. When regression analysis is performed with one independent variable, it is called simple regression; if there are two or more independent variables, it is called multiple regression.

- Delphi technique is a judgmental forecasting procedure for obtaining, exchanging, and developing informed opinion about future events. Originally, the technique was applied to problems of military strategy, but its application gradually shifted to forecasts in other context: education, transportation, housing, technology, research and development, medicine, space exploration, budgeting, and quality of life. The process is to reach a consensus without biases toward each other.
- Judgmental forecasting techniques attempt to elicit and synthesize informed judgments. Judgmental forecasts are often based on arguments from insight, since assumptions about the creative powers of persona making the forecast are used to warrant claims about the future.

3.15 Recommendation

Recommendation yields policy relevant knowledge about the benefits and costs of alternatives for the future consequences which have been estimated through forecasting, thus aiding policymakers in the policy adoption phase. Recommendation helps estimate levels of risk and uncertainty, identifies externalities and spillovers, specifies criteria for making choices, and assigns administrative responsibilities for implementing policies. The risk measurement can be both: quantitative and qualitative. The quantitative risk analysis has three major goals: (i) assess the probability of achieving specific project objectives, (ii) quantify the effect of the risks on the overall project objective, and (iii) prioritize risks by their contributions to the overall project risk. Qualitative analysis is an estimate, and is less precise than quantitative analysis, which is based on numbers and hence is more precise. However, qualitative analysis is quick and cheaper.

3.16 Implementation

Administrative agencies often are provided with broad and ambiguous statutory mandates that leave them with much room for choice in deciding what should or should not be done on some matters. Frequently those who participate in the legislative process are unable or unwilling to arrive at a precise settlement among the conflicting interests on many issues. Only by leaving some matters nebulous and unsettled can agreement on legislation be reached. Lack of time, interest, information, and expertness as well as the need for flexibility in implementation may also help explain the delegation of broad authority to agencies. Although administrative agencies are the primary implementers of public policy, many other players may also be involved and contribute in various ways to the execution of policies.

3.17   Monitoring

Monitoring provides policy relevant knowledge about the consequences of previously adopted policies, thus assisting policymakers in the policy implementation phase. Many agencies and organizations regularly monitor the outcomes and impacts of policies by means of various policy indicators in areas of housing, health, crime, science and technology, and education. Monitoring helps to assess degrees of compliance, discover unintended consequences of policies and programs, identify implementation obstacles and constraints, and locate sources of responsibility for departure from policies. Monitoring helps maintain an accurate and timely information base regarding the policy implementation process and control changes and implementation of approved amendments.

3.18   Evaluation

Evaluation yields policy relevant knowledge about discrepancies between expected and actual policy performance, thus assisting policymakers in the policy assessment phase of the policy-making process. A good example of evaluation is the type of analysis that contributes to the clarification, critique, and debate of values by challenging the dominant mode of technical reasoning.

3.19 Process of policy communication

Policy analysis is the beginning, not the end, of efforts of the policy-making process and its outcomes. This is why policy analysis has been defined as the communication, as well as the creation and critical assessment, of policy relevant knowledge.

3.20 Conclusion

Planning is an interesting discipline. By virtue of its nature, it is always changing. The planner and planning has to adapt those changes to make human living more congenial. The planners and planning has to observe changes in human living habits and incorporate in plan and planning process. Then comes the technology, which is metamorphosing human habits and behavior. Smart Cities is the prime example of human innovation and incorporating the same into day-to-day life. Planners are challenged to make that technology work for humans.

Chapter 4
Planner's tool kit

4.1 Role of community participation

Public or community participation is the involvement of people in the creation and management of their built and natural environments. Its strength is that it cuts across traditional professional boundaries and cultures. The activity of community participation is based on the principle that the built and natural environments work better if citizens are active and involved in the creation and management. The main purposes of participation are the following:

- To involve citizens in planning and design decision-making process and as a result make it more likely they will work within established systems when seeking solutions to problems.
- To provide citizens with a voice in planning and decision making in order to improve plans, decisions, service delivery, and overall quality of environment.
- To promote sense of community by bringing together people who share common goals.

Participation should be active and direct; those who get involved should experience a sense of achievement. Once planners have identified the overall goals and objectives for the participation process, planning for participation requires the following steps:

- Identify the individuals or groups that should be involved in the participation activity being planned.
- Decide where in the process the participants should be involved, from development to implementation to evaluation.
- Articulate the participation objectives in relation to all participants who will be involved.
- Identify and match alternative participation methods to objectives in terms of the resources available.
- Select an appropriate method to be used to achieve specific objectives.
- Implement chosen participation activities.
- Evaluate the implemented methods to see to what extent they achieved the desired goals and objectives.

Planners, in Indian context, may have an uphill task during public participation phase: the general public not being familiar with what kind of community they want or how to plan for future. The professionals should assess the audience and plan to educate them prior to formal public participation. There is no best solution to design and planning problems. Each problem can have number of solutions. It is recommended to involve expert and experienced facilitators to mitigate the meetings. Facilitators are trained to keep the meetings and participant focused to the issue and problems.

4.2 Surveys

Survey is collection of data and information. Collection of data and information is necessary for preparing plans. Surveys can be conducted for various purposes such as existing land use, existing population, population growth, housing, traffic and transportation system, economic activities, and social fabric. Each category can be further sub-divided to collect relevant data. There are various methods to conduct surveys, collection of data in the field, household survey, questionnaires, interviews, and mail-in surveys and other techniques.

4.3 Community visioning

Community visioning offers local communities new ways to think about and plan for the long-term future. In the simplest terms, visioning is a planning process through which a community creates a shared vision for its future and begins to make it a reality. There are five key characteristics about visioning various communities have evolved:

i. *Understanding the whole community:* The visioning process promotes an understanding of the whole community and the full range of issues shaping its future. It also attempts to engage the participation of the entire community and its key stakeholders.

ii. *Reflecting core community values:* The visioning process seeks to identify the community's core values – those deeply held community beliefs and ideals shared by its members. Such values inform the idealistic nature of the community's vision.

iii. *Addressing emerging trends and issues:* The visioning process explores the emerging trends driving the community's future and the strategic issues they portend.

iv. *Envisioning a preferred future:* The visioning process produces a statement articulating the community's preferred future. The vision statement represents the community's desired "destination."

v. *Promoting local action:* The visioning process also produces a strategic action plan. The action plan serves as the community's "road map": to move it in the direction of its vision in the near-term future.

Visioning works when the community is concerned about its future and is eager for dialogue. The key community institutions and opinion leaders are involved in the process and public is authentically engaged in the process.

4.4 Charrettes

Charrettes are an integral part of many of the urban planning and design processes. A charrette involves a multidisciplinary team of professionals developing all elements of a plan. The team works closely with stakeholders through a series of feedback loops, during which alternative concepts are developed, reviewed by stakeholders, and revised accordingly.

The word charrette is French for "cart" or "chariot". In 19th century, in Paris, it was common practice among architecture students to continue working furiously in teams at the end of the allotted term, up until a deadline, when a charrette would be wheeled among the students to pick up their scale models and other work for review, were called *en charrette*. In today's world and simple words, charrette is a design workshop – without a chariot.

The charrette is a sophisticated process that best serves controversial and complicated urban design and planning problems. Its capacity to bring all the decision makers together for a discrete amount of time to create a solution makes it one of the most powerful techniques in a planner's tool kit.

Charrettes are not a substitute for standard planning processes, which may take a longer time to complete. They are conducted to address specific problematic situation and should complement the overall planning process. The charrettes works best for situations such as:

- High-stakes projects;
- Volatile yet workable political environments;
- Complex design problems;
- Community wide impacted projects; and
- Projects that include imminent development.

A charrette is a central event of a larger project with values of:

- Anyone affected by the project has the right to provide input with potential impact on the outcome.
- Each participant has a unique contribution that is heard and respected.
- Many minds and hands make the best plan.

The term "charrette" is some time overused or misused. The following strategies are what differentiate a charrette from other planning processes.

1. *Work collaboratively:* All interested parties must be involved from the beginning. Having contributed to the planning, participants are in a position both to understand and to support a project's rationale.
2. *Design cross-functionality:* A multi-disciplinary team method results in decisions that are realistic in every step of the way. The cross-functional process eliminates the need for rework because the design work continually reflects the wisdom of each speciality.
3. *Compress work session:* The charrette itself, usually lasting for a short time (one to seven days), is a series of meeting and design sessions that would traditionally take months to complete. This time compression facilitates creative problem solving by accelerating decision making and reducing unconstructive negotiation tactics. It also encourages people to abandon their usual working pattern and think "out of the box" approach.
4. *Communicate in short feedback loops:* During the charrette, design ideas are created based upon a pubic vision and presented within hours for further review, critique, and refinement.
5. *Study details and the whole:* Lasting agreement is based on a fully informed dialogue, which can be accomplished only by looking at the details and the big picture concurrently.
6. *Produce a feasible plan:* The charrette differs from other workshops in its expressed goal to create a feasible plan. In other words, every decision point must be fully informed, especially by the legal, financial, and engineering discipline.
7. *Use design to achieve a shared vision and create a holistic solution:* Design is a powerful tool for establishing a shared vision. Drawings illustrate the complexity of the problem and can be used to resolve conflict by proposing previously unexplored solutions that represent win-win situation.
8. *Include a multiday charrette:* Most charrettes require between one to seven days. The more difficult the problem is, the longer the charrette should be.

9. *Hold the charrette on the site:* Working on site fosters the design team's understanding of local values and traditions, and provides the necessary easy access to stakeholders and information. Therefore, the studio should be located in a place where it is easily accessible to all stakeholders and where the designers have quick access to the project site.

A project may entail one or more charrettes, depending upon the size and complexity of the project. At the initial stages of the project, the designer should ask questions to the participants, not giving answers. Designer should not come with set ideas or solutions. They should develop in response to the understanding obtained through the process.

When done correctly, the charrette promotes trust between citizens and government through meaningful public involvement and education. It fosters a shared community vision by turning opposition into support. It continually strives for a creation of a feasible plan, which increased the likelihood of the project getting built by gaining broad support from citizens, professionals, and staff.

4.5 Asset mapping

The most efficient and effective way of not only presenting but also integrating information about a number of factors that must be considered in urban planning and engineering is through maps. Maps serve at least two important purposes in urban planning:

- Provide a graphic representation of the planning area
- Relate pertinent planning data to geographic location

The maps must, however, be prepared and designed specifically for planning and engineering applications. The design and proper preparation of such maps require proficiency in surveying and mapping. Surveying and mapping technology has undergone a period of rapid, indeed revolutionary, change. This change has been marked by the introduction of new instrumentation for the conduct of field surveys, such as electronic theodolites and distance-measuring devices (Electronic Distance Measuring), the development of software and the application of computers for the reduction and storage of survey data, and development of new programmetric plotters and digitizers to permit the development and use of maps in digital form. Perhaps most revolutionary has been the development of Geographic Information Systems (GIS) and Global Positioning System (GPS) technology. There also has been an increasing interest in the development and use in the urban planning of computerized, multipurpose, spatial analysis capabilities, parcel-based land information and public works management system.

A map may be defined as a flat, true scale, graphical representation of a portion of the earth's surface. In this respect, it should be recognized that the spherical surface of the earth cannot be presented on a flat surface without distortion. The map scale is defined as the relationship between a distance on a map and the corresponding distance on the surface of the earth. A map scale may be expressed as an equivalence, as a ratio, or as a graph.

The creation of a map requires three fundamental elements: (1) A system for accurately locating features on the surface of the earth; (2) A projection to reduce the spherical surface of the ellipsoid to a plane surface; and (3) A system of survey control to manifest the project used on the surface of the earth.

Two basic types of maps are required to adequately meet the urban planning and engineering needs. The first is the large-scale topographic map. Such maps accurately show the configuration and elevation of the ground, the water bodies, and other natural and cultural (manmade) features of the land and cityscapes. For city planning and engineering purposes, the topographic maps should be at scales ranging from one inch equals 50 feet to one inch equals 200 feet, and should have vertical contour interval ranging from one inch to 2 feet. In small size parcels, the scale should be 1–10 feet to observe more details of the property. The second type of map required for urban planning and engineering purposes is the large-scale cadastral maps. Such maps accurately show the location, arrangement, and dimensions of real property boundary lines, including all streets and other public rights-of-way, and all existing subdivisions. The cadastral maps should be prepared on the same map projection and at the same scale as the topographic maps.

Aerial photography provides another useful tool for urban planning and engineering. Although oblique photographs have use for general information and display purposes in planning, the most useful photographs are vertical. The aerial photo should be orthodigitized or orthophoto rectified. Conventional aerial photographs have limited use in GIS because they are not true to scale. When you look at the center of an aerial photograph, your view is the same as if you were looking straight down from the aircraft. But as you look toward the edges of the photograph, the view of the ground is no longer straight down, but from an angle. This is called a central perspective projection; scale is true at the very center of the aerial photograph, but not elsewhere. In order to create a scale correct photograph that can be accurately measured, an orthographic projection is necessary, in which the view is straight down over every point in the photograph. Orthophotographs are adjusted by computer manipulation not only for variations in flight altitude and in the tip and tilt of the aircraft during photography, but also for variations in relief. Triangular irregular network (TIN) model is often used to orthogonally rectify the scanned image file. The individual photographs are then clipped and seamlessly joined together over the entire study area. The result is a digital image that combines the image characteristics of a photograph with the geometric qualities of a map – a true to scale photographic map.

4.6 Development standards

Indian cities reflect very interesting features, viewing from the build environment. A planner, in an Indian city, encounters complex, difficult, and hard to explain urban form and layout. A planner faces complex and difficult challenges than what they are trained in, understanding the relationship between the existing built environment and the theory of urban form is analyzed. Many Indian cities have evolved over time with many internal and external forces acted simultaneously or exclusively. To establish justification and reasoning for what exist is a complex task for planners. To synthesize the design and form the cities have taken due to factors like history, incidents, accidents, themes, and concepts is a serious obstacle. At the same time, it is challenging and interesting to understand and explain the built environment to plan for the future.

At planner's desk mainly two types of assignments come for review: one, applications for the new developments on vacant lands and two, redevelopment applications or redevelopment projects. The preparation of new residential, commercial, industrial, and mixed-use development plans is comparatively has less complex issues to consider. The new development submissions, over raw lands, prepared by the engineers, architects, and planners are generally based on, one, established subdivision regulations and second, if no subdivisions regulations exist then the consultants generally make plans based on professionally established standards and personal experiences. The use of established standards and norms are easy to apply and defend. If plans are questioned on the basis of sustainability and smart development criteria, then the plan takes a different approach. The development plan preparers are equipped to answer, justify, address, support, and reasoning their proposed plan in both cases, using industry standards and using or creating standards from other sources. The second set of redevelopment plans or redevelopment projects can also use the established and accepted minimum standards and norms, provided the project has capacity to handle the existing standards. There should be sufficient land and unbuilt space available to apply minimum standards. In some cases, applicant of minimum standards may create problems. In this case, the application of established standards may be easy or may not fit easily in the application. The other standards are derived from research reports, successful projects, unsuccessful projects, borrowed standards from other regions and professional organizations (national or international), and other sources. The onus of legitimacy of the standards used for the project depends on the professional who stamp and sign the development plans. The plan preparers, in this context, have to reason with their professional ethics, integrity, intelligence, knowledge, creativity, and expertise.

They strive to create a legacy. Whether successful or unsuccessful, people would like to learn who did the project.

Standards and norms are provided for various elements. The established norms and standards are tools, not a prescription. The tool can be used accurately only if the numbers being plugged into the formula are accurate. Each user is responsible for his or her numbers – and for the estimates that will ultimately result. The professional planners are keenly aware that output from computer programs may not always reflect local conditions or circumstances. They give us an initial local conditions or first impression. Some professional judgment may be needed to interpret or refine analysis for any given community or application. For planners, urban designers, architects, and engineers, it is absolutely necessary to comprehend the size, shape, form, and daily living habits of the community. The application of standards and norms can vary accordingly. Large cities have their requirements different from small and medium size cities.

4.7   Land use distribution

For land use distribution, the basis of densities, population, and work force are employed.

Proposed land use distribution and occupation of land is for residential, commercial, markets, industrial, institutional, pubic, semi-public, open space, recreational, transport and communication, agriculture and water bodies. Also for study purposes, the city is divided in two basic categories of landmass and water bodies.

4.8   Infrastructure standards

Urban land uses are supported by public and private utilities. Providing utilities by private sector is a new concept in India. Urban development is highly dependent on the availability and quality of the utility services, which significantly influence the pattern of land use development. For water supply, sewage, drainage, storm water management, electricity, gas supply, telecommunication, and solid waste, various engineering and organizations have standards.

4.9 Social services

Education (day care centers, pre-schools, primary schools, senior secondary schools, colleges, universities, higher education), vocational education, health care centers, hospitals, nursing homes, dispensaries, worship places (planners should be careful for planning this use), libraries, community rooms, community centers, and elderly centers. Provision of police stations, police precincts, fire stations, ambulance stations, and other services.

4.10 Recreational

Theaters, performance theaters, museums, art galleries, parks, open spaces, playgrounds, sports centers, and other locally accepted recreational activities.

4.11 Traffic and transportation

Pedestrian ways, bicycle lanes, streets, alleys, roads (local, arterial, sub-arterial, collector roads), parking for cars, taxis, two wheelers, rickshaws, tongas, bus stops, bus terminals, regional bus terminals, truck terminals, integrated freight exchange centers, and other modes and other related infrastructure.

4.12 Other facilities

Cremation grounds, burial grounds, and facilities as required by the local communities must be included.

4.13 Context-sensitive solutions/design/planning

The idea of "good design" has been undergoing a transformation to include the elements of context – how new development can integrate and interact with the dynamics of the existing natural and man-made environment, and what can be done to preserve or even enhance those features. Context-sensitive design/solutions/planning (CSD) is a process for achieving design excellence by developing planning solutions that require continuous, collaborative communication, and consensus between various professionals, related agencies, and any and all stakeholders. A common goal of CSD is to develop a facility that is harmonious with the community, and preserves character, aesthetics, history, and the environmental resources, while integrating these innovative approaches with traditional developmental goals for safety, health, welfare, and performance. Here the pretext of context-sensitive design/solutions/planning is interchangeable.

It is vital and a key factor to understand a community's values for existing built environment, historic and environmental resources, scenic and aesthetic values. Applying CSD principles in development investments will create a lasting value in a community. CSD calls for innovative thinking, improved coordination and communication, and implementation process.

A determination of the discrete steps has to be taken to mobilize adequate staff or consultant resources to initiate and complete the tasks associated with managing stakeholders group, advisory committee, or other public involvement strategy. The goal of this process is to anticipate and understand the steps needed to effectively develop and transfer the needed information to numerous business, civic, institutional, and residential groups and persons in a collaborative, context-sensitive effort. This effort will seek input and feedback to consider all appropriate "context-sensitive" alternatives, and to improve a project with such inputs.

Context-sensitive system (CSS) is an important part of future planning and design projects in Indian context. Cities in India have witnessed long periods of history – in which each historic phase has left its impression on the built and natural environment. The present urban form is the result of many forces and values. The forces and values are acting the same way today. Maintaining the balance is the interesting part of the modern planning processes. The challenge is to extract the best and functional parts of the old practices and incorporate them into the modern development processes.

For the purposes of planning and design, the following guiding principles are suggested:

1. *Interdisciplinary team:* To bring the development design process the best of all possible alternatives and options, it is important to consider and create an interdisciplinary approach to project development and decision making. Project team should include multiple discipline professionals, such as engineers, land use planners, architects, landscape architects, historic preservationists, environmental resource specialists, cultural resources staff, and transportation specialists who can address the multimodal issues for the project and any other specialists related to the particular nature of the project undertaken.
2. *Community and stakeholder focus:* It is advisable an early continuous commitment to public involvement. Community residents and stakeholders play an important role in identifying local and regional issues and concerns, as well as neighborhood values. Furthermore, they have much to offer regarding strategies or solutions that may better meet and balance the needs of community stakeholders and project. These teams can be used as a conduit of information gathering and dissemination to the community they represent.
3. *Environmental sensitivity in design:* Understanding the natural and built environments, the street layouts as part of the landscape and the valued resources within that landscape, must be accomplished before engineering design processes. If there is not an existing landscape element, then it should be incorporated in the development plan. In addition, the design approach of avoiding and/or minimizing effects on important resources to the extent possible, and creating resource enhancement opportunities where impacts are unavoidable should be pursued.
4. *Historic and heritage preservation:* The understanding of the existing historic and heritage preservation to relate to the proposed project is vital in Indian context. Historic features should be recognized carefully by involving the local community and researching records. Preservation and extension of the existing design, evolved over a long time, can make the community stand out and have its own identity and uniqueness.

5. It is critical that the informed design decision making should not preclude new ideas, new ways of thinking, to ensure flexibility in development standards where it is feasible. Designers, planners, and CSD experts should be encouraged to research new, innovative, and creative solving development project needs and keep an open mind to flexibility in community settings due to the unique natural, social, and cultural context in the areas.

6. *Context-sensitive solutions is a process:* CSS is a process that should begin during early stages of development. This step can make the project cost effective and avoid any later stage mistakes. The planning, designing, and programming continues through specific period of project development, preliminary engineering, final design and construction and maintenance.

Since every project has a setting or context, CSS can be applied throughout a project's life. Key elements of the CSD/CSS process include managing diverse technical resources, incorporating meaningful public involvement, integrating collaborating solutions to develop multiple alternatives, and maintaining open and honest communications and decision-making processes that are well documented. Listening and clarification of what is being said are key components of the communication plan.

4.13.1 Steps to successful context-sensitive solutions

Management framework

CSS/CSD is a customer-focused initiative; project managers should understand that real partnership between planning department and others do not occur automatically but on a project-by-project basis. They are results of continuous, collaborative, and respectful working relationships. This is why the project management structure must be not only supportive of the CSS concepts, but also supportive of inclusive stakeholders involvement and an interdisciplinary project team. Within planning department management framework, emphasis should be on project management and developing talented, technically competent, creative and innovative project teams. The team experience is paramount to the successful implementation of the CSS/CSD process.

Interdisciplinary project team

Project team composition for CSS projects should include skill sets that bring broad perspectives, clear vision, technical knowledge, and intuitive thinking, as well as reasoned problem-solving and creative ideas. Starting with the right team that includes a variety of professional disciplines is a core element in the success of a CSD project. All project team members need to ensure that the project will progress effectively and efficiently and solutions will be delivered accordingly to the project and community needs and goals set for the project.

Early in project development, the experience, expertise, and collaborative energy of these professionals can help set the broader foundation work and context for CSS project success. Beyond the team comprised of staff and specialists, the project planner should consider and expand project team made up of representatives of the various agencies, jurisdictions who are directly involved in planning for, implementing, and/or eventually living with the results of the completed project. Other project team member can be university/college/school students, housewives, citizens, non-technical individuals, worship/spiritual centers associates, small business owners, "wallas", and other community members. The project teams should include the full range of interests and perspectives that should be addressed during the CSS project. However, not all projects are large enough to warrant large project teams, so the project manager must balance diverse team expertise and perspectives with a measure of the project's complexity.

Team self-assessment

Time and efforts are costly. Project teams, once assembled, should not be reluctant to assess themselves as individuals and as a team. Knowing the personality traits, strengths, weaknesses, preferences, and biases of the individuals on the project team is important for a project manager to appreciate the diversity and differences that will make the team strong. Project manager should strive to enhance his/her project team's performance and effectiveness through a professionally learning environment. The objective of team self-assessment is to guide participants in becoming new observers and listeners of themselves and others, and to be present in the team experience in newly self-aware and different ways. Team self-assessment could save time, money, and resources caused by trial and error management by team leaders.

Results through communication

Successful CSS project results require continuous communication with all stakeholders throughout a project's duration. Enhancing communication and trust through new awareness and discipline in conversation can also be important to a project's success. Project managers, planners, design engineers should gain new insight into how conversational network function and what this mean for the project team. Team members should acquire a basic understanding of common speech patterns – assertions, judgments, declarations, requests, offers, and promises – and how to use them to maximizing meaningful discussions. The benefit to the team and the project is clarity and discipline in team conversations. This approach can accelerate progress, enhance results, and reduce project mistakes or misunderstandings. Trust and commitment are the portals through which all CSS project teams must pass on their way to states of collaboration and creativity. Project managers and professionals must also understand the language of commitment and the elements of trust. Understanding trust and how to distinguish genuine trust is paramount to collaborative decision-making.

Identifying community values

Identifying community values can commonly be addressed through a Community Impact Assessment (CIA). A CIA is the process that evaluates the potential impacts of proposed projects on a local community. Topics that commonly fall under a CIA include: history of the community; style and nature of built environment; social integration or split; cultural integration or split; new development impacts; changes in quality of life; changes in property values; access, mobility, connectivity, separation of the neighborhood from community facilities; values of any existing worship places; historic identities; displacements; impact on community activity places; land uses; removal of urban blight; and human environment.

Sensitivities to social and cultural environmental concerns

Understanding the problems or issues: Interested parties, stakeholders, and the agency must reach a clear understanding of the project needs, issues, and problems to be resolved, so that progress can be made towards solving the project issues. Developing successful context-sensitive alternatives that will lead to context-sensitive solutions begins with a clear definition of the project. This problem definition is the first step towards developing a roadmap for obtaining CSD consensus.

Economic development projects can enhance the development or redevelopment of certain areas. These projects also need to directly involve beneficiaries, at least to keep the process from appearing to be biased.

The cities provide and create arena for social and cultural advancements. People exchange ideas and adopt new social and cultural traits and habits. Sometimes accidentally or incidentally cultures get metamorphosed. History reflects that all food consumed today are not indigenous. Like foods, social and cultural habits are imported and exported. Context-sensitive solutions should carefully assess the need of certain social and cultural habits to be preserved and how the habits of faraway places are penetrating into the local social life. The social media, Internet, television, marketing tools, and high-pressure commercial forces are changing the communities.

The project manager and planners should avoid, minimize, and mitigate to the fullest extent possible the adverse effects of the proposed programs and projects on the neighborhood, community, and natural environment; seek opportunities to go beyond the traditional project mitigation efforts and implement innovative enhancement measures. Context-sensitive solutions often appear deceptively simple, yet the holistic, multi-disciplinary, community-driven nature of CSS-based project delivery makes measurement challenging.

4.13.2 Context-sensitive solution/design/planning guidelines

Traffic and transportation:
- Landscaped medians and oversize right-of-ways
- Canopy/shady trees, historic trees, specimen trees, and clear zone policy to preserve them
- Special finish guardrails to minimize the obstruction
- Reduced clear zone behind curb and gutter in constrained areas
- Installation of directional signs
- Installation of identification signs
- Inclusion of sidewalks
- Inclusion of bike lanes
- Construction materials that blend with the environment
- Gateways, amenity corridors, and historic areas
- Neighborhood buffers, open spaces, and trails as buffers
- Scenic view sheds and tourism, gathering, and events
- Add appropriate lighting
- Provide safety environment for all types of facilities (vehicular, slow traffic, pedestrian, and bicycle)
- Traffic calming techniques
- Multimodal Approach
- Parking availability for all modes

Architecture and building design:
- Building façade
- Building realm
- Building mass
- Building style
- Building artwork
- Building details (windows, doors, entrances, arches, and outdoor stairs)
- Building scale
- Building setbacks
- Building materials, colors, and locations
- Building setback
- Historic realm and features
- Landscaping

Land use distribution:
- Smart cities must plan and project various land uses such as residential, commercial, industrial, institutional, recreational, and mixed use. The future demand of various uses must be articulately incorporated in the future land use plan.

4.13.3   Natural environment and open space

Interaction and coordination of built and natural environment should be carefully assessed through CSS. Old towns were of small size. The open space and natural environment was not too far from the city boundaries. Another salient character of the cities was absence of pollution. Either there were no cars or a meager number of cars did not emit pollutants to the cautionary level. During the expansion or redevelopment process through CSS can assist in incorporating the need of more opens spaces and creating natural environment. The stakeholders should be educated about the benefits of urban forestry and need of landscaping for the sustainability of the built environment.

4.13.4 Enhance safety

The introduction of automobiles on the old designed roads has posed serious challenges for safety of pedestrians, bicyclists, and slow moving vehicles, e.g. rickshaws. The narrowness of road width with no sidewalks (were not required in the old designs of development) has made walking dangerous due to the addition of fast moving vehicles. The redevelopment of neighborhoods through context-sensitive solutions not only preserves the old form but also must enhance road safety at the same time. A careful design consideration should suggest restricting automobile traffic, including two wheelers, in older section of a city. Further, residents in older parts of cities, with no on-site parking facility should not be allowed to own cars.

4.13.5 New creations

The planners and designers will witness the influence of modern development techniques and design elements on new developments. The new development in the form of renovation or expansion of the existing buildings or a new development connecting with the existing building especially in older sections of the historic cities should be viewed as continuation of the existing realm of buildings. The new development should, to the maximum extent, preserve the previous developments. This process will preserve the old heritage and continue to preserve the old style for the future. The older developments were more confined to social cohesiveness and mixed-use type. The continuation of this process can be supportive of the new concepts of sustainability, smart growth, and life-style neighborhoods sans automobiles. These types of developments sustain higher densities without creating congestions.

The CSS can be instrumental in preserving the built environment of the older parts of the cities at the same time help make improvements to the lacking elements. The new living habits must not destroy cities' old neighborhoods, markets, open spaces, historic traditions, building art, and culture of the community. Addition and expansion of built environment should carefully be assessed. The buildings are permanent features. The new developments on the vacant/raw lands should consider replicating the old themes with modern amenities, design elements, and improved building, designing, and planning concepts.

The planner's tool kit is to facilitate the professionals with basic understanding of the planning tools. These are just guidelines; the user can make improvements or changes according to the needs of the project or situation or circumstances. These are not rigid commandments, and this is the best part of planning profession. The experience of planning projects and implementation adds new dimension to the profession.

4.14 Underground development planning

The demands for space have resulted in cities that have spiraled upwards. In old Indian cities context, the customer base is limited and/or no surface parking spaces have resulted in underground development. For planners using underground space remains one of the great challenges for the future planning. The potential is to place unsightly car parking, highways, and shopping malls.

The feasibility or cost of an underground development depends on three main parameters:
  i. The type and form of development
  ii. The ground and groundwater conditions
  iii. The sensitivity of adjacent structures and services

Different types of underground spaces are subject to different constraints.

Cuttings for transport infrastructure are more economic when the excavated soil can be re-used.

The feasibility of tunneling is dependent on the size of the tunnel and tunneling method chosen. Near-surface cut-and-cover tunnels are generally much cheaper than deep-bored tunnels requiring specialist tunnel boring machines. However, ground movements caused by shallow tunnels are greater than those at depths. Cut-and-cover can also cause more disruption to activities on the ground surface, such as traffic, utilities, and local businesses and residents, if any.

The cost-benefit of a basement excavation often be improved by optimizing the plan area of the basement to its depth. Optimizing will also depend on the type of retaining wall uses, method of providing horizontal support and construction sequencing.

Ground and groundwater conditions should be investigated at early stages of the feasibility study since these can often have major implications on the development. Engineering solutions at an early stage, before detailed design, can often resolve potential constraints, minimizing risks and costs. For example, excavations in rock require very different methods of construction to those in soft soils, and the issues associated with the two types of ground conditions are very different. Excavation in rock generally results in very little ground movement compared with those in soft soils. High groundwater tables may require dewatering measures and additional ground support during excavation.

Feasibility should consider the possible interaction between adjacent structures, such as overlying or neighboring buildings, tunnels, foundations, or services. Not all cases require detailed analysis. An impact assessment can follow the following steps:

- Predict surface settlement contours and identify buildings where the settlements or tilts are lower than the specified limits and do not need further attention.
- Evaluate building strains and distortions and predict the likely category of damage to existing structures.
- If there is a potential of significant damage, a more detailed analysis can be performed using numerical analysis or taking into account the three-dimensional settlement.
- Mitigation measures or monitoring systems can be implemented if structures are found to be at risk.

A good knowledge of the ground conditions beneath the site reduces risks and enables cost-effective designs to be implemented. A site investigation should be designed and conducted to examine the aspects of ground behavior relevant to the underground development that is proposed. A site investigation may provide information on some of the following elements:

- Depth and extent of existing foundations
- Location of existing services
- Stratigraphy or sequence of soil deposits and rock heal level
- Unusual geological features
- Strengths, stiffness, and permeability of soil and rock strata
- Archaeological remains
- Groundwater
- Contamination or aggressive ground conditions

4.15 Project management

Planning departments gets overwhelmed by various projects. These projects are related to community planning, social planning, physical planning, and economic planning. Preparing a comprehensive plan, zoning ordinance, or assessment of parks and open spaces in the community are projects. Imagine handling of a mega project – preparation of planning and management processes for 100 smart cities. Planners and planning departments are sometimes dragged into the projects at various stages of a project. A brief description of salient features of project management is depicted here. For details on project management, reader should research additional sources.

Project management is largely conducted by performing a set of processes. Processes may be grouped into process group and knowledge areas. A project performed with a process is called process group and what management knowledge is used is part of knowledge area.

4.15.1 What is a project

A project is a work effort performed over a finite period of time with a start and finish to create special or unique results, product, or capability to offer a set of services. Because a project has a start and finish, it is also called a temporary effort or endeavor. If the project does not create the final product, it is incomplete for whatever reason. The outcome of the project must be a special or unique result, product, or service. Result is usually the knowledge-based outcome of a product; for example, the results of any analysis performed in a project. Product is a tangible, quantifiable artifact that is either the end item or a component of it, for example, computer, clock, or television. The service is when a project can create a service – mean the capability to perform service; for example, Geographic Information System or computerized development permit issuing system. Projects can be performed at various levels of an organization. They can vary in size and can involve just one person or a team or group of people.

4.15.2 What is a project management

The practice of managing projects is called project management. To be more specific, project management is the usage of knowledge, skills, and tools to manage a project from start to finish with the aim of meeting the project goals and requirements. Project management is from simple to complex status with today's globalization, fast-paced global economy, local, regional, and international competition and fast changing business, local and political environment. Cities, towns, and even villages are on the front end of globalization.

Following are few of the advantages of project management:

- Optimizes the results by creating the right balance between scope, cost, schedule, and quality
- Focuses on the established goals and objectives of the project
- Focuses on the mission and culture of the organization
- Makes optimal use of available tools, resources, and knowledge or expertise
- Assesses and responds to the internal changes in the organization and the project and explores available and new opportunities to optimize the project.
- Explores and provides related and useful information for making timely decisions.
- Helps create healthy and professional relationships with various stakeholders and interested and involved parties.

These advantages are built into the design of project management and can be harnessed through effective project management. This is because of virtue of design, project management is the implementation of management knowledge about areas such as project scope, project cost, project risk, and establishment of qualified human resources at the right time during the lifecycle of the project, such as initiating, planning, executing, monitoring, evaluation, final outcome and closing. Project management occurs in a two-dimensional space, with one dimension being the management knowledge in various areas, and the other being the project lifecycle.

4.15.3 Initiating the project

This stage defines and authorizes the project. In public sector, a project can be initiated at various levels. Local, state, or regional elected officials, administrators, and other government entities can initiate a project for planning departments directly or indirectly. In private sector, depending upon the culture of the business can initiate projects as pro-active research project or reactive project. In professional world, some direct or indirect, through push and pull factors, can generate projects. In private sector, generally profit motive and time constraints are the two main elements of assessing initiation of a project.

The project manager is named and other project details such as the purpose of the project, a high-level project description, assumptions and constraints, milestone schedule, and business or purpose case for the project are prepared.

4.15.4 Planning the project

In this stage, the project manager, along with the team, refines the project objectives, scope, requirements and develops the project management plan, which is a collection of several plans that constitute a course of action required to achieve the objectives and meet the requirements of the project. The project scope is finalized. In association at this stage, project scope management plan, a schedule management plan, and a quality management plan be prepared.

4.15.5 Executing the project

In this stage you implement the management plan, and the project team performs the work scheduled in the planning stage. All the activities being performed to achieve the project objectives and goals are coordinated by the project manager. Approved changes, recommendations, and the cracks are performed at this stage. These changes are outcome of steps of monitoring and controlling the project.

4.15.6 Monitoring, evaluating, and controlling the project

Monitoring refers to the ongoing collection and analysis of information about trends, activities, and events that could affect and impact the project's performance. Monitoring can also address whether the project or plan has been efficiently managed.

Evaluation tells whether, and how effectively, the project has achieved its intended goals and objectives. It is the measurement of project or plan performance in term of the outcomes and impacts compared with intended goals and objectives. This can also include, how efficiently allocated resources have been used and the project has been administered. The main forms of evaluations are: (i) evaluation before implementation starts, (ii) evaluation during the plan implementation, and (iii) evaluation undertaken after the implementation.

Controlling is against scope of the projects which are unapproved or initially unforeseen but somehow filtered through the process.

4.15.7 Closing of project

In this stage the project manager accepts the formal acceptance of the project or plan product, close any contract or other legal or technical documents, and bring the project to an end by official closing announcement. Closing the project includes conducting a project review for lessons learnt, and steps to improve those lessons learnt.

4.16 Project management knowledge areas

4.16.1 Managing project scope

The primary purpose of project scope management is to ensure that all the required work and only the required work is performed to complete the project successfully. This is accomplished by defining and managing what is included in the project and what not. It's a finite amount of work and will need a finite amount of time, which needs to be managed as well.

4.16.2 Managing project time

The primary purpose of project time management is to develop and control the project schedule. This step must be monitored regularly to assure the project is proceeding as planned. The actions cost, and if the actions delayed or not following the schedule, may impact the budget and timeline.

4.16.3 Managing project cost

The primary goal of project cost management is to estimate the cost and to complete the project within the approved budget. Project manager will perform the appropriated processes to accomplish the tasks of managing the projects costs.

4.16.4 Managing project human resources

The primary purpose of project human resources management is to obtain, develop, and manage the project team that will perform the project work.

4.16.5 Managing project risk

A project risk is an event that has a positive or negative effect on meeting the project objectives, if it occurs. The primary purpose of project risk management is to identify the risks and respond to these should they occur.

4.16.6 Managing project quality

Project quality is defined as the degree to which a project satisfies its objectives and requirements.

4.16.7 Managing project integration

The project is planned and executed in pieces, and all those pieces related to each other need to come together. That is where integration management comes in.

4.16.8 Managing project communication

It is absolutely imperative for the success of the project that the project information is generated and distributed in a timely fashion. It is agreeable that communication is the most important aspect of a project and the most important skill for a project manager.

4.16.9 Role of a project manager

The role of project manager is challenging. The major responsibility of a project manager is to ensure that the project objectives, goals, and requirements are accomplished on time and within established budget. Managing a project means applying project management to the project at hand, which includes initiating, planning, executing, monitoring, evaluation, and controlling, and closing the project. The project responsibilities include optimizing requirements, managing expectations, managing priorities, and managing changes.

A project manager needs to have qualities of a facilitator, point person, organizer and planner, resource manager, leader, coach and mentor, and a visionary.

4.16.10 Interpersonal skills of a project manager

The project manager must keep in mind who the decision maker is/are and work with them to ensure the success of the project. To lead the project and team, a project manager must have excellent interpersonal skills including the following:

4.16.11 Communication

A project manager is required to communicate throughout the project to perform almost anything: exchange information, resolve conflicts, and manage expectations, deliver information, and lead. Project manager, depending upon the project, must have skills to develop a communication strategy with following issues:

- What needs to be communicated?
- Who is the audience? Whom to communicate? One might need to communicate different deliverables or information to different individuals or groups.
- How to communicate? What is the medium of communication? Again, this might differ depending on whom you are communicating with.
- What is the expected outcome of communication? You need to monitor your communication and its results to see what works and what does not, so you can improve communication and communication skills.

Communication with the client should be characterized by a high level of openness and trust from the very beginning of the project. Spend time establishing how communication will work. Communication with the client tends to be more formal. The challenge is often to be assertive, particularly when requesting decisions, access, and information. Maintain an open and honest relationship with the working team. Make sure, individual members of the team, with particular assignments, are not left out and informed about the required information or decisions promptly.

4.16.12 Influencing

Influencing is getting individuals or groups to do what project manager wants them to do without necessarily having a formal authority to mandate an outcome from them. This is increasingly becoming an essential management skill in today's information economy and e-government operation. To exercise influence, one must understand the formal and informal structure of the organization.

4.16.13 Leadership

In the traditional organizational structure, the functional structure, project managers do not have formal authority over the project team members who perform the work. So there is no other choice than managing by leadership and not by authority (power or position). Managing by leadership is overall more effective and productive than managing by authority. Through right leadership, project manager can share the vision, inspire, motivate, excite, and zeal with the working team. Before you can start to motivate your team, you first have to motivate yourself; if you are not enthusiastic and energized, there is little chance that will be. Be alert to the first sign of procrastination and act quickly to ensure internal resistance is never given a chance to build up. As a project manager you are hub of all communication within the project team and stakeholders. You need to maintain communication with the client, stakeholders, and the team.

4.16.14 Networking

Networking is one of the golden secrets for succeeding as a project manager, especially in Indian context. It is important to know stakeholders, decision makers, and influencing people more than project involvement level. To network effectively, project manager should understand the influence of political and interpersonal factors. Networking is a regular practice and can be practiced through informal meetings, proactive correspondence, luncheon meetings, conferences, and workshops.

4.16.15 Politically savvy

In dealing with people and elected officials, a successful project manager is a savvy navigator through troubled waters. This skill is developed personally and by learning from others' experiences and by following traits of successful people. Project manager should take initiative, responsibility, and accountability for the project.

4.17 Management of planning department

Managing planning department is as interesting as complex. A planner may have to wear many hats in a day's work. The challenge is to know the goals of the community, understanding of the bureaucratic system, and judgment of political platform. The planners have to consider the community as priority; however, balance the act with other forces. The planner may have to make tough decision or unpopular decisions. Right judgment combined with justification and legislative process is a key to success.

Chapter 5
Education of planning

5.1 Why learn planning

Every individual plans. All actions and events are planned – consciously or subconsciously. Every individual plans for future. That future plan could be for the next moment, immediate, short range, medium range, long range, or lifelong. Similarly, it is important for an individual, family, neighborhood, village, town, city, state, and a country to plan consciously for the future. An individual or a community can lose its foothold, identity, or recognition in this four-dimensional world, without planning for future. With the understanding and knowledge of planning, we can make well-thought and well-informed decisions for the community, which will help achieve community goals. The onus is on the present generation to perform responsibly to leave this world in a better shape and position for the future generation, than we inherited it; this will help achieve ultimate goals. That's what planning is about.

5.2 How to learn planning

The techniques of planning are learned through various means:

For individuals: Planning is learned by education, personal experience, other's experiences, inherited intelligence, reading literature, preaching, sermons, and guidance from wise and experienced people.

For family: Inherited intelligence, history of the family, experiences from other families and individuals, reading literature, preaching, guidance from wise and experienced people.

For villages, towns, and cities: Planning is learnt from the planning professionals (urban planners, city planners, architects, landscape architects, engineers, and other professionals), planning experiences from other communities, books and literature, visionary community, and visionary elected officials. Communities can learn from their successes and mistakes.

Planning professionals learn about planning by attending planning training colleges and universities, attending and participating workshops, conferences, meetings, books, journals, and visiting other places.

5.3 Planning in India

In India, town planning education started in mid-50s with two pioneer schools: Indian Institute of Technology, Kharagpur, followed by School of Planning and Architecture, Delhi. At the time of this writing, there are eighteen institutions in India offering graduate degrees in the planning discipline. Some institutions offer specializations in planning such as urban and regional planning, transportation planning, infrastructure planning, environmental planning, housing, and disaster management. These educational institutions train about five hundred planners every year. According to the Institute of Town Planners of India (ITPI) in 2013, were less than 3000 registered members. It is estimated that the total number of planners in India is less than 5000. There are little shy of 8000 towns and over 640,860 villages in India, according to the 2011 census. Analyzing the available data gives two quick perspectives: (i) almost 3000 towns and 640,860 villages have no planner, and (ii) there are only 1.32 planners per 100,000 urban dwellers in India. Comparing the numbers with the

United States, there are over 40,000 urban and regional planners for 315 million people that comes to average of one planner for 8000 people. In England, one planner is for every 2700 people or 37.63 planners for every 100,000 citizens. With growing urban population and problems, India needs a large number of planners to manage and plan cities.

Further, the shortage of planners' problem is expanded when the private sector attracts trained and educated planners by offering higher salaries, benefits, and future growth potentials than the public sector. The problem becomes more acute when trained planners prefer to join international organizations and take employment in foreign countries. The demand for urban planners is acute with the national policies such as 74th Constitution Amendment, Jawaharlal Nehru National Urban Renewal Mission, Urban Infrastructure Development Scheme for Small and Medium Towns, Rajiv Awas Yojana, Environmental Improvement of Urban Slums, Mega City Project, Special Economic Zones, Delhi–Mumbai Industrial Corridor, IT Parks, Knowledge Cities, large scale residential subdivisions, Smart Cities, and other programs. Governments of all levels need trained planners to implement these programs. Now a humongous project of building 100 smart cities will need a very large number of trained and talented urban planners. Government should assess the need and incorporate in the plan to prepare and train planners and support personnel ahead, so that the plans succeed and achieve the established goals.

The Twelfth Schedule to Article 243W of 74th Amendment specifically highlights:

- Urban planning including town planning;
- Regulations of land use and construction of buildings;
- Planning for economic and social development;
- Water supply for domestic, industrial, and commercial purposes;
- Public health, sanitation, conservancy, and solid waste management;
- Fire services;

- Urban forestry, protection of the environment and promotion of ecological aspects;
- Safeguarding the interests of weaker sections of society, including the handicapped and mentally retarded;
- Slum improvement and up gradation;
- Urban poverty alleviation;
- Provision of amenities and facilities such as parks, garden, and playgrounds;
- Burials and burial grounds; cremation grounds and electric crematoriums;
- Cattle pounds; prevention of cruelty to animals;
- Vital statistics including registration of births and deaths;
- Public amenities including street lights, parking lots, bus stops, and public conveniences; and
- Regulation of slaughter houses and tanneries.

This is a very comprehensive policy approach by the Government of India directed towards rational planning of cities. Implementation of these policies can assist in mitigating many urban problems and issues, if not totally eradicate them. This can be a great start – commendable formulation of policies by the Government of India. Cities and towns should incorporate these policies in their comprehensive plan, community goals, and their day-to-day operation. Implementation of these policies can be a great start to eradicate some of the basic causes of urban problems. Urban planners, urban designers, and planning departments of cities and towns can be instrumental and pioneers in implementing these policies. They have the right tools in their possession. They can make improvements on their tools by employing support and justification from these policies from the Government of India. Planning department should integrate with other departments and organizations. Deputy Commissioners, the ultimate policy creators and implementers, should consult planning department on consistent basis to make implementation more effective and consistent with the Government of India policies. Department heads of other departments should coordinate with planning department for the same reasons. By working together for common goals, cities, towns, and communities can achieve more.

These policies should have specified role and participation of transportation, transit, and infrastructure of transportation, implementation, enforcement, and monitoring and evaluation of policies at local level. The professional staff of urban local bodies (ULBs) should include these elements in their operation. Elected officials, of all levels, should use these policies as their platform to attract voters and constituents. Government of India should revisit and review these policies by adding additional policies, incentives, financial grants, in-kind grants, programs, training models, and other locally workable tools. The government should prepare "tool-box" for the rural, small, and large towns/cities to implement these policies. The tool-box should guide and facilitate the local governments to employ these policies. Government should assemble and create teams of diversified professionals with planners as leaders to assist and train local governments and local elected officials to educate them about these policies and how they can assist in improving quality of life in their jurisdictions. Implementation is the key to success of established policies.

5.4 From where planners will come

The foremost step for every government level is to create financial and professional advancement and recognition incentives for urban / town / rural / regional / transportation / environmental / historic preservation planners and urban designers to select the urban planning discipline by offering competitive salaries, competitive benefits, scholarships for education, simple and inexpensive student loans, inviting teaching staff from overseas, making urban planning jobs more stable and respectful, creating opportunities for planners to advance professionally by giving equal or better status than administrators (they are not trained in any kind of planning), opportunities for Indian students to study abroad, creating programs to invite specialized and talented planners from abroad to train students in India. Various ministries of Government of India, such as Ministry of HRD, Ministry of Urban Development, Ministry of Housing and Urban Poverty Alleviation, Ministry of Commerce and Industry, Ministry of Rural Development, Ministry of Road Transport and Highways, and other ministries associated with population, urban / town / rural / regional development, and progress of the country should prioritize to support urban planning and related planning disciplines. Indian government should take the shortage of planning professional situation as top priority agenda item. Decision makers are experienced and aware that execution of policies is the only way to achieve goals. Following are few of the suggestions:

- Instruct every Indian Institute of Technology (IIT) to initiate urban planning and design program. IIT Kharagpur, the first IIT, was pioneer in commencing such program.
- Government of India is assigning the responsibility of 100 Smart Cities program to IIT Bombay and IIT Roorkee, where IIT Bombay does not have a planning department or planning degree on their curriculum;
- Instruct every central and union territory universities to initiate urban planning and design programs;
- Instruct every state and union territory universities to initiate urban planning and design programs;
- Instruct every newly developing engineering and architecture school to initiate urban planning and design programs;
- Provide incentives for accredited private universities to commence urban planning and design schools;
- Prepare a national level urban planning and design program to prepare planning students and faculty to compete with international planning educational institutions and job market;
- Ministry of Urban Development should establish a policy to make 100 Smart City Program led by planning team. The smart city division should be responsible for integrating with other departments, organizations, institutions, private sector, and technology specialist businesses.
- Government of India should make mandatory and establish grants with restrictions and incentives to promote planning

education. Planning should be introduced at school level. Ministry of HRD should be instrumental in starting planning schools in India.
- Central and state ministries should involve urban planners early on during policy formulation and to execution and implementation of projects and plans to monitoring and evaluation of policies and projects.
- Commissions (e.g. High Powered Expert Committee – for estimating the investment requirements for urban infrastructure and services), committees, boards, and groups related to development, transportation, and infrastructure, urban/town/rural/regional issues should be led and participated by urban planning professionals.
- Institute of Town Planners, India, (ITPI) should be pro-active, assertive, and lead to initiate planning programs at national and regional levels. ITPI should involve at national level program development and urban related issues and programs. It should guide decision makers with recommendations relevance to the planning profession, discipline, domain, and realm.
- ITPI should relax the policies of membership to attract both professional planners and non-planner individuals. It should encourage membership of other disciplines to ITPI. ITPI should offer free membership to new and non-member planners.
- Elected officials of all levels should be required to qualify of urban/town/rural planning – 101 program. The program should be mandatory and should be required right after the start of the position responsibilities. The program should be prepared and organized by the planning professionals in conjunction with other required professionals.
- Government of India should establish a research cell and program to prepare educational material related to Indian planning, Indian cities and towns, Indian regional planning, and Indian rural planning. ITPI should spear head this project. The professionals rely more on western research and literature which hardly applies in Indian context, e.g. elected officials

and administrators travel to the United States to learn about historic preservation. It should be other way round. In the United States, buildings over 50 years old could be designated as historical. Historic buildings in India are centuries old. India is enriched with historic buildings, historic sites, and historic features. India should lead the world in the knowledge of historic preservation and conservation.

5.5 Planning and other professions and disciplines

Planning professionals and other professionals such as architects, engineers (various specialities), landscape architects, urban studies, sociologists, economists, and so on should integrate and consult each other with an "open mind." No one discipline can complete the urban fabric needs. Planning is a multi-disciplinary profession, but each discipline with their knowledge, expertise, and specialization and willingness to work together can contribute to make cities, town, and villages of India more harmonious and livable.

5.6 Education, Education, Education

Every citizen has a fundamental responsibility to understand the basic dynamics of operation of local government, such as sources of revenues; capital program expenditure; contact information about the elected officials; role, duties, and responsibilities of local municipality; information about the various departments of local government; source of water; sewer system operation; solid waste management system; role of planning department; and rights and responsibilities of citizens or residents of the community. All these activities are part of local government education. Following are the recommendations:

- Right from the beginning, students at schools should be made knowledgeable about their rights and responsibilities as citizens. At young age, Indian citizens should be educated about respecting, appreciating, and feel pride of their community. Young

Indians should be trained to not to throw trash anywhere, everywhere, and places where they live. India's Prime Minister did not have to tell people of India to keep the country clean – "Swachh Bharat Mission". Planners and designers should assist schools to prepare information brochures for needed information. They can prepare graphic presentations for school children about clean spaces versus dirty places with trash, pictures of planned and designed in the community where they live and creative ideas like that. Young and adults should be educated about the harms of dumping trash everywhere.

- At college level, irrespective of any specialization, introductory planning courses should be introduced. Local planners should take that responsibility and share the various level information packages with the college students.
- All universities, engineering colleges, architecture schools, management schools, medical schools, and other educational institutions should have mandatory planning subject as part of their degree program.
- Other institutions, organizations such as Lal Bahadur Shastri National Academy of Administration and Institute of Social Sciences should incorporate urban planning subject as part of their curriculum. The program should be introductory and advanced level, depending upon the learning environment.
- Masters and dexterous of worship centers, religious/spiritual institutions, and religious/spiritual organizations should take initiative to learn about civic responsibilities to contribute to make communities better places to live and worship.
- Citizens, NGOs, informed citizens, participatory citizens, civic groups, and other civic associations should involve in the process of local government operation.

5.7 Teaching the teachers

Like metadata – teachers to make teachers. The next step is equally tedious and complex: training the trainers of planning discipline. With the advocacy and need of a large number of planners, India will need trainers of urban/rural/regional planning. Even further, to train the trainers to train the emerging planners should be equipped with right, innovative, and expertise in planning, management, and training. Government of India with right ministries should take this grave, complex, and long range situation in consideration and create a committee (typical Indian approach to tackle problems) and find practical, feasible, and effective solutions. Any further delay can make the situation more cumbersome. The settlements may become more chaotic and will create sub-standard human living conditions.

5.8 Other planning elements

5.8.1 Planning, planner, and management of planning department and cities/towns

We all make plans, usually our own. Professional planners, however, make the plan for others – generally a community. Working mainly for government, planners advise public officials on how to overcome with various uncertainties such as population growth, land use disparities, urban sprawls, slums, housing, environmental problems, and economic development.

Most planners complete two years of graduate planning education, during which they learn how to analyze the origin and patterns of human settlements, assess the individual and institutional activities that form communities. Planners learn theories of city growth, city decline, suburban expansion, neighborhood change, urban design, historic preservation, environmental assessment, regional balances, and transportation participation. Planners identify and analyze these elements through land uses. Traditional purposes of land use regulations are:

- to maintain property values
- to stabilize neighborhoods and preserve their quality
- to provide uniform regulations through each district
- to move traffic efficiently and safely
- to control aesthetics and architectural harmony

5.8.2 New vistas

- Protect environment
- Urban design to beautify the areas
- Protect economic stability and explore economic development opportunities
- Urban management
- Smart cities
- Slum improvement

Today's practicing planners are multifaceted individuals who have been academically prepared. Professional planners' judgment relies on theoretical and specialized knowledge of social, economic, political, and geographic relationships. A good planner should be able to:

- know what is a good development from the professional and public point of view;
- know what the development means in terms of the general plan;
- know the potential politics of a proposal;
- know how to apply the laws, standards, and policies in a positive way;
- know to analyze zone changes, subdivisions, and complex development; environmental and social projects by applying the ordinances, codes, design principles, and local objectives;
- know the latest trends in the profession; and
- know how to incorporate innovative and creative ideas at the right moment.

A planner should be skilled in working with public, elected officials, peers, subordinates, other professionals and departments, and in building community, and verbal and written communication.

5.9 Code of conduct of ITPI members

In India, the Institute of Town Planners, India, is the professional body. It was established in 1951 under the Companies Act. As of January 2013, about 3,000 urban and regional planners are its members.

Membership of the ITPI is one of the desirable conditions of the recruitment rules for appointment as a spatial planner in many government departments. All members of the ITPI are required to follow the Code of Professional Conduct as contained in the Memorandum, the Article of Association, and the by-laws of the Institute (ITPI 2003, pp. 29–30). These are:

Welfare of people and protection of public interest

1. Since the basic objective of planning is promotion of the general welfare, a member of the Institute of Town Planners, India, will respect this paramount consideration in his work, even in cases where it may be in conflict with the apparent interest of smaller groups or individuals.
2. The member of this Institute of Town Planners, India, will recognize that all land is a natural resource of the nation as well as the property of some individuals or groups; therefore, they will seek in advising on comprehensive arrangements of land uses and occupancy and the regulations there of to protect and promote both public and private interests, as may be appropriate to the situation, always acknowledging the primacy of the public interest.

Pledge to share knowledge

3. A member of the Institute will undertake continuing study of planning problems and their solutions and pledge himself to exchange of his opinion and knowledge with others, in the interest of both of the profession and the public.

Fair and considerate relationship with fellow professionals and pledge to charge ITPI recommended fee

4. A member of the Institute will act towards other members of the profession in a spirit of fairness and consideration. He will not falsely or maliciously injure the professional reputation of another spatial planner.
5. A member of the Institute will not compete for prospective employment on the basis of the fee charged, nor by taking advantage of a salaried position. Having stated the proposed

charges, he will not reduce the amount in order to offer a lower price than another of his profession.

6. A member of the Institute shall follow the scale of charges for professional services recommended by the Institute of Town Planners, India, and in cases where the scale cannot be applied, he shall refer such a special case to the Institute and obtain their permission to charge on a basis other than the one prescribed by the Institute.

7. A member of the Institute shall not attempt to supplant another town planner, once he has knowledge that definite steps have been taken towards the other's employment; nor will he accept an appointment while the just claim of another town planner previously employed remains unsatisfied. He will not investigate or criticize the work of another town planner for the same client without first giving the other an opportunity to explain his work. He will not advertise in self-laudatory language or in any other manner derogatory to the dignity of the profession.

Participation in a competition

8. No member or student of the Institute shall take part in a town planning competition not approved by the Council of the Institute.

Responsibility towards the client

9. Within limitations imposed by his responsibility to both public and private interests, a member of the Institute will act as faithful agent of his employer or client, whether an individual, either private party or a public agency. He will not undertake work for which he is not qualified by education or experience, nor at a price, which precludes adequate performance. He will accept no remuneration other than his establishment compensation or agreed charges for services rendered. He shall have no financial interest in the result of his work which has not been disclosed to and received the approval of the client nor shall he use for himself nor disclose to his relatives, friends, nor to any person, whatsoever private information in

the course of his professional duties which could be turned to pecuniary advantage.

10. Any estimate of work to be performed by other than him is to be considered an expression of opinion, which implies no guarantee of any kind.

Responsibility towards the employees

11. A member of the Institute will be mindful of the personal, financial, and professional welfare of his employees. He will encourage them in study, and advancement and achievement in the profession.

Responsibility towards the students

12. A member of the Institute will recognize a special obligation to students of planning and so far as is possible give them part of his time and his knowledge to the end that the high mission of the profession may be safeguarded for the future.

Know your job

To be successful and proficient in the profession, the knowledge of the job is eminent.

Integrity

Webster's dictionary definition of word 'integrity' is "the quality of being honest and fair."

People with integrity tell the truth, and they keep their word. They take responsibility for past actions, admit mistakes, and fix them. They know the laws of their organization and abide by them. For any type of a profession, "integrity" is the core requirement.

5.10 Conclusion

This profession is for selective and few people with special interests in community improvement and development. Undoubtedly, the profession is very challenging but very fulfilling at the same time. Making a difference in the community and improving the life of citizens is very rewarding.

Chapter 6
Smart cities

6.1 Introduction

Cities evolve over time; evolution is sometimes planned and sometimes unplanned. Every city has its history, heritage, culture, way of life, flavor, specialty, indigenous characteristics, and identity. Cities have to grow but at the same time has responsibility of preserving its fabric of culture, history, and style. Change is inevitable. Human dynamics change; cultures change themselves or get metamorphosed. Change brings new dimensions in many facets of human life. Change impacts the built environment. Change also initiates new process sometimes. Independent India showed the world changing India and new India by building new city of Chandigarh followed by Gandhinagar, Bhubaneswar, Navi Mumbai, Mohali, and Panchkula. Other industrial towns were built such as Ranchi, Jamshedpur, Bhilai, Durgapur, Rourkela, Raipur, Kochi, and Bhakra-Nangal. Depending upon the needs, requirements, and policies, new cities are built.

India's population and economy is growing. According to the India's latest census, 31% population is urbanized. It is not stopping. By 2030 it is estimated that India's economy will grow by five times.

Urban population of India has increased from 286 million in 2001 to 377 million in 2011. India's urban population is expected to reach 600 million (about 40% of total population) by 2031 and it is not too far away. The urban sector's share of India's gross domestic product (GDP) is expected to increase from its current 66 percent to 75 percent by 2031. This suggests that India will be at the capital of urbanization in the near future.

Cities are economic engines. Cities are agglomeration of economic and social activities. Cities provide opportunities, choices, variety, options, and cosmopolitan environment for people. Thus people flock to cities. By involving in to the urban system, people attempt to improve quality of life. From the other perspective, personal desires, choices, space limitations, growth limitations, unsustainability of and by local resources, limited economic opportunities, and restrictive growth policies make people accept the circumstances and environment and continue living in the same time frame or attempt to change the time frame by moving to suburbs, migrate, and immigrate. Population growth, needs, and consistent increasing demand can lead to building new cities.

Smart cities is a new phenomenon. Smart cities may be a shift from smart growth or sustainable growth terms used for years. The urban professionals are at infant stage of understanding the concepts such as new urbanism, sustainable development, and smart growth, a new term has been introduced – Smart Cities. Smart cities concept, from planning perspective, is discussed later in this chapter.

The recent government has introduced the concept of building 100 Smart Cities with a handsome budget allocated for this project. The concept is evolving as more ideas have been invited from other disciplines, especially technology. The plan is to build world-class, self-sustainable, with efficient mobility, efficient public transportation, safe and secure, minimal pollution level, optimized energy supply, and sustainable economy and job sector cities. This project includes making some old cities and some new cities – smart.

6.2 The concept

A smart city is that operates with technology. The basic elements of cities like water, sewer, sanitation, telephone system, electricity, trash collection, trash recycling, traffic and transport systems, and city operation use data analysis to provide smart and efficient solutions. Many other city operations such as surveillance systems, whole city Wi-Fi connected, high-speed connectivity, and efficiently operated utilities will be managed through advanced smart technology. Smart cities will be developed both vertically and horizontally. Smart cities will be equipped with innovative and smart professionals.

Cities are complex systems with thousands of activities performed every day. Presently, the quality of urban performance depends on the availability of the infrastructure and services. The infrastructure is roads, streetlights, water, sewer, storm water management. To complete the picture, cities also provide services such as city hall services, collecting taxes, cleanliness, schools, colleges, hospitals, libraries, parks and open spaces, and cultural activities. Housing, depending upon the policy, can be both infrastructure and service in Indian context. Cities strife to provide these services to retain citizens. Cities who do not care generally do not grow or if they grow then with *only* selective citizenship.

The concept of smart cities is founded on the premises of providing optimum level of infrastructure and services with device of encompassing modern urban production factors in a common framework and to highlight use of Information and Communication Technologies (ICT). Computers, sensors, and networking together makes technology framework of smart cities. The smart cities may compete with each other for providing better opportunities of employment, global connectivity, entertainment, nightlife, and advanced academic institutionship. City management, operation, livability, entrepreneurship advancement, global status, and recognition may be redefined, reconfigured, expanded, or evolve new definitions of these terms as the concept progresses. The smart city concept is essentially means efficiency with minimum human interaction.

Smart cities concept has many definitions by different organizations and institutions. They have defined which suits their operation, business culture, business goals, and availability of expertise and experts. The basic goal of private businesses is to maximize the profit. On the contrary, the responsibility of the government is not profit but provide services equitably and fairly. When government outsource or hire third party experts, the responsibility of government authority becomes multifold. The justification of spending taxpayer's money and to make sure the scope of work of the project is accomplished, at least meeting minimum expert standards. In smart city project process, the government officials and staff should be careful in coordinating planning, design, development, and technology. The term is used around the utilization of networked infrastructure to improve way of life, living conditions, improve political efficiency, economic viability, lifestyle activities, high-tech services (TV, telephone, Internet), and e-governance.

Is smart city concept being used to create urban utopia? The traditional definition of utopia is "an imaginary place in which the government, laws, and social conditions are perfect." "Utopia is a community or society possessing highly desirable or near perfect qualities." The word was coined by Sir Thomas More in Greece for his 1516 book *Utopia* (in Latin), describing a fictional island society in the Atlantic Ocean. The term has been used to describe both intentional communities that attempt to create an ideal society, and imagined societies portrayed in fiction. It has spawned other concepts, most prominently dystopia. If the understanding is such, then the policy makers, administrators, technology companies (both software and hardware), planners, engineers, architects, designers, and other related professionals must be very wary, alert, cautious, and simply careful. No city has been built based purely on pure technology operations. No empirical data, information, and measurement scale is in existence. This is not pessimistic statement but a word of caution, especially in Indian context where for centuries, cities have developed and evolved on the basis other than technology. Urban-use technology is relatively new and experts are rookies in this pavilion/stadium/arena. In order to determine use and level of technical services, models based on the data and information available and collected are developed to inject into technology systems.

6.3 Sustainability

Sustainability is a major strategic component of smart cities. Sustainability is in terms of basic resources (water), energy (electricity), land (limited supply), air quality, protection of hinterland, and interaction at global level.

Environmental sustainability is eminent in developing stages of any economy. Many lessons can be learnt from the western world's blunders during various development stages. Those should not be repeated in Indian context. Making environmental mistakes does not take long; however, correcting them sometimes takes a very long time. Resources are limited and must be used smartly. The present generation must leave world in better shape than they received for the next generation – that is sustainability.

6.4 Wireless sensor and network for smart cities

Wireless sensors and networking and computers together help to activate smart cities. The goal is to create a smartly distributed network of intelligent sensors nodes which can measure and track many parameters for a more efficient operation and management of a city. The data is delivered wirelessly and in real-time to the concerned citizens and the appropriate authorities to make well-informed decisions. For example, if a water pipe ruptures in a neighborhood, the residents will know, through electronic connections, the cause and effect. The authorities, through sensors, network, Geographic Information System (GIS), and Global Positioning Systems (GPS), will know where the problem is, and authorities can dispatch the crew in a timely manner to correct the situation or bring it under control. In this scenario valuable resources can be saved. Whereas, in the same situation, in a traditional city it may take long time to detect the problem and may take a long time to correct situation. In this scenario valuable resources can be wasted or saved.

In smart cities, vehicular traffic can be monitored in order to reduce or control congestion, divert traffic, control traffic lights, and provide movement priority to emergency response vehicles through sensors while managing from a control center. Traffic can be reduced with systems that detect the nearest available parking lots or street with no traffic or other alternative. GIS and GPS can tell emergency response team of shortest route to reach the incident site or route – not to take – because of repair work in progress. Motorists get information ahead to plan their trip, find parking spots, calculate travel time, and find shortest route for their destination; thus, they can save time, fuel, reduce congestion, make travel a pleasure and improve quality of life. In Indian context, through sensors and network, part of traditional lifestyle can be maintained. This can be beneficial to the consumer and service providers.

In traditional cities of India, many types of "wallas" (*chai, phool, sabzi, paan* vendors) actively participate in day-to-day operation of communities. Smart cities will not be gated or have manned booths to allow only certain segment of the society. The "wallas" will penetrate into smart cities. It will be interesting to assess their roles in smart cities. *Phool-walla* will deliver flowers through delivery people instead of sitting on a sidewalk or street corner, *chai-walla* will be replaced with café, newspaper stand will disappear because the news are available online and on TV. Citizens of smart cities will not be smoking because of health consciousness and environmental issues or they will import cigarettes from neighboring cities.

Through sensors, networking, and computers, various departments of smart city, e.g. administration, public works, transportation, planning, architecture, engineering, code enforcement, inspections, parks and recreation, tourism, police, senior services and cultural or special event department, can perform their duties and responsibilities more effectively and efficiently. This can reduce the cost of operation for the city thus less taxes.

6.5 Geographic information systems in smart cities

Geographic information systems is a modern way of creating maps. Old way of creating maps with hands had worked for centuries. Preparing maps manually had many limitations. Depending on the type and details of the presentation of the information, it took time accordingly. Sharing and forwarding of the maps were cumbersome and difficult. Now with the help of computers and GIS, the chores of preparing maps have become easy and convenient. GIS do much more than creating maps. GIS can integrate data and represent smartly.

Geographic information is a computer system that captures, stores, queries, analyzes, and displays geographic data. The system allows question, interprets data, and understands relationships, patterns, and trends. The system can be used to produce maps that are more accurate and attractive than those drawn by hand. GIS provides reliability for organizations which are responsible for maintaining authoritative records about the status and change in data status. GIS provides a strong framework for managing these types of records.

GIS has both qualitative and quantitative benefits. GIS benefits organizations, institutions, various departments, and citizens. For example, in a city government various departments such as community development, transportation, public works, parks and recreation, police, emergency management department, tax assessors, land records, and others can use the established database through GIS.

6.6 How GIS works

The following steps need to be taken to make GIS system work:

The applicant must know the problem to be solved or analyzed and its location. Framing the question will help to decide what to analyze and how to present the results to the recipient. The next step is the most crucial – to find data. The system needs data to complete the project. The type of data and the geographic scope of the project will help direct the methods of collecting data and conducting the analysis. The administrator must assure that the data is accurate, complete, correct, credible, valid, timeliness, reliable, readable, and maintainable. The administrator must efficiently and promptly update the data, information, and records to maintain the accurate and correctness of the information. Only thorough examination of the data provides authenticity of appropriateness of the data. This includes how the data is organized, how accurate it is, and where it came from to vouch for validity. Geographic analysis is the core strength of GIS. Depending on the project, there could be many different analytic methods to choose from. A GIS specialist can assist in selecting GIS modeling tools to make the changes and create new output. The last fundamental step is to prepare results through reports, maps. Tables and charts are shared and delivered in printed format or digitally over network or on the web. GIS can make sharp, crisp, colorful, and attractive displays. Other two important elements, besides data, are selection of GIS software and efficient and knowledgeable personnel to operate the GIS. A driver is no good without a car, so GIS needs hardware of computers with lots of memory, plotters, scanners, digital cameras, digital video cameras, printers, plotters, and copiers.

6.6.1   Benefits of GIS in Indian context

Jawaharlal Nehru National Urban Renewal Mission (JnNURM) has recommended mandatory reform to urban local bodies (ULBs) by introducing GIS. The technology is readily available; however, obtaining valid and authentic data could be a challenge. It has to start somewhere – now is the time. ULBs and policy makers should take steps by adopting GIS within their system for a better tomorrow.

6.7   GIS and smart cities

GIS can help in preparing and managing land parcel data, which is the fundamental requirement of managing and planning cities. The administration has to know the details about each parcel such as ownership, zoning, size, location, building information, utilities connected to the parcel and other features. With GIS, cities can manage tax collection and distribution of resources.

GIS is not exclusively for smart cities. Every city and village in India can use GIS and be a part of the smart city concept. GIS has many applications for agriculture sector such as detecting type of soils, using right equipment for right crop, integrating high-resolution imagery, helping in field observations, selecting right area for right amount of fertilizer distribution, selecting grazing area for the cattle, and the list goes on. The smart cities can assist hinterlands requirements or hinterland can seek GIS applications with the help of the smart cities. The smart ideas are not confined to the city limits only but go beyond. With time, the benefits of GIS can be spread beyond the smart city project territory.

The planning for urban areas has an integral element of mapping, and GIS provides the facility to prepare GIS mapping with geo-spatial analysis and solutions. GIS with the help of remote sensing and GPS can prepare more accurate maps. This should include mapping of smart cities, rural areas, and traditional cities.

6.8 The smart city model

A model of smart cities will combine various urban elements needed. Smart cities will attract investment to create smart economy, and will provide smart mobility, clean environment, smart living, and smart governance for smart and innovative people. Smart governance is simple and transparent online process that makes it establish an enterprise and run it efficiently are components of smart city model to attract investors. A smart city is with ability to create and attract investments to create employment opportunities. Next element is combination of environmental and social sustainability. In return, for residents it will be provided with quality of life, safety and security, inclusiveness, entertainment, ease of seeking and obtaining public services, state-of-the-art healthcare, quality education, and transparent e-governance which will encourage public participation.

6.9 Economic infrastructure

Attraction of innovative and creative population requires innovative and creative job opportunities. The model claims, through investments, to generate employment opportunities. The program focuses on developing industrial parks, trade centers, service centers, IT/BT parks, financial centers, mentoring and counseling centers, skill development centers, logistic hubs, freight terminals, special economic zones and export processing zones.

6.10 Governance infrastructure

Smart cities would have municipal administrative offices fully computerized and automated to deliver services efficiently, effectively, and in time. Public participation will be encouraged. Presently, public involvement in decision-making process is negligible at state and local level. Transparency in governance will be the main feature of smart cities. Social media and making information available to the citizens will be tools to operate the smart cities.

6.11 Physical infrastructure

The rapidly growing passion of owning automobiles in cities is leading to problems like congestion, deteriorating air quality, noise pollution, unsafe roads, higher energy consumption, shrinking pedestrian spaces, and dumping of junk vehicles. Walking and bicycling have been considered unsafe due to lack of safe sidewalks and bicycle lanes. Public transportation is inadequate. The smart cities will provide balance of personal automobiles and public transportation. The design will provide appropriate sidewalks and bicycle paths. The transportation system will encourage walking and bicycle use.

The model emphasizes that smart cities will provide reliable and utility services of water, electricity, telephone, ICT, and Internet facilities. These services are critical in a smart city. The services will be state of the art, round the clock, and meet threshold. They will be well maintained to make them reliable. In addition, other city services such as, drainage, storm water management, and solid waste management need to be of high quality. Solid waste management is a process of collection, segregation, transportation, and treatment and disposal system.

Sanitation is a health issue for urban residents. Lack of sanitation can cause epidemics, health issues. Un-sanitized conditions can cause morbidity. Smart cities will be designed to provide state-of-the-art sanitation for its residents.

6.12   Institutional infrastructure

In smart cities, institutional infrastructure of education, healthcare, entertainment, sports activities, and cultural activities will be of upscale, unlike traditional cities. Educational facilities will be of good quality at all levels, schools, colleges, universities, research centers, research incubators, and specialized research centers. High-quality healthcare facilities is an important factor in providing quality of life. Entertainment centers will make citizens happy with sports facilities, cultural centers, parks, and open spaces to provide healthy and active environment.

6.13   Technical infrastructure

Smart cities will be smartly equipped with Computer Information Technology (CIT), GPS, GIS, advanced sensors, networking technology, and Management Information Systems (MIS). These systems will work interactively to be effective. These systems will work together to provide better quality of life. The operation of smart cities will be a process because the technology is changing at a faster speed. The systems will need to be at par with the latest technology to be globally competitive.

6.14   Smart city project in India

The smart city concept is new in India albeit it has received a lot of attention in the last few years. Several cities in India have initiated deploying selective smart technologies to efficiently provide civic services to improve quality of life for its citizens. For example, cities like Hyderabad, Bangalore, Chennai, Surat, Indore, Mumbai, Kanpur, Coimbatore, and Mangalore have taken initiatives in traffic management system, metro rail system, communication systems, smart meters, solid waste management, GIS, property tax collection, water quality monitoring, online building-approval process. Interestingly, new cities, such as Kochi in Kerala, Gujarat International Finance Tec-City in Gujarat, and Lavasa in Maharashtra are being developed as smart model cities. In addition, seven smart cities are under development by states with foreign investment and collaboration as part of Delhi–Mumbai Industrial Corridor (DMIC). Overall, the plan is to develop two cities in each of the states in India as smart cities under phase II of the JnNURM.

Under JnNURM, ULBs have been directed to introduce GIS to achieve property tax collection efficiency, introduction of e-governance using GIS and MIS for service delivery, review of building bylaws, simplification for change in land use, computerization of land and property registration, mandatory rainwater harvesting, by-laws for reuse of recycled water, and structural reform relevant in this context. Many other recommendations have been made under the JnNURM. For additional details, the reader may consult JnNURM program enacted by the Government of India.

6.15   Telescopic view

In a democratic system, the policy makers' responsibility is to create a policy. The policy is carried over by the professionals and experts. During the formation of the policy, the policy makers consult professionals and administrative staff to make a sound, practical, and functional policy. Depending upon the nature, type, and level of implementation of the policy, the ideas and views can be obtained from other sources. The process should be done prior to announcing the policy publically. The next step is that the policy is implemented by the professionals. During the execution duration, the results of the policy are monitored for successes and failures. The evaluation of the implementation results are retrofitted with the policy to make changes to assure effectiveness of the policy. In certain circumstances, elected officials announce or create policy statements to lure voters or make themselves more popular. The voters should be aware of such events and should make the elected official accountable.

The smart cities project is at initial stages of policy formulation. Initial drafting stage is the perfect time for the policy makers and administrators to engage with professionals and experts of urban planning, rural planning, environmental planning, transportation planning, engineering (civil, mechanical, structural, transportation, geo-technical), architecture, landscape architecture, sociology, economics, physicians, and other related professionals to form a practical and achievable policy. Depending upon the nature of the policy, the organizers should involve technical experts, and professional organizations and associations. The elected officials and administrators are not fully trained in specialized fields to provide expert opinions. In the end, the results matter. How much the policy was successful in terms of achieving its goals? Many times over, in Indian context, policy makers have installed yojanas/schemes. Some are successful, some achieved limited goals, some became victims of the criticism, some became targets of the journalists and writers, some totally failed and some disappeared with time. This analysis is suggesting few lessons need to be learned. The lessons are: (i) the policy makers and administrators should invite professionals and experts at the initial stages of policy formulation, (ii) the draft policy should be reviewed, assessed, and commented by the independent third party experts, (iii) the final policy should have clear understanding of the implementation body (should not be administrative services personnel), (iv) policy structure should have time limit to achieve established goals, and (v) finally, the policy should have evaluation component attached to it. The evaluation should start with the launch of the project. The project policy should be flexible to incorporate any needed change. It is the right time that India's elected officials should start trusting professionals and experts. A deviation from the traditional system established by the colonial rulers for their own interests will be in India's interest.

Another component of smart cities equation is the innovative people of computers, sensors, networking systems, GIS, GPS, MIS and associated team of marketing and management. Many national and international technology firms, such as CISCO, SISTEMA, IBM, 3M India, Oracle India, Microsoft India, ESRI India, Intel India, Panasonic India, SANKHYA Technologies, Tech Mahindra, SAP Software and Solutions India, REPL India, GIZ India, CA Technologies India, CSR Foundation India, NASSSCOM, India Smart Grid Forum and others want to be part of the interesting and challenging project. The challenge for the ICT and related technology firms is to understand the component of technology element in the bigger picture of urban planning processes. The technology industry should incorporate in their proposals, to provide technology component of the smart cities, through three primary components of urban planning: first, planning is a process; second, the purpose of planning is to build harmonious communities where people like to live and enjoy; and lastly, the planning is taking actions today for better tomorrow. The policy makers and administrators should evaluate the level of understanding of urban, rural, and regional planning amongst the ICT and related firms and companies. The elected officials, administrators, and planners should invite these firms to display use of technology in the bigger picture of urban activities. It is very clear and proven in certain areas around the world that the technology firms are equipped with the know-how of piecemeal application of various day-to-day operational needs of a city. The next question for elected officials and administrators is to ask the technology firms "how these technology experts will work together and have consensus for final installation and implementation of various and diverse components of technology?" The dice comes back to the elected officials, administrators, and planners to challenge them of their caliber and understanding in this arena.

A city is a complex phenomenon. A city may have specific activity more prevalent but thousands of activities are performed by the city dwellers. Smart city concept is no exception. Smart cities may lure talented, innovative, and creative population but they will need services of other service providers. Those service providers may or not be interested in technology or equipped with technology or may not need technology of that level to perform and provide their services. A *chai-walla* may not need sensors but could use cell phone or computer to receive orders online and fulfill the order. *Sabzi-walla* and *doodh-walla* (milkman) could deliver orders as requested online. A resident could order dinner online from a favorite restaurant to enjoy at the ease of home. But how much technology the delivery person will need. Will the residents of smart cities worship online than going to the God's house? Will priests of a worship house deliver message through technology or traditional personal interaction? May be with use of advanced technology, students can interact with the teacher online while sitting in a study room than going to the educational institutions. The residents may play sports, with use of technology, in their bedroom than going to the field or play against someone in person or play online with the opponent from another country. The architectural and development plan could be approved by the city hall online. No visits to a doctor's clinic will be required. The prescriptions could be provided online with a delivery service, again, by delivery person. Will the residents socialize through web cameras than personally shaking hands or folding hands or hugging? Will the residents of smart cities live in isolation? The citizens of smart cities will have difficulty in assimilating in traditional cities or when visiting a village of their ancestors. The traditional Indian living will have a new definition in these cities. On the flip side of the same situation, visitors from the other traditional cities and villages will assimilate or adjust or adapt or learn to fit-in when they encounter a different way of life and living system totally different from the system they are accustomed to. The new elite group of smart cities will create a new caste system in Indian social fabric. In spite of tireless efforts by the smart and visionary leaders, administration, and many others to fix the caste system jungle, it is still deep rooted in our lives. Instead of unfolding the complex caste system, a new elite class of talented, smart, and innovative citizens will create another segregation. The new social class of smart cities may innovatively eradicate the centuries old caste system with the help of computers, sensors, networking systems, GIS, MIS, and GPS and new technologies invented in the future. The archeologists have discovered in the old cities of old civilizations that the certain sections of the city were assigned to particular class of the society and particular uses were permitted in certain areas of the city. The smart cities concept, especially in case of new cities, should be careful while designing the layout to accommodate various strata of the society.

6.16 Lessons learnt – Case of Chandigarh

The other component of this equation is the final recipient of the policy – the citizens of smart city. Have the policy makers and administrators thorough understanding of the needs and requirements of the final consumer? Policy makers need to have a feedback of the acceptance of the project by the future residents. On the one side is what policy makers want the final outcome and on the other side is how the perspective residents wants to live? The city of Chandigarh has changed in many dimensions than the Le Corbusier drew plan on the paper in the early fifties. He was promised many required urban operational facilities and services to make Chandigarh harmonious and livable. The administration did not fulfill the promises. Resultantly, Chandigarh was forced to fit in changes. Other forces of change were, one, unawareness of Indian culture, way of life, living habits, day-to-day activities and habits by Le Corbusier. He was not aware of Indian citizens' lack of civic sense, lack of habits of cleanliness, lack of organized and disciplined living, lack of sense of place, and lack of sense of pride. He did not incorporate in his plan road side and open air *chai-walla, rickshaw-walla, three-wheeler-walla, rehri-walla, dhobi-istri walla, pan-sigrat walla, road-side repair walla, road-side naai (barber), road-side (unhygienic) dhabas, boot-polish walla, road-side-massage walla, sabzi-fruit walla* and many other India's favorite entrepreneurs who are part of day-to-day urban living but are responsible for being undesirable urban use. Le Corbusier did not incorporate Indian lifestyle uses in his plan. With time these uses penetrated and occupied the space in the City Beautiful without any recognition in the master plan. These types of uses have no accommodation and recognition in Euclidian zoning system. He did not design shops for computer repairs who repairs in open, and *halwai* (sweet maker) who cooks and washes his utensils on the sidewalk but sells merchandise from the store. He did not plan Chandigarh for 960,787 people – and still growing.

May be Le Corbusier was a perfect architect, planner, and designer; but he was a Westerner and designed Chandigarh on Western standards for Western people living in the city. He tried to blend Western way of life in Indian culture. To what extent it worked?

Other force of change of Chandigarh design and layout is the excess number of people in the city than it is planned for or can hold. According to the 2011 census, 960,787 people are living in Chandigarh. The metropolitan population of Chandigarh is 1,025,682 as per 2011 census. The City was originally designed for only 150,000. Indian people are not trained to follow rules and the situation is further worsening by the administration's lack of zeal to enforce laws and regulations. Ironic and disappointing, Chandigarh has slums both within the city and around the city. Slum dwellers have moved from other areas because of better quality of life in slums of Chandigarh. Go figure.

Next force of change of Chandigarh is the shopping habits of Indian people. Local shoppers, who live in the city, and visitor shoppers, who visit the city for shopping contribute to the local commercial sector. The activity is supportive of local economy, more jobs, and more prosperity. Le Corbusier had designed Western style shopping areas. But shopping Indian way has its own charm and thrill. Shopping areas with narrow access ways, small tight shops (can accommodate only limited number of customers at a given time), street vendors, street squatters, floating vendors (sell merchandise from their pockets, arm-hangers, head on vessels), with limited or no parking facilities, no sanitation facilities, and many other interesting features of indigenous culture and way of life were overlooked by the architect. Present Chandigarh has incorporated many traditional shopping/"bazaar" elements in their Western design markets to fit to their style and taste.

Planners are equally responsible for bringing change to modify the plan and physical set up. They had no choice but to accommodate more people, more activities, more roads, and more new uses – not planned originally. City planners are sometimes helpless to enforce the plan and policies due to the pressure from elected officials and administrators. These unwritten policies and pressure from "above" make Indian cities the worst living cities in the world. One does not have to be an expert in engineering, planning, or architecture to know that the plan prepared by Le Corbusier and compare it with today's empirical design, and physical setting is certainly not what was intended in the original place. The comparative results are simple and straight. Planned city of Chandigarh has all the problems of any other traditional Indian city: traffic congestion, overcrowding, slums, air pollution, noise and light pollution, poor road conditions, crime, and many other urban blight issues.

City of Chandigarh has been tagged with satellite towns of Mohali, Panchkula, Baddi, and Zirakpur. They were not part of the original design. The birth of satellite towns are the outcome of political tug-of-war between Punjab and Haryana. Population and economic growth helped creation of satellite towns. The urban system has become complex in this area of satellite towns. Two states, one union territory, and other local governing bodies are involved in power struggle, distribution of resources, planning processes and management of various services and operation responsibilities. Resultantly, the basic concept of planned city is torpedoed and eventually the citizens are the victims. The quality of life is not what was expected from a planned city.

6.17 Forward thinking

The onus is on the urban planners, urban designers, architects, engineers, and other urban related professionals to understand the benefits and challenges of new technology; furthermore, to incorporate new smart technology into their solution toolbox to solve urban problems and plan better. The innovative technology should make life comfortable and enjoyable. The technology should help citizens to have living conditions with minimum stress or difficulty. Combining technology with day-to-day life should make life easy and convenient, not cumbersome. A city is comprised of citizens of all ages. Planners should assess the adaptability of ever changing technology by children, elderly, and people who are not technology savvy. Limited knowledge of technology and how to use the technology can be frustrating. The technology firms are, one, concerned with pushing their product, expertise, know-how, and introduce new innovations, and second, to maximize their profit. The ultimate responsibility of making technology work for citizens (not citizens working for technology) and making living safe and healthy is on the urban planners, architects, engineers, landscape architects, and other related professionals.

6.18 Planning for Smart Cities

Planning is a process. Cities evolve and grow over time. If cities are not planned and managed sensibly, then they can turn into ghost lands or may refuse to grow or may not attract desirable citizenry or may become chaos. Right from the inception of the idea of "100 Smart Cities," the policy developers, policy makers, administrators, urban planners, urban designers, architects, engineers, landscape architects, transportation planners, traffic and transportation engineers, environmentalists, economists, sociologists, and other related professionals should bring their vision and futuristic ideas together to make 100 smart cities a catalyst for the urban world. Following are the guidelines:

6.18.1 Regional perspective

The placement of 100 smart cities is evolving, starting with handful existing cities along Delhi–Mumbai Industrial Corridor stretching 1483 km between Delhi, capital of India, and business capital, Mumbai. Also planned is the Multimodal High Axle Load Dedicated

Freight Corridor (DFC) between Delhi and Mumbai, covering an overall length of 1483 km and passing through the six states – UP, NCR of Delhi, Haryana, Rajasthan, Gujarat, and Maharashtra, with end terminals at Dadri in the National Capital Region of Delhi and Jawaharlal Nehru Port near Mumbai. The project is covering a large portion of already business active corridor. The project is ripe for economic, social, infrastructure, institutional, political, and environmental impact along and beyond the corridor. The opportunities will attract more people from all over the country and overseas. The additional people will need and demand infrastructure and services. The region should prepare for regional impact keeping limited resources, inadequate, or totally absent infrastructure. The purpose of the project is to provide infrastructure needed for growth and handle growth. A regional plan should be prepared to address all the relevant elements. The Government of India should reconsider and reconfigure the corridor by extending the territory from Amritsar to Mumbai. The extended regional corridor can be beneficial for many reasons.

6.19   Suburbs and new cities

The initially proposed plan is to accommodate smart cities in the existing cities and build new cities. The existing cities have their own cultures and way of life. The suburban concept must be thoroughly understood in term of linking new development with the old city. Sociologists must evaluate social impact of new citizens on the existing culture. Establishment of harmony between the existing culture and new technologies is needed. To have harmony, these two time-separated elements must be bridged by sensible and careful planning.

The creation of new smart cities must establish the purpose of building of each new city, cultural theme of each city, design of each city, sustainability of each city, form of each city, architectural theme(s) of each city, planning and design of each city, detailed land use plan of each city, zoning of each parcel of the city, future land use plan of each city, and operation of each city.

6.20 Internal and external transportation links

Mobility design is vital for movement of people and goods. For each new city, transportation plan should be prepared to provide efficient, functional, safe, and easy mobility. Cities should be planned to be sustainable with minimum dependency on automobiles. Public transit with bike paths should connect the city throughout. Futuristic means and modes of transportation should be kept in consideration while planning for roads planners, and engineers should incorporate the regional connectivity in the master plan of 100 smart cities.

6.21 Environmental balance

Environmentalists should consider not only local but also regional environmental impact of this mega project. The project is very inviting especially when tagged with the plan to provide state-of-the-art, 24×7 services to the citizens. The transfer of people to this corridor development will have a ripple effect on the existing and future environment. The environment will be impacted during the planning and construction stages. Air quality plans, water supply sources plans, local fauna and flora plans should be prepared to protect these resources.

6.22 Social and cultural integration

Every part of India has association with its unique culture. India's heritage and different cultures are the country's pride and need to be preserved. The preservation of culture requires understanding of its relationship to people, its importance in local way of life, harmony, peaceful durations, and determination to preserve it. During the development process of this project, the project manager(s) must prepare plans for protection of social and cultural heritage throughout the corridor. Economic development is a feature of this project but sensible plans should protect social and cultural heritage.

Historic buildings, features, sites, and other related monuments should be recognized and recorded. It is needless to say that India and Indians are proud of their historic buildings and sites. Prior to any disturbance of land or buildings or features, historic preservation plan should be prepared and followed. To make the case strong, the historic preservation plan should be integrated with the zoning plan. Archeologists, local historic preservation organizations, national archeology department, national and regional chapters of archeology and historic preservation organizations, local historic preservation groups, international historic and heritage preservation organizations, planning and architecture schools specializing in historic, heritage, and cultural preservation, early on should be consulted to avoid any irrevocable damage. The plans should be prepared to take the historic treasures to the next level. Maintenance of the historic features should be integral part of the smart city development. Education of historic and heritage preservation should be inclusive of curriculum of educational institutions of smart cities. Smart cities can be catalyst of preservation for other cities, towns, and villages of India.

6.23   Cities of future and future of cities

"Bharat Hamara Desh Hai. Jaisa Banayange Vaisa Hee Banega."

"It is our county. India will be what we make of it."

The future of Indian cities and future cities of India is *now*.

Mongolians came and went, Middle Eastern and Afghans came and went, British, French, and Portuguese came and went and same with others. America, England (again), Canada, Australia, China and other developed countries are prevailing now in India with their brand name products, cars, electronics, mobile phones, water filters, air conditioners, beauty products, glossy magazines and journals, new marketing tools, big-box stores, indoor malls, highways, flyovers, outsourcing trends, and making social and behavioral changes. With the influence of these elements, Indian society is being metamorphosed for various reasons. India is on the fast track of development and growth. Keeping the following trend of development, undoubtedly, India will be among the economic leaders of the world. Forefathers of India and many great thinkers and visionaries of recent times have established strong foundation of social, cultural, economic, political, religious, spiritual, and ethical values, traits, and peculiar characteristics. The challenge of the present times is to carry on those legacies and take them to the next level. India is advancing in space technology, engineering, transportation, medical science, education, computer science, communication, and many other fields. The development and growth comes with *responsibilities*. But how we live matters. Are we taking care of our cities, towns, and villages? Are we making our cities, towns, and villages more livable with better quality of life? Are we making our cities, towns, and villages safe, healthy, aesthetically appealing, morally sound, well-being of citizens, economically viable, socially nourishing, preserving history and heritage, and planning for the future? The challenge of the present generation is to create sustainable cities for the next generation. The next generation should create communities for the next generation.

6.23.1 Mixed-use living

The analysis from the observations is evident that, in Indian context, people enjoy mixed-use living. People like proximity to services, convenient access, propinquity, closeness, and availability of activities within vicinity. Mixed-use can reduce automobile dependency thus helps improve air quality, water quality, and reduce noise level. Developments should be mixed-use oriented and new plans should retrofit the conveniences of living close to services and activities. Urban sprawl has its consequences. Suburbanites enjoy the amenities of space but sprawl has its negative impact as well. Indian sprawl will repeat the history of the West – no so much harmony as depicted in the glossy and glamorous pictures. Urban India should continue with what has worked for centuries and is proven to be working – mixed-use living.

6.23.2 Healthy living and activities

People strive to live healthy lives. This is attained through eating healthy food, exercise, living in a clean environment, personal hygiene, and other personal choices. Urban planners, urban designers, health professionals, land use planners, and policy makers can assist in achieving the goal of healthy living by every citizen. Community design elements such as provision of sidewalks, parks, open spaces, activity centers, walkable access of education institutions, especially schools, and closeness to markets can create healthy living environment. The responsible authorities should educate the citizens and market the idea of healthy living. Healthy living can reduce medical expenses. This can help reduce tax spending on services where health service is provided free by the government. It can assist in increase gross national product. Smart cities with design can maintain air and water quality for its citizens.

6.23.3 Walking mode of mobility

Build walkable communities. Sustainable urban design starts with human body and its needs. Through design, communities should be equipped with safe, convenient, comfortable, clean, and delightful sidewalks. Towns and cities should be designed so that people of all ages and abilities walk for the sheer delight of it. People choosing walking over automobile trips means no congestion, no harmful emissions, reduced noise level, no junk vehicles and parts along ROWs and open spaces. The willingness to walk is since the dawn of the humanoids, and it will continue till eternity. So why not build communities to accommodate and let humans enjoy the fun of walking.

6.23.4 Bicycle is for everyone

Bicycle is the most energy efficient mode of transportation ever invented, translating almost all of our metabolic energy into motion. Albeit we initiate with idea of walking in urban design, bicycles come in next close. The professionals should build a network of bikeways, separated both from pedestrians and motorists and other heavy traffic, use traffic education, traffic calming, and other tools to ensure that fast moving traffic do not dominate and interfere with cyclists on shared streets. Through attractive design provide safe, convenient, attractive, sufficient, and secure bicycle parking everywhere. Incorporate in design creative solutions for addressing the limitations of cycling, particularly barriers due to steep grades, rough roads, long distance travel, and weather conditions.

6.23.5 Transit for quick movement

Transit helps move large number of people covering longer distances. Transit system is cost effective, environment friendly, reduces congestion, and reduces dependency on cars. There are successful transit projects in India and in other countries. To make transit attractive to people who have choice of modes, transit must meet certain basic requirements; it must be comfortable, it must be convenient, it must be relatively fast, it must be efficient and reliable. Affordable transit attracts more patronage. Transit comes in many shapes, forms, and style. The local authorities should review the various options, costs, functionality in respect to the local conditions and then make a selection. Marketing of the system is equally important to make it a successful endeavor.

6.24 Spirituality for spiritual living

Spirituality is one of the most strong and common values among Indians. Historic buildings and sites, worship/spiritual places, and other features make this system of beliefs stronger. Spirituality is practiced individually on personal basis and cumulatively in groups. The buildings used for spirituality and worshiping are commonly visible in cities. These buildings should be studied and analyzed on the level of service they provide and should include planning elements to make them spiritual, contending, canorous, and harmonious. Spiritual experts can assist masses to shift from orthodox thinking and lifestyle to adopt to the present day needs of social, economic, political, spiritual, and behavioral dynamics. These professionals should take initiative to interact with other societal professionals to understand the sensitivity of time and incorporate in their teachings to make living more pleasant.

6.25 Integrity and honesty

Knowing one's responsibilities and duties for performing the job or assignment is a fundamental prerequisite. Combining the knowledge of and expertise of doing something with integrity, honesty, morality, probity, and righteousness in a communal platform takes the country to next level. Practicing of such values by every citizen makes day-to-day life pleasant, livable, and delightful.

6.26 Communication

The world is considered now "flat." Globalization has made the world more competitive. The urban professionals, policy makers, administrators, architects, engineers, and other professionals must train themselves in communication skills to deliver their ideas more effectively and impressively. The ideas, before implemented, must be understood and accepted by the communities. The educational institutions must incorporate communication skills in curriculum to equip the future professionals with the required needs of the real world.

6.27 India clean and beautiful

Teachers of schools, colleges, universities, and other educational institutions toil to train students for the future. In addition, every Indian student, especially when they are young, should be trained in civic sense and civic responsibilities. Some may never learn. Every citizen should be trained to understand and perform civic duties, e.g. keeping the environment clean by not throwing trash on the ground and everywhere, disposing toxins at appropriate places, keeping rivers, streams, canals, lakes, and other water bodies without any debris, trash, garbage, and pollutants (we drink that water), not allowing posters, pamphlets, signs, advertising, defacing facades, writing everywhere, and other message techniques. Every citizen should be trained to respect public property. After all, it is purchased with taxpayers' money. Municipalities should allocate budget for maintenance of public property and keep it in operational shape. Municipalities, businesses, shops, restaurants, markets, offices, institutions, service centers, activities centers, and other places should be required to keep trash receptacles on their premises. They should be accessible. They should be emptied, maintained on regular basis, and kept clean all the time.

Ironically, in the West the society is shifting their shopping style from polyethylene bags to recyclable bags versus Indian society is leaving cotton bags, "thellas", reusable "tokris", reusable satchels, to plastic bags. In America, some cities have adopted ordinances to ban use of plastic bags for bagging groceries, etc. Plastic is not a biodegradable product. Trash, heaps of used plastic bags, all kinds of garbage dumped, and people making use of outdoor as toilets along Indian Railway rights-of-way (ROWs) is a common eye-sore and embarrassing features to see while traveling by trains. Indian nationals, tourists, visitors, and people living along the corridor witness this all the time. Cleaning the Indian Railway ROWs (corridors) can be an ideal project under "Swacch Bharat" project. Surely, Mahatma Gandhi *jee* and PM Narendra Modi *jee* will appreciate it.

6.28 Green India Green

The benefits of urban trees are: reduce air pollution, produce oxygen, clean the air, reduce global warming by fighting atmospheric greenhouse effect, conserve water, reduce soil erosion, save energy, help in modifying local climate, increase economic stability, reduce noise pollution and create shelter for fauna, and other benefits. Perhaps, India is the pioneer in recognizing the benefits of trees and worshiping them. The new development is sacrificing trees in urban areas where land is valuable. Local authorities should adopt landscaping ordinance, encourage tree planting, educate citizens the benefits of urban forestry, and create associations and clubs to promote urban forestry.

The design benefits of urban forestry are: aesthetic appeal, visual discontinuity of continuous build environment, visual discontinuity of buildings, break monotony of continuous black surface of parking lots, and create harmony of built environment with nature.

6.29 Love your home, *galli*, street, neighborhood, city, town, village, and country

Humans are territorial and tribal primates. Humans have sense of belonging to a certain geographical area. We certainly not know every citizen of the city we live in. But, if some reason, we meet somewhere else, just being from the same city, we establish bonding. This bonding starts from the home we live in, and take pride. That pride needs to mix with the neighborhood. Keep the neighborhood safe, clean, attractive, and presentable, just like the home. If everyone does this, the whole city, town, village will be safe, clean, attractive, and presentable. Next, the whole country will be safe, clean, attractive, and presentable. Everyone should be proud of their neighborhood, city, town, and village – and India.

6.30 How many Indians in India

With over 1.2 billion people in India, government is struggling to provide everyone a house with toilet, a job to sustain a family, some means of transportation, proper health care, proper education for both children and adults, recreation, open spaces, and parks to provide quality of life and other services and infrastructure. Numerous "schemes", "yojanas", "plans", and "national policies" and some other projects with "attractive/fancy" names have been established since the independence. All with good intentions make path for progress. With time some of these plans have succeeded, some have succeeded partially, some expired with time, some are lost in time, and some just vanished. These plans did help to some extent – a few. The problems, issues, and challenges still exist in urban areas. Many individuals, professionals, patriotic individuals, commissions, boards, and committees have assessed the outcome of respective projects and have made recommendations to the Government of India. Recent report by McKinsey & Company and High Powered Expert Committee Report on Indian Urban

Infrastructure and Services have concluded the need of millions of dollars to provide basic services to the citizens of India. Although these reports state that the availability and trustworthiness of the data available was questionable. The costs suggested by these studies to provide infrastructure and services is acceptable. Assuming, to provide the required infrastructure and services money and resources (limited) become available without any strings attached to that.

In the real world, it will take years to equip the cities, towns, and villages with identified infrastructure and services. In Indian context, it will take even more than anticipated or hypothesized time frame in the reports. The population growth will continue and numbers are more cautionary with such a big base. The population of India was approximately 345 million at the time of independence, which has grown to 1.2 billion according to the 2011 census; a growth of over 800 million people in mere 65 years. On an average, addition of approximately 130 million people every year since independence. This population growth triggers two scenarios to consider. But before that, it must be stated that India has come a long way in many sectors such as agriculture, industry, communication, transport, computer science, medicine, and many other sectors. Many countries in the world seek assistance from India to learn know-how. India not only is self-sufficient in food supply but also exports it now. India's space agency provides payload equipment and technical instruments for other countries into the space.

1. *First scenario to consider is:* The population of the United States is 310 million according to the 2011 census. Establishing the quality of life and level of services available for each US citizen, the same level of services and infrastructure available to Indian citizen. The question is, are there enough resources available to meet the demand of over 1.2 billion people?

2. *The second scenario is:* The amount of time (years) it will take for installation of infrastructure and establishing services, by the time how much population will be added to the existing base of the population sector with 1.3 percent growth rate. The

question is "How much additional resources, infrastructure, and services will be needed to suffice additional population?"
3. *The third scenario is* a challenge to deter who gets it first – infrastructure and services? To establish criteria will be a complex task for the policy makers and administrators. The political and social powers will flex their muscles. Courts may take years to make decisions. This tug-of-war may further delay allocation of resources like other national projects lingering in doldrums.

The moral of the statements through analogy is: In a jungle, with hard work, a path is cleared to reach destination. Next morning, path again gets covered with the plants, bushes, and trees.

The crux of the issue is to have certain number of people, which are sustainable. Keep in mind the resources are limited. The social, political, religious, spiritual, and other beliefs may not support control of number of people. Force in a democratic system is not an acceptable mean. "Education, education, education" is the tool to help achieve the goal of sustainable population in India. Educate masses on quantity versus quality.

There is a shift of paradigm to build new cities from reflection of independent India, industrial town, capital towns to a new concept of smart cities. Central government, administration, planners, engineers, hi-tech firms (national and international) should be very careful in preparing the foundation of this paradigm. Technology should not manage people – people should manage technology. Individually or as a way of life of society, living habits, basic culture, day-to-day operations and day-to-day life may get influenced or some extent metamorphosed by the technology but the basic human needs and requirements remain the same and carefully preserved.

Each Indian citizen should consider what kind of country they want to live in and what kind of country they want to leave behind for their children.

Let us make our India a beautiful place to live, work, play, learn, worship, invest, and raise a family.

Chapter 7
Land use planning

7.1 Introduction

Cities of old civilizations show that certain land uses were placed at certain part of the city. We can speculate the reasoning now. The reasoning points towards harmonious and functional relationship between various uses. During those days, the population was much less and number of social, economic, political, recreational, and other activities in a city were limited or at much smaller scale. Residents of the cities remained mainly confined within the city boundaries or extended beyond the hinterland area of the city. People walked to places or used animals as faster mean of travel or carts to travel and move goods. Fear of attacks from outside tribes made erection of walls and moat. In northern India, there are many examples of cities – even medieval era cities – built walls and gates along the city boundaries. The Romans had to rebuild city boundary walls because of the growth of the population. The allocation of land uses, in the older cities, perhaps was made by kings, queens, priests, citizens, or then city planners. They seem well thought, organized, and planned.

City needs to organize various uses. The times have changed and progressed. People are more dynamic. Today, it is possible to have breakfast in Delhi, lunch at Mumbai, high coffee in Chennai, dinner at Kolkata, and back to Delhi on the same day. It is common that someone working a full-time day job is pursuing a postgraduate program during the non-working hours and also performing arts or entertainment activities. People have more desires and resources now. Way of life has shifted from only being a full-time farmer. A farmer can have a white-collar job and manage a smart digital lifestyle at the same time. A seasonal farmer with latest technical equipments, digital technology, and advanced know-how may be a full-time elected official in a city. Present societal system offers more choices, options, and opportunities for their residents. All these elements make cities more complex and interesting. The urban planners and urban designers have many challenging responsibilities to allocate various land uses in a city, in such a manner that citizens enjoy and are happy living in the city. Is it more difficult than said? Well-thought, well-organized, well-planned, well-designed, and well-consensual allocation of land uses can make living convenient, comfortable, and harmonious. This is only one part of the big puzzle. Other parts are: implementation of the goals, follow the rules, consistency of actions, revisiting the plans as the society changes it needs and requirements, and flexibility component in the plan. In addition, specific authority figure for accountability, full support to the plan, fairness in implementation with required power and tools, enforcement authority, and continuous process of understanding of human behavior, activities, and continuous process of understanding and incorporating citizen's needs and requirements in the plan. Next, very important part of the puzzle is availability of sufficient resources for the cities to make them livable and economically viable. The last but the integral part of the puzzle is the will to grab the bull by the horn. The system needs educated, trained, expert, experienced, passionate, motivated, and zealous professionals, administrators, and elected officials and citizens.

7.2 Uses, land, and planning

Local land use planning can be viewed as high-stakes tyranny of competition over a community's future land use pattern. Competition among the competitors to gain adoption of land use plans can be brutal. Their ultimate goal and motive is – profit. This game sometimes becomes a jigsaw puzzle between the rational uses of land versus the motive uses.

There are main five land use classifications: residential, commercial, industrial, institutional, and agricultural. Each category can be divided in to sub-categories. For a city, all uses can be displayed on a map. The purpose of land use map is to know the existing uses in the city. To understand land uses, two types of maps are prepared. First, existing land use map, and second, future land use map. Existing land use map consists of existing uses on each parcel or plot of land. Combination of previously prepared maps, records of rezoning, business license records, windshield survey, foot-survey, graphic records, and other local sources can assist in preparing the existing land use map. Prior to that, classification and sub-classifications of each major use must be established, e.g. single-family detached, single-family attached, multi-family, town-homes, duplexes, condominiums, flats, duplex, four-plex, kutcha homes, slums, and *jhuggies* (local names vary); similarly establishing sub-categories for each major land use prior to conducting surveys and preparing maps. The existing land use plan helps prepare the future land use map. Future land use map is the planning and allocation of land uses in the future. Comprehensive plans are the best document to keep this record for cities. Comprehensive plans keep records of other social, economic, and physical features of the city. Thus connects to the land use maps. The purposes of future land use map are as follows:

- To create balance between various uses in a city;
- To address any imbalance between land uses;
- To create complimentary land uses next to each other;
- To segregate noxious uses from other uses, e.g. industrial next to residential;
- To allocate uses in areas in need of certain uses;
- To meet the community land uses goals established in the comprehensive plan; and
- Guiding document to follow to achieve community's goals.

The land use planning arena can be confusing and frustrating even to the experienced professionals. Rather than following an orderly and rational procedure of adopting land use plans derived from scientific studies aimed at overall community interest, planning can appear to be an ad hoc process based on biased or misleading perceptions about reality. Long-range ideas may fail with time. Because of the permanent development, sometimes it is hard to change the course, even though detected timely. The interfering forces, social and political, can change the established goals through the implementation process. Later on, during the monitoring and evaluation of the project, it is impossible to justify the cause.

7.3 Capabilities, values, and planning

The planning process by planners evaluates the professional capabilities and values. The planners should be:

(a) *Visionary:* They must look beyond immediate concerns and issues of the community. They should understand the needs of the future generation. Planners must envision and shape the scope and character of future development. They should identify and comprehend the existing and emerging needs, and incorporate such a way in plans to ensure that those needs will be met. Planners may have to diversify their outlook towards the community from local to regional to national level. Planning is a process; planners should remain active with visionary thinking to continuously create scenarios for advancing visions of future urban form.

(b) *Comprehensive:* Planners should investigate the links among the local groups with similar goals. These groups sometimes work parallel without interacting and collaborating. Comprehensive and collaborating thinking can break barriers of parochial thinking.

(c) *Fair:* Planners should provide opportunities to interested groups on fair basis. Fairness involves analyzing plan alternatives concerning the impact on different groups. Planners should participate in educating the groups about the steps and purposes of processes. The achievement of consensus early on can help the planners in implementation of the plan.

(d) *Innovative:* Planners should be creative and innovative. Policy makers, administrators, professionals, and citizens look to their planners for new approaches to address and solve the problems. Innovative thinking will challenge planners to consider actions previously unconsidered, reconsider the alternatives did not mature, reexamine communities values, broaden their perspective, make young and future generation part of the collective hope, and act on the future generation's behalf. Planners should not be timid about advocating change in the plan-making process and plans.

Rational planning offers a systematic forward progression from initial stages of goal setting to forecasting impact of various alternatives and selecting the alternatives that best achieve the public goals, to implementation. The steps of rational planning could be the following:

1. Establishment of the idea to do the rational planning with continuous momentum;
2. Identify issues, assumptions, strengths, weaknesses, and assumptions;
3. Establish a vision statement and a mission statement;
4. Establish goals in association with stakeholders, community leaders, interest groups, and citizens;
5. Collect data, relevant information, and analyze it;
6. Revisit goals and revise them based on the data analyzed;
7. Determine objectives to achieve goals;
8. Develop alternative plans, evaluate consequences of each alternative to achieve the vision and goals;
9. Select and adopt the preferred alternative with a consensus;
10. Implement the plan, in which the land use plan is adopted and carried out, incorporate in the comprehensive plan; and

11. Monitor and evaluate the plan as it progresses. In which the progress and development is compared with the established objectives of the plan, and amend the plan.

Relationship between land use values of stakeholders, their planning programs, and outcomes constitute the land use planning process.

7.4 Types of land uses

7.4.1 Residential

Residential use is the most used land in a city. The type, size, and location of residence depends upon various factors: income level, family size, social status, proximity to work, permanent residence, temporary residence, rental choice, and personal choices. Due to the shortage and lack of variety of housing, in Indian context, people accept whatever is available than picking what actually meets their needs. Residential area should have ancillary land uses of small markets providing services needed on regular basis. Inclusionary zoning to accommodate various income level residents should be part of the land use allocation process. People with resources tend to move out of the core areas. This process is known as urban sprawl, suburbanization, and suburbia. It provides more physical space to the suburbanites, open environment than core areas, security, safety, and social status in some cases.

Cost of sprawl

Because of development and growth, like Western countries, India is on the track of facing several environmental challenges most of which are related to the sprawling development patterns caused by the expanding urban areas: residential, commercial, and industrial development along transportation corridors and on farmland in and around cities. Many factors are responsible for urban sprawl, such as growing number of people, increased buying power, ineffective and liberal policies, congested cities, lack of regional development policies, expensive real estate in cities, higher taxes, inefficient supply of utilities, inefficient services, pollution, crime, and deteriorating quality of life in cities. Urban sprawl has its impact such as:

- Expanding cities are converting prime farmland, forests, open spaces, water bodies, temporary water bodies, and other natural areas to housing subdivisions, industrial parks, technology parks, shopping malls, and office parks at an alarming rate;
- The physical sprawling has preceded faster than new infrastructure (water, sewer, storm water management, roads) and services (educational facilities, streetlights, activity centers for all ages) can keep pace.
- Sprawl has taken over the limited resources to manage new system thus neglecting maintenance of older infrastructure and services.
- The sprawling land use patterns are fueled by heavy energy consumption by cars, trucks, and other auto vehicles.
- Sprawl has led to serious environmental degradation both within the cities and outside the cities.
- Sprawl has caused hazardous waste and solid waste over larger areas.
- Sprawl has triggered land issues such as non-compatible land uses, non-complimentary uses, sporadic development, haphazard development, and undesirable uses.
- Sprawl has created a false development market by creating land speculation.
- Sprawl has impacted wild fauna and flora, wildlife habitat, ecosystem, and biodiversity.

7.4.2 Commercial

Commercial uses are intense. Customers need services provided by retailers. Depending on the hierarchy of the settlement, commercial uses can offer certain level of services to the residents. For certain higher level of choices and specialized products, the citizen may travel to a city providing next level of services, choices, and specialized products. In Indian context, market concept is a feature combined with mixed-use development, which can create sustainable communities. Other commercial uses are office use, office warehouse uses, up-scale office use, and office-service use.

7.5   Retail mall / Big-box retail

Retails mall is a new concept in India but in practice for years in the Western world. Retail malls have been a challenge to the planners to justify as a compatible use with surrounding uses. Malls are concentrated retail centers providing variety of products and services. Many retail outlets especially upscale businesses, being located in malls, attract fancy and rich customers. Malls are pride commercial places in a city. Initially they have to assemble parcels to create enough space to build a mall. Malls attract rich customers from nearby and far off places. These customers use cars to access shopping malls. Malls have to provide sufficient parking area to retain the auto owner customers. If measured by the Western standards, malls use lot of land to provide parking. The parking areas are paved and create impervious surface. This causes storm water runoff, point source pollution, and are concentrated air pollution centers. Underground parking has other challenges of air pollution, cost to install exhaust systems, expensive to build and maintain, excavation during construction can damage existing neighboring buildings. Malls generate higher real estate values for the surrounding lands. But the negative side of higher values works negatively by discouraging entrepreneurs with limited resources to start their businesses. In certain cases, this has led to higher vacancy rates of buildings. Higher land values encourage small property owners and small business owners to make a quick profit without realizing permanent loss of income and loss of business. Economies of scale and to recover high building costs, malls attract high end retailers and build multistory structures. Multistory malls change the skyline. They bring new dimension to the built environment. Malls built on city extensions generally take up prime agricultural land.

Big-box retail is one business in one building providing number of products and services. Again, this is a new concept of shopping in India, but in practice for a long time in the West, examples are Wal-Mart, K-Mart, and Woolworths. There are lots of similarities between the malls and big-box retail centers, such as occupation of large real estate, big size buildings, encourage car ownership and use, big parking areas, large areas for delivery and pick-up facilities to accommodate large trucks or delivery vehicles, negative and positive impact on local small- and medium-size businesses, attract rich customers, increased real estate values, and a new shopping phenomenon. Some big-box shoppers have to pay membership fee to shop at their facility. This system bars customers with limited resources or smaller needs. Psychological impact is impulse shopping – buying more than needed.

Planners, designers, and traditional business entrepreneurs must learn lessons from the West prior to encouraging and developing shopping malls and big-box retail centers. Because of the awareness among people about sustainability, environment cautiousness, negative impacts of such uses, and negative experience of shut down, empty structures, unsuccessful malls and big-box buildings, communities have to pay a price for that. Empty and boarded buildings are not only eye-sore for the communities they attract undesirable uses and invite criminal activities.

These uses are taking away the traditional shopping style of Indian culture and way of life and introducing Western way of shopping. The time will be the best judge of this new trend using lots of resources. These are white elephants to operate and maintain – or can the existing market systems redefine, redesign, and reconfigure to retain and lure customers to maintain centuries' old tradition of market concept. Existing business practices need to be changed by understanding new marketing style, needs of the customers, and understanding the competition. Customer service practices needs new shape and style. Honesty and commitment is the new name of customer retention. Planners and designers should evaluate traditionally successful shopping practices and incorporate modern facilities and attractions to that. Business communities/small retailers should cumulatively invest in the research to improve their operations and adopt the recommendations. They should be supportive of the suggested changes. The time is not far away that they will be only seen sporadically in unattractive places if they do not adapt required changes of time.

7.6 Wholesale / warehouse

Wholesale and warehousing are needs of businesses in the cities. The level of services, size of cities, and nature of activities determine the location and size of wholesale and warehouse development. This type of land use is generally on the periphery of city boundaries. However, for perishable goods the wholesale locations are generally near the population concentration.

7.7 Temporary and mobile vendors

Mobile, temporary, seasonal, event-time, or permanent street/sidewalk/open-space vendors are part and parcel of day-to-day life in Indian cities. They play a vital role in an everyday Indian culture and activities. Meeting friends or strangers at the "*chai-walla*" at the corner of neighborhood 'galli' (small street), picking up flowers while going home from the "*phool walla or walli*" who comes in the evening just before you are returning home, make your kid run to "*istri-walla*" or "*dhobi*" to iron your clothes instantly, get quick snacks from the "*pakore walla*" or "*pav-bhaji walla*" or "*idli-walla*" to give break to your spouse from cooking is a daily routine. In Indian city culture, there are many "wallas" actively participating in a citizen's way of life such as "*sabzi-walla*," "*paan-sigrut* (cigarette) *walla*," and *mochi* (cobbler), "*doodh-walla* (milkman)," "*garri* (coconut) or *challi* (maze/corn) *walla*," "priest or palmist on the road side," and with other local names of such service providers; they offer services quickly, efficiently, cost-effectively, comfortably, conveniently, on-demand, and instantly. They are smart service providers, who know when you require their services. They may be located on the sidewalk, open space, in front of closed or unoccupied buildings, street corner, under a tree, and on some cleverly selected site. Some vendors are mobile by walking, bicycles, *rehris*, push carts, or selling merchandise from a bag carried on their back. Stop. Western urban planning and design books or authors do not cover these uses as a land use. As a matter of fact, in certain communities they are outright considered as illegal. The code enforcement staff will remove them instantly, if someone attempts to perform these types of uses. But they are fully accepted in Indian context. Let us preserve them by recognizing as legitimate and authentic business and entrepreneurial operations. They contribute to the local economy and provide services within walking distances.

These vendors, whether they are temporary, permanent, seasonal, or mobile, should be identified and make part of the development/comprehensive plan. They contribute to the local economy by self-employment and paying their dues. They provide services to the community. They generate revenue like other established businesses. Elected officials, administrators, urban planners, urban designers, and law enforcement entities should accept them as legitimate, legal, and lawful operations and provide legal identity for their operations and assign a land use designation.

7.8 Institutional

Institutional uses are post office, police station, fire station, city hall, courts, libraries, and public building providing services to the citizens.

7.9 Industrial

The land use plans should identify various types of industries such as heavy industries, medium industries, light industries, small-scale industries, cottage and home-based industries and other industries active in the local areas.

7.10 Digital industry

With expanding territory and use of computers and its other electronic systems, local land use plans should identify them as a separate category. This attempt can be a pioneer endeavor to guide building of smart cities. Telecommunication towers and satellite dishes are few of such uses.

7.11 Environment and planning

The environment is made up of three main land uses: natural areas that provide environmental services of water supplies, wet lands, wildlife, riparian regions, coastal areas, national parks, forests, wilderness areas, and other natural areas; second, working area include, mines, farms, and recreational areas; and finally, built environments of towns, cities, villages, public spaces, transportation system, and water and sewer facilities.

The assignment of an environmental planner is to apply his/her expertise in natural and health sciences to land use planning and decisions. Environmental planners are also involved in preparing environmental assessments or in the development of environmental land use plans. In all cases the work of environmental land planners is done in a difficult setting where political, social, economic, and opponent groups must be taken into account. Like any aspect of planning, environmental land planning is an art and science. Limited resources and conservation and city planning contributed to the development of land use planning. Other reasons for environmental planning is the sensitivity of the environment towards results of the human activities such as noxious industries, emission of polluting gases by automobiles, release of pollutants, disposal of solid waste, storm water mixed with pollutant runoff to natural water sources, septic tank discharges, noisy surroundings, light glares, and other known and unknown factors.

7.12 The ecology

Ecology can be defined as the study of the relationship between an organism and its environment. The context of environmental land planning is made up of a broad and complex set of institutions, changing science(s), laws, practices, and the sensitivity of the specific physical space and built environment. Environmental planning is multi-disciplinary activity in which the planner's primary task is to collect the wealth of available information and expertise and apply it either to the project or problem. Planners must not only have solid grasp of natural and health sciences but must also have comprehension of the holistic dynamics of planning process which includes political, social, economic, and legal factors. Ecology directs that everything in the nature is connected to everything. Empirical examples have shown that extraction of excess water in one area for either human use or irrigation, dried up the water in another area.

7.13 Environmental planning

Any planner should be sensitive to environmental values and incorporate those values in to the planning process. But environmental planning is becoming a specialized field in itself. As mentioned earlier, the environmental planners bring elements of natural and health sciences to the planning process. That means, the planning process must include three broad goals into the development plans and land use regulations: first, to protect people and property from natural hazards; second, to protect people and property from manmade hazards, and third, to protect and maintain important natural and manmade values.

A hazard is a natural or manmade feature or process or outcome that threatens safety, health, or welfare of people and/or their property. The chemical stored for industrial use or transported from one area to another or for use in chemical processing plants can be substantial manmade hazard. An environmental planner may suggest to defining the hazard zone, identifying the population and property potential for damage, and preparing risk or emergency preparedness plan by suggesting minimizing population density, relocation plan of the residents, and minimizing incompatible land uses within or adjoining areas.

A value is a natural or manmade feature or process that enhances health, safety, or welfare of the people or their property. For example, an industrial plant proving number of jobs adds value to the community. It ought to be protected as value-adding property.

The most significant work of environmental land use planners falls into three categories – preparation of land use plans, assessment of the proposed developments, and preparation of land use regulations. In the preparation of the land use plans, the most common methodology that planners use is land suitability analysis (LSA). To assess proposed developments, planners prepare environmental assessment. In land suitability analysis, planners evaluate the appropriateness of the land for various uses. For example, a planner might use land suitability analysis to identify various alternative sites for a proposed solid waste disposal. The planner may study large area to identify various locations for the project. After selecting alternative sites, a detailed environmental impact study is prepared to determine more precise location. LSA is more on a general level, versus environmental impact study is more detailed study of various elements with a mitigating program of various unfavorable conditions.

Land Suitability Study is an analysis associated with a variety of methodologies and applications. The first tool provides maps showing the appropriateness of land areas for various land uses. Since suitability is dictated partially by environmental criterion, the maps show land suitability associated with environment. Land suitability analysis includes the following steps:

- Selecting and defining a classification system for all resources within a land area
- Classifying the land area according to the system
- Selecting and defining a classification system for land use
- Comparing each of the classified land uses to each of the classified land areas

Land suitability study may include numerous classifications of land uses, but not limited to, such as, soil details, geologic, hydrology, topography, physiographic, historic, botanic, and zoological. Each element can sub-details for various aspects. For each of these, planner makes a value and hazard evaluation.

7.13.1 Environmental impact assessment

Environmental impact assessment (EIA) is generally conducted to evaluate the proposed land use in a specific site. EIA is more detailed than land suitability study and often includes evaluation of various alternatives to the proposed proposal, to certain extent assessment of irreversible impact, and recommendations to minimize or mitigate the negative impact. Environmental impact study covers wide range of applications. Heavy industries, large residential subdivisions, airports, regional bus terminals, religious sites of magnitude, sewage plants, solid waste collection sites, and other large landscape projects are the ripe candidates for EIA. These studies can be required in small areas or project in environmentally sensitive areas, e.g. projects near wetlands, rivers, and lakes. Intensity of the study depends on the context of the project; however, generally EIA studies cover: existing or current conditions, identification of alternatives to accomplish the objectives, enumerate the assessed impact of each alternative, identify the preferred alternatives and method used to select it, assess the impact in details for the selected alternatives, and list possible actions to minimize negative impacts of the selected.

The planners must understand the complexity and magnitude of the project prior to assessing the environmental impact. The alternatives and recommendations must evaluate the mitigating scenarios in social, economic, political, and total environmental considerations. Another element to be part of the study and recommendation is the future. Future in terms of short, medium, and long range. A dry cleaner's operation, releasing chemicals, or a petrol pump with leaky underground tanks may have long-range impact.

Quick approach methodologies are simply quick responses to EIA requirements at preliminary stages or for small projects. A checklist is a refinement of quick approach including expert elements. These are generally pre-established questionnaires from research studies or other projects. In a matrix, proposed actions are identified. The severity of the impact is noted. Network methodologies offer an in-depth investigation of the environmental impacts. Each element is studied in details and then cumulative impact is identified.

7.14 Environmental land use regulations

Through regulations, the plans can be implemented. Land use regulations are generally part of zoning ordinance or subdivision regulations. Entities can prepare separate regulations governing environmental considerations. Land use regulations are generally based on the same evaluation of values and hazards that guide the land use plan. The fundamental purpose of establishing regulations is to protect or maintain resource areas or process that have value and to protect people and properties from hazards associated with resource areas or processes.

Typical resource areas are wetlands, water bodies, and woodlands. The ordinance identifies the functions to be protected. Then to develop regulations that will perform so. In developing such regulations, the planner must ensure that they are clearly twined with public interest – that they show specific public health, safety, and welfare issues.

7.15 Sustainable water supply and planning

Water is very special resource needed by humans, animals, and plants to stay alive. Water provides essential wildlife habitat, enables crops to grow, and is important in many manufacturing processes. People use water to drink, bathe, clean clothes, and cook. Dirty water spreads diseases and poses a variety of health threats. Water is a renewable resource that is replenished through the water cycle. But some water supplies, especially groundwater, are essentially nonrenewable because they recharge themselves very slowly.

The planners should identify the location, amount, and quality of water supplies and protecting them over time are essential actions in planning for the future of a community. Water supply planning is vital for places experiencing rapid population growth and development, and especially where water is scarce. Applying water use standards is a good start to estimate needed water supply. In Indian context, planners should count the number of slum dwellers in the city and around it. It is estimated that one out of three urban dwellers lives in slums. They may have direct access to municipal water or not, but they do use water. They get water from somewhere. Municipalities install water taps especially in low-income communities. Since they do not pay for the utilities, they may abuse the system. The water use on such facilities must be recorded and kept account for. Someone pays for it – other citizens of the city. This increases cost of supply of water for the municipality. To recover cost, municipalities charge more to the residents – pay for the utilities.

Another new feature in cities, towns, and villages is installation of water storage tanks, generally on the rooftop. The tanks once filled with the help of an electricity-generated power supply, provides continuous water supply to the residents. This system gives a false impression or notion of endless supply of water to the residents. This may lead to the habit of using water more than needed or required. Irresponsible citizens may waste precious water through this feature. Excess discharge of water into the municipal sewer system may cost municipalities more to treat water before discharging in to the natural water systems. The excess use of water because of roof top storage tanks means there is more extraction of water from the available sources. This could impact ecology imbalance and water supply imbalance in situ and or in other areas. In reality, water resource is limited and should be used responsibly, carefully, and restrictively. Environmental planners should take in to consideration the following for water sustainability.

7.16 Hydrology

Only 3% of the earth's water is fresh. Water supply depends upon the hydrologic cycles of precipitation and evaporation. A key concept in water availability is the replacement period, or time it takes for water to replenish itself through the hydrologic cycle. Masses, right from early on, should be educated about the water resource. Water resources should be protected, by sharing information on harms of throwing garbage, trash, toxins, hazardous chemicals, clothes, and other materials and pollutants in to the natural water system. They not only impact clean drinking water supply but aquatic life as well. Non-point pollutants also add pollutants to water systems. Cars, trucks, and other vehicles using petrol and petroleum products (oils), if not maintained, can discharge toxin on roads. They can mix up with the storm water runoff and mix with surface and subsurface water. This can impact water quality.

7.17 Watersheds and surface water

A watershed consists of the land area that drains into a particular river system, including its tributaries. Most watersheds consist of several smaller watersheds and eventually drain into the ocean. As a caution, some studies or inventories are conducted at too great a scale – too many watersheds are considered. The slope and soil type of watersheds affect how much water infiltrates and how fast water runs off. Comprehensive plans and ordinances that involve day-to-day land use decisions more directly affect water resources at the sub-watershed scale. The influence of impervious cover on hydrology, water quality, and biodiversity is most evident at the sub-watershed scale where the influence of individual development projects is easily recognizable. Urban development generates significant amount of paved surfaces, such as streets, sidewalks, roofs, parking lots, and driveways that prevent infiltration of water into the soil. Local municipalities should adopt ordinances to demolish dilapidated, unsafe, old buildings and structures in the city. The foundations and flat surfaces should be removed too to make land porous.

7.18 Sustainable air quality and planning

Air is a resource we take for granted because it is everywhere around us. Emissions by automobiles, industries, home heating/cooking, and other sources have made public aware of the quality of air we breathe. Clean air is enjoyable. Dirty air can increase the effects and frequency of illnesses, such as asthma attacks, chronic bronchitis, emphysema, lung cancer, and circulatory problems. Smog (combination of fog and smoke) can make visual hazards, respiratory problems, and can damage crops, buildings, and trees.

The atmosphere serves several purposes, including providing necessary oxygen for humans and animals. Besides humans other sources of air pollutions are volcanoes, meteorites, and forest and brush fires. Human factors are cars, trucks, airplanes, factories, industries, incinerators, power plants, gas stations, dry cleaners, burning coal.

Human activities release sulfur dioxide, nitrogen oxides, carbon monoxides, carbon dioxide, mercury, and soot. Winds carry pollutants from one area to another. Air, like water, has an ability to assimilate pollution. Air pollution occurs when the assimilative capacity is exceeded. Factors that impact the concentration of air pollution are as follows: the amount and rate of pollution released by local stationary and mobile sources, prevailing wind direction and speed, climate, topography, and vegetative cover. Polluted air does not recognize political boundaries. Once air is polluted it is not easy to clean up. Few of the pollutants of air are:

(a) *Nitrogen Oxide:* It is a reddish brown gas that mainly comes from exhaust of cars, trucks, and buses and from factory smokestacks. is a main ingredient in smog, which can reduce visibility and cause lung damage, bronchitis, and asthma attacks. Combining with water vapors, it forms nitric acid, which falls from sky as acid rain. It causes damage to lakes, water bodies, and trees.

(b) *Sulfur Dioxide:* The primary sources of sulfur dioxide are coal-fired electrical plants, paper, metal factories, and burning of gasoline. This toxic gas can harm lungs, and reduce visibility as well as can damage plants. Mixed with water vapors can cause acid rain.

(c) *Carbon Monoxide:* Carbon monoxide is a colorless, odorless gas that is poisonous to human beings. Carbon monoxide is a by-product of the internal combustion engine and most of the CO comes from automobiles. It reduces the ability of blood to deliver oxygen to the body's cells, muscles, and tissues. In large amounts, without ventilations, carbon monoxide is fatal.

(d) *Carbon Dioxide:* Carbon dioxide is the major "greenhouse gas" to which the recent worldwide rise in average temperature has been attributed. Climate warming in turn can change ocean levels, weather patterns, and functioning of ecosystems. Carbon dioxide is naturally present in the atmosphere as part of the earth's carbon cycle. Human activities are altering the carbon cycle. Human related emissions are responsible for the increase that has occurred in the atmosphere since the industrial revolution.

(e) *Lead:* Lead is a heavy metal that, when airborne, can cause developmental disabilities in children, neurological problems, and cancer; and is also harmful to wildlife. Airborne lead pollution can result from peeling paint, lead smelters, and the manufacture of lead storage batteries.

(f) *Particulates:* Particulates come in the form of microscopic dust, soot, smoke, and tiny bits of minerals, such as asbestos. Particulates emanate from fireplaces, smokestacks, processing plants, farm fields, cars, buses, and diesel trucks. Particulates are the primary cause of haze that reduces visibility. More importantly, they are leading air pollution health threats, causing nose and throat irritations, respiratory ailments such as asthma, and premature death. Both children and elderly are especially vulnerable to particulate pollution.

(g) *Toxic chemicals:* Toxic chemicals pose serious health threats to humans and other living organisms. Toxic chemicals that are often released into the air include mercury from coal-fired power plants, perchloroethylene from dry-cleaning plants/shops, and dioxin from the incineration of medical waste.

(h) *Radon gas:* Radon is a naturally occurring substance that is released as a colorless, odorless gas from decomposing uranium or radium in rock. The radioactive gas can seep into the homes and buildings. Radon can cause lung cancer.

7.19 Environmental land regulations

For most planners, the heart and soul of environmental land use planning is in the regulations that implement those plans. Land use regulations usually appear in zoning ordinances or subdivision regulations, although some jurisdictions adopt separate ordinances governing environmental matters. Land use regulations are generally based on the same evaluation of values and hazards that guide the land use plans. That is, regulations are designed to protect or maintain resource areas or processes that have value, and to protect people or property from hazards associated with resource areas or processes.

7.20　Conclusion

You cannot fool Mother Nature. Protecting the nations' built or natural environment is every citizen's responsibility. The multifold human activities of today are the causes for future's effect. The present generation must think for the coming generations. There is no such thing as "free lunch." Every human action has its results and consequences. Everything in the nature is connected to everything – the butterfly effect.

Chapter 8
Zoning

8.1 Introduction

Many countries around the world use zoning to control land uses. Zoning is the basic means of land use control employed by the local governments. Zoning is implemented through ordinance – zoning ordinance. The purpose of the zoning ordinance is to promote safety, public health, general welfare, moral, aesthetics, and to protect and conserve the value of the buildings and spaces, and encourage the most appropriate use of the land.

8.2 Definition of zoning

Zoning has been variously defined. It has been stated that zoning consist of "a general plan to control and direct the use and development of property in a municipality by dividing it into districts according to present and potential use of property." Definitions have not always been adequately served and the best concept of zoning is broadest. In its original and primary sense, zoning is simply the division of a city into districts and the prescription and application of different regulations in each district. These regulations may be called "zoning regulations." The primary purpose of zoning is to segregate uses that are thought to be incompatible. In practice, zoning also is used to prevent new development from interfering with existing uses and/or to preserve the "character" of a community.

8.3 The objectives

The objectives of zoning are the following:
- Improve the public health, safety, convenience, and welfare of its citizens
- Improve aesthetics, moral, and environment
- Preserve historic buildings, sites, features, and monuments
- Preserve heritage and culture
- Preserve natural features, landscape, and promote cleaner environment
- Plan for the future development of communities to the end that transportation systems be carefully planned
- Develop new community centers with adequate roads, utilities, health, educational and recreational facilities
- Recognize the need for basic resources and the needs of agriculture, industry, and commercial activities in future growth
- Provide various types of residential areas with healthy surroundings for family life
- Preserve agricultural and forest land
- Assure the growth of the community is consonant with the efficient and economical use of public funds

8.4 The purpose of zoning

In order to achieve the objectives of zoning, zoning regulations be designed to give consideration to the following purposes:
- Reduce or present traffic congestion in the public streets;
- Facilitate the creation of a convenient, attractive, functional, and harmonious communities;
- Protect against the destruction of or encroachment upon historic areas;

- Facilitate the provision of adequate police and fire protection;
- Provide for adequate light and air for healthy environment, convenience of access, and safety from fire, flood, impounding structural failures, crime, and other dangers;
- Protect against the overcrowding of land, undue density of population in relation to the community facilities existing or available, obstruction of light and air, danger and congestions in movement of people and goods and transportation, or loss of life, health, or property from fire, flood, panic, or other dangers;
- Facilitate the provision of adequate police and fire protection, disaster evacuation, civil defense, transportation, water, sewerage, flood protection, schools, parks, forests, playgrounds, recreational facilities, health care facilities, airports, railway stations, bus terminals, and other public requirements;
- Promote economic development activities that provide desirable employment, and diversify and enlarge the tax base;
- Promote the creation of affordable housing suitable for meeting the current and future needs of the locality as well as a reasonable proportion of the current and future needs of the planning district within which the community is situated;
- Eradicate the exiting slums, if any, and develop strategy to curb invitation to slums in urban areas;
- Promote general health awareness, obesity conditions, and healthy living conditions; and
- Provide reasonable protections against cantonment areas, military basis, and military installations.

8.5   Implementing zoning

Zoning requirements are described in two documents: the zoning map and the text as zoning ordinance. The requirements are then executed through professional staff, planning commission, the board of appeals, and the governing body. Each entity has its role and responsibilities through the process of implementation.

8.6 Zoning map and zoning ordinance

The zoning map shows the boundaries and labels of the zone in which the community has been divided. The map is legally adopted as supplement to the zoning ordinance. To determine how a particular parcel is zoned refers to the map. The zoning map must be updated with every change of zoning. The installation of zoning map on the Geographic Information Systems (GIS) can be done quickly, cheaply, and efficiently. The management of the maps through administrator can reduce mistakes, over writing, duplication, and maintain consistency and validity of data and maps. GIS also can help reproduce maps, show attributes, topology links, and buffering quickly and cost effectively. In some projects time is of the essence. GIS can also help delivery and communication of required information to distant participants.

The zoning ordinance is the text law of zoning requirement of the local government. A local law may be called an ordinance, a resolution, or zoning regulations. The local governing body enacts zoning control laws for the local community. Zoning ordinance is amended from time to time through rezoning or change of text either by the citizens, property owners, professional staff, board members, or governing body. Many reasons could be responsible for amendment to the zoning ordinance.

8.7 Districting

The basis of traditional zoning techniques lies in the division of the municipal areas into districts or zones. Land uses are traditionally divided into four basic categories: residential, commercial, industrial, and agricultural. Depending upon the size and functions of the city, a city may have many sub-categories. Metropolitan cities may have extended sub-categories to separate districts for more details and refinement. Under use regulations, there are typically three categories of allowed uses: principal uses, which are generally "out right" or "uses by right," allowed in the zone without further review and without any limitation other than the bulk, intensity, and density requirements of the zone; accessory uses, such as storage buildings, garages, and other outbuildings, which are allowed only as uses incidental to the principal uses; uses that are allowed by special exception or some other form of special approval process.

8.8 Variety of districts

In early zoning, the basic division was into residence, business, and manufacturing districts. These groupings are still prevalent in the modern ordinances but the refinements within each broad category or additional classifications are quite extensive. In Indian context, additional categories have been addressed here. The professionals may associate more categories or leave some sub-categories depending on the local community land uses, way of life, culture, and activities.

8.8.1 Residential

Residential districts have, by and enlarge, been established to separate low-density and high-density uses, for example, the separation of single-family homes from multiple unit apartment buildings. The basic classification of residential uses are single-family detached, single-family attached, multi-family, duplexes, triplexes, four-plexes, group housing, *chawls*, flats, high-rises, town-homes, and condominiums. Through imagination, other categories can be established. Each category must be defined crisply in the zoning ordinance to avoid any confusion. The intensity of use is the criterion of distinguishing residential use districts. Setbacks and other bulk requirements vary as the intensity of use is allowed to increase. For purpose of regulations, condominiums, apartments, and fee simple townhomes are designations of different types of ownership, not different types of land use. Another interesting and challenging example is defining "single-family." In the West, commonly accepted definition is "no more than 4 or 5 people living together related or not related." In Indian context, the definition of "single family" may include other people living with the single family, such as paying guest, extended family, relatives, servants, and domestic help. In some instances, servants and domestic-help living with their families within the principle single-family household is another explanation for definition of single family. The definition of "family" is the true instrument to control densities and overcrowding of buildings and overcrowding of neighborhoods (Fig. 8.1).

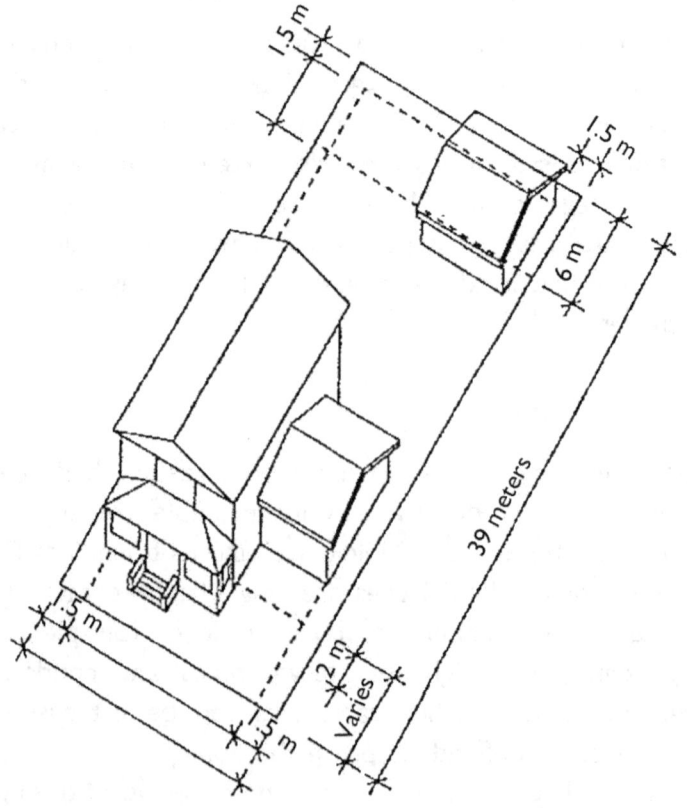

Figure 8.1 Single-family detached

8.8.2 Commercial

In a city, there are multiple levels of commercial zoning, corner store, small convenience store, small market, large market, large stores, shopping malls, box stores, warehouses, *godowns* (underground or above ground storage spaces), offices, banks, high impact commercial uses as auto dealerships, hotels, and all other commercial uses. Like residential zoning, commercial zoning is almost cumulative from one commercial district to another. While planning a commercial zone, access to various modes for people and goods must be considered comprehensively. Areas must be designed to handle loading and unloading conveniently without interfering with the daily traffic. Easy and convenient customer access must be part of land use design.

To determine the amount of land to be allocated to office buildings, employment is considered a more suitable indicator than population. Because persons employed in office are not enumerated by location, representative categories need to be chosen, such as employment in finance, insurance, and real estate and in professional and related services. Daytime population is another unit of measure that is used for estimating nonresidential space requirements.

In Indian context, it is noticed that main thoroughfares are used for commercial purposes. Mixing of high-speed traffic with commercial uses, pedestrians and slow-moving traffic can cause unsafe conditions for both shoppers (pedestrians) and moving traffic. The problem is extended by allowing commercial activities along highways. Whether on temporary or permanent basis, in both instances it is incompatible and unsafe. Commercial uses along main roads should not be allowed. Another recently cropping up use of rights-of-way along highways is retail sale of fruit and produce. This creates dangerous and unsafe conditions for the flowing traffic by drivers of exiting for purchase of goods and merging with fast-moving traffic. This use should not be allowed and strict regulations should be enforced. Sale of goods, especially by children, at the intersections and traffic lights is dangerous for the sellers and drivers. This practice should be prohibited. *Dhabas* (roadside restaurants), retail stores, souvenir centers, local specialty item outlets, including, surprisingly, worship/spiritual places are cropping up along the highways. Once businesses established, they are difficult to be removed or displaced. Businesses and property owners along main streets either do not have or cannot afford to provide required parking. Vehicles parked along main road generally occupy a driving lane. This makes congestion bad to worst. Land being expensive adjacent to roads, landowners avoid providing parking spaces thus creating congestion and confusing situations.

Another feature of commercial uses, in Indian context, is the use of public rights-of-way for profit purposes without compensation to the local authorities or appropriate approval such as open-air *dhabas* (street side restaurants), barbers, fruit and vegetable juicers, magicians, palmists, fortunetellers, priests, counselors, and vendors and squatters, and sometimes entertainers occupy areas for performances. Planners with engineers should seek practical solutions to these types of uses along roadsides.

8.8.3 Industrial

The land uses for industries can be subdivided into heavy, medium, light, minor or cottage or local scale industrial usage. One of the original purpose of zoning was to separate industrial uses from residential uses. The industries, depending upon the type, can be noxious and noisy.

Light industrial districts generally include uses such as warehouses, glass, ice making, and light assembly plants, which have little or limited impact on the surrounding land uses, especially neighborhoods. Truck traffic and visual impact is limited; however, planning and design should include green belt buffers or urban forests.

Heavy industrial uses include metal mills, large bottling plants, cement plants, large food processing plants, and manufacturing facilities, which are likely to create noise, odor, or smoke that can affect surrounding areas. Planning of heavy industrial uses require many details about the specific industry to mitigate impact. Industries generating smoke should be located in relation with the wind direction and season.

Medium industries can be oil mills, cotton mills, sugar mills, and other types of industries. Again, design must consider vegetative screening and buffering between other uses through transitional uses. Berms can also be suggested with landscaping along. However, landscaping is hard to maintain on berms.

Minor industries can be small bottling plants, dairies, bakeries, computer assembly or repair uses. These uses may have less impact but still requires screening and buffering from other uses.

Many communities use performance standards to distinguish among type of industrial uses. Industries create jobs and add to gross national product. These must be evaluated accordingly to allow them in an area.

8.8.4 Institutional

Also known as civic zone. Institutional uses are government buildings, schools, colleges, universities, post offices, city hall or municipality buildings, museums, libraries, and zoo. These uses are complimentary to residential uses being proximity to residential zoning.

8.8.5 Agricultural

Agriculture can be subsistence, choice, need, hobby, or a special activity. There are three types of agricultural zoning: agricultural zoning in rural areas without development pressure; agricultural zoning that is a temporary or holding zone where development pressure is increasing; and agricultural zoning that is designed to preserve agricultural land in a developing area. Agricultural rural zoning, in general, is simply obvious use of land for agriculture. Such zoning can be valuable for the subsistence of the population. Agricultural zoning is extremely important in rural areas. Maintaining the use of agriculture is a sensible use of land till the time of development. Land used for agriculture provides food. Other benefits are stop storm water run-off, grown product contributes to the local economy, and provide jobs. Agricultural zoning in urban areas can be used for buffering purposes between different uses, e.g. between residential zoning and industrial zoning. This zoning in cities can help maintain eco-balance in the developed areas. In densely developed urban areas agricultural use is not feasible. In Toronto, Canada, local communities negotiated with the utility companies, who own large tracts of vacant land under the transmission lines, to allow neighboring residents to use the land for kitchen and hobby gardening. The program not only provides organic food to the growers but helps in storm water run-off management.

8.8.6 Historic districts

Another biggest industry of India is tourism. Tourism industry generates revenue for all levels of economic sector and creates jobs. The qualitative benefits are enormous. People come from all over the world to visit, study, research, and for other purposes. The historic buildings, historic sites, historic features, and historic monuments are big attractions. History and historic buildings keep present generation attached to century's old civilization and culture.

Historic districts are created to preserve history, culture, buildings, and other related features. Historic preservation ordinance with special architectural control are easy ways to preserve the integrity of historic buildings. It is important that architectural controls in a historic district be based on carefully determined standards. Every city should prepare a list, duly researched, of historically important places and sites. An ordinance to preserve them should be in place. Individual historic buildings can be historic district itself. An overlay district is another alternative to assimilate historic buildings and sites spread over area. The ordinance may include controls for building material, colors, façade design and proportion, roof treatment, elevations, entry design, verandahs, open spaces around buildings, landscaping, and other architectural elements depending upon the local requirements.

8.8.7 Religious, spiritual, and worship places

Spirituality is one of the oldest export industries of India. Planning and designing new religious, spiritual, and worship centers and redeveloping existing religious and worship center may be a new category of uses with new challenges for administrators, urban planners, urban designers, architects, landscape architects, and environmentalists. Uses at religious/spiritual places are very intensive. Their influence extends beyond walking distances. Some are of international importance. Believers, devotees, worshippers, and performers of all kinds gather or visit many religious and worship places. Trees, trees along rivers, trees in the middle of the road (with colored ribbons, fire, ashes, color powders), river sites, stylish stones, and pretty much any object, with little creativity, can take the identity of a worship center. With due respect to GOD, gods, and goddesses people should be careful making any entity or a site a worship center. During old times, this action of believers might have been acceptable without any reservations. But with complex dynamics, putting some deity or other belief everywhere, anywhere, on road islands, any wall, or middle of the road may not be acceptable or appropriate.

Worship centers conglomerate people of various sizes, shape, and status. Some worship centers attract large number of people thus need to be equipped to provide human need services accordingly. A common site, at worship places, is unplanned settings of retail stores, souvenir outlets, food places, beggars, assembly places, many "wallas" (*chai, phool*, etc.), and others depending upon the worship place, way of life, and local customs. Worship places have concentrated use of various activities.

Worship places are asset to the local community and society as a whole. They fulfill spiritual and religious needs of the community. Worship places should be equipped with other social and cultural facilities such as senior learning center, senior activity centers, meeting places, children's activities places. Worship places' operators and managers should participate in local community requirements such as, planning, social activities, and informational educational activities. They should participate in finding solutions to make people self-reliant, instead of allowing or encouraging them to ask for alms or begging for charity. Society is as strong as its weakest citizen. Because of people's trust and faith in them, worship places can play a vital role in correcting many social, cultural, economic, environmental, and psychological problems. Planning schools should prepare and organize programs for people associated with worshiping places to educate them about the purpose and need of planning and how they can be instrumental in improving quality of life of citizens.

Communities should recognize and record the existing worship/spiritual places. The number of people visit them, the number, duration, and length of events/festivals they hold, and other related information. The new worship/spiritual places should adhere the zoning requirements as established by the local government. They should not be exempted. Worship places should obtain approval from the planning department. Planning department should have zoning bulk requirements, parking, and commercial uses along and around, landscaping, access way, entrance, traffic management, and other safety issues in place. For existing worship/spiritual places, each entity should be reviewed on the basis of safety, traffic management, utility provisions, landscaping, parking, event planning, and other design requirements. Reciprocally, installing religious or worshiping objects everywhere and anywhere may not be appropriate and respectful. Code enforcement department should be strict about this.

8.9 Planned unit development

A planned unit development (PUD) is typically land development of minimum acres with construction and use often differing from that permitted under the strict term so the applicable zoning classification. During the process a detailed plan is submitted. Once approved, the development conforms to the detailed plan. The purpose of PUD zoning classification is to provide flexibility in large-scale developments which otherwise could not be developed under the applicable zoning classification. In many instances, the PUD combines what would otherwise be applications for multiple variances and special uses into one plan. The final development may combine several different uses such as a shopping center, a club, a park, multiple residential and single-family residential, a golf club, and a day care. Not all PUDs include non-residential uses, nor do all planned unit developments contain clustered housing with common open space.

Planned Unit Development has advantages of allowing a better quality development. This can be desired development than strictly following zoning ordinance. The development can be designed to take advantage of the unique characteristics of the area and coordinate living, commercial, recreational, and design imaginations within one development. It permits a large area to be developed at one time without the need to seek a large number of zoning changes. In addition, more restrictive controls can be attached with the development, such as requiring adherence to an aesthetically pleasing architectural design.

Being so flexible, PUD allows for purely arbitrary decisions which do not permit uniform and orderly development of the total community. Some argue, it constitutes a "contract" zoning, which is unlawful because it restricts the exercise of police power by contract. And, the development conflicts with the comprehensive plan and may constitute as "spot zoning."

8.10 Mixed-use development / new urbanism

Mixed-use developments are characterized by:
- More than two significant revenue-producing uses such as, housing, retail, office, civic, or cultural. These uses may be integrated or may not be. They may act independently of each other.
- The activities significantly have physical and functional interaction with intensive use of land.
- The activities are close knit to encourage pedestrian traffic or uninterrupted pedestrian traffic.
- A planned development with nexus of scale of uses, types of uses, and appropriate densities.

Interestingly, cities in India are/were dominantly mixed-use type. Commercial activities are in close proximity to residential uses. Different types of uses selected their activity time, vacated the premises for the next uses; for example, the produce vendors occupied the premises till late morning for interaction with the consumers for that particular services. At mutually agreed time deadline the vendors leave. The space is available for the next operation of retail stores. This mutual agreement created a scenario of running multiple businesses at the location without any conflict. The system worked perfect. No competition of type of customers and no competition between the types of businesses exist. They were complimentary. In some areas, there were more than three or four levels of different uses but complimentary to each other.

The customers had advantages of time saving, money saving, and conveniently acquiring services. (Fig. 8.2)

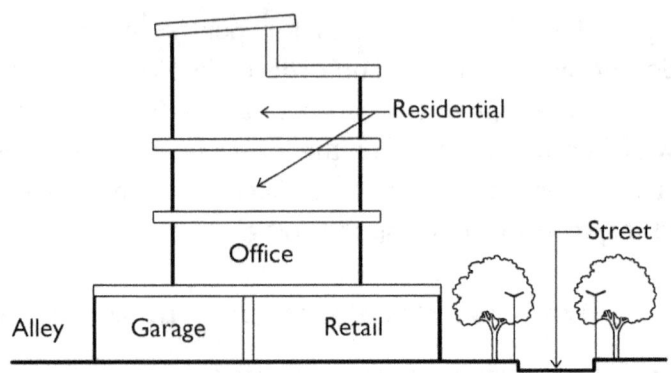

Figure 8.2 Mixed use

In Indian context, it is (still) common to have multiple uses in one building: residential, commercial, office, even industrial. In the West, urban planners struggle to convince citizens about the benefits of mixed-use development. People rely too much on automobiles. They prefer to drive miles to get services than walk few steps. People understand and are aware of the issues related to mixed-use living. Historically, the automobile industry lured the people to buy cars and advertised fun of driving cars. With time people became habitual of use of cars. Now it is hard for planners to change that habit of people. The history of West is being repeated in India. The mistakes of the Western development are being replicated in Indian cities.

There are many social, economic, and environmental benefits of mixed-use development. The proximity of services saves many automobile trips thus save environment. Mixed-use development provide healthy living environment. Interestingly, majority of urbanites, in India, are accustomed to mixed-use living environment. Indian cities are catalyst to the rest of the world, especially for Western countries, for mixed-use environment. Urban planners and designers should advocate for mixed activities places over malls, large markets, spacious single-family developments, and gated communities. From the viewpoint of the urban environment, the design of mixed-use projects, because of their typical size, density, diversity, and cohesiveness, requires more skillful urban design expertise. By accepting mixed uses, the citizens make the job of planners and designers easy. But they should take this accepted system to the new level to make it more inviting, functional, and useful for majority of urban population.

Architecture of buildings of mixed-use developments should be complementary to local architectural style. Vernacular architecture should be associated with the new development. The diversified history and time periods have developed varied architectural designs in various parts of India. Planners, architects, and designers should take note of the architectural styles around, preserve it and blend it with the new developments. Creation of courtyards along main streets can be a component to incorporate small businesses ("wallas") within bigger picture of mixed-use development. Courtyards can also provide gathering spaces for local residents. Signage of the mixed-use area should be very integrating, small scale, with acceptable colors, and complimentary with overall design. Mixed use can be associated with the transit system to invite additional users. Automobile use discouraging developments like, urban villages, smart growth, sustainable development, smart places, active living spaces, new urbanism, walkable communities, and related types of developments should be planned and installed.

8.11 Non-conforming uses or buildings

A non-conforming use is a use which is lawfully existed prior to the enactment of a zoning ordinance and which is maintained after the effective date of the ordinance, although it does not comply with the use restrictions applicable to the area in which it is located.

A non-conforming building or structure is a building or structure which lawfully existed prior to the enactment of a zoning ordinance, and which is maintained after the effective date of the ordinance, although it does not comply with all of the regulations of the new ordinance.

A non-conforming use and non-conforming building can be meaningful to make decisions. The distinction is most important as it relates to elimination of use or structure.

A correctional decision should include amortization. In other words, some or suitable time duration must be built into to make the use or building in conformance or remove the use or building.

8.12 Exclusion of named uses

This category, only the specific uses named were prohibited, includes any use which had not been named was permitted as a matter of right. This was true regardless of how incompatible the new use was with the permitted uses. The zoning ordinance preparer must provide proper verbiage to protect the ordinance from such happening.

8.13 Cumulative use restrictions

This characteristic is from early zoning creations. This was "cumulative" or "pyramiding" of permissible uses. In this regard, any use permitted in a more restrict district was permitted in a less restrictive district. For example, single-family residences were permitted in heavy manufacturing districts because almost everything was permitted in heavy manufacturing district. This technique may be in practice, depending upon the type of zoning ordinance.

8.14 Exclusion of those uses not specifically permitted

The modern practice in zoning is to exclude from a district all those uses not specifically listed in as permitted. In some cases the "cumulative" technique is employed by simply adding a phrase stating "those uses permitted in the X-zoning are also permitted in this zone." The question of how you determine what type of uses may properly be excluded from any given zone is not easy to answer.

8.15 Exclusionary Zoning

One of the most significant problems faced by local governments relates to the exclusion of particular uses from a given district or even from the entire municipality. It is often a very difficult planning problem to determine which uses can be excluded from given districts. In some instances, a determination is made that a particular use can be excluded from the entire municipality. One of the principal problems that arises in connection with such exclusionary zoning is in areas of economic, social class, and racial segregation.

8.16 Inclusionary Zoning

Inclusionary Zoning is also known as inclusionary housing. Inclusionary Zoning requires that a certain percentage of units in a new development or a substantial rehabilitation that expands an existing building set aside some units, as affordable, in exchange for a bonus density. The goals of the program are to create mixed-income neighborhoods, produce affordable housing for poor, seek equitable growth of new residents, and increase homeownership opportunities for low- and moderate-income citizens.

The Government of India, under Rajiv Awas Yojana, has directed that cities may legislate to make it mandatory to provide 15 percent of plot area or 25 percent of buildup area for the housing for the poor. Other countries such as USA, Canada, France and Spain have used "Inclusionary Housing" technique to ensure affordable housing for the poor by making it compulsory for the developers to make it part of the project.

8.17 Transitional Zoning

The principal purpose of Transitional Zoning is to provide transition between the low-density residential areas and on-residential uses and activities.

Through relatively strict development standards, location requirements, and use restrictions, this district is to act as a buffer between major traffic carriers and residential areas or between commercial and industrial uses, and residential areas. Within these buffer areas, the intent is to provide for office, clerical, and personal service uses which are characterized by a low or infrequent volume of direct daily customer contact, and little or no storage or exchange of products or foods on site.

8.18 Spot Zoning

Spot Zoning is one of those creatures of the law which are often used as an epithet in regard to a myriad of zoning wrongs. Spot Zoning is singling out of a parcel of land for a use classification totally different from that of the surrounding area for the benefit of the owner of the property and to the detriment of other owners. It is not in conformity with the comprehensive or development or zoning map of the community.

8.19 Development limitations

The zoning ordinance imposes different uses, intensity, density, and bulk regulations for each district. These regulations deal with issues such as the size of the plot, size of the structure, where it may be placed, and how high it may be.

8.19.1 Height

Height limitations are exactly what the nomenclature is. They are designed to limit the height of a structure in a given area. This is common type of regulation in single-family and commercial zones. The most common provisions limit buildings in single-family residential districts to certain stories and to a certain height not to exceed.

Other element to consider in height limits is the equipment limit to reach certain height of the fire department.

8.19.2 Density

One of the most common regulations in residence districts is that of limiting the number of dwelling units permitted by reference to the size of the property. This is usually done in terms of the number of units per acre, e.g. ten dwelling units per acre. In this situation, in order to determine the number of dwelling units permitted to be constructed on a given lot, one first determines the total square footage of the property and then divides by the lot area per dwelling unit factor.

The population per unit area or acres is defined as density of population. Density of units should not be used as density of population. These are two different elements representing different values. The building may be built for a family. What matters is how many people actually live in that building. This is controlled by the definition of word "family." If the structure is single family, that means it is for a family. The "family" definition from Western zoning ordinances will not work in Indian context. This is a contemporary problem facing zoning planners. The definition will explain, how many people or limiting the number of people who might live together in a single-family dwelling. The situation is very different in a college or university town. A number of students may live in a single-family dwelling but not qualifying for a family. Zoning planners have to develop an acceptable definition or multiple definitions which will fit in the local social setting. The zoning ordinance should have a clear definition of "family" and should be enforced. This method will help slow down urbanization and help control population growth.

8.20 Bulk requirements

8.20.1 Setbacks

These requirements are imposed pursuant to the power of the municipality to preserve "open space" between buildings and to satisfy the objectives of the zoning ordinance "to provide adequate light, air, and safety from fire and other dangers."

8.20.2 Front, side, rear yards

Side yards, front yard, and rear yards are what the name imply. A side yard is generally defined as that yard extending along the side lot line from the front line to the rear yard line. The rear yard is that yard extending along the full length of the rear lot line between the side lot lines from the rear of the structure or building on the lot. These requirements should be reasonable in nature. Each zoning district must be divided on its merits. In Indian context, zero lot line development is common.

8.21 Floor Area Ratio

This term refers to the relationship between the floor area of the building and the size of the lot on which the building is constructed. Floor Area Ratio is also called Floor Area Index or Floor Space Index (FSI). The floor area ratio is determined by dividing the floor area of the building by the area of the zoning lot. The higher the FSI, the more the floor area available that can be built on a plot of land. It does not increase the population of a city, but concentrate the population in a specified area. FSI is generally high in commercial areas or business districts. For example, if a building contains 5000 square meters of floor area and it is located on a 1000 square meters lot, the floor area ratio is 5.0; if, on the other hand, a building contains 1000 square meters and located on a 5000 square meters lot, the floor area ratio is 0.20 (Fig. 8.3).

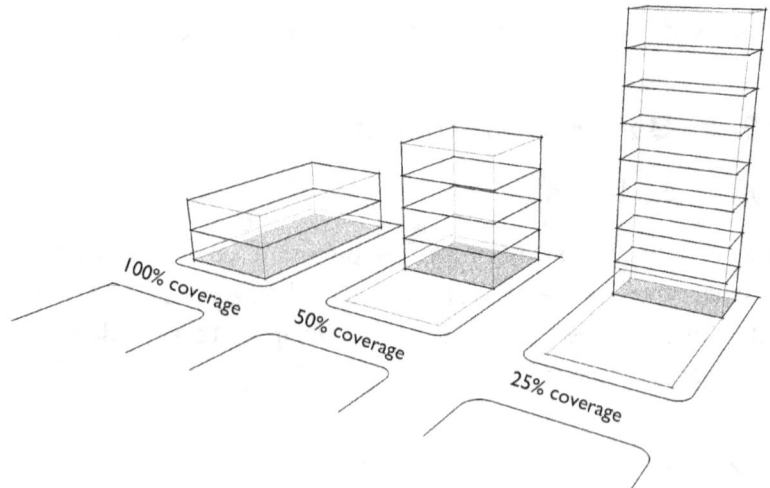

Figure 8.3 Three buildings with the same floor area ratio and equal bulk. Left diagram covers 100 percent of the site, middle covers 50 percent of the site, and the right covers 25 percent of the site.

It is important not to confuse this type of bulk regulations with the density limitation. Density determines the number of units permitted on a given lot; floor area ratio limits the size of the building.

8.22 Lot area retractions

Zoning ordinances provide that a zoning lot has not only minimum area but that the frontage of that lot on a public street be of a particular width.

8.23 Parking

Parking is generally a part of the zoning requirements. However, it can be a separate ordinance as well. Residential, commercial, and industrial uses have different standards for parking. Parking requirements vary from use to use. A movie theater, a college, or university may require different number of parking spaces compare to residential areas, which can have both off-street parking and on-street parking. Commercial areas, depending upon the use, may require additional parking spaces. In Indian context, parking is required for bicycles, scooters, motorcycles, cars, rickshaws, three wheelers, and tongas. Parking design requires engineered design entrance and exit. Parking design should consider slow- and fast-moving vehicles simultaneously.

For new developments, the property owner is required to provide space for parking. The planners and engineers should include parking provision for other modes of travel. Other elements are parking size, parking lighting, parking area landscaping, parking area striping, parking area signage, and responsibility of maintenance of parking area.

8.24 Signage

Signage regulations can stand alone as "Sign Ordinance" or part of the zoning ordinance. Signage plays an important role for the businesses to get recognized, attract customers, and establish identity, e.g. in this location since xxxx or established in xxxx. Signs are helpful to customers too to find the services. Delivery people can find the businesses with the help of signs. Attractive and creatively designed signage can be part of aesthetic appeal of the business and area. A careful choice of colors and combination of logo(s) can attract new customers as well as it is appealing.

Irresponsibly and inappropriately placed signs can create clutter. Choice of unattractive signs with incomplete message can repel customers. Too large sign or too small signs may appeal out of place to people. Too many signs together may create clutter of signs. The purpose of sign may be defeated. Signs placed inappropriately may appeal an eye-sore. Wrongly placed signs can be dangerous and cause accidents. In older areas, buildings signs may cover historic features or reduce the importance of façade. Signs not maintained can be dangerous and cause accidents. Hanging signs, if not anchored properly, can create unsafe feeling. Too bright signs can produce glare to make driving hazardous. Too high signs may not fit well with the skyline of the city. Too many signs can be distracting to the road users; can cause accidents. The LED signs have proven to be distracting to the drivers.

Signs on the private property walls in the city, along the roads, and on highways are distracting the drivers and look the area shabby, uncontrolled, and unmanaged or ill managed with lack of sense of cleanliness and design.

Too large bill-boards/signs by big companies may seem effective advertising but it covers the sky-line, covers the sky view, covers view of bird flying, covers landscaping, cover buildings (historic or with architectural expression), and create civic barriers. Too large bill-boards too close to each other even worsens the situation; these are common sites in metro cities and medium-size cities in India. Large signs can block the natural vistas in urbanized setting. Empty sign structure frames with no advertising coverage gives a skeleton and ghost town feeling. Not to mention the irresponsibility and inefficiency on the part of the advertising location owners and local government.

Private advertising signs should not be placed along public rights-of-way (ROW). ROW should only have directional and instructional signs as required and approved by the authorized departments. Private signs on street lights, utility poles, street poles, trees in the ROW, and rights-of-way should not be permitted or allowed. They should be considered illegal and should be removed at the expense of the installer and the installer should be fined. These signs not only create clutter but pose danger to the road users, pedestrians, and to others. ULBs should remove expired or unauthorized signs, and unclaimed sign frames around the city.

Signs come in many shapes, forms, and designs. There are many types of signs, such as pole signs, marquee signs, wall signs, pylon signs, neon signs, LED signs, monument signs, channel letter signs, masonry signs, flag pole signs, hanging signs, brick-mortar signs, plastic letter signs, wood signs, aluminum signs, portable signs, folding signs, flag signs, cloud signs and many other types of signs. In addition, there are permanent signs, temporary signs, seasonal signs, event signs, architectural signs, and special occasion signs.

Political signs have their own identity. Political signs are temporary in nature but depending upon the event they can be everywhere. They are hard to control because of their heritage. However, the planners can have condition to remove the political signs within certain period of time after the event/elections are over. Signs on vacant properties need some regulations. Definition of "sign" is critical in Indian context, e.g. the monumental statue of *Hanuman jee* or *Shiv jee* along the highway, is a building or a sign? They can be distracting to the road users. People tend to greet may get distracted. A study must be done to assess the impact of such creations on the road users. In the West, studies have proven that the roadside signs distract motorists and cause accidents.

The urban planners and designers should carefully develop sign ordinance. Size of the frontage is one criterion to establish allowable size of the sign. Implementation and enforcement are the keys to successful sign ordinance. Organized and maintained sign system can make look the community more beautiful and aesthetically appealing.

8.25 Traffic impact

The reports prepared for zoning purposes should include impact on existing mass/public transit, impact of cars, vehicular trips, busses, two wheelers, three wheelers, rickshaws, bicycles, pedestrians and taxis. Freight traffic should be accounted too. The study should include impact of automobiles on the non-automobile traffic.

8.26 Impact on social services

The development change should prepare reports on impact of social services of schools, colleges, universities, health centers, civic services and other local active services such as research centers and training centers.

Other services such as open spaces, play grounds, parks, recreational centers and other community should be part of the impact study.

8.27 Utilities impact

Any development should consider impact on existing system of water, sewer, solid waste management, storm water management, gas (domestic) supply, telephone, and cable services. The study should provide details of additional load on services on the existing utilities. The report should professionally provide information and evaluation on the existing capacity versus additional level of services required to maintain the level of services.

8.28 Enforcement

Control and management of building permits are the primary forms of zoning enforcement. The enforcement of the zoning ordinance and other laws is the key to manage the growth and development in the city. Most of the urban problems are due to lack of enforcement of zoning laws and building codes.

Prior to issuance of building permit, planning department and building official or engineer must consult each other. The general practice is that planning department issues the building permit. The development plans are reviewed by the planning department and building official or engineers, depending upon the local system, prior to issuance of the building permit to ensure the building complies with all the zoning requirements. Building inspector inspects the building to make sure the construction is according to the plan approved and meet the codes. National Building Codes of India is at the verge of revising the building codes.

The local governments must enforce the zoning to make it effective. Good enforcement must be prompt, consistent, fair, predictable, and firm.

8.29 Subdivision regulations

Subdivision regulation is the other principal tool of the police power that controls the development and land use. Like urban planning, good land division is both an art and science requiring a high degree of technical skill and full realization of the importance of the design to the various interests involved and affected. Good land division design requires imagination and creativity, as well as adherence to the sound principles of land planning, engineering practice, architectural elements, and landscape architecture component.

Subdivision controls regulated division of larger parcels of land into individual building lots. Generally, subdivision regulations deal with all aspects of subdivision design, including lot size, and shape, and street widths and layout. Construction standards for improvements such as streets, water mains, telephone, street lights, sewer, and sidewalks are also incorporated into subdivision controls. Some regulations contain standards for open spaces, play grounds, and recreational activities details.

Good land subdivision design should create building sites that meet the requirements of modern living. The building sites created should be not only immediately marketable, but also capable of competing favorably with future development, thereby providing stable investment. Building sites should be so arranged in relation to the rest of the community and to the natural resources base in order to provide a good environment for living, working, and recreation, and worshiping, in Indian context. The role of government should be to create conditions amenable to good land subdivision design, provide a framework for such design, and encourage and support endeavors to achieve such design.

The zoning and development control systems function almost independently. Because of relationship of zoning and subdivision regulations, the developers submit conceptual plans with department. Some communities require mandatory preliminary meetings with the developers prior to submission of conceptual plans.

Land subdivision design is a process requiring professional knowledge and experience. In undertaking a subdivision design, the designer may face the following situations that will determine the manner in which the design must be approached:

- The land proposed to be subdivided is located within a community that has not adopted a comprehensive plan or have not followed subdivision regulations.
- The land proposed to be subdivided is located within a community that has adopted a comprehensive plan, but that does not include as a component detailed neighborhood unit development plans or platting layout.
- The land proposed to be subdivided is located within a community that has adopted a comprehensive plan, and that plan includes detailed neighborhood development plans or platting layouts.

8.30   Principles of good design

Good land division design can be achieved through the effective application of following basic design principles.

(a) *Provision of external features of community-wide concerns:* The design must properly provide for certain external features of community and area wide concern that affect the proposed land division. Land division design must provide for the proper extension of arterial streets; for the location of sanitary trunk sewer, water transmission mains, and other utilities; for the preservation of major drainage ways; for adequate management of the quantity and quality of storm water runoff; for needed education and open space and park sites; and for convenient access to public transit facilities; and convenient and safe access to local market. Consideration should also be given in the design to the relationship of the proposed land division to such external factors as neighborhood, community, and regional shopping centers, places of employment, higher education facilities, and worship/spiritual places.

(b) *Proper relationship to the existing and proposed surrounding land uses:* The design must be properly related to existing and proposed land uses. Moreover, adjacent land uses must be carefully considered in design. Playgrounds, play lots, and parks and certain types of institutional uses are a definite asset and can increase the value of a land division. Others, such as railway station, bus terminals, freeways, and major streets can be asset and liability depending upon the occupant.

(c) *Proper relationship to the natural resource base:* The design must be properly related to the natural resource base. Wetlands, lakes, woodlands, specimen trees, wildlife habitat areas, areas covered by unstable soils, steep slope areas, areas with shallow bedrock or bedrock outcrop, and areas subject to special hazards, such as flooding and stream bank, bluff, ravine, must receive careful consideration in the design. In this respect, good subdivision design may present opportunities for the restoration and expansion of areas containing valuable elements of the natural resource base. Good land division design should seek to exclude intensive urban development from such areas as flood lands, seasonal streams, wetlands, woodlands, and wildlife habitat areas, utilizing such areas for recreational and open space, and thereby avoiding the creation of serious and costly environmental and developmental problems.

(d) *Proper design of internal features and details:* The land division design should pay proper attention to internal detailing. This include careful attention to the proper layout of streets, block, sidewalks, lots, play grounds, play lots, open spaces, the organization of larger subdivisions into smaller sections, and careful adjustment of the design to the topography and the natural and cultural resource characteristics of the site.

(e) *Creation of an integrated design:* Design elements that may contribute to an integrated design include focal points such as historic buildings, historic features and structures, specimen trees, and local school or public building, thematic architectural design of homes and other buildings.

This system provides an established system to be followed by the developers, builders, contractors, and citizens. The established subdivision regulations make the system fair for everyone and easy to manage.

8.31 Aesthetic and architectural control

The zoning ordinance may promote aesthetic appeal of the development by installing regulations for material type, color, design, and architectural guidelines and other related elements. These control, if implemented, can make difference to older parts of the city, historic areas, and around historic buildings.

8.32 Zoning in operation

The implementation of the zoning ordinance required three activities: rezoning; the review of variances, appeals, and special exceptions; and enforcement. The approved zoning district map must be in place prior to initiation of any activity.

8.32.1 Rezoning

The most important and most common zoning action of any local government is the map amendment or rezoning of land. The model zoning act provides no effective administrative mechanism for map amendment or rezoning of land. The steps in the formal review process typically include submission of application, staff review, notice of planning commission hearing, preparation of staff report, planning commission hearing, planning commission action, initial governing body action, notice of governing body hearing, governing body hearing, final governing body action, and final notification to the property owner and or the applicant. Rezoning is a legislative action.

8.32.2 Variance

The second most common zoning operation is the consideration of requests for variances. A variance is when some requirement in the zoning ordinance cannot be complied. A variance allows the applicant to depart from the standard rules established in the ordinance. They are a tool to alleviate "unnecessary hardship." For example, a pre-existing lot of 3600 square meters in a zone requiring 4000 square meters minimum lot size would require a variance application. A strangely shaped lot which may not be able to meet the lot frontage requirement can apply for a variance. However, financial hardship is no ground for a variance request. Many requests for variances are generally for minor bulk variances, e.g. for set-backs.

8.32.3 Appeals

The zoning ordinance regulations extend powers to the board to hear the appeals from an aggrieved applicant or property owner where it is alleged there is an error in any order, requirements, decision, or determination made by the staff or administrator. The appeal could be for the enforcement too.

8.32.4 Special use permits

An example of a special use section of a zoning ordinance is the following:

The requested uses shall be permitted only after the passage of an ordinance granting the special use, for example:

- Similar and compatible uses to those allowed as "permitted uses" in this district
- Planned unit development
- Residence of a proprietor, caretaker, servant, or watchman, when located on the premises of the residential, commercial, or industrial use
- Radio, television, and telecommunication towers
- Landfill facility

- Car wash
- Sewage treatment plant

8.33 Form-based codes (FBC)

Built environment of Indian cities are jeweled with architecture richness. The built areas of one city after another, one street after another, one neighborhood after another, one building after another is a marvel of planning, design, and architecture. Gardens, palaces, mansions, *havelis*, forts, and other building with architectural and art details are legacies in themselves. Family residences are garlanded with art and design. Mosques, gurdwaras, temples, churches, and other worship buildings are legacies of time. A book could be filled with the examples of each category.

Ironically, the new unplanned, unthoughtful, insightful, undetermined, arrhythmic, unrhymed, and unsystematic development is covering the great architecture and art work done by the past generations. Art and design of buildings is patched up with grey plaster, facades are covered by sign boards, *chajhas* and *chatris* are eloping and disappearing fast, and verandahs and courtyards are missing in the high-rises. The history is being replaced with modern times with no detailing, art, and design work. Modern architecture is a class in itself. Selective villages have their recognizable form, architecture, design, and art work. Form-based codes can provide a compromising platform.

Zoning is a component of public policy. Policy is one of a trio of controls that shape land and building development along with design and management. Design, policy, and management vary according to the type of environment and community. Form-based codes are vision based and perspective, requiring that all development work together to create the place envisioned by the community. This requires that the community creates a detailed vision at the start of the coding process and then draft and administer the form-based codes to enforce the vision, and inherently proactive process.

Perhaps because of the envision reason, Indian cities have marvels of architecture, art, and design. In olden times, there were no zoning regulations but old civilizations (Mohenjo-Daro, Harappa) are the prime examples of planned cities, well laid out infrastructure, provision of utilities throughout the community. Now the communities follow laws, established policies, and systems. To protect and maintain cities built environment, form-based codes are the answers.

Form-based codes are holistic, addressing, public, semi-public, and private space design to create a whole place, including buildings, streets, alleys, sidewalks, parking, parks, and activity spaces. They regulate public and private development for the impact it has on the public realm.

FBC identify the local character, unique characteristics, and place based. They help create unique vision for each place. This scenario fits perfect in the Indian cities context – especially in older sections of a city.

FBC regulate the details that are most important for a successful implementation of walkable, human scale, harmonious neighborhoods. Through FBC codes, historic or new design of commercial buildings and areas can be created.

The following components of FBC can lead to achieve established visionary goals:

1. The regulating plan

    The regulating plan of FBC is for purposes of administration, direct regulation, and planning. The administration part is to identify application area to apply rules of development. Direct regulations will show actual development regulations, e.g. front façade type, building type, street frontage. Planning step is to prepare the regulating plan. The plan depicts development standards for each lot, each building, each block, or each zone. It defines critical details in the form and character of the development to reflect configuration of the public realm. The plan provides details of building mass, color, material, wall openings, alleys, parking, space between buildings and other elements depending upon the project.

2. Public space and semi-public space standards

   The recognition of the existing or envisioned character of the rights-of-ways, sidewalks, parks, and open spaces in the project area. Rights-of-ways or streets play a vital role in creating FBC areas. Streets are important in residential, commercial, and mixed-use type FBC. The design of streets should consider contextual presence than applying the standards. For walkable communities, narrow, winding roads discouraging automobile traffic may be more practical and functional than a straight four lane with boulevard. Similarly, selection of type of roads should be complimentary with the goals of the project. Wide sidewalks in commercial area with proximity to transit facility will be workable to make the project a success. Other features of design to consider are volume of traffic both pedestrian and automobiles, walking influence distance, pedestrian crossing time, width of roads, directional sign, placement of signs, parking, bicycle lanes, bicycle parking, curb type, landscaping, street lighting, street furniture, and safety elements.

3. Building-form standards

   In Indian context, for the projects with existing buildings, building form standards can make a whole lot difference. For newer areas, building-form standards are equally important because they set the standards for future. Building-form standards provide details for building placement, build-to line (front set back, generally zero in local commercial settings), aligned or staggered, space for courtyards, setbacks (side, rear, front), maximum lot width, minimum lot width, maximum building height, minimum building height, ground-floor finished level height, minimum ground-floor ceiling height, maximum building width, maximum building depth, parking (automobiles, bicycles, three wheelers, and rickshaws), parking spaces, location of parking spaces, allowed land uses, restricted land uses, and other elements.

4. Building-type standards

   During envisioning FBC for an older city section, historic building designs, art, architecture, and layout with respect to the neighboring properties must be considered. The efforts should be to maintain the realm, mass, and character of the existing building. The new buildings or remodeling of the existing should maintain the existing theme with the help of FBC.

5. Architecture and planning layout standards

   In the FBC, various architectural regulations can be integrated: complete regulation by style down to very specific details, regulations by quality and general local character, very basic regulations to achieve basic standards of quality, and no architectural standards. Massing, façade composition, windows and doors, balconies (in certain area of the country), material, and other elements and details.

   In some cases of older cities their lay out reflects history. The planners and architects have to be creative to see to what the existing plan can threshold the new activities of the present time and projected future.

6. Administration

   Last but not the least. The implementation of the plan is the key to the successful project. The architects, designers, planners, and enforcement staff should be adamant to follow and implement the FBC plan.

Local municipalities may have difficulty in adopting FBC. The suggested mitigating scenario is to be selective in choosing the areas or sections of the city and making it part of the zoning ordinance than a stand-alone ordinance.

8.34 Addressing

Before the independence of India, during Mahatma Gandhi's time, people wrote letters to him from England with address as "Mahatma Gandhi, Where ever He Is" or his picture on the envelope instead of mailing address. In the West, children write to Santa Clause, name, North Pole. In Indian context, it is common to tell your address as "live behind a temple," "live near a theater," "opposite a prominent building," "in a neighborhood," "on a street next to a big tree," "opposite big yellow building," or " ask any rickshaw-walla or scooter-walla" or address such as 1234 Krishna Street (99 Rama galli)? This type of addressing system did work for quite some time. Cities were small with limited people and limited buildings. Everyone knew everyone. Historical buildings were land marks. Associating a residence with some entity or feature was identifiable and workable. The cities are growing in leaps and bounds. The surroundings are changing fast. These vague identification marks and system can be proven dangerous and frustrating in some situations. It is about time planners to understand the significance of address identification and have a policy and system in place to assign a proper address to every building – residential, commercial, and industrial – in coordination is local India Post Manager.

8.34.1 Why addressing

Cities have grown spatially more local streets, roads, and residences, commercial places, and industrial buildings. More people live in cities. It is hard to know everyone.

Identity

Each building should have a specific address for its own identity.

Access

Proper address helps individuals to access a building without any confusion or perplexity. Appropriate addressing make jobs of delivery people (postman, pizza delivery, package delivery, visitors or guests, taxi, and rickshaw).

Orientation

Addressing helps to keep orientation for any one for some purpose. Makes one feel "not lost."

Census

To obtain authentic census information and data.

Emergency

This is the most important element of advantages of proper addressing. For emergency situations, it is eminent to find the right site of the incident for police, ambulance, fire, and emergency (disaster) management team. Emergency personnel may not be familiar with the area. The incident may be time sensitive. It is immensely important for the emergency entity to know the exact destination. A caller about the emergency situation (e.g. heart attack) must be able to tell the exact address to the operator so he or she can dispatch the personnel to the right place. With the knowledge of the right address, emergency services can select the nearest available unit to dispatch help.

Others

Addressing is the right tool for tax collectors, voting identification and counting, census, planning department, utilities departments, and school and voting districts.

8.34.2 What is addressing

Addressing is a technical policy to identify each building and/or person and each section of building to access conveniently. Addressing gets complex with multi-family buildings, buildings with joint families, high-rises, and multi-buildings on one parcel and building complexes.

The planning department (only one department should act as administrator to assign addresses) must establish a policy or procedure or system to assign an address to a building. The addressing system must avoid old-fashioned building recognitions such as, "opposite to," "next to," "behind" or "next to a phase." Prior to issuance of a building permit, the parcel must have an approved appropriate address. Each entity should have a clear address to avoid any confusion or mix-up. The department can use GIS technology to develop a policy, assign addresses, monitor, and maintain addressing for the community. The department can learn from other's experiences or any other successful addressing system specifically in Indian context. The challenge is to assign addressing in the old sections of a city. During the process, the planning department should include local post office, police, fire department, and local delivery services to assist in preparing policy and procedures.

The second important element of addressing is street name. Each street must have starting point and ending point. Street names should be short, clear, and simple. Duplication of names must be avoided.

8.35 Gated communities

Gated communities are choice of people with resources. Living in gated communities costs more. Gated communities have their own covenants to be followed by the residents. Sometimes covenants go too far to tell residents color of the building, material type, landscaping type, or mandatory fees for certain choice, whether used by the resident or not. Gates provide privacy and security, as believed by the residents.

The gates are not much of a deterrent because they are often easy to get around, scale over or left open or unlocked. Burglaries and thefts occurred even in communities were gates were manned. The communities are segregated with the rest of the community.

In Indian context, building walls around the property, commercial, institutional, or residential is generally the first step towards claiming the ownership of the property. These walls with a gate makes the property "gated." It limits the access by other people. These walls are also perception of security and privacy. These walls needs to be maintained, which does not happen. These walls also cause damming effect for storm water runoff. This condition damages walls and foundation of the buildings. Creates flooding situation at the subject property. On some places, advertisers start using walls as bill-boards. Sometimes use of dark colors and inappropriate message makes aesthetically unappealing and create clutter of the signs.

Walls and gated building in case of residential use should be discouraged. Walls on vacant lots, commercial, or industrial buildings should be maintained all the time, no bill sticking or message writing or advertising of any type should be permitted. Walls should remain with the color of material build with, e.g. cement, brick, or mud.

8.36 In-laws apartments

Another sub-category, under residential zoning district, can be in-law apartment or student apartment or grand-parent apartment. Generally they are on the back of the principal structure with private entrance. This works well if alleys are there. The entrance for this use could be from the alley than the front of the principal building. This is practical for families having parents or in-laws living with them, areas with college or university to accommodate additional flow of students or students who wants to have privacy and manage own time schedule or the property owners to have extra income. Whatever the reason or purpose, this use may be incorporated in the zoning ordinance prior to influx of any problems of overcrowding or mismanagement of the single-family zoning district.

8.37 Servants' employment and planning

Average families take pride in having at least one if no more than one servants at their disposal. Government of India, military, police, many other institutions and organizations provide servants as part of the benefit package to their employees. These servants lack vocational skills and are generally illiterate. They are not familiar with or exposed to other opportunities to make a living or improve their way of life. They will work for meager salary with no other benefits other than the mercy or kindness of the master. This is ironic, on the one hand government policy is to eradicate poverty and on the other hand low-paying jobs are created and encouraged by the same government. Whether the working class of servants started by kings and queens, maharajas, or colonial administrators, it is still prevalent and common practice among Indians, even those who can afford one. With the prosperity of selective social segment, use of domestic help is more prevalent than ever.

Servants come from poor families with no other option but to work for someone to carry on day-to-day household chores. Generally, there are no regulations of work hours, sick days, time off, casual leave, or time off on national or local holidays. In addition, there are no regulations to provide proper living spaces for the servants or their families. They could be living in garages, attics, roof top rooms, verandahs, or living in slums and commuting daily to work place. Some rich people provide servant quarters to servants and their families.

Servants should have working benefits like other working class. Servants should be allowed and permitted only to those families who can provide proper living spaces connected with utilities, enough space for family activities, toilets, and bathing facilities. Servants commuting daily and living in unauthorized places with no toilets and other facilities should be regulated and have regular medical checkups. Domestic help living in slums may carry bad bacteria and spread diseases.

Urban planners should create a recognized job category of servants. The employers of servants should be responsible for providing proper living conditions with bathroom and toilet facilities. Development plans, prior to approval, must consider provision of living facilities for servants. If not provided or needed at the time of development, then should leave space for future development or no servants shall be allowed.

8.38 Home business / home occupation

Businesses operating from home should be regulated through zoning ordinance. The purpose of having home business or occupation is to operate something to make a living or as a hobby or a passion or use of a skill or any other related purposes. But activities can cross the line by having additional traffic, deliveries, pick-ups, creating noise or inappropriate for peaceful living of neighbors. Regulating this use can provide information of happenings in the community. Home occupations/businesses should obtain permit from the planning department to ensure if the use is permitted. These uses can generate additional revenue for the local government. In general, those occupations which customarily have been given approval when conducted in the home are the professions, chiefly doctors and lawyers, and certain feminine occupations such as hair salon, dressmaking, and sewing.

The regulations for home occupation/business should incorporate sections of occupations permitted, area occupies, sale of goods, employment, accessory building, differential regulations by zone, display, transitional zoning, general regulations, traffic limits, equipment used and permits.

8.39 Planning for "wallas"

"Walla" word is attached to the type or particular service provided by someone, e.g. person providing tea service (*chai* in Indian) becomes *chai-walla*.

These service providers such as, *chai-walla, phool-walla, sabzi-walla,* phall (fruit)*-walla, pakore-walla, dhobi-istri-walla, paan-sigrat-walla, mochi-walla, repair-walla,* and other "wallas" depending upon the area, way of life, and local customs are part of day-to-day life. They provide services either at the door or in close proximity. They are part of mixed-use living. These "wallas" provide social, economic, and environmental benefits.

Social:

- Help reduce trips to various services;
- They offer convenience of shopping at home by bringing the product/service to your door-step;
- With time, they become familiar with the neighborhood and community;
- They create social bonding by knowing choices and habits;
- Floating vendors bring services to many consumers versus many consumers have to access on fixed location of service provider; and

- Certain use type provide social and gathering places of neighborhood. This can help share the information and happening in the community.

Economic:

- These entrepreneurs can start a business with very little or no capital investments;
- Since they do not have overheads of rent, utilities, and other operational expenses; thus provide with better pricing;
- They do not take physical spaces in a building thus leave those spaces for more organized and established businesses;
- They are part of local economy;
- They create jobs for themselves. They spend their earnings in the market. They are part of multiplier effect on labor and money;
- They create sub-jobs for others (in some instances).

Environmental:

- Floating vendors bring services to the consumer thus helps reduce automobile trips;
- Reduced automobile trips help environment by less emission of pollutants;
- Some service providers use no or limited utilities thus save energy; and
- Some services require no or limited utilities thus save energy.

8.40   Planning process

Planners should be creative by imagining new and different zoning and use categories for "wallas." They are part of the local economy. They contribute the local revenue directly and indirectly. Expensive real estate, no or very limited personal investment capital, non-availability or difficult availability of investment capital from other sources (e.g. banks), non-availability of collateral or assurance, and challenge to establish trust with the consumer are some of challenges for these entrepreneurs. Because of stated social, economic, and environmental benefits, local communities and planners should make them recognizable part of the system, economy, and society.

There are many types of them: floating, fixed location, seasonal operations, special hour operations, specific hours operation, special occasion operations, and local way of life operators. Planners should analyze the operational traits of these entrepreneurs. Their peculiarities, special features, habits, needs, requirements, and way of operation should be part of economic studies.

Local planning department should create a category in the zoning ordinance. If required, create sub-categories for their uses and activities. These service providers could be part of mixed-use zoning category. These service providers should be registered with the local municipality and obtain a business permit or certificate. Local planning department should oversee the issuance of such documents. The vendor should carry approval document during the business operational hours. The planning department should share that information with the local law enforcement and code enforcement departments. GIS and GPS technologies can play a vital role in managing this category of zoning ordinance. The planning department, depending upon the needs and requirements of vendors, should provide support of safety, security, operational identity, and facilities to make them part of the bigger system. Planning and design process should address such uses with creative designs and planning processes.

8.41   Telecommunication tower planning

High demand of mobile phones use requires telecommunication towers to get connected. Telecommunication towers, if placed with proper design consideration, may be that obvious. They can become part of day-to-day life like electricity poles and telephone poles. They are so common that visually they do not get special attention. But because of the height of telecommunication tower, they are noticed in the built environment.

Telecommunication towers have utilities of running mobile phone but also some challenges of having them in our backyard.

By regulating the telecommunication towers, local governments can generate additional revenue during the plan approval process, permits, redevelopment, changes to the tower, and annual business fee for running a business.

The placement considerations are safe height, co-locations, throbbing lights installation after certain height to warn air traffic, wind threshold, crash safety concerns in residential areas, noise due to generators, landscaping of tower premises, access to towers for maintenance, advertising, signage, and other micro level concerns can be addressed in the regulations.

8.42 Animals in the city

In Indian cities, humans and animals living together is a recognizable feature. Animals such as, cows, bullocks, dogs, cats, monkeys, donkeys, pigs, and goats including snakes are common features. They can be seen on roads, road intersections, vacant lots, open spaces, sidewalks and wherever they find space to settle. The pets are not part of this explanation. Pets are acceptable animals living with humans. As pets they are reared, managed, and taken care by the owners. In Indian context, animals and humans should live in harmony. It should be to certain extent. This notion was workable in old days with less number of people and smaller number of animals in a city. For long time, cities had more open space, less roads, less activities, and traffic was slow with most manually operated vehicles. Now, there are large number of animals and human beings living in cities. The increased diversified traffic has posed more threat to animals. Animals are cruelly killed by heavy traffic. Animals, without care, with diseases, malnutrition, and handicapped roam around aimlessly. They make traffic congestion situation worst.

Especially monkeys and dogs are direct threat to humans. They create havoc situations. Instinctively they gang up and if they get opportunity they attack children and individual humans. In many cities such incidents have been recorded and witnessed. These uncontrolled animals disrupt normal day-to-day life in cities, Delhi is the prime example of that. These animals scare and are threat to children. Some animals carry contagious diseases with them. Getting in contact with them can pass on the diseases to humans. Being wild and no home, they may end up anywhere after final expiration. Certain philosophies and mythological believes sometimes encourage growth of such animals. Religious/spiritual leaders should understand the sensitivity of the situation and should discourage activities promoting growth of such animals in cities. They should participate with educating people about harms and dangers of this practice.

Local government should prepare plans to stop the growth of animals in cities. The reasoning is simple and strong – safety of children and citizens. Planning department should establish rules of registering pet animals with a specified department, limit number of pets, restriction on certain species as pets, and laws for regular medical check-up of animals by vets. Cities should establish animal shelters, animal control regulations, humane societies, and other means depending upon the area and beliefs.

8.43   Farm housing

Resourceful people tend to have more than one living places, e.g. permanent home, summer home, hill station home, winter home. A new wave of owning a "farm house" is becoming popular among city dwellers. They are tired of congestion, pollution, noise, hectic life style, lack of natural environment, and other problems of city living. They seek refuge from all these problems in country side. This helps them balance their hectic lifestyle with slow pace and quite time in their farm house with country surroundings.

Building farm houses poses social, economic, and environmental challenges. Socially, instead of becoming part of the society after working for days, they take refuge away from the community. They disconnect themselves from the societal activities. By going away from the community, they miss the opportunity to contribute to the community. They could assist in improving the quality of life for others and themselves. They cut off themselves from the happenings in the community.

By building a farm house which is used on short-term basis, limited time basis, and selective basis, on a prime agricultural land, they take the right of producing food on that piece of land. It is important in the context of India with limited land and other resources with over billion people. They take away grazing land for cattle in the country side. In the absence of the dwellers the structure is of no use. May be a care taker takes care of the property with meager salary?

The building and its surroundings with a wall covers prime agricultural land for a long time. Building with a septic system discharges solid waste into the ground which mixes with the underground water which pollutes the water. The access way to the building takes additional agricultural land. Providing spaces to park cars for visitors may take additional agricultural land. People with tilling experience knows that land adjacent to a structure is not easy to cultivate. Thus additional agricultural land is wasted. The issue becomes bigger when all the agricultural land is totaled up which is used for farm houses.

Government should have policy in place to discourage cropping up of vacation houses in the country side. Farm houses should be regulated with policy and procedures to permit farm house.

8.44 Staff

Local government should have staff to support planning commission, zoning board of appeals, governing body, committees, and review boards. Staff basically performs three duties. First, the staff administers the zoning ordinance, comprehensive plan / development plan, subdivision regulations, and other related documents. Second, the staff enforces the ordinance. The responsibility to stop non-compliance and conflicting activities in the city. Third, the staff performs project reviews for the governing body, planning commission, board of appeals, committees, and review boards. All these bodies depend on staff for professional and expert reviews and opinions. In Indian context, the administrators should consult the planning department professional prior to making any development, redevelopment, land associated, transportation related, and future growth related matters. An irresponsible, incomplete, inaccurate, or inappropriate decision can lead to a bad project or rejection of a good planning idea.

8.45 Planning commission

At local government level, citizens are appointed by the elected officials for the planning commission. Planning commission is a recommending body. Their recommendations are not the final decision. A membership of five, seven, or nine is typical. The primary purpose of the planning commission is to make sure the application and process is in compliance with the established rules and regulations.

8.46 Board of Adjustment or Appeals

The most common function of the Zoning Board of Appeals or Adjustment is the consideration of requests for variances. Their decision is final in the local jurisdiction. The zoning ordinance may provide opportunity for the applicant to challenge the decision in the court of law.

8.47 Governing body

The term 'governing body' refers to the legislative branch of local government. The local government may be purely legislative or both legislative and administrative. It may be called mayor and city council, city council, town board, commissioners, or town council. Irrespective of the name, the governing body has most of the powers and responsibilities for zoning decisions. Any changes in the law would be the responsibility of the governing body.

8.48 Zoning powers

A mandatory recommendation of transfer of city functions to urban local bodies by the state governments should be implemented without delay. The conditions of urban areas is deteriorating at a fast pace. The quality of life has a downward nose dive. State governments, local governments (ULBs), administrators, urban planners, urban designers, professionals, and citizens should understand the sensitivity of the situation and work towards solving it. Managing micro level issues is not feasible and practical from state level. State level administration and politics may create system to keep watch on the performance of ULBs. Transferring of city planning functions to ULBs should be the utmost priority for the elected officials and citizens.

8.49 Pros and cons of zoning/conclusion

Zoning is a useful and effective tool of the police power. It can play important role in helping planners and local governments guide community growth and development. No matter how good or how effective the zoning in a particular community may be, land owners, developers, and individual citizens still make a variety of decisions; that influence the final land use patterns of the community.

Chapter 9
Urban design

9.1 Introduction

When we see a good design, we know it is a good design. Designing a city is much easier for an individual but persuading to other people to accept the design on same terms as designed is hard job. There are many successful urban design examples around the world. Indian city designs have been pioneer in establishing acceptable and functional urban designs and forms. People lived in harmony and appreciated aesthetics and operation of the built environment. Cities, towns, and villages, or in other words, human settlements have evolved consciously and sub-consciously. The settlement forms have taken shapes with social, economic, political, professional, and other forces. People living in areas partially accept what they inherit, partially they change certain elements, partially they keep trying to change, and partially they do not even notice the built environment. The built environment, psychologically, is fully acceptable. Certain segments of society do not think or cannot think of changing the built environment they live in. It is perfectly acceptable.

Many elements play a major role in understanding, modifying, accepting, or not making any note what so everywhere people live. They perform their day-to-day life activities. The elements are transportation, buildings, and spaces around buildings, spaces between buildings, connectivity between buildings, connectivity between spaces, landscaping, skyline, and openness to nature, amenities, aesthetics, architecture, history, culture, religious/spiritual and worship places, and other local elements. Residents select their nodes and niches where they live, work, play, worship, and perform other activities. People like to enjoy where they live. They identify reasons and options to like the places. They establish connectivity with them. They like to know the *paan-sigrat-walla*, *phool-walla*, *chai-walla* and other wallas. They establish connections with the built environment. They feel pride where they live. They like to share various elements with friends and other people about their built and natural environment.

The onus of providing a well-designed environment is on the urban designers and urban planners. The task is not easy. But the challenge is to provide the best by creating well-functional, harmonious, and aesthetically appealing spaces. People should take time to appreciate the creation. It is hard to determine the functionality of the Taj Mahal, but it is an iconic building for centuries and one of the wonders, even today. It is an architectural marvel to millions of human beings. Golden Temple, Amritsar, is a religious landmark in itself. The "Stupas" are landmark and legacy.

Urban design is a balance between urban planning, architecture, and landscape architecture. The primary concern of urban design has been with the urban form. It may manifest itself in the façade of the building, the street, the neighborhood, or the entire town.

9.2 Indian cities' context of urban design

The urban form of Indian cities is very intrinsic. The urban form of cities has taken shape based on its location, activities, historic events, political reasons, religious association, and monarchy's vision. Some urban forms are results of mix of reasons. Cities may have been formed by people who are visionaries or designers or planners. Some people gave a shape to cities just by being influential. Colony rulers may have used some planning principles, for their interests. Transportation links play a vital role in shaping cities.

For the architects, locating and designing a building is an act of urban design. Architects work with some character and form of building. Combining these two elements becomes part of urban realm. A set of buildings or extension of building with new construction gives a new shape to urban form. Each building gives its own performance, as visualized by the architect. The purpose and size of the building are important decisions. Sometimes non-architects play role in making the decisions.

The other force play in this role is urban planners. The location of uses, layout of roads, common activity places, open spaces, location of public spaces are part of urban form. Government regulations are the guiding documents in shaping urban form. Urban planners also can play a role in creating regulations with their interests, specialties, expertise, and biasness.

In democratic system, if allowed, citizens also become players in the game of shaping cities and towns. Involvement of citizens in decision-making process can be a critical situation. It depends, if the citizens are well informed about the consequences of their decision inclination. Other, if they have an open mind to listen to the professionals. The professionals may have their "narrow-minded" thoughts or limited information to make decisions. Just as urban design gives meaning and significance to urban life, so too the urban design a product of social influence. The design of a city is a very much product of social, economic, and political forces.

The combination of architects and planners can balance the act of making decisions to shape the urban form. However, including landscape architecture specialist can help boost environmental element with urban greenery appeal.

Technology in the form of automobiles, transit, telephones, computers, Internet, cell phones, and wireless technology is influencing in shaping our cities, towns, and villages. Starting with industrial revolution to steam engines to automation to computers and Internet world has given an unprecedented platform to urban form and design.

9.3 Urban form

Linear form: Cities are laid out in grid system so that they can grow in orderly fashion. The streets are in linear form bisecting a right angle. Greeks, Romans, British, American, and many other cultures have adopted this system. Many cities in India have orthogonal form. Colonial administration used this system connecting new development with the existing towns.

Organic: Many Indian cities are typical examples of organic form of cities. Organic planning is most often considered as less planned or less conscientious. It responds to more non-geometrically preconceived notion of form. This form is more driven by topography, social, political, and historical forces. The form is more need based. Organic plans have developed over time without any organized plan or thoughts of reaching a specific design. A classic example of organic design is Old Delhi.

Radial: Another system to channelize the urban form is radial system. Where the center is identified and a radial system is laid out with axial connecting lines is layout with the intent that it can be expanded and additional nodes and activity centers can be created along axial lines.

Transport network: Transportation lines from the time of movement with carts, buggies, or wagons to automobiles have been a primary factor in shaping the urban form. Transportation has been the force to make cities or settlements grow, to establish new settlements, and sometimes the root cause of converting settlements into ghost towns. The network could be roads, rails, waterways and airports. Efficient, economical, and fast air travel is impetus for modern urban form.

Communication network: Hundred smart cities concept can be the theme of creation of new urban form based on communication and services. The expansion portion of existing cities, as smart cities notion, will shape new urban form. However, a new smart city formation will be a category itself for its urban form. New technologies such as sensors, computers, networking systems, cloud systems, GIS, GPS, MIS, and other innovative technologies are new forces of creation of urban form and design.

Service network: Rural population gets attracted by the services provided in the cities. These services give a shape to the urban form. Development follows infrastructure – water, sewer, roads, and other services. Most service systems have threshold. It can provide optimum services to a certain point. It is expensive to alter the existing services because they are most underground. In Indian context, in frequent cases, they are above ground. They are visible in cities and towns. The rising costs of building new services and connecting to old services is difficult. In addition, the resources (water and energy) are in limited supply. The future development may have dramatic impact because of these and other reasons.

9.4   Economic advantages of design

Good design can generate a sense of place for residents and visitors alike. They like to associate with the place whether living or visiting. The place could be a building, set of buildings, activity centers, markets, and worship/spiritual places. With a good design real estate values go up. It has been proven by experts that a well-designed environment along with amenities and other quality of life enhancements to support economic development initiatives influence business location decisions. People visit those places more often. Businesses thrive because of attracted customers. Businesses incline to retain better designed areas as their selected work place. Active places generate and diversified revenues for the local municipalities. Colleges and universities increasingly recognize the importance of visual perception in attracting and retaining students, staff, and faculty. Well-designed neighborhoods attract professional and stable families. In return they become asset to the community. They contribute to take the communities to the next level.

Cities should integrate design with the planning to reinvent themselves as centers of cultures, social activities, religious/spiritual performances, education, health, recreation and entertainment in association with commerce and industry. Iconic designs become tools of marketing of the cities. Cities should explore and use as part of design such as topographical features (shores, mountains), lakes, rivers, waterfalls, and other natural landscapes. Many cities are either located along rivers, or rivers and streams flow through them. Riverfronts can be wonderful places for recreational use. Riverfronts can be made attractive and useful by building walkways, boardwalks, parks, and other recreational activities. The beauty can be enhanced by installing decorative and designer street lighting, landscaping with flowers and decorative trees, designer furniture, pavilions, artistically designed kiosks and concession booths, designing picnic spots and by dressing the banks of water bodies local communities can enjoy natural environment. These sites can be venues for community activities such as "*mellas* (fairs)." This arena provides ample opportunities for designers to express their creativities and talents.

In Indian context, religious places, spiritual places, worship places, and other worship features can be used as extension of design elements of new development. The religious, spiritual, and worship places should take initiative, participate, and support design element of development in surrounding areas and local communities. Many such places are treasures of art and design work. Forefathers worked hard then so we can enjoy the built environment and enjoy the creations. Such places should share portion of their revenues to maintain and enhance the surroundings.

9.5 Good design makes better places

Good urban design is a process. This process holistically incorporates five image system of the built environment – planning, architecture, landscaping, transportation, and special features. Design challenges and solutions differ for each system and for each project. The designers need to understand the purpose, distinctive attributes, goals, and potential solutions for each element. Designers also must be considerate of the context of development at every scale and size.

Planning: Planning contributes in combining various elements to organize and design a place. Setting of buildings: architecture, landscaping the place around the buildings by architects and landscape architects; transportation means, modes, and location by transportation planners; and identification of special features such as water bodies, topographic features by various professionals. Planner is a project manager for projects by confining appropriate locations to make the project functional, practical, comfortable, integrated, and enjoyable. Planners and architects can visualize the theme of the project. Planners can identify and lay compatible and complimentary uses.

Architecture: Buildings form the most visible component of urban areas. Vertical images shape our perceptions about the places, cities, and neighborhoods. The purpose and use of buildings play eminent role to shape places to live, work, entertain, recreate, worship, and many other community needs. Professionals can take this opportunity to create order and beauty. Architect Le Corbusier created iconic buildings in Chandigarh prior to build up of the city. Those buildings laid the path in urban design, form, and order. Architects with their expertise determine bulk requirements, height, appropriate material, color coordination, exterior appearance, positioning of buildings in term of sun, wind, local weather, and relationship to nearby built environment. Environmental consideration by architects by designing and developing green buildings is the new approach to sustainable built environment.

Landscaping: One of the most important elements, especially in urban environment, is the layout of greenscaping, which consists of natural open spaces, parks, playgrounds, play lots, and gardens. The assignment can be responsibility of combination of architects, planners, and landscape architects. Other professionals like, horticulturalists, hobbyist, environmentalists, and floriculturists can contribute to greenscaping designs. Parks, open spaces, and recreational facilities enhance the social interaction, livability of citizens, and urban fabric. It adds diversity to sometimes to monotonous building curtains. The flat walls next to sidewalks in continuation of roads are uninviting and without any human action. The trend of sustainability has certainly enhanced the practicality of greenscaping. The idea of including landscaping to the projects is easy to sell to investors, now being marketed for many reasons by many professionals. Designers of greenscaping try to avoid the fragmentation of natural systems that often occurs as urban regions develop and expand. People yearn for scenic natural features and recreational opportunities provided by parks, open spaces, multipurpose trails, and special features.

Transportation: Transportation systems can play a major role in strengthening communities. Transportation is vital in local and regional economies, active living, and community identity. Transportation system varies from pedestrian, bicycle, cars, buses, rental motorized vehicles, to non-motorized vehicles to trams, street cars, to waterways. These systems use sidewalks, streets, roads, highways, airports, and water bodies. The challenges are, in the modern Indian context, to accommodate various modes safely, balance competition among various modes, reduce people's preference for cars despite rampant traffic congestion, limited supply of transportation lines (streets, roads, highways, and parking spaces), provide proximity to work places, shopping areas, and activity centers, and worship places, and provide balanced network to provide access to residential areas on the outer edges of metro cities. Constructing highways, flyovers, more roads, and widening of existing roads to accommodate additional cars and traffic is the solution to the expanding traffic congestion in the cities. The other school of thought is that with building roads, highways, and flyover will make a cause lost for encouraging use of transit, bicycle, and walking. For the developing and expanding cities have lessons to learn from auto-loving societies around the world.

Innovative designs for components of transportation systems in cities, towns, and villages are much needed part of urban design. Indian cities, towns, and villages are competing with world cities. The mobility in cities needs to be efficient, safe, economical, comfortable, and enjoyable. These requirements apply to all modes used in the cities, towns, and villages. The transportation lines, at every level, should be equipped with landscaping.

Special features: Special features make project design more versatile, attractive, vibrant, and lively. Rivers, streams, lakes, ponds, coastlines, waterfronts, aquifers, rolling planes, hills, and other natural features can make the design project more attached to human scale activities. Cities, along rivers and water bodies, should attempt to capitalize on the values of scenic marvels offered by them. For example, location of Taj Mahal at River Yamuna, Varanasi on River Ganga, Kolkata on River Hooghly. There are ample opportunities in India for designers to tap the locations along water bodies. There are examples where artificially water bodies have been created and have become historic destination for example Sukhna Lake, Chandigarh; Golden Temple, Amritsar; Bahai worship place in New Delhi, and Akshardham Temple.

There are other opportunities to incorporate manmade features for designers such as fountains, sculptures, artifacts, replicas. Indian culture is rich of such creations and should use them at non-original places rather than importing Western features, e.g. Eiffel Tower, Big Ben Clock Tower or replica of Egyptian Pyramids. Such activities and features enhance and encourage art and culture in local places and among local people.

9.6 Design reflects people

For urban designers, the design of buildings and spaces as objects is often approached as an expressive activity. Unlike buildings or private landscapes, places are in the public, for the public, paid for in large part by the public, and ultimately judged by the pubic in their activities, with satisfaction or not. These characteristics throw urban design into a special category and set up different relationships among different categories and set up a different relationship among different designers, between design and owner, between client and user, which is different than one finds in individually commissioned design project. The owner or client wants to make a statement, wants a certain look, or wants to reflect a theme. However, an urban designer wants to express themselves, much as other artists or creators do.

In the public domain, activities are mostly public, social, and in motion over time, and the "client" at one level is everybody, at the other, is the public body that exercises authority over the spaces. While there are creative urban spaces designed, insisting on consideration of the larger spatial and cultural context usually improved the quality of the design of the places. Thus the designers should perceive public spaces – for the public. Ultimately the public uses it and makes a judgment on the designed space.

9.7 Design is an essential skill

Public projects are about planning, engineering, architecture, landscape architecture, and design. Private project encompasses same requisites depending upon the "client." Why does design matter in making of places? What kind of skills, aptitude, and attitude does it takes to be effective in place-making process? People either feel good or bad about their experiences and sensations in this common ground, or they simply take it for granted. There is a high level of agreement in these about the look and feel of environments that people like and prefer. Trusting one's own judgment, based on experience, expertise, and intuition about the experience of space is a reasonable starting point for engaging in its improvement.

In order to be an urban designer, one must develop and home urban design skills. The formal training and education in these skills is offered by architecture and landscape architecture schools. Some planning schools offer this training and specialization. People with urban planning or engineering background, as well as community people dedicated and with interests to the purpose, can pick up the knowledge, expertise, and conceptualization of how to design and improve the places that they care about. The design of each of the separate elements that are coordinated to create a place is not that complicated. But the complication flows from the sheer number of possible combinations and variations of these elements in a dynamic social and political context.

The principal values in formal design training for urban design lie in learning to draw, to understand and comprehend the space and human activities, to represent, to measure, to attach, and to solve holistic spatial problems. The understanding of three- and four-dimensional space approach is the next level design technique. Drawing connects the eye, the brain, and the hand into a single perceptual and conceptual tool. Drawing is important because so much of urban design is about visual communication. Skills of verbal expression can make a substantial difference. Sometimes the visual communication may have individual interpretations. Combination of visual with verbal and text completes the professional work. Measuring is important because everything in the physical world has a shape, size; and to design how the various elements of space come together to make a whole, designer must know how big they are and their shape is. Human behavior in spatial context, while varying according to the particular characteristics of the build environment and social culture, is vague but crucial element to understand to design human activity spaces.

9.8 Design in context of place

Design guidelines should be appropriate, selective, and acceptable. Before developing design guidelines, it is important to have a realistic understanding of what they are, or more importantly, what they ought to be. The "ideal" selection of guidelines may not work for a given location or project. They must address location's contextual challenges and goals. Because every community is different with varied goals and vision, the question is what aspects of design should be controlled? To establish the direct design elements, the urban designers can perform certain exercises, such as:

- Review of existing documents, comprehensive plan, subarea plans, and other documents with established vision for the community;
- Assuming there is existing stated vision, one can compare and evaluate it against existing built environment to determine the key designing elements need to addressed;
- Review of the existing regulatory documents, such as zoning ordinance and development regulations. These documents can show what is not covered as well for design guidelines; and
- Experiences from the similar type of communities.

9.9 Innovative planning techniques

Sustainability, smart growth, new urbanism, life style communities, walkable communities, smart community, green infrastructure, and other terms guide us for urban development. These ideas point towards common features of responsible, sensible, and attractive development; and they all have something to offer in terms of design guidelines. The designer may pick established definitions and policies or creates new ones depending upon the goals, purpose, site, and surrounding built environment or open spaces. The advantage of following established philosophies is that they come with set of development principles that have some relevance to site and building design and a system of metrics for assessing the effectiveness of a proposal to attain those principles. Once it is determined, what are goals and types of design elements needed, it can be achieved through amending the zoning regulations, incorporating new guidelines in the ordinance, or establishing the new regulations. A new design process can be incorporated with the amendments and changes.

9.10 Urban design perspectives

A well-designed project brings appreciation. It is subjective but with careful and thoughtful nexus of elements can become objective. The cities, towns, villages, and areas we seek to live or work or visit, or play or perform activities have certain attractive design qualities. They feature memorable buildings, human scale activities, easy and comfortable connectivity, some special features, green environment, and planned layout. All these elements coordinated to provide a healthy and inviting environment for people. Each element individually may be identifiable not as much effective as holistically.

Architectural improvement to the built environment can generate measurable economic, social, cultural, environmental, and visual value. Community decision makers invest extensive time and resources to maximize the value of a proposed project. Elected officials, bankers, investors, developers, builders, stakeholders, professionals (planners, architects, landscape architects, engineers, and transportation planners) should work together to make the project a landmark, a legacy, a monument, a creation of appreciation. A planned layout with rational placement of activity centers by urban planners must be the founding step. The projects should assess the need to add landscaping by landscape architects. The creative idea of special features by talented artists and other professionals should be part of the project. A good design is a holistic approach. (Fig. 9.1)

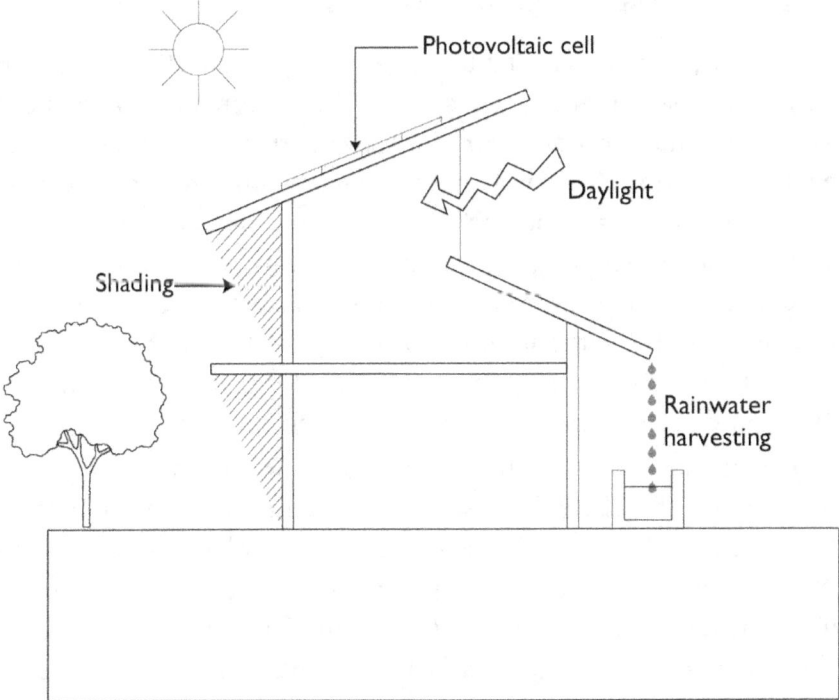

Figure 9.1 Sustainable design

It is recognized that each project has its own design merits. Some of the urban design elements are:
- Sustainability
- Human scale layout
- Manageability
- A holistic and comprehensive approach
- Seamless connectivity

- Visual value
- Place making
- Spiritual connectedness
- Social value
- Functional value
- Economic asset

9.11   Urban design controls

The two aspects of planning that have the greatest effect on urban design are development controls and public investment. Development controls provide the framework for the construction part, and public investment determines what government builds. An understanding of the urban design implication of planning decisions can add a strategic dimension to planning. It can create new opportunities for design change. Government-invested project does not have to be dull, ugly, and without touch of design. Rather public projects, well planned and designed, can be catalyst for private projects. The elements discussed can be applicable to the government projects.

For zoning to be a useful means of influencing the design of cities, the regulations must restrict somewhat the amount of development. Zoning ordinance is a useful tool to direct design-oriented development. The first phase of design control deals with land use and density. Land use and densities should not be negotiable. However, planned developments may mitigate some requirements in the initial stages of the project. Limiting floor index ratio, square footages of development, transportation requirements, infrastructure for present project and future connectivity, open space requirements, and social and economic forces remain a necessary part of development regulations. The second phase of design control shapes the physical bulk of a building. Setbacks, height limits, spaces between buildings and required open spaces are some of the examples of bulk requirements. The third phase is the performance requirements that become the basis of design of the project and design review by the authorities. These requirements can range from informal suggestions to design of façade, architectural and functional relationships to the surrounding structures, entrances, exits, and number of curb cuts, and choice of exterior materials and colors. The fourth phase control can be obtained through the use of illustrative and graphic site plans and three-dimensional models, computer graphics, and other innovative presentation of plans showing more realistic realization of the project.

The connection between land use and urban design is more sensible when a community seeks to promote development or strengthen a particular aspect of the local system, for example a new shopping center, an entertainment center, or a new worship place. The implementation of urban design should be combination of community's cultural, social, political, and economic values. A project with urban design qualities should address these variations and relationships than purely theoretical explanation of the design to market it to the impacted groups. To a large extent, its success and acceptance is dependent upon many individuals making independent decisions in such a way that they complement each other. To manage design part of the projects, there is usually public intervention or controls. Zoning is the primary tool available to control the form of urban development. There are certain types of zonings which can help manage the projects.

9.12 Restrictive zoning

The most common method of zoning control is to place development restrictions on new development. This method can apply on built environment, provided the tools are placed creatively in the zoning process. There are arguments in favor and against this tool. However, if handled professionally it can generate positive results.

9.13 Indicative zoning

This type of land use regulation instructs building community on the form the development should take. It provides guidelines for various selected elements. The administrative professional staff works very closely with the building community. This can be tricky on basis of fairness and competitive grounds. This is least practiced tool.

9.14 Incentive zoning

This zoning type should not be taken synonymous with contract zoning. Contract zoning is a legally unacceptable platform. Incentive zoning is giving incentive to the building community in exchange for certain public benefits provided by them. The incentives usually are in the form of bonus to the developer by providing more density, higher floor index ratio, quick return time for plans reviews, exemption on fees, and public recognition. The developer agrees to provide promised public amenities such as park, open space, activities center, library, and other amenity needed by the project or the community.

9.15 Performance zoning

Performance zoning gives the most latitude to the public officials in controlling urban form. Instead of a rigid list of requirements detailing what cannot be done, rather a set of urban design criteria is established to be met by the developer. The developer's proposed plan is then evaluated in terms of how well it meets the established performance criteria. It gives both the building community and the city a great deal of latitude in evaluating the proposal. The planning staff is at the stake of interpretation of both home rules and the submitted proposals. Another disadvantage is that elected officials are generally reluctant to relinquish their power and authority, even to the well-trained professionals.

9.16 Urban design plan

Urban design is the discipline between planning and architecture. It gives three-dimensional physical form to policies described above and in comprehensive plan. It focuses on the design of public realm, which is created by both public places and buildings that define them. Urban design views these spaces and buildings holistically and is concerned with bringing together the different disciplines responsible for the components of the cities into a unified vision.

Key elements of an urban design plan include the plan itself, the preparation of design guidelines for buildings, the design of public realm, which are open spaces, streets, sidewalks, courtyards, spaces between buildings, and plazas. These include massing, placement, greenery, and sun, wind, and shadow issues. The purpose of preparing an urban design plan establishes tone for goals of the plan. The urban design plans can be for mixed-use developments, market areas, worship/spiritual places, historic sites, campuses, water fronts, corridors, shopping malls, and neighborhoods. Urban design plan requires interdisciplinary collaborations among urban designers, architects, landscape architects, planners, engineers, environmental planners and engineers, transportation planners and engineers, and market analysts. The central role of the urban designer is to serve as the one who can integrate the work of a diverse range of specialists.

The main components of an urban design plan are executive summary, existing conditions, analysis drawings, report on issues and challenges, development program, urban design plan, street framework plan, open space framework plan, perspective drawings, design guidelines, phasing plan, implementation, and monitoring and evaluation.

9.17 Urban landscaping design

Landscape architecture is an aesthetically based profession founded on an understanding of the landscape. That understanding requires knowledge of the land sciences, soils, geology, hydrology, botany, horticulture, and ecology. Landscape architecture includes the art, science, and management of landscape. Landscape architects plan, design, and manage the landscape. Landscape architecture grew out of garden design. The critical difference between the two is that gardens tend to be enclosed and to be designed for the private individual, whereas landscape architecture is concerned with open space, the public realm, and the relationship between mankind's development activities and natural environment. Landscape architecture is concerned with the public good, with community values and with human development and its impact on the land.

Landscape embraces the cityscape and hence landscape architecture is also concerned with urban design.

Indian historic buildings, palaces, historic mansions, historic sites, historic gardens, and worship places are prime examples of landscape architecture. Many other international communities take pride in the art of landscape architecture, for example Japanese culture, Middle Eastern cultures, and European cultures.

The professions of landscape architecture and urban planning have a strong tradition of representation that has evolved with the profession. For a long time, this has been dominated by analog representation – primarily pencil, pen, markers, and watercolors. With the latest technical innovations digital tools have been adapted. Knowledge of analog representation plays a vital role in understanding the application of digital tools and techniques. Tools such as Adobe Illustrator and Photoshop are born directly from analog processes and tools defined by their physical counterparts. For digital landscaping, drawing preparation, computers with motherboard, processor, memory/RAM, hard drives, graphic cards, monitor, mouse and keyboard are required. Software typically describes code or computer programs that perform a specific task within a computer system. Software applications, image editing, vector editing, three-dimensional modeling, and video editing and motion editing software are used for digital landscaping representation.

Two common modes are used for storing graphic data: raster and vector. Photoshop is the primary raster-based program used in digital rendering. Programs like Illustrator and AutoCAD are primarily vector based, although these elements of both raster and vector tools are in all of the programs. Raster images are stored in a file as a set of pixels, with each pixel representing a single area of color in the drawing. When a raster image is printed, the quality of the final image is determined by the resolution of the image. In terms of printing, resolution refers to the number of pixels inch on the printed paper. If the number of pixels per inch is too low, you will be able to see the individual pixels when the image is printed. This kind of image is often referred to as a pixelated image. Higher resolution leads to a higher quality image. *Upsampling* increases the number of pixels in an image, and downsampling decreases the number of pixels in an image. *Upsampling* means adding more pixels to an image so that a larger image at a resolution that does not cause pixilation can be printed. The problem with *upsampling* is that when the program fills in these new pixels, they do not always perfectly match the existing pixels. The pixel is the smallest unit in an image, and it cannot be subdivided. The overall image is created by the combination of a large number of pixels. When an image is printed or displayed on a screen at normal resolutions, the individual pixels are so small that they are not noticeable to the human eye. When the pixels are small enough, the illusion of a continuous image is created. The number of pixels in an image determines the overall size of the raster image. If an image is said to be 1200×800 pixels, it means that there are 1200 pixels across and 800 pixels from top to bottom. Analog creations have human touch to it, versus digital creations are more controlled. Digital landscaping drawing/architecture requires experts and trained personnel.

9.18 Urban forestry

They are dynamic ecosystems that provide environmental services such as clean air and water. Trees cool cities and save energy; improve air quality; strengthen quality of place and local economies; reduce storm water runoff; improve social connections; complement smart growth; and create walkable communities. Important element of "urban ecology" is the role of trees in providing wide variety of environmental, economic, and social benefits, such as:

- Sequestering of carbon, thus contributing directly to climate change mitigation;
- Reduction of air pollution through direct deposition of pollutants and through cooling effects that reduce the formation of ozone;
- Shading of buildings, which can lower energy use and demand for air conditioning;
- Reduction of urban heat island effect. Urban heat island is a phenomenon where air temperatures in urban areas are

2–10°F hotter than surrounding rural areas due to high concentrations of buildings and pavements in urban area (and lack of natural vegetation);
- Interception of water runoff, thus buffering local water bodies from pollution and helping to control storm water overflow problems;
- Provision of natural habitat for wildlife; and
- Access to nature.

Many of these benefits, those related to air pollution, water pollution, and local cooling effects, have direct and significant effect on physical human health. There is also growing recognition that exposure to trees and green spaces provides many socioeconomic and mental health benefits, including enhanced social cohesion, increase in real estate values, improved health and recreational activities, and cultural and spiritual values.

Urbanization can result in most of the available land being utilized for building and infrastructure development. As cities grow, trees and green spaces are often lost, and with them valuable ecological services, and the benefits stemming from those services. With more people in towns and cities, there is growing need of land to construct buildings for residential, commercial, institutional, and industrial spaces in towns and cities. Existing trees are the first natural feature removed from the land. A clear land, without any vegetation, is easy and less costly for development. Developers start removing the trees for development project. If for some reason, the project is delayed, the area is prone to erosion, dust, and storm water runoff. The local government should have ordinances to place to stop this practice till the project is ready for constructing buildings. Another alternative is to install best practice management measures to control soil erosion and dust blowing. Another approach is to conduct a tree survey of the existing vegetation. That will record any specimen, hardwood, or old trees on the site. They should be preserved to possible extent and should be replaced according to the established standards. The local government should adopt Tree Preservation Ordinance with elements to protect the existing trees, replacement of removed trees, landscaping of the project area, cutting of existing trees with approval process only. With increased urbanization, urban sprawl, new smart cities, and other urban and rural activities, there are both challenges and opportunities for designing more sustainable development pathway. To aid the design of sustainable cities (for the benefit of its citizens), urban forestry should be recognized as an urban system and should be incorporated into various policy documents. A central challenge for the future is to develop strategies for "sustainable stewardship" of urban ecosystems that can support a healthy tree canopy and healthy, safe, and diverse environment for the citizens. In Indian context, the local governments, civic groups, NGOs, concerned citizens, and other interested groups can assist in protecting and enhancing urban forestry in towns, cities, and villages.

9.19   Campus communities

New IITs, central universities, state universities, and private universities and colleges are being built in India. These institutions are formed with many different types of buildings, such as classrooms, meeting rooms, offices, lecture halls, lecture auditoriums, laboratories, workshops, amphitheaters, conference halls, theaters, playgrounds, gymnasiums, recreational centers, and many other types of buildings depending on the type and nature of the educational institutions. Staff, faculty, students, and visitors fill these institutions.

Educational institutions generate economic, social, psychological, and institutional and time-released benefits. They become part of the local community, and local communities participate in various activities at these campuses. They act as lighthouse for the young generations. Local communities take pride in the local educational institutions. Educational institutions attract talented and creative people. These residents are part of making cities more social and culturally advanced. These people discourage criminal activities in the local community. Universities and colleges create psychological pride among the campus residents and local communities. Once graduated, with their knowledge and contributions, they make their campus and local communities recognizable, even in distant places. Some alumni, with their intelligent performances, put the communities on the world map. These institutions become part of the local economy. The campus community contribute to the local communities by their creative and smart contributions. Economically, they generate and increase local revenues. The money spent by the campus residents creates monetary multiplier impact. The occupants of these institutions need and demand additional services from the local economic sectors. They need more restaurants, movie theaters, retail shops, malls, worship places, and additional requirements depending on the type of the institute. These requirements create jobs, entrepreneurial activities, creative businesses, and increase land values. These institutions offer some unique opportunities, such as:

- Diverse student population. For example, IITs bring students from all over the country at one place. This foster national unity and understanding for other cultures.
- A growing focus on interdisciplinary and collaborative learning and teaching. For example, management institutes, science expert institutions, engineering campuses are adopting diversified and collaborative learning and teaching techniques.
- Educational institutions for a long time.
- Faculty, students, and staff view campus as their community. Some institutions are self-sustainable, self-contained, and self-dependent. Once on the campus, the residents feel the environment as their community. It creates sense of association, sense of pride, and sense of affiliation. For some, this feeling stays with them lifelong.
- Even temporary, for few years or limited time, students adopt local communities and become part of their activities.

9.19.1 Steps for master planning and designing a campus

Conduct needs assessment study: The project manager should conduct needs assessment of the new institute. Needs assessment study should include number of departments, nature of departments, and number of students, faculty–student ratio, staff requirements, offices, administration space needs, library, residences, recreational activities, market requirements, health center, museum, visitor's center, guesthouses, and other requirements. The interviews with various department heads from existing institutions can lay foundation for future master plan and design. The project manager should prepare comparison tables with similar type of institutions existing. A survey, by contacting existing institutions, should be conducted to learn from their successes and mistakes. An empirical visit to carefully chosen campuses can provide wealth of information. During visits, meeting with their planner, project manager, and engineer can provide additional information and an opportunity to learn from their mistakes, errors, and right actions. Needs assessment should not be a closed room endeavor with favorite friends or chief client. However, they may be consulted during the process.

Select a team: Building the team will move to initiate the master plan and design process. The team should be led by a project manager, preferably an urban planner. Campuses are like cities, only specialized in education activities. Project manager should be capable of understanding the role of each discipline and more importantly, when to incorporate a particular discipline. The project manager must be dynamic and a team builder. Project management element is discussed in this text.

Vision and goals: The project manager's first assignment is to establish vision and goals of the project. The vision should be in collaboration with the institute's head, organization's head and management team, department heads, local community's stakeholders, head of local educational institutions, local civic groups, neighboring property owners, local ULBs elected officials, ULBs department heads, police chief, local deputy commissioner, head of local hospital(s), and local, regional, state, and center government affiliated officials and recognized stakeholders. Involving many personalities early will help the project manager during the lengthy development process. The early participants will become partners during the process. They will not be surprised when the project manager, engineer, or architect approaches them for approval of the project plans.

Build a theme: Establishing a vision with a theme for the campus, buildings, and overall institutions will keep everyone focused. It can help project manager to make decisions and move forward on the path, already established. The campus should be a planned development. The horizontal and vertical scales should be decided early on. This will save time and avoid confusion at the time of master plan, design and building architecture. The project manager must consult other experts to incorporate the latest technology, know-how, and trends of the present times. Inclusion of indoor sports complex, amphitheater for large gatherings for events, airport, heliport, radio station, and a landmark building or buildings should be established early one.

The project manager, in consultation with architects and planner, should determine the style of certain buildings on the campus, namely, library, administrative division, museum, visitor's center, guest house, conference room, main entrance to the campus, to suggest a few.

Charrettes: The project manager should organize charrettes with the available professional, stakeholders, faculty, students, staff, security staff, and involve neighboring property owners and other stakeholders. This will provide many new, innovative, and creative ideas from people, very much unexpected. In charrettes, the project manager is encouraged to include spouses of faculty and staff and their grown up children (from age 12 and above). The experiences have shown that they bring interesting and unique ideas for the development. They live and experience campus life and have their ideas and observations. They must be recorded very carefully. They help in developing and designing future campus.

9.19.2 Master plan and design elements

The centerpiece: The designers should learn from previously held meetings, design workshops, charrettes, and surveys to determine the centerpiece of the project. The institute's director may/would like to have his or her office in the centerpiece building or library could be relevant choice, or a water body to welcome everyone coming to the institute. The choice of open space with lush landscaping should not be ruled out; a large water body with lots of activity spaces before laying out buildings, classrooms, theaters and workshops around it.

The spaces: The spaces around buildings must be carefully designed with inviting environment for students and faculty. The spaces should interlinked and give warmth feeling than just plain high solid walls. The buildings may be linked with covered walkways. The spaces inside the buildings provide opportunities for students of various level and faculty to interact, not segregate. This area should encourage students to mingle and provide an opportunity to exchange information irrespective of academic level.

Neighboring property owners and uses: The new master plans and designs must incorporate built environment, future development, and development under construction and vacant lands. Buildings change land into non-porous land. Prior to buildings, land is porous, rainwater flows freely, and land observes water to its capacity. There is no habitation. Even if water retains for while no damage is done. In Indian context, the first step taken by engineers is to build a wall. A good idea to protect the property and establish boundaries on land. But if not engineered property, the boundary wall can retain water on the property and disturb the natural flow of water. The logged water can damage buildings, foundations, and create other structural and problems of insects, rodents, and mold. The walls on neighboring property can cause damage on the subject property through mismanaged storm water. The development projects should be designed with engineered storm water management systems.

The projects should be designed carefully by placing complimentary uses next to uses applied on the neighboring property. The architectural themes can be complimentary with the architectural style at the next property. The developments along a road should coordinate with each other to determine the appropriate width of the road needed to accommodate total trips, types of modes, and other infrastructure along that access way.

Café and cafeteria: People with resources make decisions at golf course; students interact, socialize, relieve stress, and cram exam in the café and cafeteria. During a charrette, for a new campus, the most common idea pushed by the students, of all level, was to design for an international cafeteria. Their reasoning was that they would like to have a space where they can interact with other. They wanted a common level cafeteria where they are no intimidated by someone higher above office environment. They wanted faculty to be using that facility as well. The behavior, needs, and demands of the younger generation are changing, and architects, planners, and designers must provide what fits with the new times.

The dining halls of the student residences should be at human scale. The dining halls should be more a personal, less institutional environment than a typical university hall. Areas for delivery of foods to students must be designed to show cultured and civilized behavior. The kitchens and food preparation areas must be designed for clean, hygienic, and sanitized cooking.

9.19.3 Residences

When universities provide residences to its faculty, staff, students, guests, and visitors, it solves problem of housing. Provision of residences helps the institution to take off without the fear of accommodation of employees. This feature also attracts quality employees. Students can focus on studies than searching for accommodation. However, this feature requires more land to build housing, need more resources to build residences, need more planning to locate housing on the campus, design various types of housing for various level of employees, and location of various types of housing with respect to each other.

9.19.4 Students

For students residences the issues are single occupancy, multi-occupancy, size of room, bathroom ratio, optimum number of rooms in one building, location of student residences, and provision of types of activities in the residence buildings. Some institutions provide co-ed residences and some institutions still wonder how far girl's hostel should be from boy's hostel. This can be resolved by involving both genders during the design process. This question should be resolved by the potential residents rather than other parties.

9.19.5 Faculty and staff

The faculty and staff housing is for the families as well – spouses, children, and elderly parents. The design includes one bedroom, two bedroom, three bedroom, single family, multifamily, one story, multi-story, garages, open spaces, connectivity, parking, sidewalks, and provision of street lighting. The plan has to provide additional services, such as day care center, senior center, elementary school, middle school, play grounds, play lots, recreational centers for faculty, and recreational center for staff. The faculty and staff have different social status. They prefer to live separate with separate facilities and services. This is ironic that this practice prevails among the people who deliver the message of equality and eradicating class system. The educated elite preaches on correcting orthodox systems, social evils. The new generation planners, architects, and designers should strive to eradicate these social evils by building mixed-use developments. Educational campuses can be catalyst by designing such residences.

Category of hostel mess/dining area staff, and cafeteria staff is generally overlooked while planning for residences at educational centers. They are not provided with proper housing, bathroom, and toilet facilities. Resultantly, they seek shelters at odd places either in the dining hall or other places on the campus. Their personal hygiene and facilities to stay clean are of utmost important. Bearing and carrying bad bacteria, they can spread disease to hundreds of people they feed and come in contact with.

Another category of staff overlooked during design of housing and facilities is security personnel. Security personal work round the clock and perform duties at odd places where there are no utilities or facilities. Architects must include residences, facilities, and other requirements to perform their duties, such as observation towers, office locations at entrance, spaces for waiting visitors, and other requirements depending upon the project.

9.19.6 Market

For self-sustainable campuses, markets provide day-to-day needs of the campus residents. Campus markets should be designed to attract only campus residents but for the potential customers living in the nearby areas. They can help sustain businesses in the market. The market should meet the shopping needs of the campus population of faculty, staff, students, temporary employees, seasonal employees, and visitors. A very innovative and market design inviting people to shop, hang out, socialize, interact, relax, meet friends, and a place to enjoy activities, should be safe, vibrant, attractive, creating sense of place, colorful, well lit, walkable and pedestrian character with a style and theme. A market place should be designed to clean and well landscaped. Campus markets and local community markets should be complimentary not competitive.

9.19.7 Transportation

Any newly designed or attempting to make transition towards sustainability must confront the issue of transportation. The daily movement of people back and forth to campus in automobiles burning fossil fuels is one of the main impacts a typical educational institution imposes on the life support system on the planet. In addition, the travel pattern that students learn while in college are likely to influence their future travel choices. With a large number of young people, university/college campuses attract more students, staff, and faculty. With the increase of use of cars as personal vehicles, urban campuses face serious impact from automobile traffic and parking shortages. Efforts to tame car traffic can have multiple benefits: helping the environment, improving the livability of the campus, and other fiscal benefits to the campus administration. The following factors influence the transportation policy and practices on university and college campuses:

- The physical layout of the campus as driven by campus growth or as a new campus on vacant land, the master plan, and aesthetic considerations. Aesthetics and the value of green spaces on campus influence parking and transportation programs.
- The philosophy about transportation priorities as determined by the management or student initiatives and implementation by the administration.
- Resources available, both staff and funding, to create efficient campus transportation options.
- The physical transportation infrastructure in the surrounding regions. Local and regional connectivity to the campus.
- Residential campuses differ from commuter campuses.
- The trend of more students and employees living further from campus in order to achieve rent or home ownership savings.
- The cost of parking and/or availability of parking.

Bicycles are the most efficient form of transportation, with the lowest energy input and lowest output of pollutants and greenhouse gases. Active transportation – bicycling and walking – also can contribute to the health benefits. Everyone is pedestrian during some part of the journey to campus. The motorist walks from a parking place. The cyclist walks from the bike rack and the transit rider walks from the bus stop to class or an office. But the most healthy and most environmentally benign commute to and from a campus is a pedestrian. College students who live on campus or less than twenty minutes (walking time) or approximately on a mile from a campus should be candidate for the pedestrian mode or bicycle mode. Campuses can provide bicycle service stations on premises or near campuses. Students can rent bikes, purchase bike equipment, store bikes, and obtain repair services. Flat tire repair or replacement is a well-used service. Universities should provide free bicycles, distinguished by color for on-campus short-term use. Rideshare programs can have a significant impact under some circumstances for both staff and students.

Parking lots and structures also have site-specific environmental impacts. When installing or updating parking facilities, there are number of options that can help mitigate run-off from impervious surfaces and protect sensitive areas. "Green" parking lot techniques include minimizing the dimensions of parking lot spaces, utilizing alternative pavers in overflow parking areas. Alternative pavers consist of two broad categories: paving blocks and other surfaces. Paving blocks are concrete or plastic grids with gravel or grass inside the holes for infiltration. Porous pavements is a permeable pavement surface with an underlying stone reservoir to temporarily store surface runoff before it infiltrates into the subsoil. Other surfaces include gravel, cobbles, wood, brick, natural stone, and mulch.

The master planner can enhance the educational establishment by reviewing the regional connectivity of the institute. Students are mobile and choosy. They are willing to relocate and travel long distances to get world class education. Master planners and project managers can help them achieve their goals by providing regional efficient transportation connectivity. Air, rails, buses, and taxis are the modes for regional travel. The administration should evaluate the existing modes and choices. The campus plans should be regional in terms of transportation element. Regional transportation means can attract large number of students, staff, and faculty. Railway, bus authorities, and airport managers should be partners in preparing master plans of campuses. Connect the institutions with other local, regional, and national activity centers with sleek transportation systems.

9.19.8 Education for underprivileged

The master planners, designers, administrators, deans, directors, chancellors, faculty, staff, and students of universities/colleges should develop programs to provide education to under privileged. The underprivileged are the low level staff, peons, attendants, delivery person, drivers, go-for, watchmen, and staff and servers of dining hall, cafeteria, café, security guards, and gardeners, water supply persons and others with minimum or no education at all. The campuses are equipped with infrastructure to obtain education, such as classrooms, boards, computers, libraries, and skilled trainers. No one should be left behind for education. The program should be oriented to provide basic education and knowledge about the opportunities for them to advance in life and help achieve their goals. "The chain is as strong as its weakest link."

Create places of greater civic value by incorporating various required uses in the campus such as, libraries, health centers, amphitheaters, solar farms, horticulture, and other creative ideas. Campuses are permanent features with longevity. They are educational, economic, and social institutions part of the community for a long time.

9.20 Military bases/cantonments

Cantonment as a separate entity was designed by British. In various occupied countries, in order to live and lead life away from civilian population who were considered generally hostile to them being occupied by force. So their officers and men (who were a few in number) preferred to live and lead their life peacefully; moreover, troops were not allowed to mix with civilian population. They designed and built their separate living areas, which were like small townships. These areas, also known as civil lines, met their basic requirements. Within these areas through design, they separated living areas of officers from other ranks. Their recreational needs, play grounds and golf courses, training areas for troops, a market place for daily needs, basic education facilities and medical requirements were away from the traditional city areas. Basically it was a comprehensive livable township which had vast open areas and lot of greenery. They adopted preferably straight roads. The design did not care for existing natural and built environment. The design was for sole purpose – to separate colonists from the local population. Even at place like Delhi, there is at least 2–3°C less temperature in summers.

Size of these cantonments kept increasing as they occupied more areas and more troops were added. With the result, in India, there are cantonments all over the country, e.g. Devlali, Kasauli, Shillong, Darjeeling, Dalhousie, Shimla and many more all over India. These cantonments are governed by cantonment boards as per their by-laws which are separate from municipality laws. All the cantonments are very well managed. These are safe, secure, and comfortable livable areas.

Some of the military areas now being developed are being designated as military station/air force stations/naval stations. These are separate from cantonment stations. Need of these stations arose due to increase in military strength and relocation of certain formations and units. All these military stations have been developed on lines of modern towns. These stations meet the basic requirements of troops and their families.

The Ministry of Defense should prepare plans for new military stations/air force stations/naval stations in coordination with local compressive plans. If there is no comprehensive plan in existence, then a comprehensive plan should be initiated. The planners should pay special attention to storage of explosives, missiles, ammunition, fuel, and other hazardous and combustible materials. Air force and naval requirement can be different from the army needs. The plan should incorporate the goals and needs of the existing settlement and make sure the goals and needs of the new military station are consistent, complimentary, and compatible.

Chapter 10
Transportation planning

10.1 Introduction

Everything we do is associated with transportation. Access to goods and services require some mode of transport, irrespective of who is transporting them. Relationship of transportation and land use has a continuous debate among professionals. One school of thought is, transportation impacts choices of land uses, and another thought is land uses guide transportation. Both elements work interestingly and produce marvelous results. However, transportation is a vital function in both urban and rural areas. The transportation system provides a framework upon which a city is built. Understanding the existing transportation system is vital for planning for present and future. The purposes of transportation are to enable people to move among various sections of the city for many purposes and to move goods. The transportation system must be designed to be safe, efficient, functional, and workable. These elements must be applicable to all modes of transportation: automobiles, heavy vehicles, slow and light automobiles, manually operated vehicles, animal-operated vehicles, three-wheelers, two-wheelers, buses, trains, pedestrians, boats, and air traffic. Boats, ships, and airplanes are modes with use of water and air than land or limited use of land. Through different modes, we access work, markets, entertainment, social activities, educational institutions, health facilities, hospital and welfare places, worship places, open spaces, and other activity places or sometime just visit railway station or airport to watch people and activities. All these activities require safe, convenient, and efficient transportation system.

The cities are developed over time, sometimes consciously and subconsciously. In Indian context, the biggest challenge for urban and transportation planners is to understand operation, function, togetherness, and compatibility of slow- and fast-moving traffic on the same road in the cities. There are no dedicated rights-of-way (ROW) for heavy or motorized or fast-moving traffic, e.g. automobiles, buses, trucks, three-wheelers, scooters, and motorcycle. The road with the heavy traffic is shared with bicycles, human-driven vehicles, animal-driven vehicles, rickshaws, pedestrians, and even stray animals and motorized vehicles. On Indian roads, the movement of animals is sometimes human controlled and sometimes they wander on their own. Various modes of traffic share limited road space available and compete with each other to move safely and speedily. To access day-to-day needs and special needs of life, a smooth and efficient movement of goods is necessary. Besides convenience, travel time plays a critical role in movement of people, goods, and perishable goods. Consumers keep factors of convenience and travel time in consideration for deciding to make a trip.

Personal automobiles provide feeling of ownership, convenience, save travel time, choice of changing destinations, choice of delaying trips, privacy, control over stops and selection of trips, control over travel time, sometime even waiting area, shelter from weather conditions, family togetherness, pleasure of control, easy long distance trips, and sometimes a business meeting venue. Automobiles assist in expanding businesses and their territories. Automobiles are the mean to access incident locations for the emergency personnel and save lives in some situations. Automobiles provide employment opportunities at automobiles assembly plants, additional jobs with forward and backward linkages of units providing parts and accessories to the assembly plants, repair shops and repair service men, petrol stations, and many other automobile industry associated jobs. Automobiles assist in increasing gross national product and provide revenue sources for the local, state, and central government. Automobiles can be associated with entertainment: a Bollywood movie lead singing a melodious song in a convertible to impress someone; and for certain segment of the society automobiles can be a status symbol.

With the economic development and more disposable income, people are owning more and more automobiles. Delhi, Mumbai, Hyderabad, Bangalore are adding on an average over 300 cars each day. The challenge for urban planners and engineers are to build additional roads and parking spaces to accommodate additional automobiles. Another challenge for planners is to provide enough space to accommodate mass transit on the same road space to move efficiently and to transfer large number of citizens from one point to another. People without automobile ownership rely on public transportation to move from one place to another. To make sure mass transit moves on schedule, safely, and efficiently to maintain an acceptable level of service is another challenge faced by transport planners. If the mass transit cannot maintain schedule, timely arrival and departure, and safe travel, it can discourage ridership. This can impact the revenue collection for the mass transit organization. In metro cities a large number of people use mass transit. They cannot afford to own an automobile. People also use two-wheelers, bicycles, and walk to access places.

Economic development and additional income generates more demand of goods and services. Expanding markets and expanding consumer hinterland needs well-managed traffic and transportation system. With the ownership of the automobiles and people with more resources demand more space. This promotes urban sprawl. People living on larger spaces and away from activity centers incline to make more automobile trips for daily activities such as going to work, school or college, market, shopping, recreation, or even to a health spa. Providing and maintaining utility infrastructure can be very costly for the municipalities/ULBs. People living in larger lots with larger frontages require additional layout of electric, water, sewer, cable, fiber optic, and telephone lines. To provide services to the residents, will require additional sub-stations, pump stations, lift stations, manholes, transformers, capacitors, and generators, and regulations and maintenance of the pipes, poles, and other equipment.

Additional automobiles are escalating existing problem of congestion. To accommodate existing and additional automobiles, planners have no choice but to encroach and hijack pedestrian spaces from the existing roads, build new roads, and a new phenomenon of building flyovers. Old city sections and roads were designed primarily for pedestrians and slow-moving vehicles, and certain sections of old city definitely not for automobiles or even two-wheelers (scooters, motorcycles). Already a tight area to accommodate many modes side by side makes walking more unsafe and cumbersome. Walking is a natural and basic human right. Urban planners must strive to provide enough walking space along roads. This will help discourage use of automobiles. With old transportation modes, the movement of people was safer. Even kids could fetch things without worrying of a mishappening.

Automobiles are the main source of air pollution, toxic waste, and dumping of used tires and junk vehicles. Used tires are breeding grounds for mosquitos. Mosquitos spread diseases like malaria, dengue. Junk cars and dumped car parts in cities are an aesthetic eyesore, causes of pedestrian accidents and other accidents. The addition of two-wheelers, three-wheelers, four-wheelers, and multi-wheelers in the existing stock of automobiles on the road are noticeable changes on the Indian road system. The existing roads in the cities have limited capacity. The older parts of the cities have much less capacity because of their design and time of design and construction. The historic parts of the cities are designed for pedestrians and manually operated slow-moving vehicles, e.g. bicycles, rickshaws, and tongas. For example, the streets in the sections of Old Delhi are designed for pedestrians only, e.g. Dariba, Chotaa Chippi Wara, Kinari Bazaar, and Bhiddi

Galli. There is no room for vehicles, not even two-wheelers. Some two-wheelers owners do drive their vehicles on those narrow streets, but make other users uncomfortable and unsafe. The challenge is now to incorporate automobiles in the old and historic sections of the cities. Automobiles are pushing pedestrians, bicycles, and rickshaws to the edge of the roads, making walking and bicycling more dangerous than ever, and adding number to the fatal accidents. According to an estimate 300 people die in road accidents every day in India. Pedestrian and bicyclists are put into higher risk of accidents and more dangerous conditions by the new drivers, non-experienced drivers, reckless drivers, stunt drivers, un-trained drivers, underage drivers, careless drivers and not to mention drunk drivers. Buses, trucks, square box trucks, and other goods vehicles make situations worst. These conditions are not only a menace for planners but also make difficult for emergency situation response vehicles (Fire Trucks, Ambulance, Police) and personnel to access the incident site and reach timely to perform the responsibilities. The delays due to traffic congestion cause not only environmental damage but also loss of productive time, loss of efficiency, and unmeasurable psychological impact as well.

10.2   Roads, streets, sidewalks

The fundamental step is to classify streets according to their function for both existing city area and new planned areas. The planners must be equipped and experienced to understand the existing roads and the new proposed road system of newly planned area. However, the connectivity of old road system and new road system is equally important. The connection or merging should be functional, smooth, and easy. The drivers should not get confused while merging from the old to new traffic pattern or vice-versa. The design must include proper signage informing drivers, about the new road pattern or system. Signage design must incorporate legibility of signs at the nighttime or under inclement weather conditions for the road users.

Depending upon the existing road system and newly proposed development, the road classification can be established accordingly. Traffic engineers must coordinate with the urban planners and designers to understand the local level urban character and way of life. Urban planners and designers must take initiative to share the importance of cohesive neighborhood, continuous communities, and local character with the traffic engineers designing flyovers, expressways, and major roads. Roads can be complimentary and cohesive force to keep the community fabric seamless. On the contrary, roads can act as physical barriers and can divide the communities. Sometimes physical barriers can become psychological barriers as well. It may take a long time to bridge the psychological gap among communities. In the West, communities, planning department, and transportation department are working together to remove flyovers and expressways in the cities through Context-Sensitive Solutions. The professionals have done research and analyzed that flyovers and highways in the cities may have moved the traffic faster but divided the communities, shut down successful businesses, and destroyed the local character of the areas. Following are the proposed road classifications.

10.3 Road systems

There are various types of road systems. Each system has its own utility, and merits and demerits.

10.3.1 Grid-iron street system

The streets cross each other at right angle. The streets are generally of equal widths. They are suitable for flat areas. This system is easy for road users and accommodation of various land uses in a city format. The area can be separated as blocks to accommodate traffic and accessibility. This system is also relevant for traffic calming and accommodating more traffic without creating congestion. Through this design, land can be used to its maximum and odd shape, or irregular land portions can be avoided. With proper signage and driver responsibility, this system can reduce accident situations. This system is easy to maintain as well.

This is sometimes combined with diagonal street system. This design must be based on some criteria, e.g. direct link or communication to some landmark. Some specific uses are planned at the diagonal intersections, e.g. historic building, fountain, civic sculpture, or a park. However, the intersections can be dangerous. But with proper traffic signage and markings, the danger can be mitigated. (Fig. 10.1)

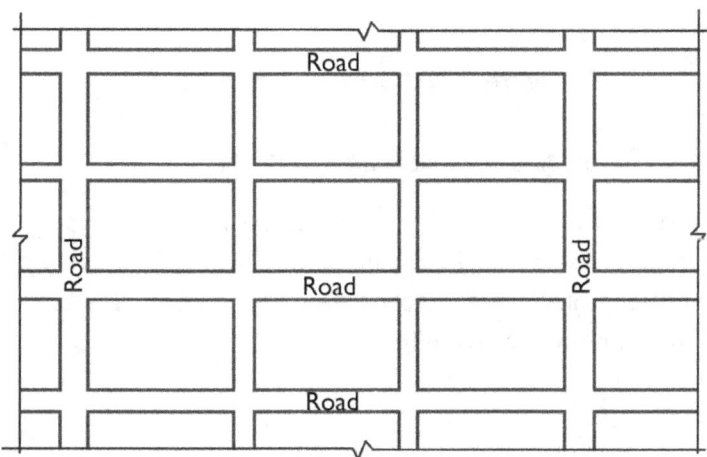

Figure 10.1 Rectangular grid-iron street system

10.3.2 Radial or concentric road system

In this system, the circular or ring roads are connected to radial roads. The system represents growth of the city in phases but continued. The hub remains the same but rest of the area grows. Radial roads of the system provide the direct access to the central part of the town. The circular roads function as the intermediary between diagonal roads and local roads. This system is more automobile oriented and functional for smaller areas and purposes. This system is not pedestrian friendly unless the streets have mixed uses. Some transportation planners have combined radial and rectangular road systems. (Fig. 10.2)

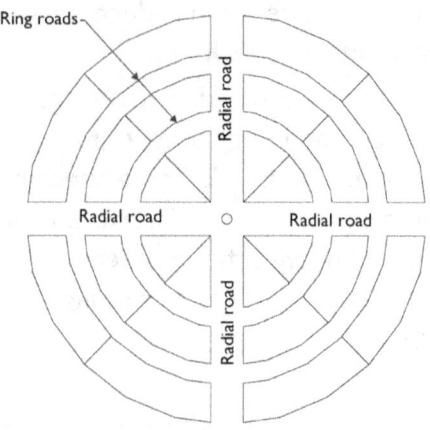

Figure 10.2 Concentric street system

10.3.3 Topographical street system

This system has roads, and development follows the topography of the area such as, lakes, rivers, hills, and seaside. This system is also known as organic street pattern. Development in this system may be planned or unplanned. (Fig. 10.3)

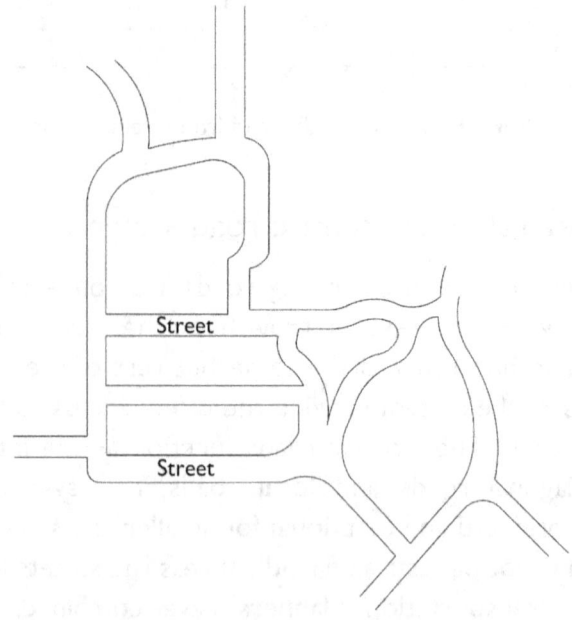

Figure 10.3 Topographical/organic street system

10.3.4 Medieval era street system

Many of the old cities of the middle ages have grown in this irregular way. Again, sections could be planned or unplanned. This system is prevalent in many old Indian cities, e.g. Amritsar, Varanasi, and old Delhi.

There are examples of irregular medieval street systems mixed or expanded with rectangular or other street systems, e.g. old Delhi and New Delhi.

10.4 Freeway

These are streets with complete control of access, i.e. no access from commercial or residential property. These streets generally carry large number of trips. No pedestrian or slow-moving vehicles are permitted to enter these streets.

10.5 Expressway

These roads are characterized by at least some degree of access control. Except in rare instances, this category is for multilane, divided roads with few, if any, intersections at grade. Expressways serve large volume of traffic. This category of roads runs through cities and connects cities.

While preparing design of the above two categories of roads. It is recommended that experts, traffic engineers, traffic planners, urban planners, rural planners, architects, landscape architects, and other professionals involve non-professionals such as non-technical citizens, housewives, young students from the local communities, and citizens. They must coordinate to work together on details of the project. The finished product must be safe, functional, efficient, aesthetically appealing, attractive, inviting, with proper signage, proper road markings, with rest areas and spaces to accommodate accident situations. The project manager must adhere to the details and ideas shared by the participants.

10.6 Arterial

This class of streets brings traffic to and from expressways and serves those major movements of traffic within or through urban areas. Arterials interconnect the principal traffic generators. This category carries large volume of traffic. Examples of arterial roads are ring roads, by-pass roads, and major roads. These roads are intended for high-speed movement of traffic.

Proper and well-designed road markings, well-planned and designed traffic signage, uniformity of traffic signage, regular maintenance, well-lit for night time traffic, guard-rails for safety and traffic control, well-designed landscaping, maintenance of landscaping, cleanliness, prompt removal of accident vehicles, removal of inoperative vehicles, and junk vehicles from the road are required features of this road classification. No direct access to commercial and residential properties be permitted.

10.7 Sub-arterial roads

Also known as major roads in an urban setting. This category connects activity nodes of the city. Commercial uses have direct access from these roads. Limited residential access to direct residential on these roads such as mixed-use building with commercial and office on the lower floors to residential uses on the upper stories of the buildings.

The planners must incorporate proper parking spaces for automobiles, non-motorized vehicles, and spaces for pedestrians. Because of commercial uses along sub-arterial roads, loading and unloading facilities must be incorporated in the design stages. Also proper signage, addressing of properties, roadside signage, individual business signage, landscaping, and pedestrian accommodation must be included in design or redevelopment phases.

10.8 Collector

This category of streets serves internal traffic movements within an area of a town and connects with the arterial system. Collectors do not handle long through trip and generally short length roads unless designed to be long. Collector roads are prime locations for commercial, institutional, and office use. Intersections of collector roads may become nodal and prominent identification landmarks.

The planners must pay additional attention of providing spacious sidewalks and safe pedestrian designs along collector roads. Design may incorporate spaces for temporary, seasonal, floating and permanent vendors and squatters. In Indian context, businesses, servicemen, and vendors like *iron/istri-walla, paan-walla, chai-walla, sabzi-walla, fruit-walla, phool-walla* and other related type must be incorporated creatively in the design process whether new planning or redevelopment or clean-up project.

10.9 Local streets

These roads are also known as minor roads. The sole purpose of the local streets is to provide access to adjacent land. There should be no through traffic on these roads. These streets make up a large percentage of the total street lengths of the carriageway. These roads carry small proportion of the vehicle miles of travel. Pedestrian traffic, sidewalks, non-vehicle traffic should be given due attention while designing, redesigning, redeveloping, and planning to accommodate additional vehicular traffic. Parking along local roads of motorized vehicles can be a nuisance. The residential areas can encounter artificial congestion along home frontages. This situation can be unacceptable to the emergency response vehicles and personnel. The store fronts can be screened with vehicles thus can lose business to potential customers. However, designing local roads carefully and maintaining already well-designed roads can be helpful in maintaining smart development for local neighborhood and discourage vehicle trips for day-to-day shopping or mundane errands by the residents.

10.10 Alleys

Alleys are spaces between the rears of structures used as access way. The primary purpose of alleys is to provide delivery and pick up space for goods without interfering with the through traffic or taking the prime parking space for customers in front of the storefront. Alleys provide safety to pedestrians without coming in contact with the heavy traffic. Alleys are also helpful to emergency response vehicles and personnel. Alleys provide additional open spaces between buildings for sunlight and air circulation. Instead of using front of the buildings for trash storage and collection, which could create smell and unsightly looks, alleys provide opportunities for that. With smart design, parking can be provided along or within alleys. This can save prime spaces along the front of the businesses. During emergency situations, alleys can be used to detour the traffic. (Fig. 10.4)

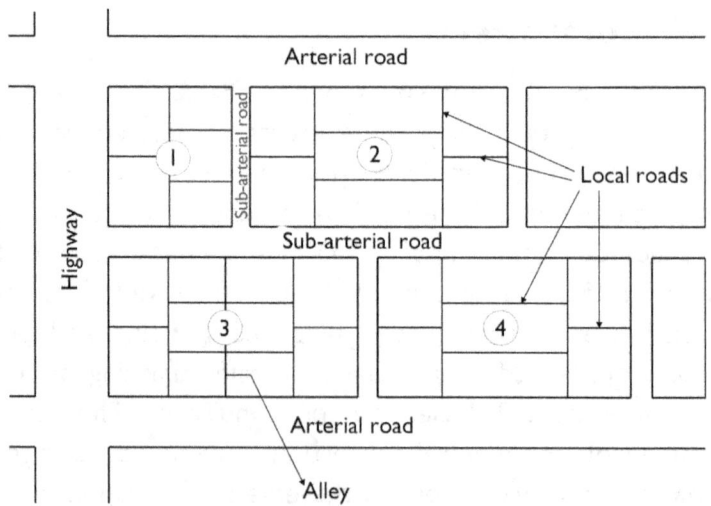

Figure 10.4 Road classification

10.11 Sidewalks

Also known as walkways, pedestrian ways, and footpath. These are paved portions on the side of the street for pedestrians. No vehicular traffic should be allowed on sidewalks. Sidewalks should be designed to be safe and inviting to people to use them. Well-lit sidewalks encourage people to use them at nighttime. Commercial area sidewalks should be wider and clear of obstruction to walking traffic.

In Indian context, sometimes sidewalks are not paved. Where there are no paved sidewalks, generally, pedestrians create their own (*kutcha*, dirt path) sidewalks. Unpaved sidewalks, especially without curb and gutter along the road, are dangerous. Moving vehicles can meander along or get off the road, can encroach the unpaved areas, and can cause accidents. Uneven surface, rough surface, trash, careless disposal of dangerous material along roads (glass, metal pieces, large objects), and unregulated encroachment can make unpaved sidewalks dangerous, difficult, uninviting, hazardous, perilous, and risky. Unpaved sidewalks can be more dangerous at nighttime for walking due to limited visibility. Unfavorable weather can make unpaved sidewalks treacherous. These sidewalks are hard to maintain. Urban planners must make a mandatory requirement of properly designed construction of sidewalks. Public Works Department, Transportation Department, Road Department, Local Deputy Commissioner, ULBs, and other locally related departments should coordinate to incorporate sidewalks in the development plan. Planning departments in coordination with Public Works Department should have an ordinance in place requiring mandatory sidewalks. Public or private projects must not be approved by the local planning department without incorporation of sidewalks in the development plan.

Use of sidewalks for business and non-business uses, from positive perspective, is part of mixed-use design, walkable community, and environmentally sustainable communities by saving automobile trips. For the local residents, sidewalks provide easy and proximate access to services, extend convenience, and support local economy. Sidewalks are meeting places for local residents. Whether it is a planned meeting at the *chai-walla* or just run into each other, sidewalks play important role in social interaction. During festivals and parades, sidewalks act as uncovered pavilion for the spectator citizens.

The planners and designers should pay extra attention while designing, redeveloping, improving, or modifying the sidewalk feature of roads. Sidewalks in urban areas, in Indian context, are very interesting and functional element. Sidewalks are used for various purposes, other than walking, such as commercial, residential, industrial, temporary use, and for night stay. Sidewalks are public rights-of-way for use by citizens who prefer to walk. Safe, attractive, spacious, and well-designed sidewalks attract and invite more people to walk. Uses other than walking make sidewalks dangerous and sometimes leave no space for pedestrians. Non-pedestrian uses must get off the sidewalks or be part of the sidewalks with creative design.

Other uses on sidewalks are acceptable activities, if incorporated creatively. Sidewalks are occupied by cobblers (*mochi*), *chai-walla, phool-walla, pan-sigrut walla, fruit-* and *sabzi-walla* (vegetable vendor), temporary and seasonal vendors, and other similar type operators. These sidewalk entrepreneurs and operators cannot afford to rent a commercial space on permanent or temporary basis or cannot afford to pay heavy rent, utility bills, and insurance premiums. In addition, they get services at no charge such as street light, free space to operate business, free cleaning of space by municipality, free water supply (from municipality tap or from other business). These uses obstruct free and safe movement of people. In certain situations, these vendors park their equipment at the edge of the sidewalk and entrance to the street (perpendicular). Sometimes at a prime business location, they take away space from safe movement of traffic on the street (especially when making turns – cause accidents), and create unsafe, awkward, and inconvenient situations for pedestrians. The vendors leave trash and unclean sites behind them; this creates odor, unsightly situations, and slippery conditions for pedestrian and invites insects and rats. This is a serious code enforcement issue for ULBs. But creative efforts can find workable solutions for both sides.

10.12 Pedestrian planning – Sidewalks

Western pedestrian facility designers use body depth and shoulder breadth for minimum space standards. A simplified body ellipse of 50 cm × 60 cm, with total area of 0.30 is used as the basic space needed for a single pedestrian. In evaluating a pedestrian facility, an area of 0.75 for walking is used as the buffer zone needed for each pedestrian. In Indian context and depending upon the area, a multilayer pedestrian space calculation may be required to accommodate more pedestrians conveniently. (Fig. 10.5)

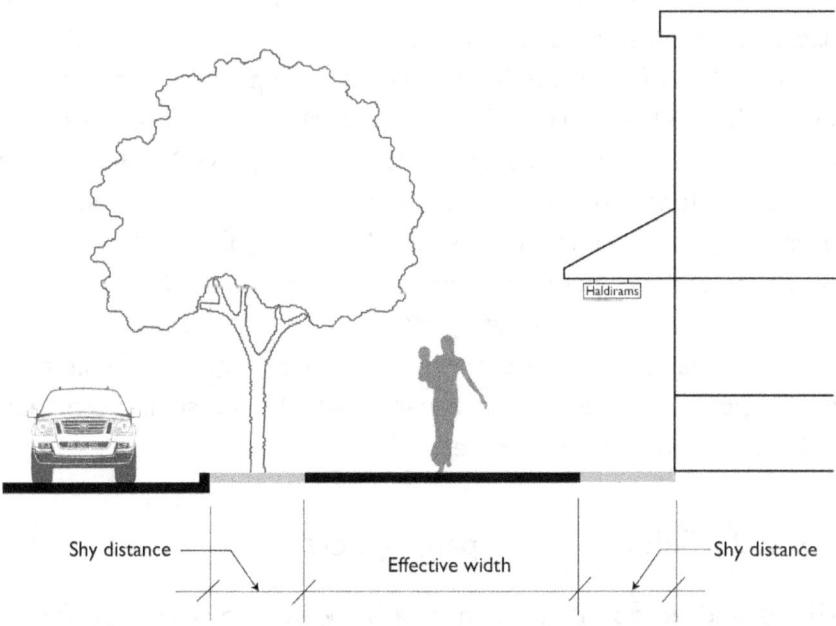

Figure 10.5 Effective side walk width can invite more pedestrian

Other design elements include:
- Wide enough to allow comfortable and multi-person walking;
- Designed for all ages of life;
- Should be kept clean – without trash, debris, junk, and spillage all the time;
- Provide well-designed and appropriate located trash receptacles;
- Landscape with indigenous species and decorative flower and trees;

- With proper, clear, and safe signage (e.g. proper height);
- Design with proper lighting; and
- Design with proper walking traffic signals (pedestrians should have priority over any other transportation mode).

10.12.1 Sidewalks as shelters

Sidewalks are for pedestrians. Some citizens, may be out of necessity, use sidewalks as shelters – day time and night time. Sidewalks are public rights of way not for individual's temporary or permanent ownership. Sidewalk laws should be enforced by the code or law enforcement agency. Through social workers, NGOs, ULBs, social and educational programs, this problem should get attention from every citizen. Occupancy of sidewalks at night time for dwelling purposes reflects negativity about the community. Not only that, once allowed, it encourages more people for the undesirable use. This may cause more crime in the city. Planning department in cooperation with other department should seek permanent solutions to this urban problem.

10.12.2 Sidewalks and panhandlers

Giving and accepting alms may or may not be legally permitted. But this is the way of life in Indian context. For whatever reasons, people like to give and accept alms. If the prospects are more to receive more alms, panhandlers select the site on permanent basis. Sometimes start living permanently with their families. These forced or volunteer dwellers have no running water, no sanitation, and no garbage collection. They do not contribute to the system but become parasites on the system and services. This is a negative reflection on the part of ULBs. Social workers, NGOs, ULBs, code enforcement and law enforcement should take the responsibility to remove this urban and human blight. May be these people need help. Agencies, institutions, organizations, and ULB should design a strategy to handle this situation by providing vocational training, education, and finding unskilled jobs and help them settle as contributing citizens. Educated citizenry and worship places activists should participate in this endeavor.

10.13 Planning and design considerations

For old areas of the city:

- Identify the study area along road/streets;
- Conduct a study of days of use, hours of use, types of uses, who uses, how long in operation, and any other peculiar local situation;
- Analyze the existing conditions, problems, issues, and challenges;
- Identify the individuals, institutions, organizations, and other entities who promote and support such activities;
- Determine the potential opportunities from the analysis;
- Select sites, locations, opportunities to retrofit the analyzed conditions and situations;
- Design sidewalks with creativity to keep people safe, without obstruction, and inviting;
- Accommodate identified uses and activities to sustain way of life and local culture;
- Designers can create small courtyards along streets and sidewalks, but away from the sidewalk, to accommodate non-sidewalk uses;
- Design should provide streetscape, street landscape, weather shelters along sidewalks;
- Design should accommodate signage for existing authentic (shops) businesses and floating businesses;
- Planning department in coordination with the urban local body must establish rules, regulations, policies, and procedures and follow them strictly; and
- Planning department should be responsible to review the performance and changes of the sidewalk every certain period of time.

For new areas of the city:

- Planners and designers must use experiences learned from the older city parts or from other cities;
- New sidewalks must be wide enough to accommodate pedestrians;
- New sidewalks should or should not be designed to accommodate other uses;
- New sidewalks should be designed keeping safety, functionality, cleanliness, design for all ages, and design for physically challenged citizens;
- New sidewalk design must consider shopping, commercial, and office uses requirements such as parking, signage, street lights, street landscaping and street furniture; and
- Local culture, way of life, and activities must be part of the planning and design process.

10.14 Cul-de-sac

This is a street with connection to another street from only one end; means a street open at only one end with sufficient space at the closed end for turning back vehicles. There is no through traffic. Mainly used by the residents of the street and visitors. Cul-de-sac streets provide privacy and minimize vehicular traffic, which results in a safe and quiet residential environment. On the other end is loop. This street design is for residential use. The use of cul-de-sac streets in subdivision design, however, requires skill and careful attention in detail. Used improperly, cul-de-sac streets may create problems related to traffic, water supply, emergency access, and drainage. Cul-de-sac streets may present pressure, taste, and odor problems in water mains if the water distribution system is not properly designed. The "loop" part must be designed considering the required turnaround radius for the delivery trucks and emergency response vehicles, e.g. fire truck, ambulance. Because of the lack of street connectivity, this design should be discouraged in the new developments. (Fig. 10.6)

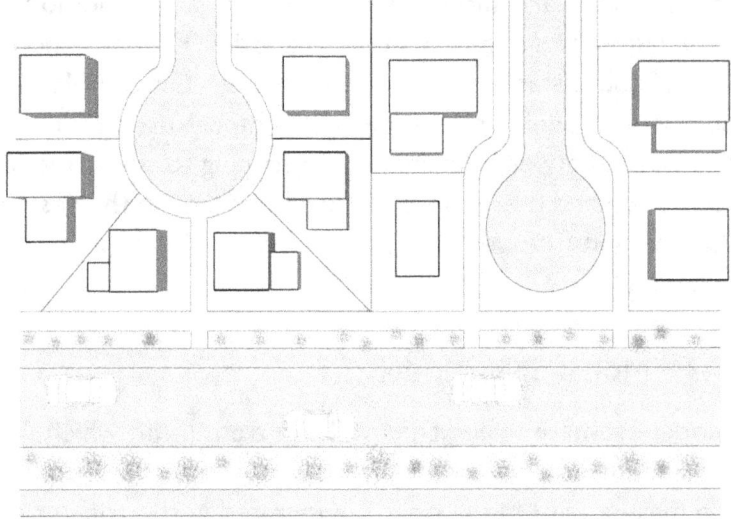

Figure 10.6 Various Cul-de-sac design

10.15 Transportation modeling

The estimation of transportation demand relies on tools that can predict one side of the land-use–transportation equation if the other side is known or presumed. Picking up the experiences from the West, now for many years planners have been developing and using models to estimate the transportation demand. Each model has several variations and limitations. There are four basic models:

10.15.1 Trip Generation Model

This estimates the number of trips generated by different types of land use. This model assesses the relationship between making trips and other elements. The elements determining the trip generation are vehicle ownership, household income, intensity of land use, and distance of the origin to the destination.

10.15.2 Trip Distribution Model

This estimates where in the city the generated trip will go. The study area is divided into zones. It analyzes trips made between the zones. In the early models, simple growth factor methods were used. The number of trips from one to another depends upon same function of the distance between two zones. "Gravity Model" and "Opportunity Model" are the most commonly used models. Trips are distributed between destinations according to the attractions of the destination and the inconvenience of travelling to the destination. The Opportunity Model predicts the probability of a trip ending in a given zone.

10.15.3 Modal-Split Model

The model estimate which trips will use transit and which will use private auto. In other words, which mode of transportation will be used to make a trip? Modal-split is integrated in the trip generation model and trip assignment model. When modal split is associated with trip generation stage, it does not take into account route characteristics. When it is related at the trip assignment stage, the modal split ignores the effects of choice of mode on the distribution of journeys. Modal-split choice or means or travel depends upon: (i) the properties of the journey, (ii) the properties of the traveler, and finally, (iii) the properties of transport system.

10.15.4 Traffic-Assignment Model

This assigns trips by each mode to actual or planned route. The selection of the route between the two zones is made by the traveler. A trip between the two zones can be determined from the network based on the minimum travel time and cost of travel between two zones.

10.16 Using the models

These models were developed in the Western world, where two modes of travel were dominant: automobiles and mass transit. Planners must critically evaluate before using these models in Indian cities. In Indian context, many transportation modes, slow and fast, work together. Land uses in the West are more segregated with specific uses in certain areas. Indian cities are more mixed-use type, which is an asset for Indian cities, provided people do not inject automobiles in them and control automobile population. In India, extensive use of automobiles is only a new phenomenon but use is very different, in certain cases, from the Western world. For example, automobile ownership in the older parts of a city is mainly to make long trips or a status symbol. There is no need of using automobiles to make short distance trips because of mixed-use land uses within walking distance, e.g. shopping, facilities, and services. In older city parts, the owners may not have parking on site or may be parking automobiles on the same premises they live. The vehicle may be parked somewhere else. Thus discouraging use of automobiles and making selective purpose automobile trips. The owners may have two-wheeler vehicles. The trip generation, trip assignment, modal-split, and trip distribution may have more or different variables.

Indian way of life, congestion on roads, proximity to services, narrow roads, joint families, inexpensive help (servants or volunteer help), and environmental issues invite walking trips, bicycle trips, rickshaw trips, *tonga* trips, or other environment-friendly modes of travel. This trend should be encouraged, marketed, and should be continued by the residents.

10.17 Land use trip generation

The complex city activities and to analyze transportation element better have enticed the need of forecasting land use, population growth, and economic activities, where the population growth and economic activities will occur.

10.18 Residential trip generation

In low-density residential development, the number of automobiles may be more than the mixed-use old section of the city or town. Traffic generation varies directly with the number of person living within the particular unit of area. The household size can also be directly related to traffic generation. Other variables to consider are family composition, household income, car ownership, other motorized vehicles ownership, non-motorized vehicles ownership, family composition, and environment awareness and availability of other modes such as three-wheeler scooter, taxi, rickshaw, tongas or other local modes of travel.

10.19 Commercial trip generation

Commercial land uses attract high intensity of trip generation. Types of businesses, location, and floor area ratio can be added to the measurement of the traffic generation. Peak travel times are critical in commercial areas. Peak hour trips, vehicle travel miles, level of commercial area can attract different types of customers with different modes of transportation. Office use has direct relationship with peak hour traffic and non-peak hour traffic. Office-use peak traffic hours are generally 7:00 AM to 9:00 AM and 4:00 PM to 6:00 PM.

10.20 Industrial trip generation

Industrial trip generation can best be correlated with employment. Industrial traffic, because of the shortness and sharpness of the peak period and its very high directional orientation, frequently constitutes much more serious problems to the adjoining roads than other land uses. Industrial traffic is more oriented towards morning or evening. Industrial traffic measurement can be tricky in Indian cities, industries being located in residential, commercial, and office use areas as well.

10.21 Recreational, religious, spiritual, and social trip generation

This category covers a wide variety of facilities and could be hard to measure. These trips are generated for destinations such as movie theaters, religious/worship places, melas (fairs), festivals, celebrations, and special events. It is common in Indian culture to make hooky trips. In some cases, big event, such as Kumbh Mela, can generate trips from all over the country even from other countries. Planners keep these vague trip generation factors in consideration, very hard to measure, associating with traffic and transportation elements while making estimates and projections.

10.22 Transportation study/survey terms

Peak time traffic: This is certain period of time when traffic count is maximum. In order to plan for maximum threshold and to know the level of traffic, this survey element is required.

Off-peak time traffic: This is certain period of time when the traffic count is low. This survey provides the details and difference between peak time traffic count and off-peak traffic count to plan the project accordingly.

Pedestrian volume: This survey tells number of pedestrians on road or facility. This element helps design pedestrian facilities and amenities along roads including width of sidewalks, pedestrian crossings, pedestrian signage, and road markings.

Average daily traffic: This survey tells average number of vehicles over 24-hour period. The details can provide average daily traffic on weekdays, weekends, Saturdays, and Sundays.

Hourly average traffic: The traffic count is conducted for peak and off-peak over a period of time to determine the maximum average traffic volume per hour. This helps for planning of traffic lanes, size of lanes, traffic signal, and other traffic elements.

10.23 Seasonal average and special events daily traffic

This survey is conducted to determine maximum seasonal volume of traffic for places of worship, entertainment, special events, and historic buildings and monuments (e.g. Taj Mahal). This survey, depending upon the project, should include other modes of transportation. This helps planners to design parking spaces, signage, access lanes to the facility, and exit plan.

10.24 Annual average daily traffic

The annual traffic represents the estimated or actual volume for the entire year. This survey is conducted to determine average annual (365 days) traffic. This survey requires 24-hour traffic count. Planners use this information to determine capacity, size, and road type. Planners may consider to include in the survey to obtain details about the speed of movement, origin-destination, and other modes of travel on the road.

10.25 Traffic volume study

This is to know the details of each type of vehicles passing the survey station. It helps in planning the roads.

10.26 Classified traffic volume

The survey may have a specific purpose to know the details of the traffic volume, types of vehicles, and other purposes such as determine causes of accidents.

10.27 Origin–destination study or survey

This survey is to determine origin and destination of trips. This survey can be specific and as detailed as planners and engineers want.

The foremost steps are to determine the purpose of the survey, goal of the survey, method of survey, and defining the study area. Various methods can be used to conduct surveys, such as roadside interview, post-card survey, home interview survey (External-Cordon Survey, External-Internal Cordon Survey), parking area survey, license-plate survey, tag or card method, commercial vehicle survey, work-spot interview method and other methods depending upon the purpose of survey. The analysis of surveys helps to seek solutions and alternatives.

10.28 Traffic congestion

The new transportation capabilities have made modern lifestyle possible and have contributed to the economic growth; the negative side of transportation capabilities is congestion. This creates debate about the advantages. Everyone complains about congestion; but behind the apparent complaint, there is a consensus that how the congestion be measured, how much is tolerable, how it costs in terms of money, social, time, and psychological, the characteristic of duration and extent of the problem. In Indian context, the relationship of slow- and fast-moving traffic makes it more challenging. Before the common use of automobiles, the movement was relatively slow. The expectation from the automobiles is to move fast. When this objective is not achieved, it becomes a problem of congestion. Historically, congestion is not a new problem. During the days of slow-moving vehicles, congestion was in existence then. There was congestion of rickshaws and tongas and slow-moving human-operated vehicles.

With the new habit of owning automobiles, the congestion in cities is likely to get worst. There is no standard or uniform expectation of how much congestion is acceptable. Using new and smart traffic management techniques, congestion can be reduced in the cities if not totally fixed. Planners should attempt to separate pedestrians and slow-moving traffic from automobile traffic. The challenge is bigger than it seems. Automobile ownership should be discouraged. People living in older parts of the cities with no parking facilities should not be allowed to own automobiles. They may own an automobile if they can justify a proper parking space on site or off site. Use of mass transit and bicycles should be encouraged. Automobile and some other users of congested areas should pay additional fees. Increasing congestion will force increased planning attention and involvements to focus on the traffic and transportation management and use of the existing system.

10.29 Safety

Around the world, over 500,000 people are killed annually in automobile accidents, and 15 million are injured. In the United

States, more than 40,000 people loose lives in road accidents. It is estimated that over 168,000 people die on roads in India. Safety is the heavily centered concern about transportation. Planners and engineers have done lot in designing safer roads. Roads and streets are well designed. Traffic signs are installed. Police men and women risk their lives to manage traffic manually. Traffic manuals are written to educate drivers by traffic engineers. Cars are equipped with safety devices nowadays. But much remains to be done. The main causes of accidents are careless drivers, driver behavior, drivers not following traffic rules, speedy drivers, adventurous drivers, underage drivers, inexperienced drivers, drunk drivers, faulty automobiles, careless pedestrians, slow and fast traffic together, careless cart/animal-operated vehicles/drivers, stray animals. Factors such as lack of street lights, ill-designed roads and streets, lack of proper traffic signage, faulty traffic signals, lack of proper traffic markings, unplanned police traffic barricades, unplanned military facilities, private traffic barricades, irresponsible traffic barricades by private property owners, and improperly designed traffic-calming techniques, e.g. speed humps, speed bumps. Illegal and improper actions by the property owners such as physical encroachment by business owners, and illegal occupation of premises along roads and sidewalks; overloading also contributes to accidents. In Indian context, other factors contributing to road accidents are irresponsible driving habits of bullock-cart operators, overloading and irresponsible driving habits of goods vehicles (trucks), distracting advertisement along streets, roads, highways, and freeways, mismanaged construction sites along roads and streets, and inclement weather (hydroplaning during rain).

Safety will continue to be a paramount concern in transportation planning. Every citizen, planning department, public works department, traffic and transportation, engineering department, police department, code and law enforcement, and other traffic and transportation related entities are responsible to perform their duties and responsibilities accordingly to reduce the accident probability to the maximum possible extent. In traffic management, improving safety while enhancing mobility, personal freedom, efficiency, aesthetics, and other transportation concerns is a continuous and ever changing balance.

10.30 Traffic-calming techniques

With use of automobiles came speed. Speed can be a challenge to safety. Socially, safety is a serious concern. Concerned citizens demand slower traffic, fewer large vehicles, no vehicles on streets not designed for automobiles even two-wheelers (scooters, motorcycles), limited access to local streets especially where children play (children should not play on streets), and slower through traffic from neighborhoods. Sometimes use of traffic-calming devices is controversial and political. Vital public services such as police, fire, ambulance, and public transit are affected. Also affected are local businesses and other users of the road.

The purpose of the traffic-calming techniques is to slow down the automobile traffic to avoid accidents and scary feeling to the pedestrians, especially along local roads and neighborhood streets. To plan and implement traffic-calming devices is expensive. In Indian context, while selecting any traffic-calming techniques, the planner must associate elements of pedestrian, bicycles, rickshaws, *tongas, rehris*, bicycles carrying other person (children, women, elderly person) and bicycles carrying goods (bicycles being used as goods transfer vehicle). The shoulder space, space between the carriageway and ROW (rights-of-way) must be considered while designing the traffic-calming project. The effectiveness of the techniques is mixed. Some of the traffic-calming devices are as follows:

10.30.1 Low speed curves

Curvilinear street design can help maintain vehicle-operating speeds within a desired range. Low speed curves are recommended in residential areas street design. The planner can adopt certain standards while designing the low speed curves, e.g. the distance between the point of tangent of the first curve and the point of the second should not exceed 155 meters (500 feet). When compound curves are used, a maximum ratio of the flatter radius to the sharper radius of 1:75:1 is recommended.

10.30.2 Traffic circles

Traffic circles are raised circular islands placed in-between intersections, cross-intersections, T-intersections, and intersections around which traffic flows. Typically, they are landscaped with ground cover, bushes, flowers, and sometime a monument to enhance the aesthetics appeal. The horizontal displacement associated with a traffic circle requires vehicles to reduce travel speed. The amount of speed reduction is positively correlated with the radius of the traffic circle and vehicle entry angle. Traffic circles are not recommended to be installed at intersections of streets that have a significant percentage of large size vehicles (e.g. trucks and busses) in daily traffic. A large size vehicle making a left turn generally cannot circulate around the island and has to make the turn in front of the island, thus increasing the chances for an accident.

There are various center island designs available. The planner should select which meets the site requirement most. Advanced circular intersection and advisory speed signs shall be installed. The advisory speed should be 20–25 km/h. The sign placement location depends upon the site conditions and other signing, but should provide adequate advance warning for drivers.

10.30.3 Median islands

Median islands are raised island placed along the roadway centerline to divert travel direction at that location. Typically, they are landscaped with ground cover, bushes, flowers, and small decorative trees to enhance the aesthetic appeal and visibility. The horizontal displacement associated with the median island requires vehicles to reduce travel speed.

Typically, the truck apron should be constructed. Mountable curb should be constructed to discourage passenger cars from traveling on the apron, while still allowing large vehicles to use the apron to make turns. Straight islands also can be used at intersections to control vehicle-operating speed. An object marker must be installed at each end of the island to guide traffic to intersection. "STOP" signs shall be used for side streets.

10.30.4 Roundabouts

This traffic-calming technique is similar to traffic circles. Roundabouts require traffic to circulate counterclockwise around a center island. Roundabouts are larger than traffic circles. Roundabouts can be used at cross-intersections or T-intersections of streets that have a propensity for traffic accidents.

10.30.5 Raised crosswalks

Raised crosswalks are elevated pedestrian crosswalks that are constructed similarly to speed humps. This alternative is used at locations that are likely to have higher pedestrian demand to cross the street. Raised crosswalks extend from curb to curb. Wheelchair ramps may be installed at each end to accommodate physically challenged citizens. Raised crosswalks should be marked as regular crosswalks. Pedestrian-crossing signs should be installed at raised crosswalks for both directions.

10.30.6 Curb exertions/chokers

Curb extensions are commonly used traffic-calming device that narrows the roadway width curb-to-curb. The curb is extended to the edge of the vehicle lane, generally at all four corners at an intersection or on both sides of a street at a midblock location.

10.30.7 Speed humps and speed bumps

Speed humps and speed bumps are both used to slow vehicles, but they have different designs and are selected for different places. These are most commonly used traffic-calming device in Indian cities.

A speed hump is a much more gently raised portion of the pavement surface extending across the entire travel width. Speed humps are typically 9 centimeters in height with 6.5 meters of travel length. Speed humps create a gentle vehicle rocking motion at low speeds, but they can jolt a vehicle at higher speeds. They should be painted to identify vertical change in the road. Sometimes they are called speed tables.

A speed bump is made of an abruptly raised portion of pavement. Speed bumps can produce substantial drive discomfort and sometimes injury. Speed bumps can damage vehicle suspension, and/or loss of control if encountered at high speed. Trucks, bus passengers, emergency response vehicles (police, ambulance, fire trucks) are likely to be affected. In Indian context, speed bumps are highly uncomfortable to bicycle riders, rehris, carts, animal-driven vehicles, bicycles riders with goods, bicycle riders with co-riders, and two-wheelers. Speed bumps can be injurious to pregnant women riding or co-riding a bicycle and can be very uncomfortable to children as co-riders and for two-wheeler riders. The purpose of speed bumps is to slow the fast-moving traffic but not to make ride uncomfortable and unsafe.

The planning department should incorporate traffic-calming devices in the development plan; establish design and construction standards; prepare traffic-calming / speed hump program policy; have spacing and location policy in place; have landscape policy (type of bushes, flowers, trees) with maintenance program; and enforce the policy strictly. No other USB or administrative authority or other department but planning department should be allowed to approve installation of speed humps and speed pumps in the city. During the resurfacing and repair of the road with speed humps and speed pumps make the project more difficult and costly. With lack of street lights and no proper markings, speed humps and speed bumps can be very dangerous, especially for two-wheel vehicles.

In our fast-paced society, slow traffic aggravates drivers. Those who have a deadline to meet – such as busy parents transporting school children or a businessman running late for a meeting – are spurred to take chances. Removing lanes and turning the road into an obstacle course creates frustration, leading to dangerous moving violations. Frustrated motorists make dangerous turns or run through red light. Drivers swerve around speed bumps into bicycle lanes to avoid damage to their vehicles. Some parents want to block off streets so their children can play on them. The flaw in this reasoning is that children should not be playing on the street in the first place. Safe play areas away from traffic and easily accessible to local communities are a much better solution. Correct the fallacy, don't legitimize it!

If safety is truly the goal, combine public safety education with an infrastructure that respects normal human behavior.

10.31 Mass/public transit

Mass or public transit plays a vital role in a city to transport large number of people. Urbanites rely on mass transit for trips to work, shopping, entertainment, worship places, educational institutions and other day-to-day activities. The no automobile ownership segment of the society depends on mass transit for mobility. The land use decision-making process must integrate with the provision of transport facilities. A walking distance hinterland for public transportation nodes must be established. The land uses within the hinterland must have higher densities. The design of the development should direct people to use mass transit. The design of the development or structure should discourage automobile ownership by providing limited garage facilities. The design should provide proximity to schools, shopping areas, entertainment, restaurants, health care facilities, social gathering places, open spaces, and providing community's basic needs within walking distance. Projects with higher densities such as mixed-use developments, walkable communities, and smart communities should be planned next to mass transit nodes. The land uses like single-family developments, large shopping malls, and large religious worship places should be avoided near mass transit nodes. These uses invite and encourage automobile ownership.

Buses are the main mode of public transit in Indian cities. They not only are practical in metro cities but also function well in small and medium cities. Planners should design new roads and remodel and redevelop old section of the city to accommodate buses. The size and maneuverability of buses must be considered. The local bus-stops should have space for buses to turn and stop for passenger pick-up and drop-off. The design should provide weather-protected passenger shelters. Bus stop shelters should be well-lit for the safety of the passengers, provide maps for the facility of riders, have proper signage to guide passengers, and have schedule to clean and maintain the premises. Advertising, bills, and graffiti should be prohibited.

To improve air quality and other environmental issues, the marketing department of the public transit should market the environmental benefits of riding mass transit than driving own automobiles. The mass transit organization should market the ideas "mass transit for everyone, not only for certain segment of society." The mass transit vehicles should be clean to encourage ridership. The maintenance of vehicles and quiet operation can invite additional ridership. The organizations should keep the vehicles exterior body advertisement free or without slogans or messages or any other writings or posters, otherwise this confuses the riders, discourage visitor riders, and repel riders not familiar with local mass transit system. The vehicles should have mellow, soft, neutral, or attractive exterior body colors with legible signage about the routes. Mass transit nodes should provide "guides" on site to assist patronage with required information. More ridership with mass transit will reduce traffic congestion; air, water, and noise pollution; reduce road accidents; and make living easy and comfortable, and pleasant.

10.32 Light rail transportation

Light rail transportation (LRT) is also known as subway, monorail, tube rail, elevated rail, and metro. This is a new public transportation system in India. The first public rail transportation system was introduced in Kolkata. Now rail system is active in Delhi, Mumbai, and Bangalore. Undoubtedly, public transportation is the most efficient way to move people and is an environment-sustainable travel mode. Light rail transit allows higher speeds by separating it from street traffic. LRT is characterized by its versatility of operation as it can operate separately from other traffic below-grade, at-grade, on an elevated structure, or together with road vehicles on the surface. Many European, American, and Canadian cities provide examples of successful LRT systems. The LRT terminals must be designed to accommodate large number of passengers, discharge of large number of passengers, multimodal connections, and connectivity to other public transit systems, safety, signage, lighting, and provision of information. Small- and medium-size cities should prepare regional LRT system to connect within the city and with other cities. It can reduce road congestion due to the automobiles.

10.33 Bus service transportation system

Connecting cities via buses plays a vital role. Urbanization is bringing people to the cities from villages and other urban areas. To stay connected with families, friends, relatives, and keep ties green with the folks, buses help keep connection. The bus fare is much less than the cost of driving a car, comparatively speaking. Various types of travel options can attract more ridership.

The planners, designers, engineers, architects, landscape architects, and other associated professionals should make the bus-stand/terminal facility passenger friendly. The design should pay attention to the needs of the passengers who are away from home and want to reach the destination. The facilities at the bus-terminal should be able to accommodate large number of people with varied responsibilities and assignments. Bus terminal facility is for: (i) passengers who come to the bus-stand to catch a bus to go to another place, (ii) passengers who get off the bus to reach to the final destination or get a connecting service, (iii) visitors for passenger pick-up or drop-off, (iv) regular staff to operate day-to-day activities of the bus stand, (v) temporarily staff or operators of buses (drivers, conductors), (vi) floating staff to help passengers with luggage or other needs, (vii) operators of connecting vehicles (*taxi-walla, rickshaw-walla, three-wheeler-walla*), (viii) business operators, vendors, squatters, and concession stand operators, and (ix) just visitors to the terminal to watch people and activities. The planners, designers, architects must provide sufficient waiting and rest areas, washrooms, and medical facilities according to the needs of the passengers and other occupants of the bus stand listed here. Bus stand facility must provide additional services of prepared food stalls, fruit stalls, gift shops, local city souvenir shops, cobbler corner, and digital corner providing power supply, Internet connections for phones, computers, and other related facilities. The architects must equip terminals with sufficient waiting areas and other related uses. In addition, they should plan to provide proper furniture and equipments to facilitate the passengers and terminal users.. The planners must keep future expansion of bus terminal facility and services in consideration while designing the project. The surrounding areas, beyond the bus stand property line, should be planned in coordination with the bus-stand facility. The uses around the bus terminal should be complimentary to the main facility. More than required parking spaces should be provided for the pickup vehicles, short-term parking, long-term parking, taxis, three-wheeler taxis, rickshaws, tongas, and bicycles. Newly designed bus terminals should have provisions of required parking. Design should provide spaces for other modes, bus stops for the local mass transit, directional signs, informational signs, police precincts, visitors and tourism assistance facilities, and other details associated with local culture and way of life. The facility should be equipped to accommodate all principles involved in the bus stop operation. If not, the facility is misused, abused, used as trash, using surrounding areas for open defecate, urination, and sidewalks for sleeping, dwelling, and other small level commercial uses. People providing connecting services generally congregate on a homemade bench installed under a tree or in a street corner, or occupying sidewalks, if not provided planned spaces for their use. The terminal facility should be well lighted and provide public phone and Internet service. The bus terminal should provide well-trained, Good Samaritan "guides" to assist passenger and terminal users.

As soon as a passenger gets off the bus will need a connecting mode to reach at the final destination. Other purpose for a traveler could be to catch a connecting bus service at that point. To reach at the local final destination, depending upon the choice of the passenger, could be a pick-up car, pick-up scooter, pick-up bicycle, taxi, three-wheeler taxi, rickshaw, tonga, or passenger may prefer to walk to the final destination if it is in close distance. For every transportation mode, planners have to pay attention to many details. The primary goal of a passenger is to reach the final destination without any hassle or discomfort or inconvenience. Through proper and detailed plan this can be achieved.

10.34 Rail transportation system

Railways make India move. Helps people reach its destinations. Unlike cars which provide privacy, ownership, and individual control, trains provide arena for multi-cultural interactions, closeness to social diversity, and exposure to different ethnic segment. Train stations are landmarks in Indian urban setting. They are social, centrifugal and centripetal points for cities, small or big, if directly connected rail line. The most interesting feature is that all segments and all strata of society travel through trains in India: rich, poor, all ages of people, and all kinds of people. Indian Railways does not ask your caste, color, creed, religion, language, ethnicity, domicile, or birth place when you travel by trains (wish all systems were like that). However, there are some facilities preferred based on gender, military affiliation, international tourist or visitor, etc. Trains are commonly used for both short and long distances. Like bus service, trains have similar advantages over personal automobiles of cost of travel, protecting environment, and avoiding hassle of self-driving. Railways have rights-of-way for movement of trains for passengers and goods. Here the focus is on passenger trains.

Historically, rail transportation system, local land uses, railway station surrounding land uses, urban form, urban development, and urbanization have played a strong relationship in Indian context. For many cities the urban form has been impacted by the rail system and level of availability of rail services. Trains have played a vital role in supporting urbanization due to the economies of travel cost, availability, dependability, reliability, and convenience.

Many features of rail transportation system are similar to bus service as discussed in the bus service transportation system section, such as needs of the passengers, requirements of the passengers, connectivity arrangements, facilities and services requirements, and railway station and outside railway station requirements. Railway stations play much bigger and complex role than bus stands in terms of passenger volume, requirements of the trains as vehicles, ROW maintenance, level of services, abrupt arrival and departure of passengers, trains with specific routes, some railway stations as junctions, some railway stations as origin point, some railway stations as final destination points, movement of personnel and goods of national security and interest, movement of large volume of goods, political and policy-making criteria, and national integration.

Railway stations are the starting points for cities. Someone could argue that City Hall is the starting point. Railway station attracts and diffuses more people than City Hall. Once the passengers leave the railway station premises, they become part of local urban fabric for social, economic, cultural, and other activities of the city. Whether permanent residents of the city or temporary visitors to the city, they become part of the local economic cycle and day-to-day life. Because of the railway activities, there are number of permanent and temporary personnel associated. They live, work, play, learn, worship, and contribute with other citizens of the city. Railway station activities impact the local activity and performance of the city. No city performs in isolation. Railways connects and allows interaction with other cities, towns, and villages.

Indian Railways policy makers, engineers, designers, planners should participate with the local urban planners, urban designers, architects, landscape architects, elected officials, business owners, civic groups to design railway stations, railway repairs and maintenance sections, railway employees residences, and other services provided and needed by the railway activities. Development of new railway stations or remodeling of previously built railway stations or improvement of existing railway stations should consider (i) impact on the immediate city, (ii) impact on the local economy, (iii) impact on the social life, (iv) impact and relationship of local social, cultural, and economic activities on the railway activities, (v) impact on the region, and (vi) present and future design elements associated with the city, local cultures, and local way of life.

The Indian Railways should plan and design both new and old railway stations keeping in mind the new life style, future needs and requirements of the passengers, and invite ideas from the local community and users of the system.

10.35 Waterways/boats means of transportation

There are areas which use local water bodies to transport people and goods. Boats and ships are no different from bus or railway service in their needs and requirements. They need adequate docking areas, proper facilities for passengers and goods, connecting services for passengers, facilities for boat operators, boat repair facilities, and protection from water hazards.

The planners should analyze the importance of local waterways and means of waterways in local context. The planning process must consider required details of the waterway transportation system.

10.36 Traffic management

Traffic management is part of the transportation planning because of volume of traffic, modes of traffic, and speed of traffic. The purpose of traffic management is to have safe, functional, smooth, and speedily movement of motorized vehicles, non-motorized vehicles and pedestrians. Traffic management helps direct the traffic to the desired routes, reduce congestion, and separate slow- and fast-moving traffic. Without traffic management, traffic can create chaos and accidents. Smooth and efficient movement of traffic increases efficiency of operation and activities. Traffic management can be conducted by traffic signals, traffic signs, and traffic markings.

Traffic control devices notify road users of regulations and provide warning and guidance for the reasonably safe, uniform, and efficient operation of all elements of traffic flow.

Traffic control devices or their supports shall not bear any advertising message or any other message that is not related or intended for traffic control.

Design, placement, operation, maintenance, and uniformity are aspects that should be carefully considered in order to maximize the ability of a traffic control device to meet the requirements of the control device. Placement of the traffic control devices should be within the road user's view so that adequate visibility is provided. Traffic control devices should be placed and operated in a uniform and consistent manner. Clean, properly mounted, legible devices in good working conditions are appreciated by the road users. Institute of Town Planners, India, should lead in coordination with other departments to establish and implement nationwide traffic management standards.

10.36.1 Traffic signals

Traffic signals are the most effective tool to manage traffic. These signals have three colors: red, yellow (amber), and green. The timing of the signals can be controlled remotely and manually. Signals can synchronized with the other signal's timing of activities. For example, the street traffic signal can be synchronized with the rail-crossing signals. Road signal could turn red prior to rail gate closing and could turn green as soon as the rail gate is lifted after train passes.

The installation of traffic signal should also take the pedestrian traffic in consideration.

Traffic signals are necessary to manage traffic at junctions or intersections. There are various patterns and designs that are used in traffic signals. Signals could be mounted on a pole or suspended on a wire between poles or signals on extended arms on the poles. In Chandigarh, administration has installed traffic signals at roundabouts. Roundabouts were planned and installed as original traffic management technique. A study should be conducted to measure the performance, effectiveness, and efficiency of these two separate but combined traffic management techniques.

10.36.2 Traffic signs

Traffic signals include regulatory or mandatory signs, warning and cautionary signs, and guide signs.

10.36.3 Regulatory signs

The purpose of the regulatory sign is to inform the road users of traffic laws or regulations, and to indicate the applicability of legal requirements that would not otherwise be apparent. The regulatory signs commonly used are "STOP," "KEEP LEFT," "TURN TO RIGHT," "SPEED LIMIT SIGNS," "PARKING SIGNS," and "DEAD-SLOW."

10.36.4 Warning signs

The purpose of warning signs is to provide advanced warning to the road users of unexpected or hazardous conditions. The warning signs commonly used are "NARROW BRIDGE," "ROAD CLOSED," "CONSTRUCTION AHEAD," "NO SHOULDER," "STEEP SLOPE OR HILL," "SHARP TURN."

10.36.5 Guide signs

The purpose of the guide sign is to inform the road user regarding positions, directions, destinations, and routes. Examples of guide signs are "NATIONAL HIGHWAY," "STATE HIGHWAY."

10.36.6 Traffic markings

The purpose of markings on the road is to provide guidance and information for road users regarding roadway conditions and manage traffic. These signs are made of words, symbols, lines, or dots. These signs use reflectors on roads, curbs, and medians. Markings are for centerline, edge line, object markers, delineation, turn markings, stop lines, pedestrian crossings, animal crossings, barricades, channelizing markings, and no passing zones.

10.37 Temporary traffic control

During events, festivals, religious celebrations, other celebration processions, constructions, repairs, and for security reasons, temporary traffic devices are installed. The installation of temporary traffic control devices are peculiar along military installations, police lines, bridges, toll booths, and other sites of national significance. The purpose of temporary traffic control devices is to provide for the reasonably safe and efficient movement of traffic and fulfilling the purpose, e.g. protecting construction workers or diverting selective traffic in case of military or security operation. There should be an advanced warning sign for the forthcoming temporary traffic control devices. Police, military, or any other security agency using barricades as temporary traffic control devices such as removable barricades, stones (in case of Indian context), bricks, cement blocks or dirt berm, flags, or manual diversion must consider safety of the road user and traffic, providing ahead warning, considering time, and weather conditions (rain, fog, or cloudy day). The responsible team must have plan in place to remove barricades, stones, tree limbs, or any other item used as a barricade – they are there for temporary reasons. These devices must be removed prior to night time for the safety of road users. Detours and diversions must be properly marked keeping in mind time and weather conditions. Detour is a temporary rerouting of traffic. A diversion is a temporary rerouting of traffic onto a temporary road or alignment placed around the temporary traffic control zone.

While installing temporary traffic control devices, other road users such as two-wheeler automobiles, three-wheeler automobiles, bicycles, pedestrians, carts, animal-driven vehicles, and human-driven vehicles, trucks, buses, and other modes must be kept into consideration for their safety and smooth flow of traffic. Proper lighting should be installed. Barricades and traffic-calming devices at the toll-booth areas must be property designed while considering signals, signs, markings, rest areas, U-turns, and physical barriers. Code enforcement authority should inspect these sites, approve their plans, and cite them if they do not follow the rules or create unsafe conditions.

10.38   Street lights

Using roads at night time need assistance of street lights to be safe. The streets should be properly illuminated. The placing of street lights, selection of type of lighting, selection of type of lighting poles, selection of spacing of street lights, and coverage of streets by street lights is critical for night time traffic and activities in a city. Some cities do not sleep, in other words cities are active round the clock. Street lights have a number of benefits, such as illumination of streets, help vehicles and pedestrians move safely and efficiently, discourage anti-civic activities, make city aesthetically appealing, make city look vibrant, and make city appealing from above.

To provide efficient and effective street lighting, planners must take into consideration the use of the road, purpose of the road, activities on the road, scale of the road, design of the buildings along the road, façade details of the road, landscaping along the road, natural and manmade features along the road and any other special or peculiar features along the road. For example, street lights in the cities of Varanasi and Amritsar should be according to the landmarks in the respective cities.

10.39   Parking

"No parking, No car". If one does not have parking space (off street or on street), one should not be allowed to purchase/own a vehicle. This should be the rule in every town and city and applicable to every citizen in India. One must provide valid evidence of availability of physical parking space on permanent basis. Obtain a non-transferable permit from the ULB, prior to owning an automobile. This should be implemented instantly and enforced strictly; no exceptions – no favors – no political backing – no administrative support – no variance.

Addition of automobiles to the already existing stock of vehicles is escalating the existing acute problem of parking spaces in Indian cities. There are cartoons showing people bribing GOD/gods/goddesses to be blessed with a parking space.

The increased resources, luring marketing techniques, availability of easy automobile loans, sincere and forceful recommendations by attractive Bollywood celebrities, and social competition enticing people to own automobiles. These marketing techniques do not suggest to have a parking space before buying and automobile. A car is an attractive social status item. Everyone, who can afford, is rushing to buy a car. Every day, in certain metro cities of India, more automobiles are sold than the number of days in a year. Automobile dealers should be legally instructed not to sell cars people sans parking – No parking, No Car.

Automobiles (cars, trucks, buses, two-wheelers and three-wheelers) occupy both horizontal and vertical space whether stationary or mobile. Automobiles use land while mobile and stationary land uses. In other words, use of automobile is a both mobile and stationery land use. Automobiles occupy road space while moving people and goods, not only the space for automobile itself but additional air space for safety from other vehicles, safety to other vehicles, safety for pedestrians and bicyclists. The roads are for sharing with other modes including pedestrian and bicyclists. Use of public rights-of-way is a privilege not a right. Vertical space matters for designing multi-level parking spaces, size of signage, and height of signage above ground, location of signage, and landscaping and streetscaping. Automobiles require parking spaces when stationary. Design process must consider these two types of automobile land uses. Nowadays, some families own multiple number of cars. In India, it is still common living as joint families in one household. Houses with joint/multiple families require multiple parking spaces. Automobiles add up additional chores of maintenance, washing, self-repair, and selling it. Some households with resources may own several automobiles not respecting environment but their showoff status. In Indian context, it is common among car owners to employ a driver to operate the vehicle. These jobs do not get paid handsomely. They are almost at the "exploitation of human resources" stage.

10.39.1 Parking facilities

In urban areas, parking is provided on-street, in surface lots, in underground garages, and in elevated decks. The dilemma is of theory of parking spaces vs. availability of parking spaces in Indian cities and towns. In Amritsar, old historic City Hall's park is converted to jammed parking lot. Furthermore, question is, are Indian cities and towns designed to accommodate automobiles, buses, trucks, non-motorized vehicles, bicycles, and pedestrian on the existing roads. These roads were designed and built for slow-moving traffic. Even if they were designed for vehicles, but then definitely not for this volume of automobiles. This means the system is stuffing more into something not built for.

For parking design, basic questions are as follows: How much parking should be provided? Where it should be located? How it should be designed? What will it cost? Who will pay for it? And who will manage and operate? According to the theory of parking spaces, there are two types of parking provision.

1. *Off-street parking:* Off-street parking is generally provided to satisfy zoning or other local government requirements. The required number of parking spaces can be based on many factors. These factors could be based on technical analysis of actual need or not. It could be based on experiences from other cities, towns, or other country or some old experience or a gut feeling, which may prove a rational approach or a failure. In the United States, sometimes an average parking supply is greater than demand.

   The off-street parking is provided at separate place from the road. This could be on a lot for specific use for parking, called parking lot. Parking decks, generally multistory, are used of parking garages. Underground parking can be multi-level too. The parking garages are generally either electronically or manually controlled. Construction costs could be heavy in this case. The multistory parking decks are a design challenge in the existing commercial areas. The design should be complimentary and compatible with the existing buildings. Another element is to consider is the design of façade at human scale level. A solid wall along the sidewalk may be uninviting or discontinuity of the fronts of the other buildings. Some decks design allows store fronts along the street to break the monotony of a solid wall. Special parking lanes are provided by the side of main thoroughfare for parking use only. This type of parking works well for temporary short-term parking, overnight parking only, or special purposes parking.

2. *On-street parking:* The automobiles are allowed to be park on the road along the road curb. This is managed through parking meters, smart parking meters, prepaid parking system, or authorized parking, e.g. local residents. This parking design takes up road space, creates congestion, and causes accidents. The roads allowing on-street parking must be wide enough to accommodate this feature. This can be a revenue source for the local government.

10.40 Parking design

Parallel parking, 45° angle parking, and right-angle parking are the most common parking spaces design. Each design has its advantages and disadvantages. Factors like availability of space, width of road, type of road, front or rear parking, types of vehicles parking, driver habits (e.g. parallel parking is difficult for some drivers), and other factors (e.g. local culture, way of life) help select the design of parking spaces. (Fig. 10.7)

So far, parking element has been addressed in terms of automobiles. For planners, parking is an acute problem in not only Indian cities but also Western world cities too. People should be encouraged to use mass transit, use of bicycles, walking, using non-motorized vehicles, using businesses offering delivery service, car-pooling, discourage personal car ownership, business/ shopping areas offering certain time periods but limited for shoppers with automobiles and educating citizens of environmental issues because of automobiles. Pedestrian-oriented (no direct automobile access) markets/shopping areas should be designed.

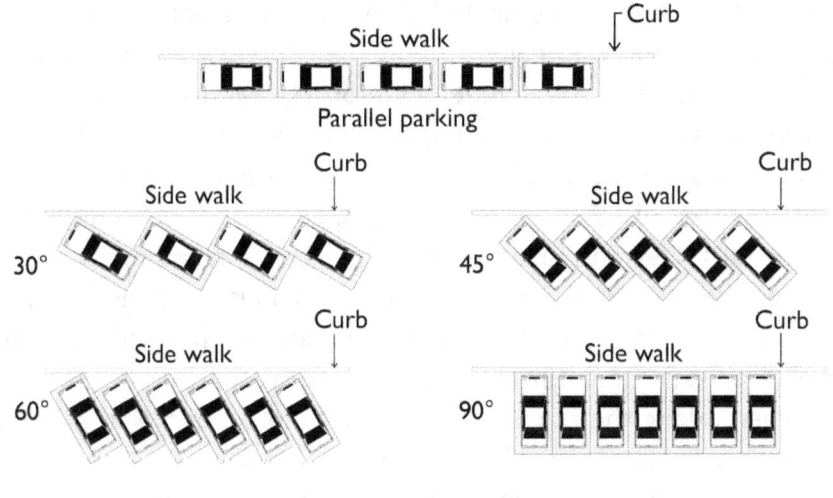

Figure 10.7 Parking design options

10.41 Shared parking

Engineers and planners should consider sharing parking options. Shared parking concept is becoming more acceptable and functional. It helps reduce cost and land consumption. Mixed-use developments typically have lower parking demands that those obtained by aggregating the demand for individual uses. To estimate share-parking requirements, parking demands for each time period can be estimated for each use and the composite demand computed. Different uses can have different times for parking use. In mixed-use development, office and retail can draw parking during day hours and residential can use parking during non-commercial hours. In Indian context, worship places should consider sharing parking with neighboring uses and vice-versa, and retail markets can consider sharing parking with nearby office operations. Shared parking concept can save land and project cost.

10.42 Taxis, three-wheelers, rickshaws, and tongas

Not everyone owns an automobile. Luckily, some provide alternate means to travel on hire basis. In Indian context, for long trips people use taxis and three-wheeler automobiles. Three-wheelers are also known as scooters, or sometimes motorcycles are converted to accommodate number of passengers to use as taxi. Innovative ideas and creative designs have invented vehicles, which are used to carry large number of passengers and goods. These are economical and fast means of transportation in Indian cities. Taxis also provide services between cities and regional connections. Taxis can be hired instantly along the road. There are sometimes pre-specified locations (planned, local municipality approved locations) or sometimes anywhere along the road, or under a tree, or unoccupied building front, or sidewalks, or public right of way locations are occupied by *taxi-wallas*. If the taxi stand location is not well designed, it causes congestion, confusion among road users, illegal occupation of public land or ROW, or unplanned use of land and premises and illegal parking or taking public rights-of-way for parking. These places are used for repair of taxis thus creating environmental issues. Generally, these locations and sites have no rest area facility, no rest room facilities, no water supply, and garbage collection system. Mobile phones have helped initiating such business anywhere along the residential and commercial areas. To protect the built environment realm and harmony and urban environment, such businesses should be regulated by the ULBs.

Rickshaw-wallas and *tonga-wallas* are commons means of transportation to hire for shorter trips in cities. They are economical and environment friendly. These transportation means help reduce automobile trips. Rickshaw use is also considered human exploitation and animal abuse in case of tongas. However, these means of transportations are in use for a long period of time and will continue in use for a long time. People with hardly any resources are inclined to become *rickshaw-wallas* or *tonga-wallas*. With the large number of human population and no veracious system to improve average human economic status, people will haul rickshaws to get ends meet. However, through intelligent and smart planning, planners can make their activities and toil comfortable to some extent. They can do the same in case of *tonga-wallas* and animals (mainly horses) tied to *tongas*.

Rickshaws play a vital role for daily commute in Indian cities. It is a common scene on Indian roads of rickshaws taking people to work, school, college, and shopping in the mornings. The same mode brings them back to their residences later. The trips are short but play a vital role in the operation of the daily economic activities of the city. Box rickshaws are designed to carry a number of school children. They are precious cargo. Engineers, planners, and transportation planners should pay special and extra attention while planning to accommodate this mode of transportation. The design should provide safety for operators and riders, separation from the fast-moving traffic, separation from automobiles, pick-up and delivery facility of passengers, parking spaces for rickshaws, rest areas for operators, public rest-rooms for the operators and passengers, and other related facilities. The design engineers should take a challenge to design safer, comfortable, and easy to operate school-children rickshaws. The engineers should design impact-resistant and balanced school-children rickshaws. These should be equipped with warning lights, warning sirens, high-rise visible flags, reflective paint and other precautionary measure. After all, they transport the future of the country. The changing technologies, making rickshaw operator's life easy, should be incorporated in the planning process.

National policies, state policies, and even local policies do not adhere to the needs and requirements to make operation of non-automobile hire services and operators part of the bigger picture planning and development processes. The local level development plans should make the operation of the non-automobile hire services and operators part of the plan. The newly developed and developing gated communities should accommodate and provide required amenities to and for non-automobile hire service providers and operators. Otherwise, they park their vehicles next to upscale, posh, and expensive development and well-designed signs and use the boundary walls to defecate, urinate anywhere, and throw trash randomly. The planners must consider requirements of *taxi-wallas, rickshaw-wallas, tonga-wallas* and other related type uses *wallas*, depending upon the local culture and way of life, while planning for the area/neighborhoods and during preparing redevelopment plans or redesigning areas. Non-motorized service facilities should be equipped with power/electricity supply, telephone connection, rest areas for operators, washroom facility for both genders, garbage collection and disposal facility, rest area and or waiting areas for the passengers, parking spaces for vehicles, and any other requirements because of local culture and way of life. Same planning and design techniques should be used in the commercial areas, markets, shopping areas, religious/worship places, recreational places, historic places, and other activity areas in the city.

10.43   Bicycles

Bicycles are not only economical and environment friendly but also good for human health. Bicycles take much less space on the road and occupy limited parking space. Bicycles are rarely the cause of fatal accident unless collision with automobiles or trucks or buses. Operation and use of bicycle do not create any noise pollution or air pollution. Bicycles are a sensible solution to the urban traffic congestion problem. In the older city parts of traditional cities of India, bicycles use should be encouraged and only means of transportation allowed, depending upon the conditions of the built environment.

The planners should design and provide bicycle parking spaces. Bicycle parking spaces should be closest or next to the facilities/buildings. Bicycle parking should be given due attention during the design process. Bicycle parking spaces and areas should be comfortable, convenient, vigilant, inviting, and safe and away from automobile parking or access, and well lighted. There are many attractively designed bicycle parking racks available and should be used to make bicycle use more inviting. (Fig. 10.8)

Figure 10.8 Suggested bike lane

While planning city roads in a city, city engineers, architects, planners and other professionals should coordinate to provide facilities and amenities to support, encourage, and sustain bicycle use. Bicycle-ride support groups should be formed in the cities. The benefits of the use of bicycles over automobiles should be marketed among citizens. Bicycle manufacturing associations should participate actively in the planning and design process. They should assist in marketing their product by educating and informing citizens of the social, environmental, economic, and health benefits of the bicycle use. They should support design and building of roads with bicycle lanes. Bicycle manufacturers should invest in research and development to make bicycles more efficient, attractively designed, improved engineering to last long, improved engineering for durability, and variety of bicycles for various uses and purposes and fit with the lifestyle of the user. One will notice, government cars provided to police officers, IAS officers, administrators, politicians, and other high-ranking officials are equipped with solid color curtains. How can they know what is existing and happening in the city with curtains on their cars? How they can make decisions without having first-hand empirical knowledge of the city and community. They should become role models for the community by using bicycles, and other professionals, civic group members, students, and citizens should join them.

10.44 Freight transportation and commodity transfer

Planners, transportation planners, and engineers need to understand the importance of freight movement in intra urban, inter urban, rural to urban, and urban to rural including global flow of goods that directly or indirectly affect the city. Freight movement is multi-modal. Freight is moved through trucks (large, medium, small size), trains, three-wheelers, boats, airplanes, two-wheelers, bicycles, animal-driven carts, manual carts/*rehris*, rickshaws, human beings, and other modes depending upon the local culture and way of life. Each mode has its own special features and advantages and disadvantages. Each mode has its own peculiarities to be understood by planners, transportation planners, and engineers. Depending upon the level of the economic activities, commercial activities, industrial products, and agricultural production of a city or a region, the type, size, and shape of freight-carrying mode depends upon it. The planners must understand the bigger freight picture of metropolitan areas or special areas, such as Mumbai, Delhi–Mumbai Industrial corridor, and international freight. In certain cases, today's businesses often require high quality transportation to assure quicker product deliveries, delivery on time, irrespective of cost. The delivery of perishable goods from hinterland may depend upon one mode versus movement of letters, documents, small packages, grains, heavy goods, may depend upon various modes prior to reaching the final consumer.

In older sections of a city, exceptions are there, roads are not designed to accommodate increased volume of automobiles. Accommodating automobiles with other modes of transportation on the same road is more challenging for planners. This creates very unsafe conditions for slow-moving traffic and especially for pedestrians.

There are three elements need to understand in transportation planning in any urban format. One, the transportation network in the existing or old part of the city; second, transportation planning for the new developments in and around the city, and finally, regional transportation lines connecting one city with other settlements.

10.45   Stray animals on roads

Cows, dogs, cats, bullocks, donkeys, monkeys, snakes, and other local animals are common sitting on Indian roads. Large and wild animals like elephants and bears are also visible in the cities. The animals as pets and under human control are acceptable to some extent. For some reasons, humans are advised to live in harmony with animals. Living in harmony with animals in countryside is understandable and justifiable. Countryside is blessed with lots of open space and no population and traffic congestion. Media covers stories about gang-attacks by stray dogs on humans. Stray dogs have killed children. How is this acceptable? Domesticated and controlled animals are part of human living.

The stray animals are in distress situations in the cities. They face unsuitable and cruel conditions and situations. A simple observation will make evident that the stray animals face dangerous situations against heavy truck, bus, and fast-moving traffic on roads. Sometimes human beings mistreat and abuse them too; some to the unacceptable cruelty level. Those animals are in search of food and safe shelter in the cities. Because of the nature of the activities on the roads, stray animals pose serious danger to themselves, humans, and traffic. Fatal accidents happen due to the presence of stray animals on the roads. The stray animals are unpredictable. It is impossible to predict the behavior of the stray animals on the roads. The stray animals on roads create hazardous and unsafe traffic conditions for all kinds of traffic: motorized, non-motorized, and pedestrians. They also make the roads and communities dirty, filthy, unhealthy, dingy, and sometime vulgar conditions. Unhealthy stray animals can spread diseases. The presence of stray animals on roads and communities reflects irresponsibility on part of the local governance and management.

Humans should be respectful and humane to the stray animals by managing them appropriately. The local governments should have animal control ordinances in place. These ordinances should be enforced strictly. Among other solutions are: building animal shelters, animal adoption facilities, veterinary solutions (neutering of animals) to curb growth, heavy fines for people feeding stray animals, fines for people releasing their animals loose, fines for people promoting unacceptable (negligence, cruelty, abuse) conditions for animals. Religious leaders should participate actively and coordinating with the local community in improving living conditions of helpless animals. Animals cannot speak for themselves.

10.46 Old city transportation planning

In older city parts, it is more intrinsic to consider space for automobiles in both positions: stationery and mobile. The roads, streets, alleys, and other access ways were not designed to accommodate automobiles. Further, the houses were not designed with one or multiple car garages, exceptions are there.

With the exception of few newly developed cities, majority are old cities. Interestingly, each city has its own history, identity, and evolution. Irrespective of how old is the city, it was not designed for automobiles. It is imperative to know the history and evolution of that settlement: the reason why the city has evolved this way. How and why the road network was laid out for that reason. Through planning process the history and design must be recorded. That should be followed to redesign, redevelop, or physical change for any reason. Planners, architects, and designers should preserve the original layout of the city streets and surrounding built environment.

10.47 Airport planning

Air travel is fast and efficient, generally no congestion, at least in the air. With growing economy and time being more valuable, both domestic and international air travel is becoming popular. Many airports in India have "international airport" designation. The cities with successful trade, commerce, and technology exchange nationally and or internationally, airports play an important role. Airports provide venue for passenger and cargo travel to and from other airports.

Planning, design, and management of airports are emerging technical fields both local and international. Airports are comprised of huge variety of facilities, systems, users, workers, rules, and regulations. Airports have serious impact on local economies, surrounding land uses, and pollution issues such as air, noise, particles, and water. A brief role of airport planning is discussed in this sub-chapter.

10.47.1 Selective definitions

Enplanements: It is used to describe the number of passengers that board an aircraft at an airport.

Deplanements: It is used to describe the number of passengers that deplane an aircraft at an airport.

Airport operation: It is used as a measure of activity at all airports, but is the primary measure of activity at general airport.

Local operation: When an aircraft takes off and lands at an airport without landing at any other airport, the aircraft is said to be performing local operations.

Itinerary operation: It is a flight that takes off from one airport and lands at another airport.

Based aircraft: It is an aircraft that is registered as a "resident" of the airport.

Airside of airport: Such as the planning and management of runways, taxiways, navigational aids, gates, and aircraft parking areas.

Flight schedule monitor: It is a primary component of collaborative decision making. Also a support tool that collects and displays arrival information, retrieves real-time demand, and schedule information, monitor ground delay performance, and provides "what-if" analysis capable of projecting arrival rates, slot availability, and departure delays.

Basic or general utility facility: Basic utility airports are designed to accommodate most single-engine and small twin-engine propeller-driven aircraft.

Airfield: This includes all the facilities located on the physical property of the airport to facilitate aircraft operations.

Airspace: Surrounding an airport is the area, off the ground, surrounding the airport, where aircraft maneuver after takeoff, prior to landing, or even merely to pass through on the way to another airport.

Landside: Components of an airport are planned and managed to accommodate the movement of ground-based vehicles, passengers, and cargo.

Terminal: Component is primarily designed to facilitate the movement of passengers and luggage from the landside to aircraft on the airside.

Ground access: Component accommodates the movement of ground-based vehicles to and from the surrounding metropolitan area, as well as between the various buildings found on the airport property.

Primary runway: The runway that is oriented into the prevailing winds.

Crosswind runway: In areas with winds that blow from various directions at sufficient wind speeds and/or accommodate primarily smaller crosswind directions. These runways are known as crosswind runways.

Runway designators: This identifies the name of the runway by the runway's orientation. The runway number is the whole number nearest one-tenth the magnetic azimuth of the centerline of the runway, measured clockwise from magnetic north. The letters differentiate among left (L), right (R), or center (C), parallel runways, as applicable.

Runway centerline: This identifies the center of the runway and provides alignment guidance during takeoff and landings.

The centerline consists of a line of uniformly spaced strips and gaps.

Runway threshold markings: This help identify the beginning of the runway that is available for lands.

Approach lighting systems: This provide the basic means for aircraft to identify runways when operating in poor weather conditions.

Visual glideslope indicators: Visual glideslope indicators are lighting systems located adjacent to runways on the airfield to assist aircraft with visually based vertical alignment on approach to landing.

Visual approach slope indicators: It is a system of lights so arranged to provide visual descent guidance information during an aircraft's approach to a runway.

Precision approach path indicator: It uses light units similar to the visual approach slope indicators, but they are installed in a single row of their two or four light units.

Runway end identifier lights: These are installed to provide rapid and positive identification of the approach end of a runway.

Runway centerline lighting systems: These are installed on runways to facilitate landing under reduced visibility conditions.

Touchdown zone lights: These are installed to indicate the touchdown zone when landing under adverse visibility conditions.

Holding areas or run-up areas: These are located at or very near the ends of runways for pilots to make final checks and await final clearance for takeoff.

Holding bays: These are apron areas located at various points off taxiways for temporary parking of aircraft.

Obstruction lights: These are implemented to warn pilots of their presence during daytime and nighttime conditions.

Location signs: These are used to identify either a taxiway or runway on which the aircraft is located.

Air traffic control tower: From control towers, air control personnel control flight operations.

Passenger handling system: This is a series of links and processes that facilitate the transfer of passengers between an aircraft and one of the modes of the local ground transportation system.

Flight interface: This provides links between the aircraft gates and passenger processing facilities.

Passenger processing facilities: The major processing activities required to prepare departing passengers for use of air transportation and arriving passengers to leave the airport for ground transportation to their ultimate destination.

Airports are among the largest public facilities in a city. Airports play significant roles in shaping economic, social, political, and planning landscape of the communities where they are located.

10.48 Economic action of airports

It is well recognized that a viable, efficient, and cost-effective transportation system is a fundamental and necessary component of a vibrant economy of a region or country. Transportation provides means to move people and goods. This movement generates trade and commerce. This movement leads to creation of employment, diversifies revenue source, and other benefits with forward linkages and backward linkages.

Aviation has a special role in intercity and international movement of people and goods. This system is complimentary to automobiles, railroads, trucks, ships, and other modes of transportation. Airports are the gateways to the nation's aviation system providing air transportation for the surrounding communities. This system connects major metro centers in much less time than taken by land means. Access to markets around the nation and world has resulted in the large and small communities reaping extraordinary economic and social benefits. Commercial air carriers provide access to air transportation between major metropolitan areas of the country. Communities without airports or sufficient air service have limitations placed on their capacity and opportunities for economic growth. The local direct economic activities generated by the regular expenditures of resident employees, the airport also stimulate local economies directly through use of local services for air cargo, food catering, airport services, aircraft maintenance, airport maintenance, ground transportation, and communication services on and around the airports. Earnings from direct and indirect economic generators further act to recycle money within the local community as money pass from one entity to another. This multiplier effect operates and generates economic money cycle in the communities with airports. Airports are source of revenue for local, state, and center level governments. They diversify the tax base for local communities. In addition, as forward and backward linkages of hotels, restaurants, shopping, and tourist attractions benefit economically from airport systems.

Airlines are capable of providing very unique services during natural and manmade hazards. Aircrafts can approach inaccessible areas to provide help and assistance to the people in disaster-impacted areas. They can provide medical help and food supply in short period of time. Sometimes, providing help is critical in disaster-prone areas. Politicians can visit the disaster-prone areas through helicopters and small planes to sympathize with the affected people.

10.49 Environmental issues of airports

Airports have great positive economic, social, and other benefits but like other built environment, airports have their share as well on the environment. The surrounding communities and natural environment gets impacted by the airports. These effects are a result of activities whose source is the airport itself and vehicles, both aircrafts and vehicles on ground, and connecting activities such as trucks, busses, and taxis.

10.49.1 Noise

Perhaps the most significant impact associated with airports is the noise that emanate from aircrafts with engines running on the ground and movements to and from the airport. Communities around the airport experience this nuisance and main source of complaints and opposition during the development of airports. Expansion of airports gives another opportunity to the neighboring communities to complaint about noise generated by the airports.

Noise is responsible for obstructing peaceful living, disturbing sleep, interfering with conversation, detracting from enjoyable use of property, and creating a nuisance. There is increasing evidence that high exposure to noise has adverse psychological and physiological effects, and the people repeatedly exposed to loud noises might exhibit high nervous tension, high stress level, and inability to concentrate.

The reduction of aircraft noise at the source, by using quieter aircrafts, is supplemented by an ambitious program to encourage compatible land uses in areas around airports, for example warehouses, storage places, and industries. Other means to mitigate noise is construction of sound barriers and sound proofing of buildings, creating and extending buffers between airports and surrounding communities, and capacity limitations.

10.49.2 Air quality

The emitted pollutants from aircrafts on ground and air, emissions from the ground vehicles and other vehicles associated with airport system reduce the air quality to a far extent. In addition, industrial facilities and operations associated with airports, including generators, HVAC systems (Heating, Ventilation, and Air-Conditioning), fossil-fueled equipments, painting materials, paving operations, construction activities, and fuel-dispensing operations all contribute to emissions of concerns to air quality. The major pollutants are sulfur dioxide, carbon monoxide, nitrogen oxide, suspended particulate matter, and volatile organic compounds such as hydrocarbons, asbestos, inorganic arsenic, beryllium, mercury, benzene, vinyl chloride, and radionuclides.

10.49.3 Water quality

An airport can be a major contributor to add pollutants to water. Sources of water pollution are domestic sewage from airport facilities, industrial wastes such as fuel spills, and high temperature water degradation from various operational plants at the airports. The installation of treatment plants at the airport facilities can help mitigate to maintain water quality. Airports should be required to prevent the discharge of any pollutants in natural environment.

10.50 Airport-planning process

At the local level, the preparation of the airport master plan for the planning of airport is the most important document. Master plan identifies the process of developing an airport with future goals. The magnitude and details of the master planning depends upon the size and purpose of the airport. The process includes support and consensus from other organizations and departments. Master planning is complex for a large airport versus for a small airport; the document and approach could be simple. Generally the master plans are for 20 years of planning horizon; however, the documents must be reviewed so often to assess the outcome of goals.

The master plan can be a guiding document for future development that will meet the aviation demand and be compatible with the community development, environment, various associated modes of transportation, and other airports. The land use section of the document should consider appropriate zoning, zoning of surrounding areas, incorporation of agricultural lands, water bodies, if any, nearby, and automobile type uses.

Other zoning requirements could include, for structures in the surrounding areas, type of roof, color of roof, building foot print orientation, shape, size, and type of windows, type and location of doors, buffers between buildings, and building of berms at appropriate locations.

In nutshell, the master plan study should include:

- Forecast of aviation demand
- Preliminary site selection
- Airside requirements
- Landside requirements
- Transportation survey
- Economic impact
- Level of various services – internal and external

- Environmental plan
- Final site selection
- Cautions against future problems and issues
- Future expansion plan for the airport and surrounding areas
- Forward and backward linkage industries
- Financial plan
- Management plan

An airport is a business like any other business. It must be planned and managed to succeed and meet the established goals.

10.51 Conclusion

A need has always existed to move people and goods between various land uses of an urban area, and to deliver certain services for those uses. An inefficient transportation system will decrease personal mobility, will be costly and time consuming, will make the urban economy less efficient, and will make the overall quality of life in an urban area less attractive. Problems currently afflicting urban transportation systems include travel and traffic peaking, facility congestion, diffused travel pattern, competition among slow and fast modes on the rights-of-way, and newly cultured dependency on automobiles. Another problem is design oriented: design and construction of roads without consideration of social, cultural, and local way of life. Traffic and transportation professionals should work together to assure that transportation act as a link between social and economic activities of a city.

Chapter 11
Historic preservation

11.1 Introduction

History is an interesting tool to learn about the past. History is vital to connect happenings of present with the past. Experiences of the past helps to design present and future. The history could be skewed and biased depending on the writer or narrator. We may not know in what context event happened in the past. The only historic truth is that events occurred. Many forces impact the compilation of the past. Interestingly, historic buildings, historic features, historic sites, and historic monuments can tell us a lot about the past. Studies and research can tell us about the design, planning, materials used, selection of colors, layout, purpose, style of era, influence of that time period, facades, interiors, subsidiary features, types of architecture, themes, connectivity, influence on the surrounding areas, influence of the surrounding areas and other related elements.

India's historic past is a big asset to India, Indians, and the world. Through various phases of history, India witnessed evolution of changing architecture, shape and form of buildings, and their influence on the way of life. India's historic features attract people from all over the world. The world and other cultures have always appreciated and recognized our culture and architectural heritage. Historic features have social, economic, psychological, and physical benefits. The focus of this chapter is on historic features, which include historically old buildings, historic monuments, sites of historic importance, and other features (historic trees, water bodies, topographical features). Social benefits are connectivity to the past, importance of heritage, cohesiveness among the community, learning experience, and guide for the future for the society as a whole. Historic features connect the present with the past. It reminds of the good and not so good happening at that time. Eternity is an ever changing element but keeping track helps community to carry on the legacies and avoid committing same mistakes. Learning and understanding heritage make communities more stable and keep them connected with each other. Cohesiveness of a society is the founding element to maintain culture and help them grow. The buildings, sites, and other features associated with spirituality provide a special service to the mankind. Economic benefits are tourism, connected economic activities, and connected services. Historic features attract local, regional, national, and international tourism. People come from various places to appreciate the features. India is rich of such places. The tourism is source of revenue for administrative entities, hospitality industry, food industry, transport industry, and other opportunities related to the specific site. Such places generate jobs and other economic opportunities. Connected economic opportunities develop due to the requirements of the historic features, e.g. manufacturing of souvenirs, printing of information brochures, manufacturing of art replicas, incentives to artists and other related opportunities. These places also can require connecting services to assist tourists, e.g. tourist guides, taxis, facility maintenance experts, and other professionals and experts depending upon the needs of the facility. Psychological benefits may not be measurable in case of historic features but do provide opportunities to people of all ages to connect to the past, spiritual attainment, and individuals may have their own definition of benefits.

There are arguments against preservation. Why commit to preserve the past when challenge is in the future? Preservationist hampers growth and development is another notion. Historic features come in the path of new development.

With the fast development we are losing many historic features. They are irreplaceable. It is our duty and responsibility as a society to preserve and protect them. These historic features are unique, deep rooted, and rich. They are the jewels of their time.

11.2 Historic districts and ordinances

Communities establish historic districts for a variety of reasons. Some create them simply as a means to protect significant historic features. Some establish historic districts to protect against specific threat of development, while others want to encourage development in the older area. Some communities use historic districts as a tool to maintain historic value of the features and others because they contribute to an improved image of the community. Examples of the various reasons can be identified in many older cities of India, e.g. Delhi, Amritsar, Madurai, Agra, and Kolkata just to name a few.

The purpose of the ordinance can also include safeguarding the historic features of the local community, stabilize and improved property values, foster civic beauty, strengthen the local economy, promote the historic district for the education, pleasure, and welfare of the citizens.

The Historic Preservation Ordinance can provide establishment of historic district, acquisition of certain resources for historic preservation purposes, preservation of historic and non-historic features within historic districts, establishment of historic preservation commission, maintenance of publicly owned resources by the local units, procedures, authority to implement, and certain types of assessments under certain circumstances, remedies and penalties, and authority to manage the publicly owned resources.

11.3 Documentation and designation of individual historic properties

There is a large amount of historic features in India. They are spread all over the country. Each feature has its own merit, significance, and importance. Interestingly, many enthusiastic preservationists have toiled to prepare extensive and intensive records of historic features. Government of India keeps records of historic features, which may not be extensive according to some preservationists. The planning department in cooperation with other experts (architects, archeologists, historians) should compile a master list for their respective areas for historic features. The list should be saved electronically. Geographic Information System can save historic features data layer with other data. GIS can help share the data with other entities without distorting the base information.

11.4 Historic buildings

For this chapter, historic features are historic buildings, historic monuments, historic sites, historic trees, historic water bodies, historic topographic landscape and others. A roaster of historic buildings and their use should be prepared. It is common in India that people pick a feature put a little fire, ribbon, incense, colored powder or paint to signify as historic feature. At worshiping places, people start donating money or other offerings, without knowing any religious, historic, or cultural value or relationships. Some people take advantage of this situation and collect money and offerings for personal benefits. This becomes their source of income. These kind of places create nuisance for traffic, nearby businesses, and for people living there. Sometimes people raise objections for development and redevelopment in that area on the subject site. These installations are placed without any approval or permission from a local authority. Local municipalities have no record of such activities. Local authorities should be cautious of these activities, keep records, place ordinance with restrictions and permits required, and enforce the law with punishment. Welfare of the citizens is the core responsibility of the local government. The consequences of these activities defy the inherit purpose of safety, health, and welfare of people. Identifying archeological and planning elements is considered for preparing historic preservation plans.

11.5 Architectural style

All buildings have certain elements that project their style of architecture. Historic buildings are commonly described in terms of their architecture. They may have historic significance attached to that. Combination of these features makes the building even more significant. There are many and varied architectural styles common in India. Depending upon the area or region, they have extended significance of their style. Experts should be involved in identifying and recording architectural style of buildings. In Indian context, type of religion, material availability, local climatic conditions, choice of the project manager, and local culture have impact on the final product.

11.6 Architectural character

Architectural character is the collection of features that give the building its uniqueness and authenticity. The character itself is not necessarily the style. It is rather a combination of things that make a building "architecturally correct," ranging from the local interpretation of the style i.e. the vernacular. The list of elements is as follows: form, massing, rhythm, and symmetry, foot print of the site, materials, primary and secondary type, texture, and color, craftsmanship, roof type, color and finish, degree of articulation, details, and finishes, windows, openings, solid-to-void ratio, doors, entrances, exits, openness, and cohesiveness.

11.7 Identify character-defining elements

The following is the list of architectural elements that define a structure. For restoration purposes these elements are important.
- Roof shape
- Roof treatment

- Towers, domes, imaret, minaret
- Horizontal and vertical shape
- Walls, including material and delineation
- Load bearing walls, including material and delineation
- Window, types and pattern, including window surrounds and reveals
- Skylight (lantern spaces, decorative sky light)
- Entrances, doors, including door surrounds and reveals
- Façades (front, side, and rear)
- Interior features such as verandah, lobby, porch, interior open square, courtyard (names differs in areas)
- Staircases, style, material, railings, gates, grills, columns, pillars

11.8 Design issues

When preserving a historic building or adding to a historic building or a new building in a historic district, an architect or designer should look carefully at the question of contextualism. Contextualism yields contemporary architecture that is sensitive to and compatible with the context surrounding it. Generally, matching, contrasting, and compatible approach is taken. In the matching approach, new architecture imitates the old is meant to fit in as coherent piece of the historic fabric. Contrasting design follows the logic that the new and old should be district because each is a product of its own era. Compatible design, the most common of the three approaches, suggest that new design be sensitive to historic structures and compatible with them in terms of, size, scale, shape, color, material, and character of the property or environment. The ordinance should provide design guidelines with administrative flexibility.

11.9 Buildings not listed

Buildings not listed in the existing records or documents or research should be included in the master list and maintained on the GIS.

11.10 Walk-through and walk-around

The walk-around and walk-through provide a thorough visual inspection of the building, site, or monument. The walk around is a critical look at every square inch of the building from the ground through the roof. This is an organized inspection with intentions of covering details.

The walk-around is an organized walk around the building, site, or monument. Each façade must be inspected thoroughly to identify the features and elements.

These exercises are applicable to the non-expert in preservation to understand the process of historic preservation.

11.11 Preservation economics

The economics of historic preservation is an important issue. Especially when there is large number of historic features. The cost/benefit analysis for maintenance and rehabilitation of a historic feature is typically more complicated than a new construction. Who is responsible for the maintenance and upkeep of the historic features? Someone once described historic preservation is an expensive art and hobby.

11.12 Other features

In India, sitting of historic monuments, old buildings, historic sites, historic trees, historic water bodies, and topographical features is common. Sometimes it is hard to determine if the building is just old or it is historical. Once a master list is prepared, maintenance and preservation share of budget should be part of the process. The cost recovery could be made with visitor's charge, taking share of sales by local businesses, or selling of souvenirs or researchers working on the feature.

Chapter 12
Utopian planning

12.1 Sustainable communities

There is lots of literature and writings available about planning and designing sustainable communities. Many other names have been employed to identify the sustainability concept, such as new urbanism, walkable communities, smart communities, livable communities, lifestyle communities, and other titles. Many definitions have been proposed to explain sustainable communities. The present urban design has official or unofficial, professional or unprofessional, and civic or non-civic fundamental responsibilities to build communities considering environment to the extent to conserve and protect resources for the next generation. Following are some of the development considerations to create sustainable communities.

12.2 Mixed-use design

In Indian context, described within this book, mixed-use development is acceptable by masses of urbanites. Developers, builders, architects, engineers, urban planners, and other professionals should give a new design element to widely accept mixed-use practices in cities and towns. Mixed use is locating shopping, stores, offices, residences, schools, worship/spiritual places, and recreation spaces within walking distance of each other in compact neighborhoods and providing pedestrian-oriented streets. Mixed use promotes free movement for all ages especially for young and elderly population, reduction in auto use, walkable and easy access to markets, safety in areas because of presence of people and propinquity, supports home occupation or telecommuting, and social activities.

12.3 Efficient use of limited land resources

With large population base and policies to provide housing to every citizen of India may be practical but will occupy lots of prime land. In addition of land for housing, more land is needed to provide services and economic activities for the habitable population. Land is required for infrastructure such as roads, streets, sidewalks, and streetlights. Land is required to grow food, grazing for animals, forests, and water bodies. Sustainable development supports the preservation of land and natural resources. These benefits result from compact building forms, infill development, vertical development, and moderation in street and parking spaces. Farmland and open spaces need to be protected from urban expansion. Compact development shortens trips, lessening dependence on the automobiles, therefore, reduce levels of energy consumptions and air and water pollution. The new wave of farm housing should be controlled by installing regulations and policies by both cities and villages.

12.4 Transportation alternatives

Pedestrian or motorist or transit user wants safe, convenient, and efficient transportation. These performance factors affect sidewalks, bicycle, and street design, parking placement, and location of buildings. Well-designed sidewalks and bike lanes protect people from vehicle accidents. People tend to use more these provisions if safe. Convenience begins with a connected network of streets that provides alternative routes with reasonable walking distances between destinations. Providing compact, mixed-use development connected with safe and convenient networks of streets, bikeways and sidewalks encourages walking, bicycling, and transit as alternatives to driving. Thus streets have less traffic congestion and less air, water, and noise pollution. Mixed uses provide convenience, density, and variety of uses necessary to support transit, and lower traffic speeds, making roads and communities safer.

12.5 Optimum use of urban resources and services

The frugality of land development supports efficient use of public and private infrastructure. Sustainable development means creating communities where more people will use existing services like water lines, sewer system, roads, schools, health facilities, worship/ spiritual places, and emergency services (police, fire, ambulance). Inefficient land use places financial burden on communities trying to provide infrastructural needs. Jurisdictions have to allocate financial resources to operate, manage, and maintain infrastructure. All developments do not have to be of the same level. Smart allocation of resources for different types of developments can support sustainability. Careful street sizing and accommodation of parking on street or on areas not fit for development or human habitation can support the cause.

12.6 Human scale designs

Community's acceptance of compact, mixed-use development and walkable access to activities requires compatibility between buildings. This approach ensures safety, privacy, propinquity, and coherence. Similar massing of buildings, orientation of buildings to the streets, presence of windows, front verandahs, front courtyards, porches, and other building elements depending on the area of development support sustainability. The provision of play areas, gardens, and play lots designed at human scale will get support from the community. In addition, planning for *"wallas,"* provision of adequate parking spaces, and balancing with landscaping contribute to successful compatibility between diverse building types.

12.7   Green built environment

Sustainability encompasses and advocates use of green materials to build per Integrated Habitat Assessment Standards. The standards are at evolutionary stages. The designs incorporating available details for green buildings will push for acceptance by the development industry. The architects and planners by supporting and marketing the green building concepts can contribute to sustainability of communities.

12.8   Green environment

The cities, towns, villages, neighborhoods, streets, roads, wherever feasible and suits, should be dressed with indigenous and locally adaptable landscaping. Decorative trees, flowery trees, and other types of landscaping should garland urban streets and roads. Vacant spaces should be planted with trees. Green environment and urban forestry has advantages for humans and animals. Green environment helps reducing pollution, storm water run-off, and soil erosion in urban areas. Aesthetic values are asset to the sustainability of communities.

12.9   Implementation

A law is incomplete on paper unless implemented. A community's ability to adopt sustainable development principles will, of necessity, require an examination of its development regulations and review process. In Indian context, development regulations can be an interesting challenge and exercise for the professionals. Elected officials and administrator must understand the purpose and goals of establishing development regulations and must support the professionals' toil to make the built environment more functional and beautiful. Ironically, because of easy and open access to Western websites, many institutions, organizations, and government websites use pictures and graphics from them to market their product and ideas. If professionals put efforts, they will find indigenous and native examples to market their product and ideas. Western entities should borrow or capture Indian examples for their project.

The existing system of review process of the development plans should be assessed. Time is money. The delay at the administrative level for review of plans can cost money to the developers and can delay the project. The review process should be streamlined to expedite the review process. The review process should incorporate requirements for pre-submittal meetings with the professionals. This step will provide opportunity for the staff to share the established development regulations with the developers and their professional consultants (architects, engineers). On reverse, it will provide opportunity for the staff to know about the details of the project going to be developed in their community. Staff can share the incentives at that point. With the assistance of the technology, the progress of the submitted plans can be posted on the website/online for the convenience of applicant to know the status of the review process. However, submission of plans online should be discouraged because staff and developer can lose opportunity to address development regulations and possible improvements to the plans prior to submittal. Delays are frustrating, costly, and time-consuming. Inflexible standards and regulations and processes may doom any innovative and creative approaches to plan, design, and development. Planned unit development process can assist relieving certain regulatory barriers and make the process easy for both developers and professional staff.

12.10 Implementation and enforcement

The next step after the approval of plans is the implementation. The development should be according to the approved plans. The developers' ethical responsibility is to implement the plans as approved. Giving benefit of the doubt, the authorized departments should be equipped with enforcement process. The enforcement should be applied equally to private and public or government projects. This uniform standard can set right examples for the private sector. The purpose of the standards and regulations are to achieve certain required goals of the community. These can be achieved only if the laws are enforced. The enforcement staff should be trained to implement the laws fairly without any favoritism. It is a tough job but communities, elected officials, and administrators should be supportive of the enforcement staff whole-heartedly. If higher authorities interfere in the enforcement, the community should question it. After all, they are part of the community and laws are applicable to everyone.

12.11 Accountability and education

Accountability is the key to make plans and design successful and sustainable. Elected officials, administrators, staff, and citizens are equal partners in preserving sustainable community. The application of sustainable standards and regulations are applicable universally in the community. Integrity, honesty, pride, dedication, involvement, accountability, responsibility, ethics, morals, and character are the elements of success for a neighborhood, community, village, town, city, state, and country.

Right type of education will bring awareness about community. Education with the sense of community responsibility and civic sense will make the job of professionals to make the communities more livable little easy. The education process should start right from the initial stages. Schools, colleges, worship places, associations, groups, civic organizations, senior citizens, and teachers should participate in learning and sharing education about the community development and building sustainable communities. Every sustainable community unit becomes part of the holistic approach to sustainable country.

12.12 Evaluation and monitoring

To ensure sustainability, continuous evaluation and monitoring process should be incorporated with the development projects. Monitoring is the process to ensure the standards and plans, as approved, are implemented accordingly. Simultaneously, the results should be evaluated in terms of established goals and objectives. If the results are not as desired, may need revisit to review the established goals.

12.13 Infrastructure planning

12.13.1 What is infrastructure

Infrastructure is the built foundation of our cities and towns. It is what citizens cannot buy or build on their own. Infrastructure includes the common places, buildings, roads, pipes, and systems that we must join together as a society to plan, finance, and maintain it. The infrastructure of our cities and towns includes the large-scale capital structures we all share that are usually publicly financed and built. Infrastructure is capital-intensive and might not be built were it not for the intervention of government. Because infrastructure is so costly, building one makes sense and usually it is owned, operated, and managed by a governmental agency.

Infrastructure can be the invisible cable underground connecting our homes to the Internet, or the mega dam that generates megawatts of electricity and protects downstream areas from flooding. It can be the library, senior citizens center, the *galli* or sidewalk and street in a neighborhood, the local playground or play lot, or the visible or invisible network of pipes and drains. Infrastructure includes schools, museums, hospitals, health centers, and municipal landfills. None of these can be bought by an individual, but are shared by the whole community; they require large-scale investment, and can last for generations. They also deteriorate over time and need to be replaced or improved.

Economists also characterize some infrastructure systems as public good or natural monopolies, which justify public investment and/or regulations if provided by a private entity. In this case, the general public see the merit of providing the good to everyone, because it's used by those who would not normally pay for the service benefits all. For example, clean water or sewage treatment results in better health and less disease for all individuals. The transportation network is also a public good, enabling industry to produce and deliver goods that are consumed by all, and enabling workforce to travel to work to produce those goods. Natural monopolies usually refer to networked facilities covering a certain territory, often so capital-intensive that developers are deterred from building a competing system. Natural monopolies are considered to have economies of scale – the large the facility and the more persons served, the lower the unit cost for everyone.

12.13.2 What are the major infrastructure systems

Water and waste: Planning for water and the removal of waste has been the concern of city builders and administrators spanning all civilizations. Ancient civilizations like China, Rome had intricate dikes and irrigation systems. Today's local planners, engineers, and administrators must know about how to transport water or how to connect existing water systems to the neighborhoods, and about purification and how to pay for it. The city builders must ensure that wastewater infrastructure is adequate for disposal of sanitary wastes. Solid waste has seen a new consciousness in past couple of decades as the quantities of wastes have paramount. A more recent concern has been the pollution and environmental degradation caused by storm water runoff. The ULBs are also getting concerned with the impact of rising coastal waters, floods, droughts, and other global warming and climate change impacts.

Streets, roads, and transportation: Transportation systems such as sidewalks, streets, roads, highways, canals, airports, railroads, shipyards, and even kutcha roads in some areas have shaped the form, and perimeter of cities are infrastructure built for movement of people and goods. Transportation is the ultimate infrastructure. Various levels of public entities work together to provide this infrastructure. However, local governments do have responsibility for streets, sidewalks, and other related infrastructure. Local officials and administrators must plan, finance, maintain, and operate the local street grid, and establish local standards for private developer when building new streets, sidewalks, bike lanes, and local markets. Local governments also control the rights-of-way for streets, sidewalks, and medians that are used by networked infrastructures. In certain cities, operation of mass transit for citizens is the responsibility of local governments.

Community facilities: Community facilities are public buildings, civic centers, libraries, public safety buildings, recreation centers, parks, playgrounds, stadiums, public pools, and other locally adopted facilities. Some exceptions are there with provisions of some facilities as private operation such as libraries, parks, sports stadiums, and hospitals.

Telecommunications, energy, and power: The provision of energy and telecommunications is crucial to the overall infrastructure system in today's urban systems. In their modern form, energy and telecommunications have been on the agendas of politicians since the independence of the country. The past two decades saw energy and telecommunications utilities pass from small-scale but highly competitive entities to large-scale operations by both public and private sectors.

12.14   Infrastructure challenges for the cities

Following are the major challenges for urban planners, engineers, and administrators.

12.14.1   Climate change and the environment

Few decades ago researchers began to notice that the temperature of the Earth was slowly increasing, that the glaciers were melting and retreating, sea levels were rising, and severe weather events were becoming more common. It has been noticed that from 1906 to 2005 the Earth's temperature had increased by 1.3 degrees Fahrenheit, with most of the increase occurring in the past 50 years. India is no exception. Monsoon trends and patterns have changed and changing regularly, floods are more common, and cyclones are more powerful and devastating, and other local climatic changes. The researchers have projected further increase in the global average temperatures of 3–7 degrees Fahrenheit by the year 2100. This will result in continuous ice and snow cover losses, and the rise of sea levels during the twenty-first century from 7 to 23 inches. Other impacts will be more extreme weather events, including increased frequency of droughts and heat waves, along with more precipitation and flooding.

Reducing energy use and carbon emissions is considered as the major means to address the issues of global warming. With increased industrialization, development, increased automobile use and urbanization, India (and China) are becoming the lead contributors of carbon emissions and energy users. Developed countries such as the United States, Germany, and the United Kingdom have been the main culprits of the contributors of greenhouse gases in the past and still continue to do the same. Infrastructure systems lie at the heart of the solutions to climate change. The design and structure of transportation systems, waste management, public facilities, and energy infrastructure directly affect energy consumption and emission of greenhouse gases. Transportation infrastructure also plays an indirect role because of its importance in facilitating more compact and sustainable development. Water supply and waste water infrastructure are the first major infrastructure systems to be negatively and seriously affected by climate change. The need to adapt to the more extreme draught and storm cycles places huge burden on older systems.

12.14.2 Capital investment needs

Large amounts of capital investment must be made in infrastructure over the coming decades to accommodate growth and to replace deteriorated infrastructure – a challenge for local administrators under any circumstances. According the Report on Indian Urban Infrastructures and Services (Ahluwalia, 2011), approximately US$ 870 million are needed to provide water supply, sewage, solid waste management, storm water drain, urban roads, urban transport, street lights, and traffic support infrastructure. This cost does not include the land costs. The recent McKinsey report estimates that US$2.2 trillion in new urban infrastructure is needed in Indian cities along between now and 2020.

High Powered Expert Committee (HPEC) Report on Urban Infrastructure and Services, Government of India, Chairperson, Isher Judge Ahluwalia, 2011. Report available at http://www.niua.org/projects/hpec/FinalReport-hpec.pdf.

12.14.3 New and unevenly distributed growth

The economic cycles may go up or down in Indian and world economy, the population growth will continue to grow and continue to drive the need for new infrastructure. The population will agglomerate in urban areas. The need and demand for infrastructure is further enhanced by the development policies, such as building 100 smart cities. These projects and incentives will make metro cities bigger and attract more migration of people from villages and small- and medium-size cities to metropolitan areas. This will increase need for more infrastructure. This will promote sprawl and more demand of infrastructure.

12.14.4 Deteriorated infrastructure

The next driver for capital investments in infrastructure is the need to replace or upgrade older infrastructure. The infrastructure has life time. In many urban areas, infrastructure built years ago has reached the end of its useful life or no longer meets current environmental standards. Many of the nation's roads, highway, streets, and bridges are in poor conditions. There are number of infrastructure disasters around the world recently. Those should be taken as warnings for the deteriorating old infrastructures.

The institutional framework to address increased demand for local infrastructure is inadequate to address future growth issues, the need to replace and upgrade existing systems, and equally inadequate to transform conventional expenditures in to one that will promote carbon-neutral cities.

Today's infrastructure must be planned, financed, built, and maintained in a patchwork of overlapping agencies and institutions, many of which have competing jurisdictions, mandates, and goals. This area is focused on the physical infrastructure. Infrastructure is required at various stages of physical development. Population and employment are the key drivers of development and growth. Population need housing and another amenities and services for day-to-day activities. The housing and employment places require power sources, telecommunication linkages, streets, roads, access ways, street lights, piped water supply, sewer system, sewage treatment plants, and other supportive activities to complete the dialing living process. Cities being economic engines must provide efficient, reliable, dependable, cost effective, dependable, and reliable infrastructure for the citizens. Infrastructure motivates citizens to create and perform more economic activities; in return, cities generate revenue by providing those utilities. Further, because of more and diversified economic activities, cities diversify their revenue sources. This makes them more stable, attractive for new businesses, new entrepreneurs, and new ventures, and incentive for viable growth. Rising incomes are also related to increased investment in transportation infrastructure: people purchase faster means of transportation alternative such as buying cars instead of walking, bicycling, taking buses, and flying instead of driving. Both roadways and airports become more congested, resulting in demand to expand these facilities. Infrastructure increases economic output, thus adds to the national Gross National Product. Infrastructure has positive impact on social structure of city. These factors give impetus to construction industry. Construction activities are hub of overall growth. Infrastructure investments are essential for functioning of economy.

Infrastructure demand is not only caused by growth, but infrastructure investments also cause growth. Business cycles correspond to periods of increased demand for infrastructure.

The planning of infrastructure is an important community decision. Inadequate infrastructure can discourage invitation to people in the community. Inadequate infrastructure can cause increase in cost for local municipality thus can drain budget without providing any benefits to the community, and badly planned infrastructure not only tie up capital but makes the planning decision look inappropriate. One local tool that can be used for sustainable cross-functional long-range infrastructure planning is the comprehensive/development/general plan. It is particularly useful for areas experiencing rapid growth. The comprehensive plan is implemented by two sets of documents: development regulations and the capital improvement plan and budget. Development regulations translate the land use designations of the comprehensive plan into more specific ordinances in order to regulate private market development. They can also provide requirements for the kind and amounts of infrastructure that the private developer is expected to provide for the project.

12.15 Infrastructure delivery

Generally, infrastructure is provided by the public entity. However, private sector is investing in installing infrastructure and providing utilities to the citizens. Their only goal is "profit." But those citizens who can afford to pay premium price for services to private sector can be model for local governments to learn from their management style and operating systems.

In developing regions, cities, towns and villages, proper planning is a necessity. To plan and decide type, scale, and distribution of infrastructure planning is required. The process needs consensus of elected officials, engineers, planners, and the community for whom the project is for.

12.16 Steps in preparation of the infrastructure plan

1. Organizing and planning process
   - Build the team
   - Prepare the preliminary budget and work-program
   - Qualification for Project/Proposal (QFP) / Request For Proposal (RFP) preparation
   - Set up the public participation process
2. Analyze baseline conditions
   - Identify the service area
   - Assemble history, inventory of existing systems and facilities
   - Develop the condition assessment for each system or facility
3. Determination of goals and objectives for the system
   - Develop goals and objectives cumulative and for each system
   - Develop level of service (LOS) standards

4. Project future demand and needs
   - Project population growth
   - Identify infrastructure system needs
   - Establish demand management considerations
   - Calculate facility requirements
   - Consult comprehensive plan with the respect to infrastructure element
   - Incorporate the information in the comprehensive plan
5. Identify and evaluate alternatives
   - Identify alternatives
   - Create spatial simulation of alternatives
   - Identify costs
   - Revise budget
   - Identify financing alternatives
   - Identify other impacts, such as social, cultural, environmental, and political
6. Adopt preferred alternatives
   - Create implementation strategy
   - Monitor and evaluate the program/project

12.17 Development regulations

The development regulations/ordinance should contain detailed requirements for on-site infrastructure improvements. A land subdivision plan should not be approved without them. Subdivision ordinances also provide a mechanism for the developer, who usually pays for and constructs the streets, sidewalks, sewers, and water lines, to transfer the title and financial responsibility for maintaining the improvements to the local government. Uniform development standards are the "guts" of the infrastructure requirements for developing areas. They generally include detailed engineering specifications for the capacity, location, placement, composition, and dimensions for the following infrastructure components:

- Streets and roads
- Sidewalks, pedestrian pathways, bicycle paths
- Community off-street parking
- Traffic control devices and signs, including street name signs
- Street and pedestrian lighting requirements
- Water mains, connections, pump stations, and fire hydrants
- Sanitary sewers, storm drainage mains, and connections
- Utility lines, poles, conduit for energy, and telecommunications
- Landscaping, including drainage and erosion control

Development standards should be prepared by engineers in coordination with urban planner. The planning department should require submission of infrastructure plans in digital format. This information should include details about the right-of-way details. Allocation of right-of-ways should keep in consideration of the future growth of the area. The connectivity element of infrastructure must be part of the future plan and growth. Either depending upon the available software in the department or both, .dwg (AutoCAD) or shape files (ArcMap, ESRI Software) should be required from the developer for the department records. These data and information should be saved in GIS. Only administrator should be authorized to manage the data and information. However, data and information should be available for use by other departments.

During the construction phase, the planning department should be equipped with the trained and experienced staff to monitor the construction. This is important not only to ensure that the contractor is accurately translating the plans and specifications into a physical reality, but to allow for progress payments to the contractor. A representative from the ULB must inspect construction and certify compliance with the design specifications. In-house engineer, architect, and planner can participate in the inspection process and share the responsibilities. A specialty firm or third party experts can also be hired to assist or completely oversee the construction process. Depending upon the size and magnitude of the project, inspection process should be decided accordingly. Local entities should take the inspection process very seriously; because only the local government/planning department/municipal engineer/architect and inspection staff is between the future owners/occupants of the property and the developers/builders/contractors. After obtaining the final occupancy permit/final approval, the builders are no longer responsible. Once the project is completed, it is the responsibility of the local government for its compliance with the local laws, requirements, and approved plans. Any non-compliance or sub-standard work or use of sub-standard material is the responsibility of the local entity. Thus, the staff should take the inspection process very seriously, without any compromise.

Cities should have an approved fee-schedule in place for plan reviews, inspections, and other associated work done by the city. Cities may also consider imposing exaction and impact fees, if law allows.

12.18 Wastewater planning

The collection and disposal of sanitary sewage for urban dwellings using pipes is relatively new concept. Earlier human wastes were collected in cesspools and privy vaults. At first, the increased flow from water closets went into the existing on-site cesspools and privy vaults, but they did not have the capacity for large amounts of water. Overflows were common. With the increased awareness came the issue of combined sewers and separate sewers. A combined sewer carries both stormwater and sanitary sewage in the same pipe. A separate system has two pipes, often running in parallel, that carry stormwater and sanitary sewage to the point of disposal. Because of poor performance of combined system, cities installed new sanitary systems and let the old sewers revert to their original purpose. Wastewater is still dumped untreated into local water bodies, with the exception of handful cities, since it is thought that running water purified itself.

A municipal sewer system is essentially a water distribution system in reverse. Today's centralized municipal wastewater system consists of a network of buried pipes for collecting sanitary sewage from households and businesses and pipes for collecting stormwater and to transport to a wastewater treatment plant. The purpose of the system is to protect the surface and ground water. The system is designed to ensure that waterborne substances – pollutants from residences, industry, and other sources that may negatively affect humans and the environment – do not get into surface or ground water sources. Conventional pollutants are human waste, food wastes, and gray water such as laundry, dishwashing, and shower water. These kinds of pollutants carried away from a home, business, or industry by the sanitary sewer. They are biodegradable. A pollutant that can cause disease in humans in called a pathogen. Toxin pollutants are harmful to animal or plant life. These are organic (pesticides, solvents, dioxins and polychlorinated biphenyls) and metals (lead, mercury, copper, zinc, chromium, silver, nickel, and cadmium). Toxic pollutants can come from households, industry, commercial and other sources. They should be pretreated and should not be discharged into the sewer system.

Wastewater collection systems are underground pipes for sanitary and stormwater. As noted earlier, these systems can be separate or combined. Preferably should be separate. The pipes leading from individual houses are called laterals. These connect to sub-mains, which generally run down the street. These in turn connect to trunk lines or interceptors, which are large lines that terminate at the wastewater treatment plant. Laterals are generally 6 inches in diameter and made of clay, concrete, or PVC. Sub-mains are usually 8, 10, or 12 inches in diameter. Trunk lines range from 15 to over 27 inches in diameter. Sewer systems have been designed to flow by gravity wherever possible. Furthermore, sewer lines are designed to flow half-full to ensure ventilation. These two facts make the physical configuration of sewer lines important. Whereas pressurized water lines can have any alignment, sewer lines need to have a specific slope, usually about 0.5–2.0 percent. Engineers indicate that flow within sewer lines need a velocity of between 2 and 10 feet per second, fast enough so that solids are not deposited, but slow enough that grit in the water does not scour the pipes and cause leaks.

Sometimes gravity alone is insufficient to carry the sewage. This occurs when the interceptor must traverse a great distance, or when the topography prohibits it. In this case, a pressurized sewer line called force main is used. Sewage flows into what is called a lift station where pressure is added. Lift stations are prone to failure, particularly during storms. They constantly need repairs. However, sometimes they are necessary in areas where elevation changes.

Manholes are also called utility access ports, are located at any changes in direction, pipe size, or slope, or any time two lines intersect. For sub-mains, manholes are usually located about every 400 feet.

12.19 Wastewater treatment

The wastewater treatment plant (WWTP) is where the sewer pipes converge. This is a centralized facility, usually located near a large water body, where the sewage is treated before being discharged into the receiving water bodies. This process removes disease-carrying organisms, harmful chemicals, and excess minerals.

There are two basic stages in the treatment of wastewater: primary and secondary. In the primary stage, solids are allowed to settle out of water in what is really a physical process. In the secondary stage, biological processes actually attack the pathogens in the water. The two most common secondary treatment techniques are the trickling filter and the activated sludge process. Regardless of which process is used, treatment is not complete until the treated wastewater has been disinfected with chlorine. Chlorine is fed into water to kill whatever bacteria are left, and to reduce odor. Done properly, chlorine will kill more than 99 percent of the harmful bacteria in the effluent. However, since after the treatment the wastewater is dumped into a natural body of water, where it becomes harmful to wildlife. Removal of excess chlorine process is called de-chlorination. This should be done before discharge to natural waters. Alternatively, some treatment plants use ultraviolet light or ozone instead of chlorine for disinfection. Some communities distribute treated water back into the community for irrigation of landscaping and washing and cleaning of streets. This water is close to potable quality – but not potable. This treated water is distributed through special colored pipes (purple color pipes) to avoid any mistake or error. This also helps municipality recover costs. The use of treated water for irrigation saves precious potable water being used for irrigation and cleaning roads and streets.

Some treatment plants are also doing tertiary treatment. Tertiary treatment is a general term for any process that removes wastewater constituents that are not removed in primary or secondary treatment. Usually, these constituents are location-specific chemicals that the local community has chosen to remove or is required to remove. Publicly owned sewage treatment plants are generally designed to treat domestic sewage. Many industrial and other non-residential uses have wastewater that is too toxic and where a discharge of this sort into the sewers would interfere with the biological processes at the treatment plant or make it impossible for the plant to recycle its used and solids.

In times of little or no precipitation, most sewers work well. But during a storm, the total volume of wastewater arriving at the treatment plan may exceed its capacity and can be discharged untreated into surface water bodies such as streams, rivers, lakes, estuaries, and coastal water. This is known as either a combined or separate sewer overflow (CSO or SSO). Another problem occurs when storm water enters the sewer pipes either from ground (called infiltration) or water is discharged into the pipes from other sources (called inflow). Infiltration can be caused by damaged pipes, joints, or connections or leakage of manhole walls. Inflow can be caused by roof leaders, cellar, yard or other drains, including sump pumps being connected to the sanitary system. It can also be caused by cross-connections from storm sewers and combines sewers or by illicit connections.

12.20 Planning for natural areas

India is a land of diversity. Diversity in religions, food, languages, customs, cultures, clothing and natural landscapes. Diverse topography with mountains, hills, rolling plains, plains, deserts, plateaus, oceans, shore lines, rivers, lakes, brooks, vistas, caves, and geological formations. These national treasures provide important sustainability, recreational, religious, spiritual, ecological, social, economic, and educational values. Careful planning, regulations, management, and land acquisition are needed to ensure that future generations can enjoy and benefit from these unique landscapes.

How to use and plan these natural resources have important implications for the economies and environments of the local areas and nation as a whole. These beautiful natural landscapes attract national and international tourists. Commercial recreation is often tied to natural features. Many religious and spiritual centers are associated with natural landscape. There is hardly any river in India which does not have historic, religious, spiritual, or local events associated with it. Kumbh Mela at the confluence of Ganga and Yamuna and mythical Saraswati is the world's biggest gathering event with over 100 million people for days. Every square inch is natural, and it is impossible to save every inch of natural landscape. With careful planning, protection, implementation, and enforcement, natural landscape can be saved to the possible extent.

There are demands for the land for farming, forestry, and mining, and for residential, commercial, and industrial uses. Striking a balance among the natural environment is one of the biggest challenges of present times that local governments face. Land is in limited supply. Suggested steps to plan for natural areas are as follows:

Inventory: An inventory of natural and environmental treasures should be conducted. The inventory should be included in the comprehensive plan. The details include their location, type, importance, and any association with historic events, if any previously done should be consulted.

Analysis: The analysis should rank natural, cultural, and historic landscapes for their importance. This analysis should be the basis for goals and objectives, action strategy, and in drafting future land use map and the zoning map.

Goals and objectives: The comprehensive plan must set realistic and achievable goals and objectives for special landscape. The overall goal should be to protect important landscape features that have aesthetics, recreational, educational, economic, and social values.

Action strategy: The action strategy should present techniques and programs for achieving the goals and objectives established.

Enforcement: The authorities must establish process to enforce the goals and objectives.

Planning for natural resources can be achieved through ordinance such as zoning and subdivision regulations. These are discussed in details in this text.

12.21   Planning for wildlife habitat

Taking and clearing land for human-use purposes has impact on wildlife habitat. Interrupting, disturbing, and diverting water bodies can have impact on aqua life. The sensitive natural landscapes such as wetlands, forestlands, floodplains, steep slopes, and coastal areas are suited to wildlife than humans. Although habitat destruction is more widely recognized cause of wild life loss, air and water pollution, diseased, and invasive species that compete with native plants and animals also pose major threats to wildlife. The expanding urban areas with additional agricultural land are increasing the interaction between humans and wildlife. Large animals are usually first species driven out by urban expansion. Many animals, like squirrels, raccoons, monkeys, and some other native animals have a way of finding ecological niches in which they can survive and even thrive around human environment.

Ecologists and biologists present biological diversity or biodiversity as a measure of the variety of plant and animal species, the population of each species, and the overall health of ecosystem. The higher the level of biodiversity, the more resilient ecosystem is. High biodiversity in turn creates very productive system that generates substantial environmental services, such as climate moderation, nutrient recycling, water purification and recharge, oxygen production, and assimilation of waste and pollutants.

Loss of biodiversity can occur when the variety of species declines, the population of one or more species decreases, or habitat comes fragmented, and here is less interaction among species. It is often difficult to predict the effects of reduction or loss of a particular species in an ecosystem. Loss of biodiversity may lead to changes in an ecosystem that may be subtle or profound. Loss of biodiversity can result from filling wetlands, ploughing, overgrazing, or paving grasslands, fragmenting habitat and migration routes with road, and siting sprawled and scattered developments, removal of forestlands, and invasion of non-native plants, insects, diseases, and animals.

Ecosystems are naturally not static. The mix of plants and animals in an ecosystem can and does change over time. But the rate and degree of change are important. Ecosystems proceed through stages called successions. To biologists and ecologists, a key concept in maintaining biodiversity and ecosystem health is critical mass. A critical mass is the minimum area of land or water needed to support a healthy number of a species and species types. A common concern among biologists, ecologists, and planners is the degree of resilience of natural environments to disruption, either from natural event such as fire, flood, or heavy rainfall or from human intrusion. Resilience is likely to be greater where there is a critical mass of plant and animal species.

Bioregionalism is a distinct collection of plants and animal ecosystems that function in certain ways and have particular needs for survival. Temperature and precipitation primarily determine most bioregions with elevations, soil types, watersheds, and microclimate as contributing factors. This concept has two main components: the protection of native plants and animal species from non-native species and maintaining native habitat in the face of development pressure.

Urban planners, environmental planners, engineers, citizens should adhere to the following principles for preserving biodiversity:
- Protect rare and ecologically important plants and animals.
- Monitor for biodiversity impacts. Willingness to learn and manage adaptability as a substitute for lack of information.

- Consider an ecosystem view. Piecemeal sites do not exist in isolation but as part of local and regional ecosystems.
- Maintain and mimic natural ecosystem processes to the maximum possible extent.
- Protect communities and ecosystems.
- Minimize habitat fragmentation.
- Promote native species and native biological and genetic diversity.
- Restore ecosystems, communities, and species.

Local planning for plants and wildlife habitat protection can be achieved through following the steps of conducting inventory, analysis, establishing goals and objectives, action strategy, incorporating strategies in zoning ordinance, subdivision regulations, creating supporting groups/associations and provide financial incentives for protecting wildlife habitats.

12.22 Planning and managing wetlands

Historically, in the United States wetlands were viewed as swamps, wasteland, and land with little value that could be drained, dredged, and filled and either farmed or developed for various purposes. More than half of the original wetlands in the southern states have been filled in.

Wetlands are vital natural resources that provide a variety of environmental services: aquifer recharge, flood protection, stormwater absorption, erosion control, filtering of sediments and pollutants, fish and wildlife habitat, carbon sinks, and open space. Wetlands hold enormous amounts of carbon and thus are important in regulation of climate as well as recycling carbon. Wetlands remove significant biological oxygen demand, which leaves more oxygen available for fish and wildlife. By acting as reservoir, wetlands accumulate and then slowly release the water they retain, either into streams and rivers or into groundwater to recharge aquifer. Wetlands act as a buffer between the land and waterways. This process is especially helpful in maintaining water supplies during times of draught.

Wetlands vary in their size, location, type, plant and animal species, and value to the environment. There are two general types of wetlands: inland and coastal. Inland wetlands are referred to as fresh water or palustrine wetlands, and are found along rivers and streams (riparian wetlands), in depressions surrounded by dry land. Coastal wetlands are known as tidal or estuarine wetlands.

Local planning for wetland protection can be achieved through following the steps of conducting inventory, analysis, establishing goals and objectives, action strategy, incorporating strategies in zoning ordinance, subdivision regulations, creating supporting groups/associations and provide financial incentives for protecting wildlife habitats.

12.23 Coastal zone management

India's coastal areas have remarkably rich and diverse natural, land, and water resources. Coastal waters include bays, estuaries, marshes, lagoons, inland lakes, and oceans. Estuaries are coastal water bodies where fresh water and salt water meet. These unique, oxygen-rich environments support aquatic life that provides essential links in the food chain. Salt marshes and tidal wetlands offer important waterfowl habitat and migratory flyway stops. Beaches are popular recreation spots for swimming, surfing, and relaxing environment. Sport fishing, boating, snorkeling, and scuba diving are also popular past times. The challenges of coastal zone management are population growth and development, managing coastal recreation, improving water quality, waterfront development, and pollution prevention.

India's coastline ecology is being impacted by the growing population. Increased human activities such as dredging, various types of pollution, discharge from ships and other vessels, sand mining, excessive fishing, and discharge from industries are the reasons coastal zone needs attention. The Ministry of Environment, Forest and Climate Change has issued Coastal Regulations Zone Notification in 1999 and 2011. Objectives of the Coastal Zone Notification 2011 are:

1. To ensure livelihood security to the fishing communities and other local communities living in the coastal areas;
2. To conserve and protect coastal stretch; and
3. To promote development in a sustainable manner based on scientific principles, taking into account the dangers of natural hazards in the coastal areas and sea-level rise due to global warming.

Coastal Zones are classified as Ecological Sensitive (CRZ-I), Built-up Area (CRZ-II), Rural Areas (CRZ-III), and Water Areas up to the Territorial Waters and the Tidal-Influence Water Bodies (CRZ-IV). Coastal Regulation Zone extends up to 12 nautical miles (about 22 km) and the tidal influenced water bodies have been included under the Coastal Regulations Zone areas in order to control the discharge of untreated sewage, effluents, and disposal of solid wastes as such activities endanger the fish and their ecosystem, conserve and protect habitats in the marine area such as corals and coral reefs and associated biodiversity, marine sanctuaries and biosphere reserves, sea grass beds, etc., which act as sparing, nursery, and rearing ground for fish and fisheries, regulate activities in the marine and coastal waters such as dredging and sand mining.

Other highlights are: The "no-development zone" has been reduced from 200 meters from the high-tide line to 100 meters, but exclusively to meet the increased housing demands of fishing and coastal communities; Floor Space Index (FSI), which was restricted to between 1.25 to 1.66 has been increased to 2..5; CRZ 2011 introduces the participation of local communities in coastal management plan, a feature absent in the 1991 notification. Thus, communities living along the country's 7500 km coastline will have a say in developing coastal regions in which development has been allowed.

Ecological Sensitive Zone (RCZ-1) includes:

(a) Areas that are ecologically sensitive and geomorphological features which play a role in maintaining the integrity of the coast:

(i) *Mangroves:* if the mangrove area is more than 1,000 square meter, a buffer of 50 meters along the mangrove shall be provided

(ii) *Coral and coral reefs,* and associated biodiversity

(iii) *Sand dunes*

(iv) *Mudflats* that are biologically active

(v) *National parks, marine parks, sanctuaries, reserve forests, wildlife habitats* and other protected areas under the provisions of the Wild Life (Protection) Act, 1972 (53 of 1972), Forest (Conservation) Act, 1980 (69 of 1980) and Environment (Protection) Act, 1986 (29 of 1986), including biosphere reserves.

(v) *Salt marshes*

(vi) *Turtle nesting grounds*

(vii) *Horseshoe crab habitats*

(viii) *Sea grass beds*

(ix) *Nesting grounds of birds*

(x) *Areas or structures of archeological importance and heritage sites*

(b) Areas between the low tide line and high tide line

The established regulation should be implemented and regularly monitored and evaluated. Local planning for coastal resources can be managed through incorporation of steps of inventory, analysis, goals and objectives, action strategy, zoning ordinance, development regulations and capital improvement programs.

12.24 Planning for natural hazards and natural disasters

Natural disasters include floods, hurricanes, cyclones, typhoons, heavy rains, snow and ice storms, avalanches, landslides, sink holes, beach erosion, earthquakes, volcanic eruptions, wildfires, drought, and tsunamis. Disaster is a sudden and dramatic emergency. Natural disasters are not confined to limited population base, they can cover larger areas and impact both human lives and properties. Animals and wildlife is impacted too. Natural disasters demonstrate time and again human limitations and control over nature. While not all losses of property and life can be avoided, however, careful planning and design for the location, type, and adapted material of development in and near hazard-prone areas can reduce losses.

When disaster strikes, the demands facing threatened communities are obvious and compelling. People must be protected to the maximum extent possible. Victims need attention and must be cared for. Basic services must be restored earliest possible. Next, properties and physical structures must be protected, repaired, and replaced. An affected community must respond immediately and vigorously. Local individuals, groups, and organizations take initiative to respond quickly with available resources. The immediate response may not be efficient or comprehensive.

Responding to an event is very different from an expectant or possible event. To most people, natural hazards are not major concern until a disaster occurs. Moreover, public knowledge about most hazards is limited. It is local communities that must deal directly with the immediate disaster problems, and yet it is difficult to prepare readiness for local areas. Disasters are viewed more intensely from the national level. Push for the emergency preparedness comes from the top to down – from national, to regional to local levels. All of this points to preparedness for disasters and emergencies at various levels.

Emergency or disaster preparedness can make an important and noticeable difference if a disaster occurs. Such preparedness should be based on an understanding of what typically happens during disaster. Even a modest preparedness, prior to disaster, makes a difference. Another factor is to know the local and regional population base and built environment in the area. Any environment-sensitive activities, if there are any, in the area will need specialized attention.

The first days following a disaster or emergency events are typically very dynamic because the local, national, and international media sharply and swiftly focus attention on the immediate need of victims and because of the health and social risks and order.

12.25 Principles of disaster preparedness

The goal of disaster preparedness is the quick and rapid restoration of normal way of life. Attempts must be made to anticipate and project possible impact of various hazards and to prepare countermeasures to neutralize the impact. Following are some of the principles that could be considered:

- Preparedness and improvisation of emergency management
- Preparedness is continuous process
- Preparedness reduces unknown during an emergency
- Preparedness is based on knowledge and education
- Preparedness directs appropriate action
- Modest planning is a reasonable goal
- Preparedness directs the entities with responsibilities
- Preparedness prepares for certain unknowns and other preparedness needs

A checklist for preparedness needs:

- Disaster and emergency preparedness drills and exercises
- Understanding the type and nature of forthcoming disaster
- Warning the public and timely communication with public
- Notifying the entities responsible for participating in the action plan
- Mobilizing the emergency personnel and resources
- Taking protective actions
- Providing care and assistance to victims and not victims yet
- Restoring the essential public services
- Assessing the damage
- Informing the public and victims throughout the recovery process of steps
- Records keeping of happenings and lessons learned

- Planning the possible extent recovery
- Coordinating emergency management activities
- Monitoring and evaluation

12.26 Emergency/disaster preparedness

12.26.1 Preparation of emergency/disaster preparedness plan

The local municipalities should prepare an emergency preparedness plan. The plan should be for the area, not confined to political boundaries. The plan should cover minimum elements of purpose, scope, location, situation, organization, concept of operations, executions, responsibilities, responsibilities and tasks, responsibilities and tasks of each department and organization, updating time line, execution of post disaster, and monitoring and evaluation.

12.26.2 Role of planning department

The local, state, and national level planning departments should lead in preparing the disaster/emergency preparedness plans for the communities. Planning departments are equipped with basic information, data, and details for preparing plans such as, basic maps, road maps, land use maps and data, records of types and use of buildings, population details of the area, location of services, type of services, infrastructure layout maps, maps with location of community services, aerial photos, remote sensing information, records of approved development plans, records of proposed development plans, records of zoning, parcel information, development permits/licenses, historic buildings, sites, and features, GIS to reproduce maps, plotters and printers to generate copies of needed information, risk management information, environmentally sensitive maps and records, land uses with environmentally sensitive structures, and records of other related information. Planners keep tract of economic, social, and cultural activities of the region – beyond city limits.

The planning departments should consider saving and storing such data, maps, information and other details on third party servers or cloud system, in the event the planning department gets impacted by a disaster.

Planners are trained to know their areas, cities, and regions of responsibilities. They are trained to know the strengths, weaknesses, and sensitivities of the region and cities. Planners are trained to integrate and coordinate with other departments, organizations, and institutions. They are required to keep records of civic groups, associations, groups, NGOs, and other related entities in the region. Some planners are specialized in disaster management discipline. Decision makers should consider all these factors while assigning the authority and responsibilities of disaster management. In addition, the planning departments are permanent-established public departments, which can oversee monitoring and evaluation exercises. Planning department may create a specialized division to manage disaster management operation.

12.27 Solid waste and recycling management

To maintain quality of life in cities, refuse discarded by the citizen must be collected, transported, treated, and disposed. The process must be efficient, functional, and cost effective. Environmental issues are important throughout the process. Solid waste is a major source of environmental pollution in Indian cities, towns, and villages. It is estimated that over one-third of the total waste in remains uncollected in Indian cities. The bigger problem of solid waste in Indian cities is its spread all over streets, roads, open spaces, sidewalks, in front and around buildings, bus terminals, railway ROWs, and even vertical (trees, buildings, and overhead wires). Waste disposal and collection services are inadequate, archaic, antiquated, or non-existent in cities, towns, and villages. The combined effect of the non-existence of collection services, inefficiency in collection, and unscientific disposal creates water pollution, odor pollution, insanitary conditions, air pollution, and unhealthy conditions for humans. This uncontrolled widespread of waste is also the cause of diseases among stray animals and even domesticated animals. This impacts quality of food supply for humans. Indian administrative system lacks incentives for waste reduction, reuse, and recycling.

12.28 Waste generators

Irresponsible citizens: Irresponsible citizens throw unwanted items as trash everywhere and anywhere without realizing the consequences of that. Street food providers, street vendors selling various types of merchandises, irresponsible habits of people, no respect for environment, and with sense of someone's responsibility to clean the space are responsible for generating controllable waste.

Household: Households are generator of various types of solid and liquid waste. Households with commercial activities generate additional waste.

Small businesses and industries: These generate both municipal and process waste, some of which may be hazardous. Offices, restaurants, and various "wallas" operators generate waste.

Manufacturing industries: These generate municipal solid waste.

Hospitals and healthcare facilities/services: These generate municipal waste along with hazardous waste mixed with body fluids, chemicals, and sharp objects.

Construction sites: These generate waste of such as concrete, bricks, metals, wood, and other construction materials.

Worship places: These are responsible for generating waste because of the traditions, rituals, ceremonies, events and other activities.

Each city, town, and village should be responsible for efficiently collection of waste and safely disposal of its own waste. The communities should penalize excessive waste, uncontrolled disposal, and indiscriminate dumping. The Government of India through the Ministry of Environment, Forest and Climate Change constituted a National Waste Management Council and offered following mandates:

1. Promotion of collection, collation, and publication of information regarding the availability of waste technologies and markets for recoverable materials.

2. Analysis of information for overcoming constraints to use available technologies for both waste utilization and waste minimization and identification of areas in which new technologies need to be developed.
3. Offering advice to the government, industry, and such other sectors on different aspects of waste management and on incentives/distinctive that may be needed to facilitate waste utilization.
4. Recommendation to the government research and development schemes for developing new technologies.
5. Advising government on fiscal and regulatory measures to promote waste utilization.
6. Promoting awareness among the public about different aspects of solid waste.

Central Pollution Control Board (1995) identified the following priorities:

1. Utilization of solid waste from resource recovery.
2. Selection of proper sites for waste disposal on the basis of environmental impact assessment.
3. Application of appropriate technology for solid waste through (a) proper design of landfills, and (b) incineration of garbage for power generation, wherever feasible.
4. Greater use of solid waste for anaerobic digestion/biogas generation, composting, etc.
5. Use of solid waste for fuel.
6. Recycling of paper, plastic, glass, battery waste, etc.
7. Provision of facilities for disposal of hospital waste.

12.29 Solid waste management and sustainability

Reduction: The reduction of solid waste depends upon the effective consumer education, regulations, and incentives. This need not result in change or reduced quality of life. Municipalities should ban certain kinds of packaging that are not biodegradable. For example, plastic takes hundreds of years to break down. Children should be, early on, educated in schools about the consequences of solid waste. Every citizen in the city should be educated about the solid waste hazards. The neighborhood association should be given incentives for control of waste. Customer/consumer-oriented businesses should be mandated to keep trash containers accessible to general public and must be maintained all the time (e.g. petrol stations/pumps, restaurants, banks, markets, and public places). The designer should design attractive, practical, and easy to maintain trash receptacle. Local municipalities should design and market/provide dumpsters with city logs and slogan of pride for keeping the city/town/village clean. Citizens should be fined on the spot for littering.

Reuse: Reuse means that a product can be used again with little or no processing. Reuse is the next best strategy to reducing overall consumption of goods. Reusable outlets should be encouraged, or environment conscientious organizations should take lead on this venture. Old shopping styles of using cloth or plastic bags should be incentivized and reintroduced. Designers should create attractive and durable bags with interesting slogans and colors. They should be marketed with the help of, e.g. Prime minister or Bollywood celebrities while shopping using reusable bags instead of "brooming" for a photo shoot. Children should be educated right from the beginning about using of reusable products to save the environment for their future.

Recycling: Recycling is the reuse of materials to make new products, for example making shopping bags from the newspaper paper. By reducing the need to harvest, mine, and process virgin material, recycling conserves wood, plastic, minerals, paper, oil, energy, and water. Recycling saves on landfill expenses and cleanup costs. Private entrepreneurs should explore opportunities in making profit by recycling products. Citizens should be educated about using recycled products.

Return: The solid waste should return soil back by composting or digesting organic wastes. Plant, wastes from kitchen, garden, and agricultural production and animal wastes are sources of key nutrients for the agricultural system and their proper utilization is important to food supply and sustainable development.

Combustion: Waste-to-energy facilities employ controlled combustion of solid waste for the purposes of reducing its volume. Combustion can destroy bacteria and viruses in wastes as well as harmful compounds. Combustion can reduce the volume of solid waste up to 90% thereby conserving landfill space. It also offers the possibility of recovery of energy in the form of steam or electricity. Technologies are available to safely dispose of waste combustion ash residues.

12.30 Sanitary landfills

The disposal of waste on the land continues to be a predominant method used to manage waste. The open dumping of waste on the land without adequate controls can result in serious public health, and safety problems and severe environmental impacts.

A sanitary landfill is engineered structure that is designed and operated to protect public health and the environment. Sanitary landfill technology has advanced very rapidly over the past decade. Landfill technologies equip landfills with leachate collection systems, linear systems, systems with control of landfill gases, ground monitoring, closure and post closure care. Since land disposal of solid waste is practiced on such a wide-scale basis worldwide, it is important that the best available technologies be used.

12.31 Other strategies

- It is important to understand that wastes are simply discarded products, and the design and use of product can have significant impact on the nature of waste that is produced. Recycling and reuse can be enhanced by designing products so that components and material can be easily separated.
- Product stewardship involves taking responsibility for a product throughout its entire lifecycle including responsibility of management of water after the product is discarded.

- Establishment of environmentally sound and sustainable treatment and disposal facilities.
- Rigorous enforcement of environmental laws and standards.
- Public participation and education.

12.32 Conclusion

Urban areas act consistently and constantly to improve service delivery. The ultimate goal for local governments is to provide quality services and protection to its citizens. Sometimes choices and decision making is tough between balancing environment with the development.

Chapter 13
Smart rural planning

13.1 Introduction

640,000 plus villages and shy of 8000 cities in India. Many research reports on urbanization and/or development start with something like this "Indians have believed that India lives in village – much of India still lives in villages, and villages and agriculture are important for Indian economy and society." These statements are true, valid, and stand good. The latest census of 2011 has counted that 377 million people live in urban areas or 31% of Indian population lives in urban areas. Simple mathematics – majority of population with 69% of share of India's population still lives in villages. Projections estimate that by 2030, 50% of the population will live in cities and towns. The questions raised are: Are cities and towns preparing for that? Do they have resources to accommodate additional population and fulfill their expectations and dreams? Visit to Indian cities indicates that they are not only economic engines but swallowing more and more people irrespective of the threshold to provide infrastructure and services. People from rural areas are attracted to the cities and towns for many reasons, such as opportunities, choices, options, variety, and with the hope of better quality of life. Urban areas and urbanites complain about the problems of human congestion, shortage of housing, traffic congestion, pollution (air, water, noise, and light), insufficient infrastructure, deteriorating quality of life, and insufficient social services. But this is a one-sided pull factor. Villagers are leaving a vacuum in areas they are moving from.

Rural areas have many opportunities if not as much as urban areas. They offer very attractive social, economic, environmental, and psychological opportunities; unparalleled to cities and towns. The shape, size, style, and form of opportunities in rural areas are different from cities and towns. But they are as inviting and promising as in urban areas. However, rural area has to change with times and adopt certain traits to make rural areas more attractive. They have to assess and recognize their potentials. The villages have to be creative and dynamic to garnish their assets to make their settlements more enjoyable and comfortable. Elected officials, decision makers, budget specialists, administrators, planners, and ruralites have to focus on the potential opportunities in rural areas. Ruralites have to dress rural area by making them attractive to retain themselves in villages and attract people from cities to live in villages. In short, smart rural planning can fix these problems to a large extent if not totally eradicate them.

In developed countries 70% to 80% country's population is urbanized. India is becoming more and more urbanized. Imagine, if just half of the country's population moves into the cities. The number of people in cities will be approximately 1.3 billion divided by 2 (650 million). Cities in India already are in turmoil and distressed. This is a generalized statement. Many urbanites with resources enjoy urban way of life. They will not trade that for anything. Various researches and reports indicate that to provide certain level of service to the urbanites, central government needs millions and trillions of American dollars. Keep in mind, these are only reports – not action plans. On dedicated terms, by the time the resources needed, which is still up in the air, become available for implementation, there will be need of more money because of the inflation, increased cost of material, and other added costs, such as land value. That still does not promise that the urbanites will be happy and enjoy their lives in the cities.

Again, the elected officials, decision makers, budget specialists, administrators, planners, and ruralites should prepare, revise, update, and refurbish the rural development portfolio with smart villages or smart rural areas concept.

13.2 What makes rural

Rural or village is a small unit of settlement, which is self-contained and self-sustainable to some extent. The main economic activity is agriculture. Agriculture includes land to grow food, domesticate animals to fulfill the needs of the family and beyond, for example, milk, eggs, and meat requirements. Agriculture includes staple crops, specialized crops, fruit, vegetables, and other crops to meet the day-to-day needs of the hinterland.

In rural areas, majority of people live in simple basic houses. Rarely, some live in large houses or mansions. Wealthy land owners have large housing or a house in a town as well.

The population size of villages varies. But this varied size can help plan with hierarchy as criteria. Various levels of rural settlement can be criteria to allocate resources and services.

The rural settlements are comprised of land owners, labor, and marginal trade and commercial activities. Because of mechanization, rural areas are equipped with petrol pumps, repair shops, rental services, and seeds and farm supply centers. Villages with relatively large size offer additional commercial services which are used by residents of nearby villages of relatively small size.

Villages offer many environmental, social, and economic advantages over cities, such as fresh and clean air, openness, desirable or very low densities, connection to the nature, quite living, beautiful surroundings, fresh produce, and stress-free way of life, no hustle-bustle, no congestion and an individual's outlook of the country side.

13.2.1 Social fabric

In Indian context, the social fabric of villages is complex and even more complex depending upon the region. Sociologists and geographers keep detailed account of local social fabric of villages.

13.2.2 Responsibilities

The benefits stated "fresh and clean air, openness, desirable or very low densities, connection to the nature, quite living, beautiful surroundings, fresh produce, stressless way of life, no hustle bustle, no congestion, and an individual's outlook of the country side" come with responsibilities on the part of local administration and local citizens of rural areas. The responsibilities are to maintain these benefits and not allow to metamorphose these assets with urban styles.

13.3 Smart approach

The rural area should become aware of smart planning and processes. The villagers should take initiative, in this globalization and competitive world, to learn about smart techniques to make their habitat sustainable and firm. The firmness and sustainability means, the rural areas should maintain their character, at the same time change to adapt modern features to live through time – not become ghost villages or disappear from the map.

13.4 Regional understanding

The villages, in situ, are relatively of small size, with limited population and with limited economic activities. However, each village has its merits, potentials, opportunities, and issues. Some villages provide specialized products or items, e.g. during a visit to a village, learnt that the village specializes in producing organic seed varieties. This attracts people from distant areas. The state level planning department should prepare regional plans with focus on villages and rural areas. The plans should focus on identifying specialties of villages and areas. The plans should provide ideas and connections to promote and market those specialties. Through economic development specialists, farmers should be educated regarding additional opportunities. They should be exposed to external markets. The villagers should be educated about the basic sector of the economic world to get optimum return for their product or services.

Regional plans should establish hierarchy of the settlements. The plans should identify the level of those services that should be provided by the respective settlements. Regional plans should explain the identity of settlements and locational potentials in terms of regional setting.

The regional plan should incorporate Regional Transportation Plan either as part of the mother plan or as a separate plan to identify the existing transportation facilities. The plan should provide scheme to connect every village with local, regional, state, and national level road infrastructure. The plan should provide railroad connectivity with villages.

The plan should identify regional and national level opportunities for their produce, product, food items, and other items and services to facilitate farmers and villagers of the opportunities around the area.

The plans should list of services needed in the area. Hierarchical order should be used to establish the type of services needed and level of services needed. This may help to avoid any duplication or overlap of services, cost effectiveness, and rational allocation of resources to reach maximum number of villagers.

The regional planners should employ their experiences, expertise, knowledge, and creativity to add the needed elements in the regional development plans. They can incorporate a checklist for the preparation of village level comprehensive plan. Rural areas may be able to afford hiring of a qualified planner. The regional development plan can guide them to improve their settlements.

13.5 Future role of rural settlements

The villages, like cities, can be economic engines by participating actively in the gross national product. The villages are part of certain economic activities, though not recognized or the credit goes to the cities, such as raw food for the processed food prepared in cities. Grain grown in the villages but mass distribution is done in the cities; raw materials to process cooking oils comes from farms; cotton comes from farms to make clothing – made in cities, and the list goes on. It is not true that rural areas are not economic engines. Urban areas collect, sort, process, and distribute the goods and services.

The rural areas should take initiative to install equipments to make the final product or final consumable goods in their areas. For example, if the area is rich in producing potatoes – they should install factory to make potato chips, potato starch making factory or potato sauce making factory or other creative ideas to convert raw goods into final consumable product. Sweets made with milk, in cities, come from hinterland. Wheat flour grinded and packed in cities comes from rural areas. Cigarettes and *biddies* may be made in cities but tobacco comes from rural areas. Fish may be packaged in cities, but comes from rural and coastal areas. If the processing plants are installed in the rural areas, closer to the raw material, this will provide employment to the local people, generate more revenue, provide forward and backward linkage advantages, and, above all, recognition of the rural areas as part of national economic engine (GNP). Once people find employment opportunities locally – in the rural areas – they will not migrate to the cities and towns. The research is skewed when it is concluded that villages are not as strong economic engines as cities.

Indian rural areas have bright and promising future. The guiding steps:

1. The central government should establish a high powered expert committee, similar to the High Powered Expert Committee for Estimating the Investment Requirements for Urban Infrastructure Services, to research and establish needs and requirements in the Indian rural areas.

   The committee should provide infrastructure and services' standards and/or guidelines for rural areas.

The committee should provide list of opportunities for economic growth in rural areas.

The committee should be chaired by rural/regional/urban planning professional. The committee should be multi-disciplinary with majority of planning professionals. The multi-disciplinary sub-committee representing each state should be represented by planning professionals.

2. The states should take lead in preparing regional development plans with goals to explore economic opportunities in rural areas with mission to retain rural population in rural areas.
3. The nearby Urban Local Bodies (ULBs) should actively participate in this endeavor to manage urban sprawl, slums, congestion and other urban issues and problems due to the migration from rural to urban areas. The benefits of this project may outperform the cost.
4. The rural areas should cooperatively hire experts and consultants to prepare plans and guide them to become self-sustainable by exploring possible and feasible economic opportunities. The consultants can suggest to make rural areas vigilant and become active part of the Gross National Product (GNP) system. This will make recognize rural areas as active economic engines like cities.

13.6 Rural comprehensive plan

The rural planning is almost synonymous with urban/town planning. The application of principles is relatively same but at smaller scale. Certain uses and applications may differ, such as minimum lot size, building structures on farm land, and use of agricultural land. Some conditions and restrictions may differ. The planning processes are the same.

The villages and/or rural areas should prepare comprehensive plans. The comprehensive plans can follow the same by cities and provided here. The comprehensive plans for rural areas are less detailed and less complex. The vision and goals and objectives must be established in association with the settlement residents. This will provide consensus, support, and expedite the implementation of goals and objectives.

The study of elements of existing features of population, housing, services, and utilities may not need much detailing. The preparer should be careful of projecting and forecasting of various elements. The check list of problems, issues, and concerns will assist in developing solutions.

The element of economic development will require special attention. Experts should be involved, if needed, to understand the local, regional, state, and national level economic gears.

Local, regional, state, and national level transportation connectivity of the economically active area is vital to ship and dispose of perishable goods within reasonable time. While assessing existing roads and streets and future needs of roads and local streets, the use and size of agricultural equipment, farm equipment, other locally used equipment and local daily traffic should be considered.

13.7 Redevelopment plan

Villages are organism like cities and towns. But they grow at much slower pace than cities. This is a healthy sign for villages. The originality in terms of form, layout, architecture, art, style, and structural layout of the settlement must be preserved to the possible extent. The plan should record the history of the local residents as narrated by the local and elderly population. The local historic features, such as buildings, old trees, specimen trees, sites and other features must be preserved and recognized in the text and on the site with plaques, etc.

The new development should be carefully planned, integrating, meshing, and nexus with the existing built environment. The open spaces, parks, and play lots should be creatively carved without disturbing harmony.

The housing element is as important in rural areas as in cities. The planers and architects should study the existing stock of housing and needed housing stock in very near future, short-range, and long-range need.

13.8 Smart rural areas

The rural areas have many innovative options to become smart rural areas, unlike cities.

- The plans should provide list of innovative energy sources in rural area produced from local byproducts.
- The choice of using wireless technology. If a service provider is installing a telecommunication tower in the area, the rural area residents should negotiate with the service provider to offer service to the resident at no cost or nominal cost, in exchange of allowing to install telecommunication structure.
- The planner should install GIS technology in rural areas for farmers. GIS can keep soil database, crop distribution, fallow areas, and crop rotation.
- GIS can manage ground moisture content, presence of harmful insects and mildew.
- GIS can manage status of specialty cultivated rows, monitor health of individual crops, adapt to sunlight, slopes.
- GIS can accurately estimate variable yields, help maximizing crop production.
- GIS can assist in harvest analysis, selection of prospective planting sites, in-field data collection and determining irrigation requirements.
- GIS can manage land data, information about new varieties, and fertilizer distribution.
- GIS can assist in determining crop selection for the whole village/area wide. Farmers do not have to guess who is growing what and when.
- The rural areas can come at par with smart cities by installing same systems in their settlements. Number of villages can pool together to make the system cost effective and enjoy economies of scale.
- With smart technology in rural areas, young population and students can learn the use and operation of new technologies and be competitive.

- Rural areas should incorporate innovative technologies in their day-to-day life, solar energy, wind energy, husk energy production, and energy from animal waste.
- Rural areas should use construction alternatives invented by Central Building Research Institute, Roorkee, and National Building Code of India.
- Smart technology can connect rural area residents with global world.

13.9 Conclusion

Smart villages can be catalyst for traditional cities to become smart cities. Together, smart villages and smart cities of India can become world leader to fill the gap of urban and rural spaces.

Each and every Indian citizen should pledge:

To make every city, town, village to be the most beautiful place to live, work, play, learn, invest, worship and raise a family in the most beautiful place on earth – India.

Chapter 14
Making India good to great

14.1 Urban overview

Cities are economic engines. Cities are social and cultural cradles. Cities are political and administrative arenas. Cities are dynamic places offering opportunities, choices, and variety. Cities are symbols of pride and status. Cities show how we live. Cities reflect local culture. Cities must be preserved. Cities must be cared. Cities must protect their infrastructure and services. Cities must preserve its history and heritage. Cities must be sustainable. Cities must respect its hinterland. Cities must interact with other cities. Cities must grow. Cities must manage growth wisely. Cities must take themselves seriously. Cities must plan for present and future.

The urban sector's share of the country's gross domestic product (GDP) is expected to increase from its current 67 percent to over three quarters of the total in 15 years. This makes the case that India's urbanization will be grown in the coming decades. This dynamic change presents long laundry list of opportunities and challenges. Must reiterate, cities offer engaging opportunities and fascinating challenges. According to the latest 2011 census, the urban population is 377 million with 31 percent of its share. There has been about six times increase in India's urban population from 62 million in 1951 to 377 million. The number of cities has grown from 5480 in 2001 to 7933 in 2011. Already the number of metropolitan cities with population of 1 million and above has increased from 35 in 2001 to 50 in 2011 and is expected to increase further to 87 by 2031. By the next census more than 41 percent of its population is likely to be residing in urban centers, which is not too far. Over the last two decades, India's urban population has increased from 217 million to 377 million and is expected to reach 600 million by 2030. As projected by UN report – "India is at the brink of an urban revolution." Besides natural growth, people are adding to cities with migration from rural areas.

The current pattern of urbanization is largely taking place on the fringe of cities, much of it is unplanned and outside the purview of city codes and bylaws and is imposing high costs on ULBs. Unprecedented growth is leaving local governments and central government with critical infrastructure shortage and service gaps. According to the High Powered Expert Committee recommendation (March, 2011), a total investment of US$822 billion (2009–10 prices) (₹39.2 lakh crore) is required to build infrastructure and services of water, sewerage, solid waste, management, urban roads, traffic support infrastructure, storm water drains, and street lighting – cost of land not included. Ahead of that is McKinsey's report suggesting need of US$2.2 trillion to improve infrastructure in Indian cities. Urban air pollution is projected to become the top environment cause of premature mortality. Recent estimates show that the cost of environment degradation, largely driven by sprawling cities, is reducing India's GDP. Many research studies, reports, articles, books, and other research activities claim that urban areas are experiencing increased population congestion, traffic congestion, under provision or shortage of infrastructure, under provision or shortage of services, air pollution, water pollution, noise pollution, lighting glare, shortage of housing, increased crime and drug use, slums, increased stray cattle population, deteriorating quality of life, immeasurable psychological impact on citizens, and compromised sustainability. These are alarming conditions for urban areas and its citizens. ULBs have mountainous tasks to manage and operate them. The reader must not get the notion that nothing is being done. Again, ULBs, states, and central government are working hard to provide necessary utilities and services to the citizens. The main challenge is to bridge gap between the fast rate of urbanization and the speed at which infrastructure and services are installed and provided.

In Indian context, unplanned and haphazard growth and development has triggered four types of urban areas. Depending upon the nature of the project, these can be further sub-divided for detailed studies. For example, slums can be classified according to the level of utilities and services they have.

Affluent urban areas: These are the areas occupied by citizens with ample resources, elite, rich, politically supported people, elected officials, affluent professionals, top level administrators, foreign dignitaries (in case of Delhi, Mumbai, Kolkata, Chennai, Hyderabad, Bangalore and some other cities) and their help (servants, watchmen, cooks, domestic help, drivers, chauffeurs, gardeners, and runners). The peculiar urban setting is – piecemeal distribution of affluent areas. They are located at the prime real estate areas of the city. Most of them live in gated homes or communities. Either they own them or lease them or provided by entities they work for. The areas are equipped with quality infrastructure, state-of-the-art services, and up-scale shopping areas, well-maintained roads and communication, and areas are well protected for safety.

Mid-level living areas: These are for the middle-class citizens, which include professionals, teachers, engineers, doctors, professors, businesspeople, entrepreneurs, and other middle-income people. They are spread all over the city. They live where affordable housing, educational institutions, infrastructure, and services are available. They also prefer mixed-use areas for easy access to services. These areas are equipped with markets, shopping centers, services, and proximate access to other day-to-day needs. Generally, services and infrastructure are of second quality.

Poor-level living areas: These are for people who live on margins with limited infrastructure and services. These people could be teachers, postmen, policemen, policewomen, services providers, small businessmen, "wallas," small entrepreneurs, small job performers, drivers, servants, and people with limited income. They share common shopping areas and markets. They generally are in more shady areas. They generally commute to work places. They select inexpensive or second-class and -hand services. They are part of the society to "make things happen."

Slums/ghettos/jhuggis/choppar: Different names in different areas. They are not desired in cities, but interestingly they are part of every city. According to one estimate, 25% our India's urban population lives in slums. These residents live with no or marginal infrastructure and services. They live in sub-standard human conditions. They are found everywhere and anywhere in the city: on vacant lots, government/public lands, private properties, sidewalks at night time, in front of closed shops at night time, intersections of roads, special slum areas, railway stations, bus stands/terminals, under bridges, buildings under constructions, incomplete or abandoned buildings, river banks, and wherever they can find a spot to install a head cover with access to water. Interestingly, Indian Railways is the big promoter of slums. Indian Railways premises, ROWs, railway stations, extended areas of railway stations, and other railway properties are heavens for slum dwellers. They get free place to live with free ample round-the-clock water supply, electricity, shelter, human sympathy, and services. They go this far to give birth to babies and raise families on the Indian Railway premises without paying a penny. Ironically, a citizen has to purchase a "platform ticket" prior to entering the Indian Railway station (platform) or has to pay a hefty fine, if caught. These slum dwellers get many services totally free of charge. They do not even need to purchase a platform ticket – they are exempted by an unwritten law – or every taxpayer pays for their services. Slum dwellers own mobile phones but have no electricity supply. They use second party public and private sources to charge their phone. There are many other such examples in India where public properties are being used to house slums. Are we encouraging slums in India?

14.2 Fairness and equity

Every citizen is entitled to fairness and equitable access to infrastructure and services in a city. Availability of clean drinking water, electricity, sewer, solid waste services, safety, education, health services, well-managed roads, clean roads, clean environment, and other day-to-day life sustainable requirements should be fairly and equitably available. Provision of these services and infrastructure makes people prefer to live in cities. Every city should assess itself to determine the threshold of services and level of services available on regular and consistent basis. Municipalities should conduct surveys to learn about the level of services provided to the citizens and strive to improve the services to provide quality of life to the citizens. ULBs should contract third party consultants to evaluate their operation and performances. The consultants should provide with recommendations to improve the quality of life of citizens to ULBs.

14.3 Urban diffusion

Overcrowding of population, shortage of suitable housing, aging housing, aging infrastructure, expansion limitation due to existing built environment, availability of limited resources, expensive real estate, competition for limited opportunities, deteriorating environment have prompted to create a program to handle the existing conditions of Indian cities. Urban diffusion of people to other and new cities will carry with it – jobs, opportunities, infrastructure, and services to other areas with potentials and opportunities of quality growth, balanced development, and absorption of externalities.

14.4 Assumptions and reality

With sincere and honest toil, efforts, and planning, existing cities can be brought up to the acceptable level of quality of life. Provided they have zeal, commitment, and determination.

However, if the existing large cities improve quality of services in a short period of time, they may attract more in migrants from rural areas. This may cause imbalance between the impact of in migration with the desired level of achievement of goals.

14.5 The urbanization model

14.5.1 Issue and background

The number of people living in cities is growing faster than they can sustain. There are acceptable standards of infrastructure and services need to be provided to the citizens to maintain an acceptable level of quality of life. The infrastructure includes water, sewer, roads, streets, streetlights, and other infrastructure, and services include educational institutions, health services, libraries, and recreational facilities (these have been covered in detail in this text). Resultantly, urban areas are experiencing increased population congestion, traffic congestion, under provision or shortage of infrastructure, under provision or shortage of services, air pollution, water pollution, noise pollution, lighting glare, shortage of housing, increased crime and drug use, slums, increased stray cattle population, and immeasurable psychological impact on citizens and compromised sustainability. This mean deteriorating quality of life.

Urban population is growing since the independence so are number of cities and towns. The challenge is to create acceptable balance between the growing urban population and growing number of cities and towns and provide a certain level of services and infrastructure.

14.5.2 Theme of the model

1. Provide quality of life in every existing city, town, and village in the country.
2. Improve quality of life in each and every village, town, and city in the country.
3. Balance the urbanization and development in the country by:
   (a) Diffusion of the urban population from the already pressured urban area to the potential towns, cities, and villages;

(b) Shift of future rural to urban (existing and already pressured) migration to the potential relatively small towns, small cities, and large villages;

(c) Retention of rural population in rural areas; and

(d) Reversing migration from towns and cities to rural areas.

14.5.3 The cascading process

There are nine primary action categories of this model. Each category is sub-detailed. Each sub-category is equipped with working details. These are intertwined throughout the process.

1. Site selection
2. Transportation and communication
3. Zoning assignment
4. Comprehensive approach
5. Infrastructure and services
6. Housing
7. Commercial and industrial
8. Marketing and incentive
9. Transparent governance

14.5.4 Pillars of the model

Following are basis of each primary action category:

(1) Site selection

- Select existing small and medium size towns and cities with potentials to attract and install diffused population and opportunities. Through this process new cities can be created as well.
- Select other areas in relation to small and medium towns and cities to attract and install diffused population and create opportunities.
- The diffused population and opportunities will be from the big magnet cities (e.g. Ahmedabad, Pune, Mumbai, Indore,

Kolkata, Hyderabad, Vijayawada, Delhi, Chennai, Chandigarh, and likewise cities) to selected areas.
- Central government and state governments collaboratively give incentives (e.g. tax credits) to citizens adopting established policies to balance the urbanization and development.
- ULBs and local governments will be equipped with professional staff. Traditional management system by traditional administrative personnel should be totally restricted.

Site selection plan

(a) Small and medium size towns and cities and large villages or other areas with potentials of growth and with opportunities to accommodate additional population.
(b) Areas with acceptable topography.
(c) Areas with available and needed natural resources.
(d) Areas with easy and vulnerable access to existing transportation lines.
(e) Areas with proximity to the requirements of the proposed business plan, e.g. raw material and availability of both skilled and unskilled work force.
(f) Coordination with Transportation and Communication Plan from initial stages and throughout the process.

(2) Transportation and communication
- The selected areas will have potential to be efficiently connected with local and regional transportation system.
- The selected areas will have efficient intra or internal (other cities) transportation system.
- The selected areas will have potential to be efficiently connected with – from local extension to – national level transportation system. The areas should have potentials to be well-connected through roads, rails, air, and waterways (where applicable).
- The selected areas should have potential to be efficiently connected with the state-of-the-art communication system – locally, regionally, nationally, and internationally.

Transportation and communication plan

To meet the fundamental prerequisites, preparation of transportation and communication plan is recommended with the following steps:

(a) Inventory and analysis of potential existing small and medium size towns and cities and other areas, e.g. large villages, identification of topographically challenged areas, and identification of opportunities for certain modes of transportation.

(b) Establishment of goals and objectives of the transportation plan depending upon the local needs and development plan.

(c) Environmental studies must be conducted for the area to protect the local and regional environment and maintain eco-balance.

(d) Transportation plan with alternatives in coordination with environmental studies and site selection plan.

(e) Transportation plan includes roads, rail, buses, air, and waterway (if available).

(f) Transportation plan includes various modes of transportation such as, bicycle, two-wheelers, three-wheelers, cars, transit, rickshaws, sleek inter-city modes, animal-driven vehicles, human-driven goods vehicles, and pedestrians.

(g) Transportation plan includes freight transportation system.

(h) Implementation and maintenance plan must be in place prior to adoption of the plan.

(3) Zoning assignment

The right assignment of various land uses at the new sites is vital. This can be achieved through appropriate zoning assignments to land parcels. Initially, establishment of zoning districts to manage the development process is the foremost step. The zoning assignment must be equipped with trained and experienced staff to implement and enforce the law. No use or operation shall be permitted unless it meets the established policies and ordinances. The purpose to establish policies and ordinances is to balance urbanization and development. GIS technology can assist in maintaining the land parcel data and prepare and maintain zoning maps and existing and future land use maps.

Zoning assignment plan

(a) Establishment of zoning districts for the existing uses and activities for every city, town, village, and special areas.

(b) Identification and establishment of zoning districts for the proposed development areas and activities for every city, town, village, and special areas.

(c) Establishment of zoning text details for each district.

(d) Careful identification and establishment of bulk area requirements for each zoning district.

(e) Identification and establishments ordinances for various planning elements such as parking, signs, landscaping, towers, animal control, environmental, and others as needed.

(f) Establishment and adoption of development/subdivision regulations.

(g) Coordination with other plans such as comprehensive plan, transportation plan, and site selection plan.

(h) The zoning ordinance must be equipped with the provision of administrative approval process of the use application.

(4) Comprehensive approach

The areas must be studied and analyzed comprehensively in its strengths, potentials, prospects, weaknesses, and challenges.

The comprehensive approach will encompass and coordinate with other elements of the built and unbuilt environment.

Comprehensive approach plan

(a) Establishment of principal idea of preparation of comprehensive/development plan.

(b) Establishment of mission, vision, goals, and objectives of the comprehensive plan.

(c) Establishment of elements needed to be incorporated in the plan.

(d) Preparation of doable, implementable, practical, and functional projects with identification of responsible entity, practical timeline, and source of resources.

(e) Built-in mechanism for monitoring and evaluation of the plan.

(f) Continuous coordination with other plans and entities of various levels – local, regional, state, and national.

(5) Infrastructure and services

The selected sites must provide state-of-the-art infrastructure and services to the existing and potential population. The policy must establish priority to provision of infrastructure (water supply, sewerage, solid waste management, storm water management, street lights, urban roads, urban transport, and traffic support infrastructure) in areas selected to adopt this model.

Priority to provision of services (schools, colleges, health centers, hospitals, recreational activities, parks, and open spaces) in the areas selected to adopt this model. No exceptions unless approved by a committee or board. The committees and boards must consist of diversified membership.

Infrastructure and services plan

(a) Preparation of plans to provide state-of-the-art infrastructure and services (water supply, sewerage, solid waste management, storm water management, street lights, urban roads, urban transport, traffic support infrastructure and schools, colleges, health services, hospitals, recreational activities, performance places, parks, and open spaces) in coordination with comprehensive plan/development plan, transportation plan, site selection plan and other plans on as needed basis.

(b) Commitment and availability of financial resources needed to implement the plan.

(c) The plan should be facilitated with future expansion and connectivity.

(d) The plan must be equipped with the qualities of Smart Cities concept.

(6) Housing

The policy must establish firm guidelines for the provision of sufficient and adequate housing of various types for all income levels and different social sectors in areas selected to adopt this model. Incentives to developers with inclusionary housing plans should be made part of zoning assignment.

Housing plan

(a) Housing plan, an integral part of the comprehensive plan, must be incorporated in detail.

(b) Plan should include inventory of the existing stock, analysis, projections, and provisions of various types of housing for various income level groups.

(c) Provisions of incentives and requirements to build housing through employers. Making the housing part of the total entrepreneurial project.

(d) Provisions of incentives for private building of housing stock.

(e) Provision and incentives for including smart technologies in to the new housing construction, e.g. rainwater harvesting, zero solid waste management.

(f) Incentives for design of housing equipped with renewable energy sources such as solar.

(g) Diverting money available through PPP, "yojanas", schemes, and plans.

(h) Encouraging other organizations, involved in housing projects, to participate and implement this model.

(7) Commercial and industrial

The sites must be made attractive by providing for commercial activities to meet day-to-day activity needs. These commercial areas must have "Indian Market Concept" layout and design. There should be public and private incentives for entrepreneurs to initiate and participate in commercial activities. Pedestrian markets should be designed with other activities associated with them. The incentives should be streamlined to assist the people interested in participating in commercial activities.

Commercial incentives plan
   (a) Plan to provide day-to-day need services (shopping, retail, restaurants, cafés) within the area.
   (b) Plan commercial area with a theme and architectural style.
   (c) Plan for businesses to be complimentary with the existing businesses.
   (d) Partnership with banks, insurance companies, and other lending institutions to promote this model.

Industry and industrial incentives plan
The land uses at sites must identify industrial areas for diversified land uses and economic sector for skilled and unskilled jobs. This will also strengthen the revenue sources. The industries should be complementary to the local raw materials and work force. The industrial areas must be connected with efficient transportation system. The transportation links should be regional and national level. Depending upon the industry type, links may be on international level. Incentive programs for establishing and promoting industries must be marketed.

(8) Marketing and incentives
Provision of incentives and marketing to promote the urbanization model and make it a success. The model should be marketed nationwide. Carefully articulated incentives should be available with easy access.

Marketing and incentives plan
   (a) Preparation of effective plan to attract private–public partnership for various projects associated with the urbanization model.
   (b) Preparation of effective incentives plans to attract investments.
   (c) Preparation of effective marketing plan to invite investments, invite projects, invite people, and invite entrepreneurs.

(9) Transparent governance
Community trust should be established by installing transparent governance. The model should provide democratic local home rule

system with transparent operation to build trust among the citizens. ULBs should oversee the management of the city. State and center government should only act as guides and check progress and success of the model.

Transparent governance plan

(a) Establishment of Transparent Government system.
(b) Establishment of e-government in the area.
(c) Establishment of open and easy communication between various entities of the area.
(d) Establishment of policy to place planning/town and country planning department to manage the project(s).
(e) Establishment of process to educate planners in administration and budgeting.
(f) Establishment of process to educate administrators in planning discipline.
(g) Establishment of easy, simple, expeditious system for business operators and professionals to obtain business/operating license/permit with nominal fee. This includes every business types and operations in the area such as, all 'wallas,' squatters, repair technicians, doctors, engineers, home occupations, home businesses, tailors, welders, and the list goes on.
(h) Establishment of policy-making planning department overseeing the issuance of business licenses/permits. Planning department must review the application with the zoning map to evaluate if the proposed use is permitted in the zoning district.
(i) Establishment of "moratorium" of allowing a new business/ operation in the existing cities and towns. An effective system and carefully designed policy to discourage people to initiate new businesses or occupations in the existing metropolitan cities. The policy must be enforced strictly.
(j) Establishment of policy in the small and medium size cities to allow, support, and encourage new business, occupations, and professions.
(k) Establishment of the policy to allow new businesses, provided they meet the established standards.

(l) Establishment of standards to allow new businesses providing adequate housing to employees, hiring employees with possession of adequate housing, businesses with right zoning of operation, businesses with appropriate space to operate activities, businesses providing adequate parking, and so on.

(m) Establishment of policy to encourage businesses to move to newly identified potential areas (small and medium size towns).

In conclusion, urbanization model is creating opportunities in the identified areas, preparing respective plans, imposing moratorium on opening new businesses.

14.6 Slums to utopia model

Substandard of living in cities is impacted with migration of rural poor to urban areas. These migrants do not have adequate housing equipped with utilities in cities. Proper type of housing is beyond their means. Affordable and reasonable housing is not available for them. This inclusion of people to cities gets the title of "urbanization." This is a false urbanization. This is further enhanced by natural growth of cities. There are sporadic success stories of people becoming rags to riches but they are rare. These urbanites are deprived of the basic human survival needs and services. These residents cannot afford to acquire and pay for housing, utilities, and services. These immigrants settle and build affordable structures with a roof of whatever discarded material they find from trashed sites. These structures are, sometimes, excellent examples of creativity, imagination, cleverness, originality, and innovation and ingenious ideas and human endurance. Slum dwellers find their niche in urban area to create a shelter to survive and fit into the urban heaven. This could be any place such as under a tree, under a bridge, unoccupied building, sidewalk, vacant lot, railway station, worship places, bus terminals, or public spaces.

There is lot of research material available telling how much slums in the various cities of India, e.g. Mumbai 57%, Delhi 45%, Ahmedabad 25% and on an average one out of three urbanites is a slum dweller or on average in every city a quarter of its population live in slums. In any respect, there are too many slums. Substandard living conditions in slums are not acceptable at any scale. A number of world level organizations and institutions are suggesting and interfering with national polices and plans to support plans to shed substandard living of human beings. There are some successes in helping people to get out of slum conditions. But still there is a big ocean of slums out there.

There are plenty of opportunities for the slum dwellers to get motivated to improve their living conditions. NGOs, local, regional, state and central governments, and various organizations, institutions, including international entities participate and collaborate to improve the living conditions for the people residing in slums. Many years ago, economists adopted the slogan, "India is a rich country inhabited by poor people." Many treatises were written to justify this statement. They were true on their part. The new slogan for economists now is, "India is a rich but poor country inhabited by too many people." Resources are limited. No new land is made. Excess exploitation of resources create imbalances – natural or manmade. The present generation of slum dwellers must make firm decisions considering how it is going to impact their children in the future. The most commonly used definition of sustainability and sustainable development is development that meets the needs of the present without compromising the ability of future generations to meet their own needs. If more people are pushed into a house than it is built for, will certainly create chaos; in the same way more people than a country can sustain will create problems and imbalances.

In Indian cities, many migrants are jamming into substandard housing, poorly served infrastructure and social services, while ubiquitous new districts of isolated superblocks provide a shallow and unsustainable urban life. With the new economic cycle, the gap between rich and poor is growing. Slum dwellers are occupying both public and private land. Slums are growing in spite of many active programs, projects, schemes, and "yojanas" at various levels.

The housing demand for cities, for many decades, has been met through a combination of formal (legal) and informal (illegal) supply of housing. Some researchers believe that this is to be expected in a developing and urbanizing economy. The agreement is only to a certain extent. The careful planning, implementation, enforcement, monitoring, and evaluation of the policies, projects, and plans are the tools to handle community needs right from the beginning – before they become a problem – especially in case of slums. Educating citizens about the cause and effects of actions by the citizens can help reduce and mitigate the impact of unplanned actions.

As 31 percent of nation's population choose to live in cities, according to the 2011 census, is changing the human conditions irreversibly. From rural areas and small scale intimate societies based on subsistence economies experiencing change. More urbanites now becoming increasing part of globally connected, fast-paced societies, with thousands of strangers and with remote natural environment is norm. This successful urbanization is leading to provide better quality of life; simultaneously it is the venue of consistent poverty, diseases, conflict, and environmental deterioration. Studies have shown that the slum communities remain at subsistence level, perpetually dependent upon political patronage, and sympathy of the haves-society. The understanding of poor people's survival in urban areas is important because it is not cost free. Poor people sustain themselves by procuring essential goods and services themselves (some cases partial by the government): by fetching water, negotiating for food, waiting for medical assistance, commuting for many hours to job, etc. Most of their time is spent in acquiring basic necessities that keep them going but that do not typically cumulate in terms of knowledge, skills, or wealth. This is a wasteful use of people's time: people can be creative, entrepreneurial, and progressive. This life cycle has short-term and long-term impact on the society as a whole and to the individual slum dwellers and slum households.

The slum dwellers, like other humans or urbanites, have families and children. Adults can make choices and decisions. Like other children, children of slums depend upon their adults to make decisions for their lives. These adults might have made a well-thought decision to move to urban areas for a better quality of life compared with where they came from. But urban areas did not welcome them by providing basic needs of housing, utilities, and services. These children are raised in an environment which is depressing and humiliating. Deprived living conditions of slums may have lifelong psychological impact on these children. They do not have access of amenities and facilities as compared to children of haves-families in a city. They witness and observe haves-children having fulfilling lives. Slum children may not have access to schools not to mention balanced and nutritious food. When they grow up, what and how will they contribute to the society? Their outlook towards life and society may be different from haves-children. They will be citizens of India with what level of ambition and zeal. Slums must be tackled seriously and replaced with decent, clean, and proper housing and amenities. Children of slums must be educated for their and society's future. They are national asset like haves-children.

The country of Taj Mahal, monumental palaces, great forts, massive mansions, estates, extraordinary architectural buildings, astonishing, stunning, and amazing worshipping buildings and places, beautiful villages, and home of God, gods, and goddesses is now tarnished and tainted with the unacceptable living conditions for too many Indian citizens – called "slums." The mythology of taking care of God's best creation – mankind – stands at the test of time. One of the strongest philosophies of Indian culture – care of mankind through mutual actions – needs rejuvenated identification and definition. The procrastinating or ignoring or in situ an issue is not a solution at least in case of – slums.

14.6.1   The reality

Two totally opposite forces are at tug-of-war in Indian cities. The first force is the attraction of cities for jobs, opportunities, choices, variety, and hope for better quality of life. These are the pull factors for masses to move to cities from rural areas. Where they do not have high-paying jobs or land ownership or other reasons to improve their life-style. The opposite force is incapability of cities to provide proper and sufficient housing, infrastructure (water, sewer, power, roads, streets, garbage disposal facilities) and services (education, health care, recreation). But this force is not working as "push" factor for the migrants. Rather, these immigrants accept and compromise with what they have and try to assimilate in the local environment economically and socially. The migrants seek any opportunity to fit into the urban system. They accept whatever is available to survive. Thus create slums. These two elements are the basis of "slums to utopia" model.

The migrants are moving to the cities but the cities are not ready for them. The number of migrants is much higher than the supply of housing, sanitation facilities, water, and other services cities are equipped with to provide. The ratio between the two is disproportionate. This imbalance is creating slums. Another factor is that the pay level of jobs for new migrants is very low. They do not have qualifications and skills to get high-paying jobs. With what they make, they cannot afford to rent or buy proper housing. These migrants from rural areas lack education and skills required for better paying jobs, and training for specialized jobs. The situation is further deteriorated for the poor migrants when cities do not offer opportunities to make a positive change in their lives. Sociologists and economists may agree that these new migrants are "exploited" in urban areas by the urban system. The lack of basic education bars the new comers to avail the opportunities available to get educated, if any. Consequently, they end up taking low-paying jobs and can only afford to live in slums.

Slums can very easily become poverty traps that force poor households into vicious cycle of deprivation and underdevelopment. Land in urban areas is very costly and beyond the means of the poor people to purchase it. In order to seek shelter and living quarters, they build their own temporary shacks by illegally occupying lands. On account of a lack of secured tenure, low-income households are deterred from making significant investments in living conditions improvements. These temporary shelters lack water supply, electricity, sanitation, sewer, toilets and other facilities enjoyed by other settled city dwellers. Slum dwellers have no choice but to defecate outdoors. As a result, people are exposed to a bacteria brew that often sicken them. This situation impacts people who are living in proper housing with toilets as well. Children are more prone to diseases because of exposure to bacteria. Living in illegal (informal) housing makes low-income households vulnerable to a variety of social, economic, and political forms of exploitation that are likely to further push their incomes down. Having to live under a constant threat of eviction, they also have to pay a higher social and psychological cost.

The government operations have to be based on fairness and equity. Citizens can and should question government policies if they are skewed or biased or lop sided. The inquiry is extended; how it impacts them; how the tax payer's money is spent; should people with limited resources be extended help by the government; should people with limited resources help themselves; why people with limited resources be helped; should they help themselves; give them "fish" or "fishing-rod." Are slums results of negligence, irresponsibility, incompetency, inability on the part of implementing institutions and staff; is the government policy to make cities slum-free or remove slums in the cities is impotent; are politicians responsible for slums because of their support to get votes from slum dwellers?

The slum dwellers living in sub-standard conditions in cities are national level concern. They are churning high level wheels to correct the problem. International organizations use their sticks to stir the pot. Sometimes it is questionable if the international organizations are "good-Samaritan" or have double standards or have hidden agendas. The same people living in villages in straw huts or *kutcha* structures do not stir enough commotion. They may not own land in the village to build a structure but has space to build a sustainable structure to live with the family. Let us use this scenario as acceptable and adoptable.

14.6.2 Cascading push process

Local action

The process to manage slums must be the responsibility of the local level planning department. Planning departments are equipped with the tools required to initiate the slum management process, e.g. GIS, maps, land records, and details about the existing infrastructure and services and city records. The department prepares and manages comprehensive plans and other community plans. A different entity, handling slums projects, may have to reinvent the wheel. Planners are trained to integrate, manage, implement, enforce, monitor, and evaluate the projects. Planners are trained to have better understanding of the community as a whole; understanding of built environment and natural environment. State level departments, even state level planning departments, may not be familiar with local planning and slum issues. Center level slum removal or slum improvement policies may be practical or functional on paper. They are not familiar with the local slum issues. Like cities, slums are different from each other. Each slum portions have their own identity and has its own list of problems and issues. Central government should only direct and provide resources and coordinate the slums issues with the local governments. State government planning department should only act as liaison between the central government and ULBs. Slum problem is not only recognized in metro cities but are also undesirable in small and medium size cities. The involved parties in this process must take initiative to experience the slum conditions by preparing a program for decision makers, policy makers, administrators, local elected officials, and stakeholders to associate with the slum dwellers by living with them to experience first-hand day-to-day life in slums. The central government should prepare program for elected officials, administrators, higher level managers, experts, stakeholders, IAS practitioners, trainers and trainees and citizens to experience slum living for at least certain period of time by living in slums, with slum dwellers. The planning department must have strong implementation arm to carry out the plans and policies.

Regional action

The central, state, regional, and local level planning departments, transportation departments, communication department, engineering departments, infrastructure related departments, and public service departments, and other associated departments should be ready with transportation plans, infrastructure plans, public services plans, historic preservation plans, environmental sustainability plans, and other related plans depending on the area. These plans must be practical, functional, sustainable, implementable, and operational. The plans must be prepared in consideration of the available resources. The funds must be committed and appropriated by the responsible entities. The plans should be flexible with scenario to expand, extend, and modify the projects on as needed basis. The plans should be prepared with future in consideration. The plans must be flexible to adapt technology changes, economic changes, and social and cultural changes with time, to the possible extent. The plans must have "enforcement" element incorporated with provision of enforcement policies, procedures, and trained staff. The enforcement must be community oriented. The enforcement should not be like a police action or military attack. The citizens should be respected during the enforcement, not harassed. After all, they are citizens of free India, may be poor.

The policies, through incentives, should direct the availability of opportunities in rural areas and small towns. In addition, low-paying jobs, dead-end jobs, and irresponsible jobs should be eradicated with time. According to the India's Planning Commission, poverty level was earnings of 37 Indian rupees per day. Go figure.

The enforcement should be a priority for the local government. Before writing the prescription for the disease, it should be stopped spreading. In other words, no new slums should be allowed to install and new additions of population to the slums should be stopped, at any cost, except natural growth. Even that should be stopped by educating the existing population. The analogy is "if a path is cleared in a jungle, next morning it is covered again with bushes." What good those efforts are?

Community involvement

Slum communities have to be communicated with organized, structured, and well-planned strategies. The plans should be motivation oriented to make positive changes in lives, not only for present slum dwellers but for the younger population. Ideally, a participatory, trustful, collaborative, and interactive relationship has to be established with the community. The local community politics and the project location's politics and dynamics must be skillfully incorporated in the project process.

Identification

The existing settlements must be surveyed and measured and recorded on GIS for validity and authenticity. It is recommended to prepare detailed maps of each slum area.

The planning department should keep, update, and maintain records of vacant lands and occupied lands through land use maps.

Through a check list, each slum settlement should be surveyed to record-existing conditions.

Existing information from other agencies, departments, institutions, and organizations should be collected and organized. This information can be used to prepare strategies to seek solutions to the issues.

Any land ownership disputes or claims should be very clearly recorded and addressed. Land disputes and legal involvement can not only increase cost but can delay the project, which is more costly.

Project planning

For each settlement project, financing has to be available and monitored.

Trained, efficient, and dedicated planning, architectural, engineering staff should be available to prepare proposals for each settlement. These proposals should be coordinated with the regional plans.

Building community should be selected, appointed, and ready to act on the proposals. The building community should be prepared to get their work certified and approved. The building community should be aware of innovative technologies and ideas.

Advance checks

The settlement must be assigned with proper addressing for each unit with its residents. This will help keep, maintain, and update the records. Local India Post (Post Office) should be involved in this process and should support the community endeavor. This will allow to establish direct connection with the residents.

The project manager/planner should involve other service providers to the citizens, such as mobile phone services, dish services, local phone services, automobile registrations, and driver license issuance agency should participate in this process. They should support the process by restricting issuance of new connections at these sites. Once the project is operational, these organizations should not renew any connections, certifications, membership, etc. Extensions may be provided with the authorization of the project manager/planner. They must be honest.

Local governments and utility supply authorities should support the planning process by managing the services they provide in coordination with the project manager, such as water supply, sewage, electricity, and solid waste management by restricting the services. Once an occupant moves, the connections should not be renewed or issued to a new occupant.

Local banks and other lending companies can be supportive in this venture; like other entities, they should similarly participate in the process.

Local educational institutions, police department, deputy commissioner's office, magistrate's office, and other local entities can assist and participate in the process.

Local Chamber of Commerce, Rotary Clubs, Lions Clubs, Kiwanis Clubs, YMCA, YWCA, business associations, women's groups, networking groups, lawyers' association, educational institutions, and other civic organizations should be encouraged to participate. This will help spread the message of improving Indian cities, not only locally but nationally.

Local media should be made partners in this process. They can play a vital role in this process by sending a positive message. Some community members rely on the media to obtain information and participate behind the curtains. Local media includes magazines, journals, newspapers, televisions, social media, and Internet news.

The media must be contacted by the project manager prior to the action and get their support. After all, the media staff live in the community too – it is their community.

The imminent step

The local planning department should be responsible for issuing business/occupation licenses for any and all type of business/occupations/professions in the city/town/village. Business license is an approved document from the local government authority/ULBs legally permitting to allow operation of a business/occupation/profession. The planning department should prepare a process methodologies based on fairness, equity, and legal requirements. The licenses should be renewed annually. The requirement of business license should be from mobile vendor to multi-national corporation. The business license application must be reviewed to assure the use is permitted in the zoning district. The applications are only approved if they meet the requirements.

The applications for new ventures should require to provide the information if the entrepreneur and employees have appropriate housing facilities. Appropriate housing should include, at least, a bedroom, kitchen, bathroom, and latrine. In Indian context, a third party should conduct a field research. There should be limit on the number of mistakes by the company.

This process can also assist in implementing many other legal requirements for various types of businesses, such as if the restaurant has proper dish-washing and hand-washing facilities, toilets for customers, trash disposal facilities; a *"chai-walla"* has running water facility to operate hygienic and sanitized operation; and a street vendor has a trash collection gadget attached to its operation vehicle.

The households who employ servants or domestic help should get certification from the medical experts and approved by the planning department. The department should be responsible to oversee the process of hiring only those with proper living conditions. These personnel have to be honest. They live in the same community. Some diseases are contagious or air-borne. They do not stop at the property line.

The offices that employ people with low-paying positions (attendants, peons, go-for, watchman, *chaukidars*, runners, delivery persons) should follow the same procedure and process.

The existing entities operating prior to the enacting of the law and other non-profit or non-business employers have to adhere the same laws and policies. However, they can amortize. Existing businesses must comply with the same rules and should be amortized over a certain period of time to meet the requirements. This can be very difficult but communities have to start somewhere.

This process can reduce and mitigate the slums situation to certain extent. Understandably, it is a slow-moving process model. Undoubtedly, it is monumental task. It is not feasible for an individual entity to correct the problem; however, it can be achieved with the cooperation of the other entities.

No turning back for settlement dwellers once provided with opportunities to change the way of life. A system should be established, through education and training, to move forward for the citizens to assimilate with the new way of life.

The process can be expedited by collaborating with the urbanization model described herein. The planning departments should prepare themselves for this monumental task. This endeavor may create opposition and vocal environment for ULBs. The settlements and coming generations will be admirable of these efforts. But planners must work with honesty, integrity, ethically, professionally, character, and morality. The confidence, dedication, and determination of the professionals are the tools for success.

14.7 Human growth and planning

Population is a very personal and individualistic decision-making process. But cumulatively, it impacts the country and whole system. In recent years, India has made significant progress in diffusing modern agricultural practices, building new industry, commerce, advancement in technology, and developing natural resources, all of which has increased national wealth. However, in a country which has rapidly expanding population, much of the newly created wealth must be used to provide food, housing, and other basic services for the additional people. With one-third population under the age of 15, the government must build educational institutions, day care centers, and hospitals. Therefore, the growing wealth is going primarily to provide a reasonable standard of living for an expanding population. Further, will employment be available to these 375 million children when they are old enough to work? The existing level of physical infrastructure and social services are struggling to maintain acceptable level of services for pleasant living. If the rate of population growth is faster than the speed of providing infrastructure and service, then the victory is beyond imagination.

Education, Education, Education: the general population should be educated about the consequences of having more children than they can afford. The orthodox system of bearing more children was much according to the needs of the time and worked. The new generation should be responsible of their decisions about family size. The national policies should be aggressive in spreading the message through education. Can India afford to have China-like population policies? Perhaps not. India's administrative and implementation infrastructure is very weak. National policy should require mandatory education of the couples prior to getting married about family planning and means to control birth of children. The education system should stress on quality than quantity. In this process, the religious institutions, religious leadership, and religious staff authorized to perform marriage commitments can assist in helping control the population growth. This action will require training and education of the religious community. Once educated, they can play a vital role in controlling population growth. The young people should be educated to be self-responsible about bearing the number of children. The young people should evaluate what kind of world they are inheriting and what kind of world they want to leave for their children.

14.7.1 Optimum population

What is the optimum size of the nation's population? The answer is simple. For every citizen of India, a suitable and respectable employment, adequate and proper living space, adequate privacy, physical accessibility, adequate open space, structural stability and durability, adequate security, security of tenure, adequate basic infrastructure, such as water supply, power, sanitation, waste management, and sewer, quality health care facilities, quality environment, transportation facilities, adequate recreational facilities, quality educational facilities, adequate social services, and safe, morally sound and aesthetically appealing living conditions, and ethical and transparent political and administrative system. The word "adequacy" is subjectively used here. It varies from person to person, community to community, city to city, and country to country. This determination depends on specific social, cultural, economic, age-specific, gender-specific, and environmental factors. Certain researchers and citizens hold government responsible for providing adequate requirements. They are correct but to some extent. Individual citizens should take initiative to improve their quality of life. The first step is: control of population growth – which is more individual's responsibility. Allowing government in one's bedroom is not a good idea and tolerable.

The present and near future's shift towards technology is changing the shape and form of job market. The shift is towards technology, skilled, education-oriented, and specialization-oriented jobs. Unskilled, labor, and other non-technical jobs are vanishing fast. The dependency is inclining more towards computers, technology, and innovative and creative ways of doing activities. Computers, ICT, sensors, networking, GIS, GPS, MIS, and other innovative technologies are being implanted in cities and day-to-day lives. Job sector is demanding more technically trained personnel. There will be more demand for people with innovative and creative ideas. Traditional job market is shrinking. Humans are not needed to perform many activities. Drones will be making deliveries instead of human couriers and postmen. Banking is done online instead by tellers. Google is designing driverless cars. Taxis will be driverless but will still take where passenger wants to go. There will be no need of servers in the restaurants. The patrons can order food on the electronic gadget provided on the table. If cities provide public bicycles, this may reduce need of rickshaws if not totally remove them from streets. Indian Railway is providing state-of-the-art seat reservation services. This reduces long lines to make reservation or hire someone to stand in line to make reservations. This trend is a caution for illiterate, non-technical, and unskilled segment of the society. The other factor impacting this scenario is the advanced knowledge of technology among Indians, both at home and other countries. These specialized professionals are making changes in leaps and bounds in India, in every sector. They are discovering niches in the Indian market to invest in their talents. This trend make the future further dim for non-technical, non-skilled, and uneducated segment of the society. Present times and trends are "wake-up" calls for the uncontrolled growth of population. Poor people will be further left behind, because of their limited resources they cannot invest in themselves or in their children. They spend their limited resources on acquiring basic necessities of life. Even if some do, by the time they catch up, the children of "haves" already have advanced further. It is hard to imagine the victory for haves-not children. The depicted picture sound depressing, but it is not, if the poor segment of the society take initiative to control the number of their children and invest in the right education of their children. This can be achieved through educating them. India, country as a whole, should think on the same lines.

The concept of public–private partnership (PPP) or only private investment in infrastructure and services. The fundamental doctrine of private sector is – maximization of profit. Private sector or shareholders of companies providing utilities to the citizens would like to have return for every penny of investment. In other words, nothing will be free. Indian municipalities provide, some times and some places, free water and sewer to the needy neighborhood. Individual citizens are not billed for that. However, someone pays for it. It is unlikely that private companies will allow use of services without any profit. The question is, how it will impact the poor segment of the society. They cannot afford to pay for those services. Unless there is a built-in policy or provision to allow use of utilities and services without any cost. This is very unlikely to happen. Poor and meager resource citizens should be very worried and concerned about the government's policy to encourage PPP projects. The situation is further worsen for un-skilled, labor, uneducated, and other related segment of society with meager resources. The foreign investments will not focus on the poor people. They will be pushed aside more than ever. These investments will focus on segment society which can give maximum return on their investment.

Non-governmental agencies can play a vital role, in Indian context, to make a difference in improving the quality of life for citizens by educating people. However, the opposite side should be watchful of NGOs' prerogative agenda and goals. They should assess, if they match, meet, or contradict the established community goals. An irresponsible action by NGOs can cause more damage than good for the community. NGO leadership should be community savvy and be patient to work in collaboration with the local entities.

Government of India is made of Indians. Every Indian should be responsible for their actions and respectable to each other. Every Indian should bear the responsibility of what India is. Every Indian, irrespective of rich or poor, should contribute to make India great, with diligent, responsible, dedicated, and honest efforts.

14.8 Salient features of making India good to great

Irrespective of being a traditional city or smart city or a village, to push them to being good to great requires commitments and determination by the communities. To make them functional and operational, settlements need to have commitment of providing basic services. Not only capitals, union territories, university campuses, and hospitals, but every household should be equipped with the required basic human needs.

14.8.1 Power/electricity

Without power nothing moves or happens. Energy is the key to economic development. Traffic lights do not operate without electricity. Without power, they create more dangerous conditions. Mobile phones need electricity for charging batteries. Cities should be equipped to provide electricity round-the-clock. Modern renewable energy sources should be retrofit in the modern day living.

14.8.2 Water

Water is a basic human need. Settlements should be equipped to provide round-the-clock clean potable water. Rivers, lakes, and other water bodies should be protected from getting polluted. Citizens should be educated to protect water resources.

14.8.3 Environment

Human health is precious. Human health should be protected by providing clean air, clean water, peaceful living (noise pollution), and eco-friendly environment. Citizens should be educated to protect the environment for sustainability.

14.8.4 Affordable housing

Settlement should have plans to provide affordable and proper housing to everyone. Slums are disgrace to human race. New technologies should be used to build structures.

Settlements should be equipped with service toilets for both genders until the system is prepared to provide housing for everyone. Citizens should be educated about the spread of diseases by outdoor toilets.

14.8.5 Education

Every citizen should have access to basic education, irrespective of social, gender, and financial status. The chain is as strong as its weakest link.

14.8.6 Healthy foods

The system should provide healthy organic foods to the citizens by checking the use of insecticides, pesticides, fertilizers, and other toxic chemicals which are harmful to human health.

14.8.7 Transportation

The settlements should be connected with safe, efficient, and functional transportation. Various modes should have respective space identity on the rights-of-ways.

14.8.8 Transparent government

The government is by the people and for the people. Government operation should be fair and equitable. Every citizen should trust the government – local, state, and center or the government should be trustworthy. The citizens should be educated about the rights and responsibilities and responsibilities of voting.

14.8.9 Opportunities

The system should provide opportunities for every citizen for jobs, entrepreneurship, and advancement and improve quality of life.

14.8.10 Children, elderly, and widows

This segment of the society is dependent on the young active population to perform day-to-day activities of life. Children are the foundation of future and elderly have paid their dues to the society. The system should provide needed services to them.

Because of the cultural heritage, widow segment of the society needs extra care by the society.

14.8.11 Open spaces

Human beings of all ages need open spaces for various types of activities. Exercise to relaxation to spirituality, open spaces are part of human living and should be given due recognition in settlements.

14.8.12 Green environment

Green helps sustain the environment. Wherever possible trees should be planted.

14.8.13 Work integrity/work ethics

The system should invest in training the workforce in work integrity and work ethics. Punctuality, discipline, accountability, timely performance, and honesty are the other names of greatness.

14.8.14 Clean/hygiene/sanitation

As a society, sanitation and hygiene is important to avoid spread of diseases. Keeping the settlement clean by practicing of not throwing trash and defecate anywhere and everywhere. Solid waste management should be part of the settlement management.

14.9 Conclusion

Each and every Indian citizen should pledge:

> *To make India a beautiful place to live, work, play, learn, worship, invest, and raise a family.*

Conclusion

"Bharat Hamara Desh Hai. Jaisa Banayange Vaisa hee Banega."
"Bharat is our county. It will be what we make of it."

Many external cultures have come to India and gone such as Mongolian, Middle Eastern, Afghan, British, French and Portuguese and others. They made India their home for centuries. They left their impressions on villages, towns and cities, planning, buildings, architecture, gardens, open spaces, food, dresses, language, and many other day to day life activities. May be we were selective in choosing what was considered "good" for us. But India and Indians survived and protected its culture and heritage. Now, it is our country. We are the planners, designers, protectors, custodians and in-charge of Bharat. The present times, again, are challenging us to adapt the globalization culture but at the same time protect and maintain our Indianship. The responsibility must be handled carefully and articulately. Presentation of our life style culture and stewardship must show the world we care and are serious about our Indian way of life. We must protect our built environment, natural environment, and human activities, irrespective of location, size, shape and form of the living environment. Each entity – villages, towns, cities and metro cities – must understand their role and identity in the national picture. Each entity must take responsibility to make them sustainable. Citizens should plan and manage entities to make better than they inherited and hand over to the next generation to be proud of their inheritance. Our legacy should be next generation's legacy with time. Like other elements of cultures; mathematics, astronomy, astrology, physics, chemistry, science, medical science, technology, communication, transportation, education, spirituality, religion, simplicity, culture, civilization and many others, our living style and habits and quality of life should be of prime concern of each and every Indian. The lifestyle associated with convenience, simplicity, environmental respect, mutual respect, harmony with nature, harmony with build environment, and closeness should be the platform of future development. We must plan today for the future.

LET US MAKE OUR INDIA A BEAUTIFUL PLACE TO LIVE, WORK, PLAY, LEARN, WORSHIP, INVEST, AND RAISE A FAMILY.

Index

74th Constitution Amendment Act, 29
   twelfth schedule to article 243W, 82–83

A

Address identification significance, 178
Affluent urban areas, 337
Agricultural rural zoning, 153
Agricultural zoning, 153
Air pollutants
   carbon dioxide, 142–143
   carbon monoxide, 142
   lead, 143
   nitrogen oxide, 142
   particulates, 143
   radon, 143
   sulfur dioxide, 142
   toxic chemicals, 143
Air pollution, 142
Air traffic control tower, 277
Aircrafts
   emitted pollutants, 280
   noise, 280
Airfield, 276
Airlines, 279
Airport
   air quality, 280
   airside, 275
   economic action, 278–279
   environmental issues, 279–281
   master planning, 281–282
   noise, 279–280
   operation, 275
   planning process, 281–282
   planning, 274–278
   water quality, 280–281
Airspace, 276
Alternative pavers, 220
Annual average daily traffic, 246
Approach lighting systems, 277
Arthashastra, 18
Asset mapping, 54–56
Average daily traffic, 245
Aviation, 278

B

Based aircraft, 275
Basic or general utility facility, 276
Basic plan structure, 29–35
   assumption, 31–32
   goals, objectives, and assumptions, 31
   plan preparation, data needed, 32–33
   vision statement, 32
Bicycle (s), 270–272
   manufacturing associations, 271

parking spaces, 270
–ride support groups, 271
Big–box retail, 131–132
Big–box shoppers, 132
Box rickshaws, 269
Built environment, 2
Bus service transportation system, 255–257
Bus stand facility, planning, 256
Bus terminal facility, planning, 255–256
Buses, weather–protected passenger shelter, 254
Business communities/small retailers, 132–133

C

Campus communities, 211–221
    building a theme, 214
    building the team, 213
    café and cafeteria, 216
    campus markets, 218
    charrettes, 214
    designing a campus, master planning, 212–214
    education to under privileged, 220–221
    educational institutions, 211–212
    faculty and staff housing, 217–218
    faculty residences, 216
    master plan and design elements, 214–216
    master planner, 220
    needs assessment study, 212–213
    students residences, 216–217
    transportation, 218–220
    vision and goals, 213–214
Central perspective projection, 56
Chandigarh
    design and layout change, 110
    Euclidian zoning system, 110
    shopping habits of Indian people, 110
    urban blight issues, 111
Charrettes, 51–54
    situations, 52
    differentiating strategies, 52–54
City (ies) See also Smart cities
    as a legal entity, 6
    as a physical organism, 6
    as a social cradle, 5–6
    as an economic entity, 3–4
    basic services required, 364–367
    economic base, 5
    employment structure, 5
    informal sector or informal economy, 5
    institutional structure, 6
    substandard living conditions, 349–350
    urban function
        education, 5
        exchange, 4

extraction, 4
government, 4
manufacturing, 4
religion/spiritual, 5
City designing
  settlement forms, 191
  well-designed environment, 192
Cities development plans *See also* Development plans
  capital investment needs, 299
  capital investments in infrastructure, 300
  climate change and the environment, 298–299
  construction activities, 301
  deteriorated infrastructure, 300
  development regulations, 301–302
  infrastructure challenges, 298–302
  infrastructure delivery, 302
  infrastructure demand, 301
  infrastructure planning, 301–302
  new and unevenly distributed growth, 300
  reducing energy use and carbon emissions, 299
  transportation infrastructure, 299
City planning organizations, 14
Classified traffic volume, 246

Coastal Regulations Zone areas, 31
Coastal waters, 313
Coastal zone management, 313–315
Coastline ecology, 313–314
Columbian Exposition of 1893, 23–25
Columbian Fair, 23–24
Combined or separate sewer overflow (CSO or SSO), 308
Commercial
  air carriers, 278
  area sidewalks, 234
  trip generation, 244
  uses, 130–131
  zoning, 150–152
Commodity transfer, 271–272
Community, power structure, 6
Community and stakeholder focus, 61
Community Impact Assessment (CIA), 64–65
Community visioning, 51
  addressing emerging trends and issues, 51
  envisioning a preferred future, 51
  key characteristics, 51
  promoting local action, 51
  reflecting core community values, 51
  understanding the whole community, 51
Comprehensive/development/ master plan, 33

coordinate local decision-making process, 34
direction towards long-range future, 35
guidance to property owners and developers, 34
informed constituency, 35
plan, 33–34
whole community, 34
Context-sensitive solutions (CSS), 60, 62
community values, identification, 64–65
continuous communication, 64
guidelines, 66–67
interdisciplinary project team, 63
management framework, 62–63
natural environment and open space, 67
new creations, 68
road safety, 68
social and cultural environmental concerns, 65–66
social cohesiveness, 68
team self-assessment, 63–64
Conventional aerial photographs, 56
Crosswind runway, 276
Cul-de-sac streets, 240, 240f
Customer service practices, 132

D

Delphi technique, 46
Deplanements, 275
Design guidelines, 201
Development design process, 61
Development regulations/ordinance, 303–305
Development plans *See also* Cities development plans
accountability, 295
education, 295
enforcement, 294–295
evaluation and monitoring, 295
implementation, 294
infrastructure planning, 296–298
infrastructure systems
community facilities, 298
streets, road, and transportation, 297
telecommunications, energy, and power, 298
water and waste, 297
natural monopolies, 296–297
progress monitoring, 294
review process of existing system, 294
Digital industry, 134
Digital landscaping drawing/architecture, 209
Disaster or emergency events, 316–317

E

Early zoning creations, 160
Early zoning, 149
Ecological Sensitive Zone (RCZ–1), 314–315
Ecology, 135
Emergency or disaster preparedness, 316
  plan, 317–318
  planning departments' role, 318–319
Empty sign structure frames, 166
Enplanements, 275
Environmental impact assessment (EIA), 137–138
Environmental impact study, 138
Environmental land planners, 135
Environmental land planning, 135–136
Environmental land regulations, 143–144
Environmental land use planners, 136–137
Environmental land use regulations, 138–139
Environmental planner, 135
Environmental planning, 136–138
Environmental sensitivity in design, 61
Eternity, 284
Evolution
  city of Athens, 21
  Egyptian cities, from 5000 B.C., 21
  European new towns, 23
  Greek civilization (750–350 B.C.), 21
  Hellenistic civilization, 21
  Medieval cities, 22
  mercantilism, 22
  Middle Ages, 22
  Polis, 21
  Renaissance cities, 23
  Rome, 21–22
  Spanish colonial new towns, 23
Exclusionary zoning, 160–161
Existing
  business practices, 132
  land use map, 126
  land use plan, 126

F

False urbanization, 349
Flight interface, 278
Flight schedule monitor, 275–276
Floor Area Ratio/ Floor Area Index or Floor Space Index (FSI), 164
Form–based codes (FBC), 174
  administration, 177
  architecture and planning layout standards, 177
  building type standards, 176–177
  components, visionary goals, 175–177

public space and semi–public space standards, 176
    regulating plan, 175
Formal regions, 39
Freight movement, planning required, 271–272
Functional region/ nodal or polarized region, 39
Functional relationships, 39
Future land use map, 126

G

Gated communities, 180–181
Geographic Information Systems (GIS), 10
  geographic analysis, 101
  how it works, 100–101
  mapping with geo–spatial analysis and solutions, 102
  and smart cities, 101–102
  specialist, 101
Good city planning, 13–14
"Good design", 59
Good land division
  construction standards, 169
  design
    community–wide concerns, provision of external features, 170–171
    existing and proposed surrounding land uses, proper relationship, 171
    integrated design, creation, 171–172
    internal features and details, proper design, 171
    natural resource base, proper relationship, 171
  land subdivision design, 170
  zoning and development control systems, 169–170
Good planning, 8
Good urban design
  architecture, 197
  landscaping, 197–198
  planning, 196–197
  special features, 198–199
  transportation, 198
Governing body, 188
Green built environment, 293
Green environment, 293
"Green" parking lot techniques, 220
Gross domestic product (GDP), 335
Ground access, 276

H

Habitat destruction, 310
Hanging signs, 166
Historic
  and heritage preservation, 61
  districts, 154, 285
  features, 284–285
  ordinance, 285
  preservation ordinance, 154, 285
  preservation plan, 28
Historic buildings, 286–287
  architectural character, 287
  architectural style, 287

buildings not listed, 288
character–defining elements, 287–288
compatible design, 288
contrasting design, 288
design issues, 288
preservation economics, 289
walk–around and walk–through, 289
Historic preservation
connected economic opportunities, 284
economic benefits, 284
Holding areas or run–up areas, 277
Holding bays, 277
Hourly average traffic, 245
Housing needs, 28
Human growth, planning
education, 361
optimum population, 362–363
Public–Private Partnership (PPP)/ private investment in infrastructure and services, 363
improving quality of life, role of NGOs, 364
Human habitats, 39
Human scale designs, 292
Human settlements, 21
Hydrology, 140–141

I

Incentive zoning, 206
"Inclusionary Housing" technique, 161
Inclusionary zoning, 161
India
100 Smart Cities, planning, 112–113
regional perspective, 112–113
bicycle, 117–118
building walkable communities, 117
community design elements, 117
create sustainable cities for the next generation, 115–116
healthy lives, 116–117
mixed use living, 116
municipalities, budget for maintenance of public property, 119–120
spiritual living, 118
spirituality, 118
transit for quick movement, 118
urban sprawl, 116
Indian cities
communication network, 194
organic planning, 194
radial system, 194
service network, 195
transportation lines 194
urban form, 194–195
Indian Railway station (platform), 338

Indicative zoning, 205
Industrial traffic measurement, 244
Industrial trip generation, 244
Indus Valley civilization, 17
    excavations, 17
    functional drainage system, 17–18
    grid pattern, 17
    living quarters, 17
Infiltration, 308
Informed design decision–making, 62
Infrastructure plan, 29
In–laws apartments/or student apartment or grand–parent apartment, 181
Institute of Town Planners of India (ITPI), 81, 86
    code of conduct, 90–93
    participation in a competition, 92
    pledge to share knowledge, 91
    recommended fee, fair and considerate relationship, 91–92
    responsibility towards the client, 92–93
    welfare of people and protection of public interest, 91
Institutional uses, 134
Itinerary operation, 275

J

JNNURM, phase II, 105
Judgmental forecasting techniques, 46

L

Land suitability analysis (LSA), 137
Land use
    classifications, 126
    distribution, 58
    map, 126
    planning arena, 127
    planning, 124–125
    plans, 133
        preparation, 137
    regulations, 139
    trip generation, 243
Landscape architecture, 207–208
Landside, 276
Large–scale cadastral maps, 55–56
Large–scale topographic map, 55
Laws of the Indies, 23
Le Corbusier, 109, 110, 111, 197
Learning environment, 88
LED signs, 166
Level of service (LOS), 302
Limited land resources, efficient use, 291
Local comprehensive planning, 35
Local entities, 304–305
Local government operations, recommendations, 87–88

Local land use planning, 125–127
Local operation, 275
Location signs, 277
Long–range ideas, 127
Low–density residential development, 243–244

M

Manholes, 307
Map scale, 55
Maps, 54–55
Market area, 28
Mass/public transit, 253–254
Mid–level living areas, 337
Migrants to basic amenities ratio, 353
Mixed–use development / new urbanism, 157–159
  architecture of buildings, 159
  creation of courtyards, 159
Mobile vendors, 133–134
Modern architecture, 174
Multiple regression, 45
Multistory parking decks, 266

N

National Commission on Urbanization, 2
Natural areas' planning, 308–310
  action strategy, 310
  analysis, 309
  commercial recreation, 309
  enforcement, 310
  goals and objectives, 310
  how to use and plan, 309
  inventory, 309
  natural environment, striking a balance, 309
Neighborhood
  'galli' (small street), 133
  cohesive, 228
  compact, 291
  maintain cleanliness, 121
  mixed income, 161
  planning programs, 10
  redevelopment, 68
  safe, clean, attractive, and presentable, 121
  values, 61
  well–designed, 195
"No parking, No Car" instructions, 264
"No–development zone", 314
Non–automobile hire services and operators, local level development plans, 269–270
Non–conforming building or structure, 159
Non–conforming use, 159–160
Non–motorized service facilities, 270
Non–point pollutants, 140

O

Obstruction lights, 277
Off–peak time traffic, 245
Off–street parking, 265–266
Old city transportation planning, 274
On–street parking, 266
Orthophotographs, 56
Overlay district, 154

P

Parking
- decks, 265
- design, 265, 266–267, 267f
- facilities, 265–266
- garages, 265
- provision, 265
- space, 263

Passenger
- handling system, 277
- processing facilities, 278

Paving blocks, 220

Peak time traffic, 245

Pedestrian planning
- sidewalks, 236
  - design elements, 237–238
  - multilayer pedestrian space calculation, 237

Pedestrian volume, 245

Pedestrian–oriented (no direct automobile access) markets/shopping areas, 267

Performance zoning, 206

Plan
- authority, 29
- elements, 35–38
- core, 30

Planned unit development (PUD), 156–157

Planner's day, 9–11

Planners, 7–8
- applications for new developments on vacant lands, 57
- development standards, 56–58
  - application of established standards, 57
  - development plan, 57
  - established standards and norms, 57
  - new development submissions, 57
  - professional judgment, 58
  - redevelopment applications or redevelopment projects, 57
  - standards and norms, 58
- education, 12
- role, technical knowledge to the projects, 9
- skills, 12–13

Planning
- as a team effort, 14–15
- education, 80
- for family, 81
- for individuals, 81
- for villages, towns, and cities, 81
- how to learn, 80–81
- monetary savings, 15

Planning 101, 7f

Planning degree
- master's–level graduate, 12
- Ph.D, 12
- undergraduate degrees, 12

Planning departments, 71

Planning knowledge, 11

Planning process by planners, 127

Planning profession, 11–12
Planning professionals, 81
Policy adoption, 44
Policy analysis, 42
    methodology, 43
    multiple disciplines, 42
Policy analysts, 44
Policy analytic procedures, 43
Policy argumentation and debate, 43
Policy assessment, 44
Policy communication, 48
Policy formation, 44
Policy implementation, 44
Policy making, 42
    problem structuring, 44–45
    process, 44
Policy relevant knowledge
    administrative agencies, implementation, 46–47
    conjecture, 45
    forecasting, 45–46
    prediction, 45
    projection, 45
    recommendation, 46
    monitoring, 47
    evaluation, 47
Policy relevant information, 43
Political activities, 44
Political signs, 167
Polluted air, 142
Poor–level living areas, 337–338
Poorly planned or unplanned urban growth, 14–15

Porous pavements, 220
Precision approach path indicator, 277
Presentation skills, 10
Presentations, 10
Primary runway, 276
Priority capital improvement plan, 29
Private advertising signs, 166
Private project, 200
Private sector planners, 11
Product stewardship, 323
Professional planners, 8–9, 89–90
Project, 71–72
    closing, 74–75
    controlling, 74
    evaluation, 74
    execution, 74
    initiating, 73
    planning, 73–74
    monitoring, 74
Project manager
    communication, 77
    communication with the client, 77
    influencing, 78
    interpersonal skills, 77
    leadership, 78
    networking, 78
    planning department, 79
    role of, 76
Project management, 10, 72–73
    knowledge areas, 75–79
    project communication, 76
    project cost, 75

project human resources, 75
project integration, 76
project quality, 76
project risk, 76
project scope, 75
project time, 75
Public or community participation, 49–50
Public policy analysis, 42
Public sector planners, 11
Public transit marketing department, mass transit environmental benefits, 254
Public transportation nodes, walking distance hinterland, 253
Publicly owned sewage treatment plants, 308

Q

Qualitative risk analysis, 46

R

Rail transportation system, 257–259
Redevelopment areas
  plans, 40–42
  revitalization strategies, 41
Regional comprehensive plan, 40
Regional geography, 38
Regional identity, 38–39
Regional plans, 38–40
Regression analysis 45
Residential area, inclusionary zoning, 129

Residential trip generation, 243
Residential use, 129–130
Restrictive zoning, 205
Retails mall, 131–133
Rickshaws, 269
Rickshaw–wallas and tonga–wallas, 268–269
  intelligent and smart planning, 269
Rights of way (ROW)
  Indian Railways, 120
  public, 166, 264
Runway
  centreline, 276–277
    lighting systems, 277
  designators, 276
  end identifier lights, 277
  threshold markings, 277

S

Sanitary landfills, 323
Satellite towns, 111
Servants
  employment and planning, 181–182
  need for working benefits, 182
  no fixed regulations, 182
Sidewalks
  and panhandlers, 238–239
  as shelters, 238
  entrepreneurs and operators, 236
  for business and non-business uses, 235

occupancy at night time, 238
urban areas, 235–236
Shared parking
mixed–use development, 267
"Sign Ordinance", 165
Signage regulations, 165
Silpa–shastra, 16
Slums, substandard living conditions, 350
Slum children
need to educate, 352
Slum dwellers
defecating outdoors, 353–354
deprived living conditions, 351–352
sub–standard living conditions, national level concern, 354
Slum management process, 354–355
Slum management
advance checks, 357–359
appropriate housing, 359
existing settlements, identification, 357
local media's role, 358–359
project planning, 357
regional action, 355–356
Slum planning, 15
Slums/ghettos/jhuggis/choppar, 338
"Slums to utopia" model, 353

Smart cities, 48, 94 See also City (ies)
benefits and challenges of new technology, 111–112
concept, 96
economic infrastructure, 103
environmental sustainability, 98
geographic information systems (GIS), 100
governance infrastructure, 103
historic preservation plan, 115
innovative technology, 112
institutional infrastructure, 104
intelligent sensors nodes, 98
mobility design, 114
need for environmental balance, 114
need for social and cultural integration, 114–115
need to recognize monuments, 114–115
physical infrastructure, 103–104
project process, 97
public transit, 114
sustainability, 98
technical infrastructure, 104
understanding suburban concept, 113
urban performance, 96

vehicular traffic monitoring, 99
wireless sensor and network, 98–99
Smart City model, 102
Smart city planning, 15
Smart governance, 102
Smart rural areas, planning, 325–334
    guiding steps, 330–331
    redevelopment plan, 332
    regional transportation plan, 329
    regional understanding, 328–329
    rural comprehensive plan, 331–332
    rural settlements, 327, 329–331
    ruralites, 326
Smart service providers, 133
Social satisfaction, 6
Society, cohesiveness, 284
Solid waste, 319
    management and sustainability, 321–323
Spatial centers, 38
Special parking lanes, 266
Speed hump, 252
Spiritual experts, 118
Spot zoning, 162
Sprawling land use patterns, 130
Stray animals on roads, 273–274
    hazardous and unsafe traffic conditions, 273
    unhealthy stray animals, 273–274
Street lighting, planners, 263
Street lights, 263
Suggested bike lane, 271f
Sustainable air quality, 141–143
Sustainable communities, 290
Sustainable development, 292
    implementation, 293–294
Sustainable stewardship, 211
"Swachh Bharat Mission", 88

T

Taxi stand location, 268
Taxis, three–wheelers, rickshaws, and tongas, 268–270
Temporary traffic control, 262–263
    barricades and traffic calming devices, 262–263
    detours and diversions, 262
    devices, 262
    proper lighting, 262
Temporary vendors, 133–134
Terminal, 276
Too large bill–boards/signs, 166
Touchdown zone lights, 277
Tourism industry, 154
Town planning
    British period till the independence of India, 19–20
    Buddhist period, up to 320 A.D., 18
    civil lines, 20
    evolution, 16–48

Indus Valley civilization, 17–18
medieval period, 14th century, 19
Moghul period, 1526 to very early 18th century, 19
New Delhi, capital of colonial India, 20
Vedic period, up to 400 B.C., 19
Traffic–calming devices, 249
Traffic–calming techniques, 249–253
    curb exertions/chokers, 251
    curvilinear street design, 249
    low speed curves, 249–250
    median islands, 250–251
    raised crosswalks, 251
    roundabouts, 251
    speed humps and speed bumps, 251–253
    traffic circles, 250
Traffic congestion, 247
    discourage automobile ownership, 247
    encourage use of mass transit and bicycles, 247
    smart traffic management techniques, 247
Traffic management, 259–261
    guide signs, 261
    regulatory signs, 261
    traffic control devices, 260
    traffic signals, 260–261
    traffic signs, 261
    warning signs, 261

Traffic safety, 247–249
    traffic signs, 248
Traffic volume study, 246
Transitional zoning, 161
Transportation
    alternatives, 291–292
    needs, 28
    planning, 223
    alleys, 233–234
    –and design considerations, 239–240
        arterial roads, 232
        collector roads, 232–233
        congestion of additional automobiles, 226
        expressway, 231
        freeway, 231
        grid–iron street system, 228–229
    local streets/minor roads, 233
        mass transit, 225
        medieval era street system, 231
    –Modal–Split Model, 242
    modeling, 241–242
        personal automobiles, 224–225
        providing and maintaining utility infrastructure, 225–226
        radial or concentric road system 229
        road systems, 228–231
            roads, streets, sidewalks, 227–228

sidewalks, 234
sub-arterial roads, 232
topographical street system, 230
–Traffic-Assignment Model, 242
   travel time, 224
–Trip Distribution Model, 241–242
–Trip Generation Model, 241
Tree Preservation Ordinance, 210–211
Triangular irregular network (TIN), 56

U

Unattractive signs, choice, 166
Underground development planning, 69–71
   basement excavation, cost-benefit, 70
   cut-and-cover, 69
   feasibility of tunnelling, 69
   feasibility or cost, 69
   ground and groundwater conditions, 70
   ground movements, 69
   impact assessment, 70
   near-surface cut-and-cover tunnels, 69
Uniform development standards, 303–304
United States
   city beautiful movement, 25–26
   city efficient movement, 26
   Economies of scale, 27
   Greenbelt Towns, 26–27
   new urbanism, 27
   refinement of zoning, 27
   smart growth, 27
Unpaved sidewalks, 234
Urban agglomeration, 3
Urban areas, agricultural zoning, 153
Urban design, 191
   built environment, architectural improvement, 202–203
   elements, 203–204
   formal design training, 200–201
      Indian cities, urban form, 192
   Indian cities', 192–193
   innovative planning techniques, 202
      perspectives, 202–205
Urban design controls, 204
   Government-invested project, 204
   land use and density, 204
   land use and urban design, 205
   performance requirements, 204–205
   physical bulk of a building, 204
   zoning ordinance, 204
Urban design qualities, 205

Urban development, 58
Urban diffusion, 339
Urban ecology, 209
Urban environment, 1–2, 158–159
Urban forestry, 209–211
    design benefits, 120–121
Urban heat island, 209–210
Urban landscaping design, 207–209
    storing graphic data, 208
    raster images, 208
    pixelated image, 208
    upsampling, 208–209
Urban local bodies (ULBs), 15, 84, 101, 195, 167, 213, 226
    alternate transport, regulation, 268
    climatic concerns, 297
    code enforcement issue, 236
    contracting third party consultants, 339
    development regulations, 304
    negative reflection, 238
    non–transferable permit, 263
    performance, 190
    rural settlements, 331
    slum management, 355
    utilities and services to the citizens, 337
Urban land uses, infrastructure standards, 58
Urban planner, 16
Urban planning, 1
    and engineering, aerial photography, 56
Urban population, 340
Urban trees, benefits, 120
Urbanization model, 2, 340–348
    cascading process, 341
    commercial incentives plan, 347
    comprehensive approach plan, 344–345
    housing plan, 346
    industry and industrial incentives plan, 347
    infrastructure and services plan, 345
    marketing and incentives plan, 347
    site selection plan, 341–342
    theme, 340–341
    transparent governance plan, 348–349
    transportation and communication plan, 342–343
    zoning assignment plan, 343–344
Urban–use technology, 97–98
Utopia, 97

V

Vishvakarma, 16
Vishwakarmaprakash, 19
Visual approach slope indicators, 277
Visual glideslope indicators, 277

W

Walls and gated building, 180–181
Waste generators, 320–321
Wastewater collection systems, 306
Wastewater planning, 305–307
  centralized municipal wastewater system, 305–306
  conventional pollutants, 306
  municipal sewer system, 305
  toxic pollutants, 306
  toxin pollutants, 306
Wastewater treatment plant (WWTP), 307–308
  primary stage, 307
  secondary treatment techniques, 307
  tertiary treatment, 308
Water storage tanks, installation, 140
Water supply planning, 139–140
Water use standards, 139
Waterways/boats means of transportation, 259
Way of life, 125
Well-designed sidewalks and bike lanes, 291
Well-lit sidewalks, 234
Wetland protection, local planning, 313
Wetlands, planning and managing, 312–313
Wholesale, 133
Wildlife habitat planning, 310–312
  biodiversity loss, 311
  bioregionalism, 311
  ecosystems, 311
  preserving biodiversity, 311–312

X

X–zoning, 160

Z

Zoning Board of Appeals or Adjustment, 188
Zoning, 145
  building permits, control and management, 168–169
  bulk requirements, 163
  commercial uses, 151–152
  development limitations, 162–163
  heavy industrial uses, 152
  implementing, 147
  institutional uses, 153
  light industrial districts, 152–153
  map, 148
  medium industries, 152
  minor industries, 152
  objectives, 146
  ordinance, 148, 163
  planners, 163
  planning schools, 155
  powers, 188–189
  purpose, 146–147
  residential districts, 149–150
  single–family household, 150

spirituality, 154
worship centers, 155
worship places, 155–156
Zoning ordinances
    aesthetic and architectural control, 172
    appeals, 173
    implementation, 172–174
    lot area retractions, 165
    rezoning, 172
    special use permits, 173–174
    variance, 173
Zoning purposes
    traffic impact, 168
    utilities impact, 168
Zoning requirements
    design, 165
    parking, 165

www.ingramcontent.com/pod-product-compliance
Lightning Source LLC
Chambersburg PA
CBHW071235300426
44116CB00008B/1052